COMMANDING
VOICES OF
BLUE & GRAY

General William T. Sherman, General George Custer,

General James Longstreet, and Major J. S. Mosby, Among

Others, in Their Own Words

EDITED BY

BRIAN M. THOMSEN

A Forge Book
Published by Tom Doherty Associates, LLC
175 Fifth Avenue
New York, NY 10010

www.tor.com

Forge® is a registered trademark of Tom Doherty Associates, LLC.

Library of Congress Cataloging-in-Publication Data

Commanding voices of blue & gray : General William T. Sherman . . . [et al.];
edited by Brian M. Thomsen.—1st ed.
    p.   cm.
"A Tom Doherty Associates book."
ISBN 0-765-30583-6
1. United States—History—Civil War, 1861–1865—Campaigns—Sources.   I. Sherman,
William T. (William Tecumseh), 1820–1891.   I. Thomsen, Brian.

E470 .C6975   2002
973.7'3—dc21

2002026070

First Edition: December 2002

Printed in the United States of America

0   9   8   7   6   5   4   3   2   1

For library collections (print, not electronic) that preserve
the actual printed words of those who were there

The editor is grateful to William Terdoslavich for providing introductions to the excerpts in this volume.

Contents

Introduction—Commanding Voices

W hen we think of accounts of the Civil War on the printed page, our first thoughts are usually of such classic literary novels as *The Red Badge of Courage* or *Andersonville* or *The Killer Angels,* or perhaps such best-selling potboilers as *Gone with the Wind* or *Gods and Generals.*

We might even think of some classic works in the short form like the stories and sketches of Ambrose Bierce (who, unlike most of his literary contemporaries, actually served and saw heavy action) or perhaps the war poetry of Walt Whitman.

Today we are also blessed with epic nonfiction narratives by Shelby Foote and Bruce Catton, not to mention James M. McPherson's *Battle Cry of Freedom,* or even Ken Burns's mammoth PBS miniseries *The Civil War* . . . but these are all recent, many years after the events recounted.

What about nonfiction accounts closer to this great crucible of American history itself?

The first work to come to mind is obviously the account by a former president and leading Union general.

Personal Memoirs by U. S. Grant was distinctive and praiseworthy (some believe it the greatest military memoir of command), and indeed it was a huge bestseller that secured not just Grant's reputation, but his family's financial stability as well.

Grant was not alone in penning a personal account of the War Between the States, however. Indeed, many others saw the printed word as their opportunity to have their say for both fun and profit.

Some, like William Tecumseh Sherman, did it as an exorcism of the hell of war as he fought it.

Others, like McClellan from the North and Hood from the South, saw it as an opportunity for self-justification and a chance to recast the facts in a manner more palatable to their own sizable egos.

Others like Custer did it for plain old cash and notoriety.

Indeed, the war memoir became a publishing cottage industry where anybody of sufficient rank or privilege could take a stab at memoir stardom and publishing infamy. The results were markedly mixed, with more misses than hits for the most part.

Some of these writings are remembered because the authors went on to some other fame after the war, such as Custer and his ill-advised confrontation and demise at the Battle of Little Big Horn or Lew Wallace going home to write the bestselling chariot-and-sandal epic of the time of Christ, *Ben-Hur*, or Abner Doubleday somehow getting credit for inventing baseball.

Others, such as those by Sherman and Longstreet, are remembered as masterpieces of the memoir genre itself for their insights into the minds of complex men, their identities, and their perceptions of the events that surrounded them.

Some filled their stories with exciting tales of raiding and bushwhacking that bordered on the outlawed (as with Mosby's raiders, some of whom went on to short-lived careers as wanted felons), while others concentrated on the day-to-day operations that they witnessed and/or had a hand in.

And still others (such as Jubal Early) seized the opportunity to have one last stab at the Lost Cause and eulogize the bravery of a South that never was and a victory that never could have been achieved.

Commanding Voices of Blue & Gray draws from all of these accounts to try to provide an overview of the accounts of the war itself as seen and/or remembered by those who not only took part in it but also shaped the events and strategies that impacted so many other lives.

Theirs were the voices of command.

And these are their words.

The Civil War as they recalled it.

—Brian M. Thomsen

COMMANDING
VOICES OF
BLUE & GRAY

The Civil War is replete with stories of unpromising men rising to meet their challenges and vanquishing them. Abraham Lincoln leads this parade. With nothing but two terms in the U.S. House of Representatives and a lost Senate race to show for his national experience, Lincoln assumed the presidency facing the worst crisis in our nation's history. In war, nations must be guided by a grand strategy that unifies political and military means. Very early in his first term, Lincoln showed that he could define the Union's political aims while understanding what had to be done militarily to achieve those goals.

From the Message to Congress in Special Session

BY ABRAHAM LINCOLN

JULY 4, 1861

Fellow Citizens of the Senate and House of Representatives: Having been convened on an extraordinary occasion, as authorized by the Constitution, your attention is not called to any ordinary subject of legislation.

At the beginning of the present presidential term, four months ago, the functions of the Federal Government were found to be generally suspended within the several States of South Carolina, Georgia, Alabama, Mississippi, Louisiana, and Florida, excepting only those of the Post Office Department.

Within these States, all the forts, arsenals, dockyards, custom-houses, and the like, including the movable and stationary property in and about them, had been seized, and were held in open hostility to this government, excepting only Forts Pickens, Taylor, and Jefferson, on and near the Florida Coast, and Fort Sumter, in Charleston Harbor, South Carolina. The forts thus seized had been put in improved condition, new ones had been built, and armed forces had been organized and were organizing, all avowedly with the same hostile purpose.

The forts remaining in the possession of the Federal Government in and near these States were either besieged or menaced by warlike preparations, and especially Fort Sumter was nearly surrounded by well-protected hostile batteries, with guns equal in quality to the best of its own, and outnumbering the latter as perhaps ten to one. A disproportionate share of the Federal muskets and rifles had somehow found their way into these States, and had been seized to be used against the government. Accumulations of the public revenue lying within them had been seized for the same object. The navy was scattered in distant seas, leaving but a very small part of it within the immediate reach of the government. Officers of the Federal Army and Navy had resigned in great numbers; and of those resigning a large proportion had taken up arms against the government. Simultaneously, and in connection with all this, the purpose to sever the Federal Union was openly avowed. In accordance with this purpose, an ordinance had been adopted in each of these States, declaring the States respectively to be separated from the National Union. A formula for instituting a combined government of these States had been promulgated; and this illegal organization, in the character of confederate States, was already invoking recognition, aid, and intervention from foreign powers.

Finding this condition of things, and believing it to be an imperative duty upon the incoming executive to prevent, if possible, the consummation of such attempt to destroy the Federal Union, a choice of means to that end became indispensable. This choice was made and was declared in the inaugural address. The policy chosen looked to the exhaustion of all peaceful measures before a resort to any stronger ones. It sought only to hold the public places and property not already wrested from the government, and to collect the revenue, relying for the rest on time, discussion, and the ballot-box. It promised a continuance of the mails, at government expense, to the very people who were resisting the government; and it gave repeated pledges against any disturbance to any of the people, or any of their rights. Of all that which a President might constitutionally and justifiably do in such case, everything was foreborne without which it was believed possible to keep the government on foot.

. . . The assault upon and reduction of Fort Sumter was in no sense a matter of self-defense on the part of the assailants. They well knew that the garrison in the fort could by no possibility commit aggression upon them. They knew—they were expressly notified—that the giving of bread to the few brave and hungry men of the garrison was all which would on that occasion be attempted, unless themselves, by resisting so much, should provoke more. They knew that this government desired to keep the garrison in the fort, not to assail them, but merely to maintain visible possession, and thus to preserve the Union from actual and immediate dissolution—trusting, as hereinbefore stated, to time, discussion, and the ballot-box for final adjustment; and they assailed and reduced the fort for precisely the reverse object—to drive out the visible authority of the Federal Union, and thus force it to immediate dissolution. That this was their object the executive well understood; and having said to them in the inaugural address, "You can have no conflict without being yourselves the aggressors," he took pains not only to keep this declaration good, but also to keep the case so free from the power of ingenious sophistry that the world should not be able to misunderstand it. By the affair at Fort Sumter, with its surrounding circumstances, that point was reached. Then and thereby the assailants of the government began the conflict of arms, without a gun in sight or in expectancy to return their fire, save only the few in the fort sent to that harbor years before for their own protection, and still ready to give that protection in whatever was lawful. In this act, discarding all else, they have forced upon the country the distinct issue, "immediate dissolution or blood."

And this issue embraces more than the fate of these United States. It presents to the whole family of man the question whether a constitutional republic or democracy—a government of the people by the same people—can or cannot maintain its territorial integrity against its own domestic foes. It presents the question whether discontented individuals, too few in numbers to control administration according to organic law in any case, can always, upon the pretenses made in this case, or on any other pretenses, or arbitrarily without any pretense, break up their government, and thus practically put an end to free government upon the earth. It forces us to ask: "Is there, in all republics, this inherent and fatal weakness?" "Must a government, of necessity, be too strong for the liberties of its own people, or too weak to maintain its own existence?"

So viewing the issue, no choice was left but to call out the war power of the government; and so to resist force employed for its destruction, by force for its preservation.

It is now recommended that you give the legal means for making this contest a short and decisive one: that you place at the control of the government for the work at least four hundred thousand men and $400,000,000. That number of men is about one-tenth of those of proper ages within the regions where, apparently, all are willing to engage; and the sum is less than a twenty-third part of the money value owned by the men who seem ready to devote the whole. A debt of $600,000,000 now is a less sum per head than was the debt of our Revolution when we came out of that struggle; and the money value in the country now bears even a greater proportion to what it was then than does the population. Surely each man has as strong a motive now to preserve our liberties as each had then to establish them.

A right result at this time will be worth more to the world than ten times the men and ten times the money. The evidence reaching us from the country leaves no doubt that the material for the work is abundant, and that it needs only the hand of legislation to give it legal sanction, and the hand of the executive to give it practical shape and efficiency. One of the greatest perplexities of the government is to avoid receiving troops faster than it can provide for them. In a word, the people will save their government if the government itself will do its part only indifferently well.

It might seem, at first thought, to be of little difference whether the present movement at the South be called "secession" or "rebellion." The movers, however, well understand the difference. At the beginning they knew they could never raise their treason to any respectable magnitude by any name which implies violation of law. They knew their people possessed as much of moral sense, as much of devotion to law and order, and as much pride in and reverence for the history and government of their common country as any other civilized and patriotic people. They knew they could make no advancement directly in the teeth of these strong and noble sentiments. Accordingly, they commenced by an insidious debauching of the public mind. They invented an ingenious sophism which, if conceded, was followed by perfectly logical steps, through all the incidents, to the complete destruction of the Union. The sophism itself is that any State of the Union may consistently with the National Constitution, and therefore lawfully and peacefully, withdraw from the Union without the consent of the Union or of any other State. The little disguise that the supposed right is to be exercised only for just cause, themselves to be the sole judges of its justice, is too thin to merit any notice.

With rebellion thus sugar-coated they have been drugging the public mind of their section for more than thirty years, and until at length they have brought many good men to a willingness to take up arms against the government the day after some assemblage of men have enacted the farcical pretense of taking their

State out of the Union, who could have been brought to no such thing the day before.

This sophism derives much, perhaps the whole, of its currency from the assumption that there is some omnipotent and sacred supremacy pertaining to a State—to each State of our Federal Union. Our States have neither more nor less power than that reserved to them in the Union by the Constitution—no one of them ever having been a State out of the Union. The original ones passed into the Union even before they cast off their British colonial dependence; and the new ones each came into the Union directly from a condition of dependence, excepting Texas. And even Texas, in its temporary independence, was never designated a State. The new ones only took the designation of States on coming into the Union, while that name was first adopted for the old ones in and by the Declaration of Independence. Therein the "United Colonies" were declared to be "free and independent States"; but even then the object plainly was not to declare their independence of one another or of the Union, but directly the contrary, as their mutual pledge and their mutual action before, at the time, and afterward, abundantly show. The express plighting of faith by each and all of the original thirteen in the Articles of Confederation, two years later, that the Union shall be perpetual, is most conclusive. Having never been States either in substance or in name outside of the Union, whence this magical omnipotence of "State Rights," asserting a claim of power to lawfully destroy the Union itself? Much is said about the "sovereignty" of the States; but the word even is not in the National Constitution, nor, as is believed, in any of the State constitutions. What is "sovereignty" in the political sense of the term? Would it be far wrong to define it "a political community without a political superior"? Tested by this, no one of our States except Texas ever was a sovereignty. And even Texas gave up the character on coming into the Union; by which act she acknowledged the Constitution of the United States, and the laws and treaties of the United States made in pursuance of the Constitution, to be for her the supreme law of the land. The states have their status in the Union, and they have no other legal status. If they break from this, they can only do so against law and by revolution. The Union, and not themselves separately, procured their independence and their liberty. By conquest or purchase the Union gave each of them whatever independence or liberty it has. The Union is older than any of the States, and, in fact, it created them as States. Originally some dependent colonies made the Union, and, in turn, the Union threw off their old dependence for them, and made them States, such as they are. Not one of them ever had a State constitution independent of the Union. Of course, it is not forgotten that all the new States framed their constitutions before they entered the Union—nevertheless, dependent upon and preparatory to coming into the Union.

Unquestionably the States have the powers and rights reserved to them in and by the National Constitution; but among these surely are not included all conceivable powers, however mischievous or destructive, but, at most, such only as were known in the world at the time as governmental powers; and certainly a power to destroy the government itself had never been known as a governmental, as a merely administrative power. This relative matter of national power and State rights, as a principle, is no other than the principle of generality and locality. Whatever concerns the whole should be confided to the whole—to the General Government; while whatever concerns only the State should be left exclusively to the State. This is all there is of original principle about it. Whether the National Constitution in defining boundaries between the two has applied the principle with exact accuracy, is not to be questioned. We are all bound by that defining, without question.

What is now combated is the position that secession is consistent with the Constitution—is lawful and peaceful. It is not contended that there is any express law for it; and nothing should ever be implied as law which leads to unjust or absurd consequences. The nation purchased with money the countries out of which several of these States were formed. Is it just that they shall go off without leave and without refunding? The nation paid very large sums (in the aggregate, I believe, nearly a hundred millions) to relieve Florida of the aboriginal tribes. Is it just that she shall now be off without consent or without making any return? The nation is now in debt for money applied to the benefit of these so-called seceding States in common with the rest. Is it just either that creditors shall go unpaid or the remaining States pay the whole? A part of the present national debt was contracted to pay the old debts of Texas. Is it just that she shall leave and pay no part of this herself?

Again, if one State may secede, so may another; and when all shall have seceded, none is left to pay the debts. Is this quite just to creditors? Did we notify them of this sage view of ours when we borrowed their money?

If we now recognize this doctrine by allowing the seceders to go in peace, it is difficult to see what we can do if others choose to go or to extort terms upon which they will promise to remain.

The seceders insist that our Constitution admits of secession. They have assumed to make a national constitution of their own, in which of necessity they have either discarded or retained the right of secession as they insist it exists in ours. If they have discarded it, they thereby admit that on principles it ought not to be in ours. If they have retained it by their own construction of ours, they show that to be consistent they must secede from one another whenever they shall find it the easiest way of settling their debts, or effecting any other selfish or unjust object. The principle itself is one of disintegration, and upon which no government can possibly endure.

If all the States save one should assert the power to drive that one out of the Union, it is presumed the whole class of seceder politicians would at once deny the power and denounce the act as the greatest outrage upon State rights. But suppose that precisely the same act, instead of being called "driving the one out," should be called "the seceding of the others from that one," it would be exactly what the seceders claim to do, unless, indeed, they make the point that the one, because it is a minority, may rightfully do what the others, because they are a majority, may not rightfully do. These politicians are subtle and profound on the rights of minorities. They are not partial to that power which made the Constitution and speaks from the preamble called itself "We, the People."

It may well be questioned whether there is to-day a majority of the legally qualified voters of any State, except perhaps South Carolina, in favor of disunion. There is much reason to believe that the Union men are the majority in many, if not in every other one, of the so-called seceded States. The contrary has not been demonstrated in any one of them. It is ventured to affirm this even of Virginia and Tennessee; for the result of an election held in military camps, where the bayonets are all on one side of the question voted upon, can scarcely be considered as demonstrating popular sentiment. At such an election, all that large class who are at once for the Union and against coercion would be coerced to vote against the Union.

It may be affirmed without extravagance that the free institutions we enjoy have developed the powers and improved the condition of our whole people beyond any example in the world. Of this we now have a striking and an impressive illustration. So large an army as the government has now on foot was never before known, without a soldier in it but who has taken his place there of his own free choice. But more than this, there are many single regiments whose members, one and another, possess full practical knowledge of all the arts, sciences, professions, and whatever else, whether useful or elegant, is known in the world; and there is scarcely one from which there could not be selected a President, a Cabinet, a Congress, and perhaps a court, abundantly competent to administer the government itself. Nor do I say this is not true also in the army of our late friends, now adversaries in this contest; but if it is, so much better the reason why the government which has conferred such benefits on both them and us should not be broken up. Whoever in any section proposes to abandon such a government would do well to consider in deference to what principle it is that he does it—what better he is likely to get in its stead—whether the substitute will give, or be intended to give, so much of good to the people? There are some foreshadowings on this subject. Our adversaries have adopted some declarations of independence in which, unlike the good old one, penned by Jefferson, they omit the words "all men are created equal." Why? They have adopted a temporary national constitution, in the preamble of which, unlike our good old one, signed by Washington, they omit "We, the People," and substitute, "We, the deputies of the sovereign and independent States." Why? Why this deliberate pressing out of view the rights of men and the authority of the people?

This is essentially a people's contest. On the side of the Union it is a struggle for maintaining in the world that form and substance of government whose leading object is to elevate the condition of men—to lift artificial weights from all shoulders; to clear the paths of laudable pursuit for all; to afford all an unfettered start, and a fair chance in the race of life. Yielding to partial and temporary departures, from necessity, this is the leading object of the government for whose existence we contend.

I am most happy to believe that the plain people understand and appreciate this. It is worthy of note that while in this, the government's hour of trial, large numbers of those in the army and navy who have been favored with the offices have resigned and proved false to the hand which had pampered them, not one common soldier or common sailor is known to have deserted his flag.

Great honor is due to those officers who remained true, despite the example of their treacherous associates; but the greatest honor, and most important fact of all, is the unanimous firmness of the common soldiers and common sailors. To the last man, so far as known, they have successfully resisted the traitorous efforts of those whose commands, but an hour before, they obeyed as absolute law. This is the patriotic instinct of the plain people. They understand, without an argument, that the destroying of the government which was made by Washington means no good to them.

Our popular government has often been called an experiment. Two points in it our people have already settled—the successful establishing and the successful administering of it. One still remains—its successful maintenance against a formidable internal attempt to overthrow it. It is now for them to demonstrate to the world that those who can fairly carry an election can also suppress a rebellion; that ballots are the rightful and peaceful successors of bullets; and that when ballots have fairly and constitutionally decided, there can be no successful appeal back to bullets; that there can be no successful appeal, except to ballots themselves, at succeeding elections. Such will be a great lesson of peace: teaching men that what they cannot take by an election, neither can they take it by a war; teaching all the folly of being the beginners of a war.

Lest there be some uneasiness in the minds of candid men as to what is to be the course of the government toward the Southern States after the rebellion shall have been suppressed, the executive deems it proper to say it will be his purpose then, as ever, to be guided by the Constitution and the laws; and that he probably will have no different understanding of the powers and duties of the Federal Government relatively to the rights of the States and the people, under the Constitution, than that expressed in the inaugural address.

He desires to preserve the government, that it may be administered for all as it was administered by the men who made it. Loyal citizens everywhere have the right to claim this of their government, and the government has no right to withhold or neglect it. It is not perceived that in giving it there is any coercion, any conquest, or any subjugation, in any just sense of those terms.

The Constitution provides, and all the States have accepted the provision, that "the United States shall guarantee to every State in this Union a republican form of government." But if a State may lawfully go out of the Union, having done so, it may also discard the republican form of government; so that to prevent its going out is an indispensable means to the end of maintaining the guarantee mentioned; and when an end is lawful and obligatory, the indispensable means to it are also lawful and obligatory.

It was with the deepest regret that the executive found the duty of employing the war power in defense of the government forced upon him. He could but perform this duty or surrender the existence of the government. No compromise by public servants could, in this case, be a cure; not that compromises are not often proper, but that no popular government can long survive a marked precedent that those who carry an election can only save the government from immediate destruction by giving up the main point upon which the people gave the election. The people themselves, and not their servants, can safely reverse their own deliberate decisions.

As a private citizen the executive could not have consented that these institutions shall perish; much less could he, in betrayal of so vast and so sacred a trust as the free people have confided to him. He felt that he had no moral right to shrink, nor even to count the chances of his own life in what might follow. In full view of his great responsibility he has, so far, done what he has deemed his duty. You will now, according to your own judgment, perform yours.

He sincerely hopes that your views and your actions may so accord with his, as to assure all faithful citizens who have been disturbed in their rights of a certain and speedy restoration to them, under the Constitution and the laws.

And having thus chosen our course, without guile and with pure purpose, let us renew our trust in God, and go forward without fear and with manly hearts.

Memoranda of Military Policy

(Written after the defeat at Bull Run)

JULY 23, 1861

1. Let the plan for making the blockade effective be pushed foward with all possible dispatch.
2. Let the volunteer forces at Fort Monroe and vicinity under General Butler be constantly drilled, disciplined, and instructed without more for the present.
3. Let Baltimore be held as now, with a gentle but firm and certain hand.
4. Let the force now under Patterson or Banks be strengthened and made secure in its position.
5. Let the forces in Western Virginia act till further orders according to instructions or orders from General McClellan.
6. [Let] General Frémont push forward his organization and operations in the West as rapidly as possible, giving rather special attention to Missouri.

7. Let the forces late before Manassas, except the three-months men, be reorganized as rapidly as possible in their camps here and about Arlington.
8. Let the three-months forces who decline to enter the longer service be discharged as rapidly as circumstances will permit.
9. Let the new volunteer forces be brought forward as fast as possible, and especially into the camps on the two sides of the river here.

(Added on July 27, 1861)

When the foregoing shall have been substantially attended to:
1. Let Manassas Junction (or some point on one or other of the railroads near it) and Strasburg be seized and permanently held, with an open line from Washington to Manassas, and an open line from Harper's Ferry to Strasburg—the military men to find the way of doing these.
2. This done, a joint movement from Cairo on Memphis, and from Cincinnati on East Tennessee.

It is with humility that Jefferson Davis assumed the office of the presidency of the Confederate States of America. He had much to be humble about: Davis was a West Point graduate, Mexican War veteran, former senator from Alabama, and secretary of war. Davis possessed more ability on paper than did his counterpart, Abraham Lincoln. In his inaugural address, Davis argued that an unrestrained federal government emanating from Washington drove the southern states out of the Union. Yet those same federal powers would be duplicated in Richmond, as Davis strived to maintain a losing struggle against a nation led by a more humble president possessing more ability than credentials.

Jefferson Davis's First Inaugural Address

ALABAMA CAPITOL BUILDING, MONTGOMERY, FEBRUARY 18, 1861

G*entlemen of the Congress of the Confederate States of America, Friends and Fellow Citizens:*

Called to the difficult and responsible station of chief executive of the provisional government which you have instituted, I approach the discharge of the duties assigned to me with an humble distrust of my abilities, but with a sustaining confidence in the wisdom of those who are to guide and to aid me in the administration of public affairs, and an abiding faith in the virtue and patriotism of the people.

Looking forward to the speedy establishment of a permanent government to take the place of this, and which by its greater moral and physical power will be better able to combat with the many difficulties which arise from the conflicting interests of separate nations, I enter upon the duties of the office to which I have been chosen with the hope that the beginning of our career as a Confederacy may not be obstructed by hostile opposition to our enjoyment of the separate existence and independence which we have asserted, and, with the blessing of Providence, intend to maintain. Our present condition, achieved in a manner unprecedented in the history of nations, illustrates the American idea that governments rest upon the consent of the governed, and that it is the right of the people to alter or abolish governments whenever they become destructive of the ends for which they were established.

The declared purpose of the compact of Union from which we have withdrawn was "to establish justice, insure domestic tranquillity, provide for the common defense, promote the general welfare, and secure the blessing of liberty to ourselves and our posterity;" and when, in the judgment of the sovereign States now composing this Confederacy, it had been perverted from the purposes for which it was ordained, and had ceased to answer the ends for which it was established, a peaceful appeal to the ballot box declared that so far as they were concerned, the government created by that compact should cease to exist. In this they merely asserted a right which the Declaration of Independence of 1776 had defined to be inalienable; of the time and occasion for its exercise, they, as sovereigns, were the final judges, each for itself. The impartial and enlightened verdict of mankind will vindicate the rectitude of our conduct, and He who knows the hearts of men will judge of the sincerity with which we labored to preserve the Government of our fathers in its spirit. The right solemnly proclaimed at the birth of the States, and which has been affirmed and reaffirmed in the bills of rights of States subsequently admitted into the Union of 1789, undeniably recognize in the people the power to resume the authority delegated for the purposes of government. Thus the sovereign States here represented proceeded to form this Confederacy, and it is by abuse of language that their act has been denominated a revolution. They formed a new alliance, but within each State its government has remained, the rights of person and property have not been disturbed. The agent through whom they communicated with foreign nations is changed, but this does not necessarily interrupt their international relations.

Sustained by the consciousness that the transition from the former Union to the present Confederacy has not proceeded from a disregard on our part of just obligations, or any failure to perform every constitutional duty, moved by no interest or passion to invade the rights of others, anxious to cultivate peace and commerce with all nations, if we may not hope to avoid war, we may at least expect that posterity will acquit us of having needlessly engaged in it. Doubly justified by the absence of wrong on our part, and by wanton aggression on the part of others, there can be no cause to doubt that the courage and patriotism of the people of the Confederate States will be found equal to any measures of defense which honor and security may require.

An agricultural people, whose chief interest is the export of a commodity required in every manufacturing country, our true policy is peace, and the freest trade which our necessities will permit. It is alike our interest, and that of all those to whom we would sell and from whom we would buy, that there should be the fewest practicable restrictions upon the interchange of commodities. There can be but little rivalry between ours and any manufacturing or navigating community, such as the Northeastern States of the American Union. It must follow, therefore, that a mutual interest would invite good will and kind offices. If, however, passion or the lust of dominion should cloud the judgment or inflame the ambition of those States, we must prepare to meet the emergency and to maintain, by the final arbitrament of the sword, the position which we have assumed among the nations of the earth. We have entered upon the career of independence, and it must be inflexibly pursued. Through many years of controversy with our late associates, the Northern States, we have vainly endeavored to secure tranquillity, and to obtain respect for the rights to which we were entitled. As a necessity, not a choice, we have resorted to the remedy of separation; and henceforth our energies must be directed to the conduct of our own affairs, and the perpetuity of the Confederacy which we have formed. If a just perception of mutual interest shall permit us peaceably to pursue our separate political career, my most earnest desire will have been fulfilled. But, if this be denied to us, and the integrity of our territory and jurisdiction be assailed, it will but remain for us, with firm resolve, to appeal to arms and invoke the blessings of Providence on a just cause.

As a consequence of our new condition and with a view to meet anticipated wants, it will be necessary to provide for the speedy and efficient organization of branches of the executive department, having special charge of foreign intercourse, finance, military affairs, and the postal service.

For purposes of defense, the Confederate States may, under ordinary circumstances, rely mainly upon their militia, but it is deemed advisable, in the present condition of affairs, that there should be a well-instructed and disciplined army, more numerous than would usually be required on a peace establishment. I also suggest that for the protection of our harbors and commerce on the high seas a navy adapted to those objects will be required. These necessities have doubtless engaged the attention of Congress.

With a *Constitution* differing only from that of our fathers in so far as it is explanatory of their well-known intent, freed from the sectional conflicts which have interfered with the pursuit of the general welfare, it is not unreasonable to expect that States from which we have recently parted may seek to unite their fortunes with ours under the government which we have instituted. For this your Constitution makes adequate provision; but beyond this, if I mistake not the judgment and will of the people, a reunion with the States from which we have separated is neither practicable nor desirable. To increase the power, develop the resources, and promote the happiness of a confederacy, it is requisite that there should be so much of homogeneity that the welfare of every portion shall be the aim of the whole. Where this does not exist, antagonisms are engendered which must and should result in separation.

Actuated solely by the desire to preserve our own rights and promote our own welfare, the separation of the Confederate States has been marked by no aggression upon others and followed by no domestic convulsion. Our industrial pursuits have received no check. The cultivation of our fields has progressed as heretofore, and even should we be involved in war there would be no considerable diminution in the production of the staples which have constituted our exports and in which the commercial world has an interest scarcely less than our own. This common interest of the producer and consumer can only be interrupted by an exterior force which should obstruct its transmission to foreign markets—a course of conduct which would be as unjust toward us as it would be detrimental to manufacturing and commercial interests abroad. Should reason guide the action of the Government from which we have separated, a policy so detrimental to the civilized world, the Northern States included, could not be dictated by even the strongest desire to inflict injury upon us; but otherwise a terrible responsibility will rest upon it, and the suffering of millions will bear testimony to the folly and wickedness of our aggressors. In the meantime there will remain to us, besides the ordinary means before suggested, the well-known resources for retaliation upon the commerce of an enemy.

Experience in public stations, of subordinate grade to this which your kindness has conferred, has taught me that care and toil and disappointment are the price of official elevation. You will see many errors to forgive, many deficiencies to tolerate, but you shall not find in me either a want of zeal or fidelity to the cause that is to me highest in hope and of most enduring affection. Your generosity has bestowed upon me an undeserved distinction, one which I neither sought nor desired. Upon the continuance of that sentiment and upon your wisdom and patriotism I rely to direct and support me in the performance of the duty required at my hands.

We have changed the constituent parts, but not the system of our Government. The Constitution formed by our fathers is that of these Confederate States, in their exposition of it, and in the judicial construction it has received, we have a light which reveals its true meaning.

Thus instructed as to the just interpretation of the instrument, and ever remembering that all offices are but trusts held for the people, and that delegated powers are to be strictly construed, I will hope, by due diligence in the performance of my duties, though I may disappoint your expectations, yet to retain, when retiring, something of the good will and confidence which welcome my entrance into office.

It is joyous, in the midst of perilous times, to look around upon a people united in heart, where one purpose of high resolve animates and actuates the whole—where the sacrifices to be made are not weighed in the balance against honor and right and liberty and equality. Obstacles may retard, they cannot long prevent the progress of a movement sanctified by its justice, and sustained by a virtuous people. Reverently let us invoke the God of our fathers to guide and protect us in our efforts to perpetuate the principles which, by his blessing, they were able to vindicate, establish and transmit to their posterity, and with a continuance of His favor, ever gratefully acknowledged, we may hopefully look forward to success, to peace, and to prosperity.

The Civil War made George Armstrong Custer a war hero, and he gained popular immortality making his "last stand" with a portion of his 7th Cavalry at the Little Big Horn.

But he had to start somewhere, and that was at West Point, where he was a cadet in the pre–Civil War class of 1861. Custer describes in sad detail how his graduating class was divided by the war's inevitable arrival. It was the breakup of the United States played out in miniature, with cocky Southern cadets cheerfully leaving the Army and Northern cadets stoically sulking as war clouds gathered. Despite the disappointment, Custer the young glory seeker is ordered to go where the action was about to happen.

From West Point to the Battlefield

BY GEORGE ARMSTRONG CUSTER

In June, 1857, I entered the Military Academy at West Point as a cadet, having received my appointment thereto through the kindness of the Hon. John W. Bingham, then representing in Congress the district in Ohio in which I was born, and in which I had spent almost my entire boyhood. The first official notification received by me of my appointment to the Military Academy bore the signature of Jefferson Davis, then Secretary of War in the cabinet of President James Buchanan. Colonel Richard Delafield, one of the ablest and most accomplished officers of the Engineer Corps, occupied the position of superintendent of the Academy, and Lieutenant-Colonel Wm. J. Hardee, of the cavalry, afterward lieutenant-general in the Confederate army, was the commandant of the Corps of Cadets.

During the four years spent by me at West Point there were stationed there, either as officers in the capacity of instructors, or as cadets, several who afterward became more or less distinguished in the war of rebellion. Of these I now recall Lieutenant James B. Fry, post adjutant; Lieutenant John Gibbon, post quartermaster; Lieutenants George L. Hartsuff and Charles L. Griffin, instructors of artillery; Lieutenants M. Schofield and Cyrus B. Comstock, instructors of natural philosophy, etc.; Lieutenants Wm. B. Hazen and Alex. McD. McCook, instructors of infantry tactics; Lieutenant Godfrey Weitzel, instructor of engineering. These all achieved, a few years later, the rank of major-general in the Union armies, and commanded either armies or corps, or filled equally responsible and honorable positions. Of those whom I remember as instructors, and who, casting their fortunes with the forces of the South, afterward attained high rank, and who were then captains or lieutenants, were Charles W. Field, John Pegram, Fitzhugh Lee, Cadmus Wilcox, and John Forney. Of those who were cadets with me between the years of 1857 and 1861, there were quite a number who became more or less distinguished during the war. Of those who fought for the Union were Hardin, Merritt, Kilpatrick, Ames, Upton, and McKenzie, each of whom within less than three years from the date of his departure from the Academy won by bravery and distinguished conduct on the field of battle the star of brigadier-general. Most of these attained before the termination of the war the high grade of major-general. Among those joining the Confederate force who rose to distinction were Wheeler, Rosser, Young, Robertson, and Kelley, all of whom became general officers and rendered highly important service in the cause for which they battled. It is somewhat remarkable that these five general officers held commands in the cavalry, as did also three of the six—Merritt, Kilpatrick, and McKenzie—named on the Union side—to which list I might add my own name—thus showing that the cavalry offered the most promising field for early promotion.

A few months prior to the breaking out of the war, Beauregard, then a major of Engineers, was ordered to West Point as superintendent of the Academy; but whether because he foresaw the events of the near future, or from other motives, he applied to be relieved from the effect of the order. His application was granted, and he took his departure after a sojourn of but a few days.

Among the noticeable features of cadet life as then impressed upon me, and still present in my memory, were the sectional lines voluntarily established by the cadets themselves; at first barely distinguishable, but in the later years immediately preceding the war as clearly defined and strongly drawn as were the lines separating the extremes of the various sections in the national Congress. Nor was this fact a strange or remarkable one. As each Congressional district and territory of the United States had a representative in Congress, so each had its representatives at the Military Academy. And there was no phase of the great political questions of the times, particularly the agitation of the slavery question as discussed and maintained by the various agitators in Congress, but found its exponents among the cadets. In fact the latter as a rule reflected the political sentiments of the particular member who represented in Congress the locality from which the cadet happened to hail. Of course there were exceptions to this rule, but in the absence of any clearly formed political sentiment or belief of his own, it seemed to be the fashion, if nothing more, that each particular cadet should adopt the declared views and opinions of his representative in Congress. Hence it was no difficult matter to find exponents of the greatest political extremes; from the sturdy and pronounced abolitionist, hailing from New England, or perhaps the Western reserve in Ohio, to the most rabid of South Carolina nullifiers or Georgia fire-eaters. While the advocates for and against slavery were equally earnest and determined, those from the South were always the most talkative if not argumentative. As the pronounced abolitionist was rarely seen in Congress in those days, so was his appearance among the cadets of still rarer occurrence; besides it required more than ordinary moral and physical courage to boldly avow oneself an abolitionist. The name was considered one of opprobrium, and the cadet who had the courage to avow himself an abolitionist must be prepared to face the social frowns of the great majority of his comrades and at times to defend his opinions by his physical strength and metal. The John Brown raid into Virginia stirred the wrathful indignation of the embryonic warriors who looked upon slavery as an institution beyond human interference; while those of the opposite extreme contented themselves by quietly chuckling over the alarm into which the executive and military forces of the entire State were thrown by the invasion led by Brown, backed by a score or two of adherents.

The Presidential campaign which resulted in the election of Abraham Lincoln was not more hotly argued and contested by the regular stump speakers of either party than by the Northern and Southern cadets in their efforts to re-echo the political sentiments of their respective sections. The Republicans of course espoused the cause championed by Lincoln and Hamlin and the extreme Democrats announced themselves as under the banner of Breckinridge and Lane. A son of the latter was a member of my class, and occupied an adjoining room. The more moderate of the Democrats declared for Douglas and Johnson, while a few neutrals from the border States shouted feebly for Bell and Everett. The Breckinridge army of Southern Democrats did not hesitate to announce, as their seniors in and out of Congress had done, that in the event of

Lincoln's election secession would be the only resource left to the South. So high did political feeling run among the cadets, or a portion of them, that Mr. Lincoln was hung in effigy one night to a limb of one of the shade trees growing in front of cadet barracks. The effigy was removed early in the morning—so early that few of the cadets or professors even knew of the occurrence.

It seemed to have been part of the early teaching of the Southern youth, that the disruption of the Union was an event surely to be brought about. As an illustration of this I remember that Congress had appointed a committee in 1859, I believe, to visit West Point, and determine whether the course of study should continue to be five years, or be reduced to four. This committee was composed of two United States Senators, two members of the House, as many officers of the Army. Jefferson Davis, then a Senator from Mississippi, and a member of the Military Committee of the Senate, was a member of this special committee. The cadets, anxious to render their detention at the Academy as brief as possible, were warmly interested in the result of the committee's labors and investigation, and hoped ardently that the report would induce Congress to shorten the term of study from five to four years. To their great disappointment, however, it was soon after announced that the committee had reported in favor of continuance of the five-year system of instruction. It was believed by the cadets that this conclusion had been reached through the great influence of Jefferson Davis in the committee; an influence which his military ability, and particularly his experience and high reputation won while filling the office of Secretary of War, had properly given him. Whether justly or not, the disappointment of the cadets was loudly expressed when in groups by themselves. In one instance when the subject was being discussed a Georgia cadet, afterward distinguished in the war, indulged in the most bitter invectives against Davis, whom he charged with being the person responsible for detaining us an additional year in the Academy, concluding his execration by verbally consigning the object of his youthful ire to a locality hotter even than his native State. The next moment, however, he corrected himself in the most solemn manner by remarking, "No, I'll take that all back; for I believe the day is coming when the South will have need of Mr. Davis's abilities."

In looking back over the few months and years passed at West Point immediately preceding the war some strange incidents recur to my mind. When the various State conventions were called by the different States of the South with a view to the adoption of the ordinance of secession, it became only a question of time as to the attempted withdrawal of the seceding States. And while there were those representing both sections in Congress who professed to believe that war would not necessarily or probably follow, this opinion was not shared in even by persons as young and inexperienced as the cadets were. War was anticipated by them at that time and discussed and looked forward to as an event of the future with as much certainty as if speaking of an approaching season. The cadets from the South were in constant receipt of letters from their friends at home, keeping them fully advised of the real situation and promising them suitable positions in the military force yet to be organized to defend the ordinance of secession. All this was a topic of daily if not hourly conversation. Particularly was this true when we assembled together at meal time, when, grouped in squads of half a dozen or more, each usually found himself in the midst of his personal friends.

I remember a conversation held at the table at which I sat during the winter of '60–'61. I was seated next to Cadet P.M.B. Young, a gallant young fellow from Georgia, a classmate of mine, then and since the war an intimate and valued friend—a major-general in the Confederate forces during the war and a member of Congress from his native State at a later date. The approaching war was as usual the subject of conversation in which all participated, and in the freest and most friendly manner; the lads from the North discoursing earnestly upon the power and rectitude of the National Government, the impulsive Southron holding up pictures of invaded rights and future independence. Finally, in a half jocular, half earnest manner, Young turned to me and delivered himself as follows: "Custer, my boy, we're going to have war. It's no use talking: I see it coming. All the Crittenden compromises that can be patched up won't avert it. Now let me prophesy what will happen to you and me. You will go home, and your abolition Governor will probably make you colonel of a cavalry regiment. I will go down to Georgia, and ask Governor Brown to give me a cavalry regiment. And who knows but we may move against each other during the war. You will probably get the advantage of us in the first few engagements, as your side will be rich and powerful, while we will be poor and weak. Your regiment will be armed with the best of weapons, the sharpest of sabres; mine will have only shotguns and scythe blades; but for all that we'll get the best of the fight in the end, because we will fight for a principle, a cause, while you will fight only to perpetuate the abuse of power." Lightly as we both regarded this boyish prediction, it was destined to be fulfilled in a remarkable degree. Early in the war I did apply, not to the abolition Governor of my native State, but to that of Michigan, for a cavalry regiment. I was refused, but afterward obtained the regiment I desired as a part of my command. Young was chosen to lead one of the Georgia cavalry regiments. Both of us rose to higher commands, and confronted each other on the battlefield.

On December 20, 1860, South Carolina formally led the way by adopting the ordinance of secession; an example which was followed within the next few weeks by Mississippi, Alabama, Florida, Georgia, Louisiana, and Texas, in the order named. As soon as it became evident that these States were determined to attempt secession, the cadets appointed therefrom, imitating the action of their Senators and representatives in Congress, and influenced by the appeals of friends at home, tendered their resignations, eager to return to their homes and take part in the organization of the volunteer forces which the increasing difficulties and dangers of the situation rendered necessary. Besides, as the Confederate Congress was called to meet for the first time at Montgomery, Alabama, February 6, 1861, and would undoubtedly authorize the appointment of a large number of officers in the formation of the Confederate armies, it was important that applicants for positions of this kind should be on the ground to properly present their claims.

No obstacle was interposed by the Government to prevent the departure of the cadets from the South, although it seemed to me then, as it does now, strange that the Government did not adopt measures which would prevent the opponents of the national authority from availing themselves of the services and abilities of those who had been educated at the public expense. They knew the purpose of these cadets, like that of the many officers of the army who resigned, was to serve against the Government, and had a just and unquestioned claim, according to the terms of their oath of office, upon their loyalty and faithful service until freed from their allegiance by the acceptance of their resignation or their discharge. They could have refused to accept the resignations of all persons in the military service when there was reason to believe that such persons intended to aid the public enemy. Without the exercise of any greater or more questionable authority than that frequently exercised at a later period of the war, the Government could have promptly arrested and confined every person, of whatever rank in the military service, who tendered his resignation in the face of the enemy or in anticipation of a coming conflict. Thus the South would have been shorn of its chief military strength by being deprived of all its great military leaders. A few rash, thoughtless men might have fled to the seceded States, but the vast majority, being bound to the National Government by the solemn obligations of their oaths, would have rendered obedience, even if distasteful, to the demands of the national authority, until that authority should consent to release them from their obligations of duty, as it did by accepting their resignations. To have done otherwise would have been to commit the double offense of perjury and desertion; and I have too high an opinion of the sense of honor which governed the men who afterward became the gallant but mistaken leaders of the Confederate armies, to suppose them capable of this.

One by one the places occupied by the cadets from the seceding States became vacant; it cost many a bitter pang to disrupt the intimate relations existing between the hot-blooded Southron and his more phlegmatic schoolmate from the North. No schoolgirls could have been more demonstrative in their affectionate regard for each other than were some of the cadets about to separate for the last time, and under circumstances which made it painful to contemplate a future coming together. Those leaving for the South were impatient, enthusiastic, and hopeful. Visions filled their minds of a grand and glorious confederacy, glittering with the pomp and pageantry which usually characterizes imperial power, and supported and surrounded by a mighty army, the officers of which would constitute a special aristocracy.

Their comrades from the North, whom they were leaving behind, were reserved almost to sullenness; were grave almost to stoicism. The representatives of the two sections had each resolved upon their course of action; and each in a manner characteristic of their widely different temperaments, as different as the latitudes from which they hailed. Among the first of the cadets to leave West Point and hasten to enroll themselves under the banner of the seceding States, were two of my classmates, Kelley and Ball of Alabama. Kelley became prominent in the war, and was killed in battle. Ball also attained a high rank, and is now a prominent official in one of the most extensive and well-known business enterprises in this country. They took their departure from the Academy on Saturday. I remember the date the more readily as I was engaged in—to adopt the cadet term—"walking an extra," which consisted in performing the tiresome duties of a sentinel during the unemployed hour of Saturday; hours usually given to recreation. On this occasion I was pacing back and forth on my post, which for the time being extended along the path leading from the cadets' chapel toward the academic building, when I saw a party of from fifteen to twenty cadets emerge from the open space between the mess hall and academic building, and direct their steps toward the steamboat landing below. That which particularly attracted my attention was the bearing aloft upon the shoulders of their comrades of my two classmates Ball and Kelley, as they were being carried in triumph from the doors of the Academy to the steamboat landing. Too far off to exchange verbal adieux, even if military discipline had permitted it, they caught sight of me as step by step I reluctantly paid the penalty of offended regulations, and raised their hats in token of farewell, to which, first casting my eyes about to see that no watchful superior was in view, I responded by bringing my musket to a "present."

The comrades who escorted them were Southerners like themselves, and only awaiting the formal action of their respective States on the adoption of the secession ordinance to follow their example. It was but a few weeks until there was scarcely a cadet remaining at the Academy from the Southern States. Many resigned from the border States without waiting to see whether their State would follow in the attempt at secession or not; some resigned who had been appointed from States which never voted to leave the Union; while an insignificant few, who had resolved to join the Confederate forces, but desired to obtain their diplomas from the academic faculty, remained until the date of their graduation. Some remained until long after the declaration and commencement of hostilities; then, allowing the Government to transport them to Washington, tendered their resignations, and were dismissed for doing so in the face of the enemy. Happily the number that pursued this questionable course did not exceed half a dozen.

At no point in the loyal States were the exciting events of the spring of 1861 watched with more intense interest than at West Point. And after the departure of the Southern cadets the hearts of the people of no community, State, town, or village beat with more patriotic impulse than did those of the young cadets at West Point. Casting aside all questions of personal ambition or promotion; realizing only that the Government which they had sworn to defend, the principles they had been taught from childhood, were in danger, and threatened by armed enemies, they would gladly have marched to battle as private soldiers, rather than remain idle spectators in the great conflict.

As the time for the inauguration of Mr. Lincoln approached, rumors prevailed, and obtained wide belief, to the effect that a plot was on foot by which the inauguration of Mr. Lincoln was to be made the occasion on the part of the enemies of the Government, of whom great numbers were known to be in Washington, for seizing or making away with the executive officers of the nation, and taking possession of the people's capital. Whether or not such a scheme was ever seriously contemplated, it was deemed prudent to provide against it. The available military resources of the Government amounted to but little at that period. Lieutenant-General Scott, then commander-in-chief of the army, issued orders for the assembling at Washington of as large a military force as circumstances would permit. Under this order it became necessary to make a demand upon the regular military forces then employed at West Point. A battery of artillery was hastily organized from the war material and horses kept at the Academy for the purpose of instruction to the cadets. The horses were supplied by taking those used by the cadets in their cavalry and artillery drills. The force thus organized hastened to Washington, where, under the command of Captain Griffin—afterward Major-General Griffin—it took part in the inaugural ceremonies. Then followed the firing upon Sumter, the intelligence of which waked the slumbering echoes of loyalty and patriotism in every home and hamlet throughout the North.

It is doubtful if the people of the North were ever, or will ever be again, so united in thought and impulse as when the attack on Sumter was flashed upon them. Opponents in politics became friends in patriotism; all differences of opinion vanished or were laid aside, and a single purpose filled and animated the breast of the people as of one man—a purpose unflinching and unrestrained—to rush to the rescue of the Government, to beat down its opposers, come from whence they may. In addition to sharing the common interest and anxiety of the public in the attack upon Sumter, the cadets felt a special concern from the fact that among the little band of officers shut up in that fortress were two, Lieutenant Snyder and Hall, who had been our comrades as cadets only a few months before.

As already stated, the time of study and instruction at West Point at that period was five years, in the determination and fixing of which no one had exercised greater influence than Jefferson Davis—first as Secretary of War, afterward as United States Senator and member of a special Congressional committee to consider the question as to whether the course should extend to five years or only include four. There was no single individual in or out of Congress, excepting perhaps the venerable Lieutenant-General at the head of the army, whose opinions on military questions affecting the public service had greater weight than those of Jefferson Davis up to the date of his withdrawal from the Senate in January, 1861. As a Secretary of War he displayed an ability and achieved a reputation which has not since been approached by any of the numerous incumbents of that office, if we except Secretary Stanton. It is doubtful, however, if his administration of the duties of the war office in time of a great war like that of the rebellion, would have been successful. His strong prejudices for and against particular individuals, as illustrated in later years, would have tended to embarrass rather than promote a great cause.

In the general demand in 1861, not only from the National Government, but from States, for competent and educated officers to instruct and command the new levies of troops then being raised, in response to the call of the President, to oppose the rebellion, it was decided by the authorities at Washington to abandon the five years' course of instruction at the Military Academy, and reestablish that of four years. The effect of this was to give to the service in that year two classes of graduates for officers instead of but one. By this change the class of which I was a member graduated, under the four years' system, in June, while the preceding class was graduated, under the five years' rule, only a couple of months in advance of us. The members of both classes, with but few exceptions, were at once ordered to Washington, where they were employed either in drilling raw volunteers or serving on the staffs of general officers engaged in organizing the new regiments into brigades and divisions. I was one of the exceptions referred to, and the causes which led me in a different direction may be worthy of mention. My career as a cadet had but little to commend it to the study of those who came after me, unless as an example to be carefully avoided. The requirements of the academic regulations, a copy of which was placed in my hand the morning of my arrival at West Point, were not observed by me in such manner at all times as to commend me to the approval and good opinions of my instructors and superior officers. My offences against law and order were not great in enormity, but what they lacked in magnitude they made up in number. The forbidden locality of Benny Havens possessed stronger attractions than the study and demonstrations of a problem in Euclid, or the prosy discussion of some abstract proposition of moral science. My class numbered upon entering the Academy about one hundred and twenty-five. Of this number only thirty-four graduated, and of these thirty-three graduated above me. The resignation and departure of the Southern cadets took away from the Academy a few individuals who, had they remained, would probably have contested with me the debatable honor of bringing up the rear of the class.

We had passed our last examination as cadets, had exchanged barrack for camp life, and were awaiting the receipt of orders from Washington assigning us to the particular branches of the service for which we had been individually recommended by the academic faculty. The month of June had come, and we were full of impatience to hasten to the capital and join the forces preparing for the coming campaign. It is customary, or was then, to allow each cadet, prior to his graduation, to perform at least one tour of duty as an officer of the guard, instead of the ordinary duties of a private soldier on guard. I had not only had the usual experience in the latter capacity, extending over a period of four years, but in addition had been compelled, as punishment for violations of the academic regulations, to perform extra tours of guard duty on Saturdays— times which otherwise I should have been allowed for pleasure and recreation. If my memory serves me right, I devoted sixty-six Saturdays to this method of vindicating outraged military law during my cadetship of four years. It so happened that it fell to my detail to perform the duties of officer of the guard in camp, at a time when the arrival of the order from Washington officially transforming us from cadets to officers was daily expected. I began my tour at the usual hour in the morning, and everything passed off satisfactorily in connection with the discharge of my new responsibilities, until just at dusk I heard a commotion near the guard tents. Upon hastening to the scene of the disturbance, which by the way was at a considerable distance from the main camp, I found two cadets engaged in a personal dispute, which threatened to result in blows. Quite a group of cadets, as friends and spectators, had formed about the two bellicose disputants. I had hardly time to take in the situation when the two principals of the group engaged in a regular set-to, and began belaboring each other vigorously with their fists. Some of their more prudent friends rushed forward and attempted to separate the two contestants. My duty as officer of the guard was plain and simple. I should have arrested the two combatants and sent them to the guard tents for violating the peace and the regulations of the Academy. But the instincts of the boy prevailed over the obligation of the officer of the guard. I pushed my way through the surrounding line of cadets, dashed back those who were interfering in the struggle, and called out loudly, "Stand back, boys; let's have a fair fight."

I had occasion to remember, if not regret, the employment of these words. Scarcely had I uttered them when the crowd about me dispersed hurriedly, and fled to the concealment of their tents. Casting about me to ascertain the cause of this sudden dispersion, I beheld approaching at a short distance two officers of the army, Lieutenants Hazen and Merrill (now Major-General Hazen and Colonel Merrill of the Engineer Corps). I sought the tent of the officer of the guards promptly, but the mischief had been done. Lieutenant Hazen was the officer in charge on that particular day, whose duty it was to take cognizance of the violations of the regulations. Summoning me to his presence, near the scene of the unfortunate disturbance, he asked me in stern tones if I was not the officer of the guard; to which I of course responded in the affirmative. He then overwhelmed me by inquiring in the same unrelenting voice, "Why did you not suppress the riot which occurred here a few minutes ago?" Now, it had never been suggested to me that the settlement of a personal difficulty between two boys, even by the administering of blows, could be considered or described as a riot. The following morning I was required to report at the tent of the commandant (Lieutenant-Colonel John F. Reynolds, afterward General Reynolds, killed at Gettysburg). Of course no explanation could satisfy the requirements of military justice. I was ordered to return to my tent in arrest. The facts in the case were reported to Washington, on formal charges and specifications, and a court-martial asked for to determine the degree of my punishment.

Within a few hours of my arrest the long-expected order came, relieving my class from further duty at West Point, and directing the members of it to proceed to Washington and report to the Adjutant-General of the Army for further orders. My name, however, did not appear in this list. I was to be detained to await the application of the commandant for a court-martial to sit on my case. The application received approval at the War Department, and a court was assembled at West Point, composed principally of officers who had recently arrived from Texas, where they served under General Twiggs, until his surrender to the Confederate forces. The judge advocate of the court was Lieutenant Benet, now Brigadier-General and Chief of the Ordnance Corps. I was arraigned with all the solemnity and gravity which might be looked for in a trial for high treason, the specification setting forth in stereotyped phraseology that "He, the said cadet Custer, did fail to suppress a riot or disturbance near the guard tent, and did fail to separate, etc., but, on the contrary, did cry out in a loud tone of voice, 'Stand back, boys; let's have a fair fight,' or words to that effect."

To which accusations the accused pleaded "Guilty," as a matter of course, introducing as witnesses, by way of mitigation, the two cadets, the cause of my difficulty, to prove that neither was seriously injured in the fray. One of them is now a promising young captain in the Engineer Corps.

The trial was brief, scarcely occupying more time than did the primary difficulty.

I dreaded the long detention which I feared I must undergo while awaiting not only the verdict, but the subsequent action of the authorities at Washington to whom the case must by law be submitted.

My classmates who had preceded me to Washington interested themselves earnestly in my behalf to secure my release from further arrest at West Point, and an order for me to join them at the national capital. Fortunately some of them had influential friends there, and it was but a few days after my trial that the superintendent of the Academy received a telegraphic order from Washington, directing him to release me at once, and order me to report to the Adjutant-General of the Army for duty. This order practically rendered the action and proceedings of the court-martial in my case nugatory. The record, I presume, was forwarded to the War Department, where it probably lies safely stowed away in some pigeonhole. What the proceeding of the court or their decision was, I have never learned.

I left West Point on the 18th of July for Washington, delaying a few hours that afternoon on my arrival in New York to enable me to purchase, of the well-known military firm of Horstmann's, my lieutenant's outfit of sabre, revolver, sash, spurs, etc. Taking the evening train for Washington, I found the cars crowded with troops, officers and men, hastening to the capital.

At each station we passed on the road at which a halt was made, crowds of citizens were assembled provided bountifully with refreshments, which they distributed in the most lavish manner among the troops. Their enthusiasm knew no bounds; they received us with cheers and cheered us in parting. It was no unusual sight, on leaving a station surrounded by these loyal people, to see matrons and maidens embracing and kissing with patriotic fervor the men, entire strangers to them, whom they saw hastening to the defence of the nation.

Arriving at Washington soon after daylight, Saturday morning, the 20th of July, I made my way to the Ebbit House, where I expected to find some of my classmates domiciled. Among others whom I found there was Parker, appointed from Missouri, who had been my room and tent-mate at West Point for years. He was one of the few members of my class who, while sympathizing with the South, had remained at the Academy long enough to graduate and secure a diploma. Proceeding to his room without going through the formality of announcing my arrival by sending up a card, I found him at that early hour still in bed. Briefly he responded to my anxious inquiry for news, that McDowell's army was confronting Beauregard's, and a general engagement was expected hourly. My next inquiry was as to his future plans and intentions, remembering his Southern sympathies. To this he replied by asking me to take from a table near by and read an official order to which he pointed.

Upon opening the document referred to, I found it to be an order from the War Department dismissing from the rolls of the army Second Lieutenant James P. Parker, for having tendered his resignation in the face of the enemy. The names of two others of my classmates appeared in the same order. Both the latter have since sought and obtained commissions in the Egyptian army under the Khedive. After an hour or more spent in discussing the dark probabilities of the future as particularly affected by the clouds of impending war, I bade a fond farewell to my former friend and classmate, with whom I had lived on terms of closer intimacy and companionship than with any other being. We had eaten day by day at the same table, had struggled together in the effort to master the same problems of study; we had marched by each other's side year after year, elbow to elbow, when engaged in the duties of drill, parade, etc., and had shared our blankets with each other when learning the requirements of camp life. Henceforth this was all to be thrust from our memory as far as possible, and our paths and aims in life were to run counter to each other in the future. We separated; he to make his way, as he did immediately, to the seat of the Confederate Government, and accept a commission under a flag raised in rebellion against the Government that had educated him, and that he had sworn to defend; I to proceed to the office of the Adjutant-General of the Army and report for such duty as might be assigned me in the great work which was then dearest and uppermost in the mind of every loyal citizen of the country.

It was not until after two o'clock in the morning that I obtained an audience with the Adjutant-General of the Army and reported to him formally for orders, as my instructions directed me to do. I was greatly impressed by the number of officials I saw and the numerous messengers to be seen flitting from room to room, bearing immense numbers of huge-looking envelopes. The entire department had an air of busy occupation which, taken in connection with the important military events then daily transpiring and hourly expected, and contrasted with the hum-drum life I had but lately led as a cadet, added to the bewilderment I naturally felt.

Presenting my order of instructions to the officer who seemed to be in charge of the office, he glanced at it, and was about to give some directions to a subordinate near by to write out an order assigning me to some duty, when, turning to me, he said, "Perhaps you would like to be presented to General Scott, Mr. Custer?" To which of course I joyfully assented. I had often beheld the towering form of the venerable chieftain during his summer visits to West Point, but that was the extent of my personal acquaintance with him. So strict was the discipline at the Academy that the gulf which separated cadets from commissioned officers seemed greater in practice than that which separated enlisted men from them. Hence it was rare indeed that a cadet ever had an opportunity to address or be addressed by officers, and it was still more rare to be brought into personal conversation with an officer above the grade of lieutenant or captain; if we except the superintendent of the Academy and the commandant of the corps of cadets. The sight of a general officer, let alone the privilege of speaking to one, was an event to be recounted to one's friends. In those days the title of general was not so familiar as to be encountered on every hotel register. Besides, the renown of a long lifetime gallantly spent in his country's service had gradually but justly placed General Scott far above all contemporary chieftains in the admiration and hero worship of his fellow countrymen; and in the youthful minds of the West Point cadets of those days Scott was looked up to as a leader whose military abilities were scarcely second to those of a Napoleon, and whose patriotism rivalled that of Washington.

Following the lead of the officer to whom I had reported, I was conducted to the room in which General Scott received his official visitors. I found him seated at a table over which were spread maps and other documents which plainly showed their military character. In the room, and seated near the table, were several members of Congress, of whom I remember Senator Grimes of Iowa. The topic of conversation was the approaching battle in which General McDowell's forces were about to engage. General Scott seemed to be explaining to the Congressmen the position, as shown by the map, of the contending armies. The Adjutant-General called General Scott's attention to me by saying, "General, this is Lieutenant Custer of the Second Cavalry; he has just reported from West Point, and I did not know but that you might have some special orders to give him." Looking at me a moment, the General shook me cordially by the hand, saying, "Well, my young friend, I am glad to welcome you to the service at this critical time. Our country has need of the strong arms of all her loyal sons in this emergency." Then, turning to the Adjutant-General, he inquired to which company I had been assigned. "To Company G, Second Cavalry, now under Major Innes Palmer, with General McDowell," was the reply. Then, addressing me, the General said, "We have had the assistance of quite a number of you young men from the Academy, drilling volunteers, etc. Now what can I do for you? Would you prefer to be ordered to report to General Mansfield to aid in this work, or is your desire for something more active?" Although overwhelmed by such condescension upon the part of one so far superior in rank to any officer with whom I had been brought in immediate contact, I ventured to stammer out that I earnestly desired to be ordered to at once join my company, then with General McDowell, as I was anxious to see active service. "A very commendable resolution, young man," was the reply; then, turning to the Adjutant-General, he added, "Make out Lieutenant Custer's orders directing him to proceed to his company at once"; then, as if a different project had presented itself, he inquired of me if I had been able to provide myself with a mount for the field. I replied that I had not, but would set myself about doing so at once. "I fear you have a difficult task before you, because, if rumor is correct, every serviceable horse in the city has been bought, borrowed, or begged by citizens who have gone or are going as spectators to witness the battle. I only hope Beauregard may capture some of them and teach them a lesson. However, what I desire to say to you is, go and provide yourself with a horse if possible, and call here at seven o'clock this evening. I desire to send some dispatches to General McDowell, and you can be the bearer of them. You are not afraid of a night ride, are you?" Exchanging salutations, I left the presence of the General-in-Chief, delighted at the prospect of being at once thrown into active service, perhaps participating in the great battle which every one there knew was on the eve of occurring; but more than this my pride as a soldier was not a little heightened by the fact that almost upon my first entering the service I was to be the bearer of important official dispatches from the General-in-Chief to the General commanding the principal army in the field.

I had yet a difficult task before me, in procuring a mount. I visited all the prominent livery stables, but received almost the same answer from each, the substance of which was, that I was too late; all the disposable horses had been let or engaged. I was almost in despair at the idea that I was not to be able to take advantage of the splendid opportunity for distinction opened before me, and was at a loss what to do, or to whom to apply for advice, when I met on Pennsylvania avenue a soldier in uniform, whom I at once recognized as one of the detachment formerly stationed at West Point, who left with those ordered

suddenly to the defence of Washington at the time of Mr. Lincoln's inauguration, when it was feared attempts would be made to assassinate the President
elect. Glad to encounter any one I had ever seen before, I approached and
asked him what he was doing in Washington. He answered that he belonged to
Griffin's battery, which was then with McDowell's forces at the front, and had
returned to Washington, by Captain Griffin's order, to obtain and take back
with him an extra horse left by the battery on its departure from the capital.
Here then was my opportunity, and I at once availed myself of it. It was the
intention of this man to set out on his return at once; but at my earnest solicita-
tion he consented to defer his departure until after seven o'clock, agreeing also
to have the extra horse saddled and in readiness for me.

Promptly at seven o'clock I reported at the Adjutant-General's office,
obtaining my dispatches, and with no baggage or extra clothing to weight down
my horse, save what I carried on my person, I repaired to the point at which I
was to find my horse and companion for the night. Upon arriving there I was
both surprised and delighted to discover that the horse which accident seemed
to have provided for me was a favorite one ridden by me often when learning
the cavalry exercises at West Point. Those who were cadets just before the war
will probably recall him to mind when I give the name, "Wellington," by which
he was then known.

Crossing Long bridge about nightfall, and taking the Fairfax C.H. road for
Centreville, the hours of night flew quickly past, engrossed as my mind was
with the excitement and serious novelty of the occasion as well as occasionally
diverted by the conversation of my companion. I was particularly interested
with his description, given as we rode in the silent darkness, of a skirmish
which had taken place only two days before at Blackburn's ford, between the
forces of the enemy stationed there and a reconnoitring detachment sent from
General McDowell's army; especially when I learned that my company had
borne an honorable part in the affair.

It was between two and three o'clock in the morning when we reached the
army near Centreville. The men had already breakfasted, and many of the regiments had been formed in column in the roads ready to resume the march; but
owing to delays in starting, most of the men were lying on the ground, endeavoring to catch a few minutes more of sleep; others were sitting or standing in
small groups smoking and chatting. So filled did I find the road with soldiers
that it was with difficulty my horse could pick his way among the sleeping bodies without disturbing them. But for my companion I should have had consid-

erable difficulty in finding my way to headquarters; but he seemed familiar with the localities even in the darkness, and soon conducted me to a group of tents near which a large log fire was blazing, throwing a bright light over the entire scene for some distance around. As I approached, the sound of my horse's hoofs brought an officer from one of the tents nearest to where I halted. Advancing toward me, he inquired who I wished to see. I informed him that I was bearer of dispatches from General Scott to General McDowell. "I will relieve you of them," was his reply; but seeing me hesitate to deliver them, he added, "I am Major Wadsworth of General McDowell's staff." While I had hoped from ambitious pride to have an opportunity to deliver the dispatches in person to General McDowell, I could not decline longer, so placed the documents in Major Wadsworth's hands, who took them to a tent a few paces distant, where, through its half-open folds, I saw him hand them to a large, portly officer, whom I at once rightly conceived to be General McDowell. Then, returning to where I still sat on my horse, Major Wadsworth (afterward General Wadsworth) asked of me the latest news in the capital, when I replied that every person at Washington was looking to the army for news, he added, "Well, I guess they will not have to wait much longer. The entire army is under arms, and moving to attack the enemy to-day." After inquiring at what hour I left Washington, and remarking that I must be tired, Major Wadsworth asked me to dismount and have some breakfast, as it would be difficult to say when another opportunity would occur. I was very hungry, and rest would not have been unacceptable, but in my inexperience I partly imagined, particularly while in the presence of the white-haired officer who gave the invitation, that hunger and fatigue were conditions of feeling which a soldier, especially a young one, should not acknowledge. Therefore, with an appetite almost craving, I declined the kind proffer of the Major. But when he suggested that I dismount and allow my horse to be fed I gladly assented. While Major Wadsworth was kindly interesting himself in the welfare of my horse, I had the good fortune to discover in an officer at headquarters one of my recent West Point friends, Lieutenant Kingsbury, aide-de-camp to General McDowell. He repeated the invitation just given by Major Wadsworth in regard to breakfast, but I did not have the perseverance to again refuse. Near the log fire already mentioned were some servants busily engaged in removing the remains of breakfast. A word from Kingsbury, and they soon prepared for me a cup of coffee, a steak, and some Virginia corn bread, to which I did ample justice. Had I known, however, that I was not to have an opportunity to taste food during the next thirty hours, I should have appreciated the opportunity I then enjoyed even more highly.

As I sat on the ground sipping my coffee, and heartily enjoying my first breakfast in the field, Kingsbury (afterward Colonel Kingsbury, killed at the battle of Antietam) informed me of the general movement then begun by the army, and of the attack which was to be made on Beauregard's forces that day. Three days before I had quitted school at West Point. I was about to witness the first grand struggle in open battle between the Union and secession armies; a struggle in which, fortunately for the nation, the Union forces were to suffer defeat, while the cause for which they fought was to derive from it renewed strength and encouragement.

Just a good ol' boy having a good ol' time, John Mosby spent his Civil War years in northern Virginia raiding Union rear areas, raising hell, and causing a ruckus. Fighting for a cause he believed in, Mosby led his small force like a gang of frat house boys off on a scavenger hunt. Mosby figured loyal Southerners would be more likely to volunteer to fight a "fun" war with him for a brief spell than enlist and suffer discipline and the tedium of camp life. This says a lot about human nature.

For Mosby, victory lay in tying down as many Union soldiers as possible guarding rear areas instead of fighting. Between the daring raids and the hilarious cock-ups, Mosby happily "won" his war at the Union's expense, keeping all war booty to supply his own meager troop.

Excerpt from *Mosby's War Reminiscences*

BY JOHN S. MOSBY

Chapter II.

"O! shadow of glory—dim image of war—
The chase hath no story—her hero no star."

—BYRON, DEFORMED TRANSFORMED.

After the first battle of Bull Run, Stuart's cavalry was engaged in performing outpost duty on our front, which extended from the falls above Washington to Occoquan, on the lower Potomac. There were no opportunities for adventurous enterprise. McClellan's army was almost in a state of siege in Washington, and his cavalry but rarely showed themselves outside his infantry picket line. We had to go on picket duty three times a week and remain twenty-four hours. The work was pretty hard; but still, soldiers liked it better than the irksome life of the camp. I have often sat alone on my horse from midnight to daybreak, keeping watch over the sleeping army. During this period of inaction, the stereotyped message sent every night from Washington to the northern press was, "All quiet along the Potomac."

While I was a private in Stuart's cavalry, I never missed but one tour of outpost duty, and then I was confined in the hospital from an injury. With one other, I was stationed at the post on the road leading from Fall's Church to Lewinsville, in Fairfax. At night we relieved each other alternately, one sleeping while the other watched. About dusk, Capt. Jones had ridden to the post and instructed us that we had no troops outside our lines on that road, and that we must fire, without halting, on any body of men approaching from that direction, as they would be the enemy. The night was dark, and it had come my turn to sleep. I was lying on the ground, with the soft side of a stone for a pillow, when I was suddenly aroused by my companion, who called to me to mount, that the Yankees were coming. In an almost unconscious state I leaped into my saddle, and at the same instant threw forward my carbine, and both of us fired on a body of cavalry not fifty yards distant. Fortunately, we fired so low our bullets struck the ground just in front of them. The flash from my carbine in my horse's face frightened him terribly. He wheeled, and that is the last I remember about that night. The next thing I recollect is that some time during the next day I became conscious, and found myself lying on a bed at the house of the keeper of the toll-gate. Capt. Jones and several of the men of my company were standing by me. It appears that the night before Stuart had sent a company of cavalry to Lewinsville for some purpose. This company had gone out by one road and returned on the one where I had been posted. My horse had run away and fallen over a cow that was lying down, and rolled over me. The company of cavalry coming along the same way, their horses in front started and snorted at something lying in the road. They halted, some of them dismounted to see what it was, and discovered me there in an insensible state. They picked me up and carried me into the village, apparently dying. I was bruised from head to foot, and felt like every bone in my body had been broken. I had to be carried to Fairbay Court House in an ambulance. There is a tradition that when Capt. Jones looked on me that night he swore harder than the army in Flanders. The feelings he expressed for the officer in fault were not so benevolent as my Uncle Toby's for the fly.

While the cavalry did not have an opportunity to do much fighting during the first year of the war, they learned to perform the duties and endure the privations of a soldier's life. My experience in this school was of great advantage to me in the after years when I became a commander. There was a thirst for adventure among the men in the cavalry, and a positive pleasure to get an occasional shot "from a rifleman hid in a thicket." There were often false alarms, and sometimes real ones, from scouting parties of infantry who would come up at night to surprise our pickets. A vivid imagination united with a nervous temperament can see in the dark the shapes of many things that have no real existence. A rabbit making its nocturnal rounds, a cow grazing, a hog rooting for acorns, an owl hooting, or the screech of a night hawk could often arouse and sometimes stampede an outpost or draw the fire of a whole line of pickets. At the first shot, the reserve would mount; and soon the videttes would come running in at full speed. There was an old gray horse roaming about the fields at Fairfax Court House during the first winter of the war that must have been fired at a hundred times at night by our videttes, and yet was never touched. I have never heard whether Congress has voted him a pension. The last time that I was ever on picket was in February, 1862. The snow was deep and hard frozen. My post was on the outskirts of Fairfax Court House, at the junction of the Washington road and turnpike. I wore a woollen hood to keep my ears from freezing, and a blanket thrown around me as a protection against the cold wind. The night was clear, and all that's best of dark and bright. I sat on my horse under the shadow of a tree, both as a protection from the piercing blast and as a screen from the sight of an enemy. I had gone on duty at midnight, to remain until daybreak. The deep silence was occasionally broken by the cry of "Halt!" from some distant sentinel, as he challenged the patrol or relief. The swaying branches of the trees in the moonlight cast all sorts of fantastic forms on the crystal snow. In this deep solitude, I was watching for danger and communing with the spirit of the past. At this very spot, a few nights before, the vidette had been fired on by a scouting party of infantry that had come up from McClellan's camps below. But the old gray horse had several times got up a panic there which raised a laugh on the soldiers.

Now I confess that I was about as much afraid of ridicule as of being shot, and so, unless I got killed or captured, I resolved to spend the night there. Horatius Cocles was not more determined to hold his position on the bridge of the Tiber, than I was to stay at my post, but perhaps his motives were less mixed than mine. I had been long pondering and remembering, and in my reverie had visited the fields that I had traversed "in life's morning march when my bosom was young." I was suddenly aroused by the crash of footsteps breaking the crust of the hard snow. The sound appeared to proceed from something approaching me with the measured tread of a file of soldiers. It was screened from my view by some houses near the roadside. I was sure that it was an enemy creeping up to get a shot at me, for I thought that even the old horse would not have ventured out on such a night, unless under orders. My heart began to sicken within me pretty much like Hector's did when he had to face the wrath of Achilles. My horse, shivering with cold, with the instinct of danger, pricked up his ears and listened as eagerly as I did to the footsteps as they got near. I drew my pistol, cocked it, and took aim at the corner around which this object must come. I wanted to get the advantage of the first shot. Just then the hero of a hundred panics appeared—the old gray horse! I returned my pistol to my belt and relapsed into reverie. I was happy: my credit as a soldier had been saved.

A couple of days after this my company returned there, as usual, on picket. On this same morning Stuart came, making an inspection of the outposts. It happened that there were two young ladies living at Fairfax Court House, acquaintances of his, who did not like to stay in such an exposed situation, and so Stuart had arranged to send them to the house of a friend near Fryingpan, which was further within our lines. At that time the possibility of our army ever retiring to Richmond had not been conceived by the rank and file. Stuart had then become a brigadier-general, and Capt. Jones had been promoted to be colonel of the 1st Virginia cavalry. Although I served under Stuart almost from the beginning of the war, I had no personal acquaintance with him before then. He asked Capt. Blackford to detail a man to go along as an escort for the two ladies. I had often been invited to the house of one of them by her father, so I was selected on that account to go with them. I left my horse with my friend Beattie to lead back to camp, and took a seat in the carriage with the ladies. This was on the 12th of February, 1862. It began snowing just as we started, and it was late in the afternoon before we got to Fryingpan. I then went in the carriage to Stuart's headquarters a few miles off, at Centreville. It was dark when I got there. I reported to him the result of my mission to Fryingpan, and asked for a pass to go back to the camp of my regiment, which was about four miles off on Bull Run. Stuart told me that the weather was too bad for me to walk to camp that night, but to stay where I was until next morning. He and Generals Joseph E. Johnston and G. W. Smith occupied the Grigsby house and messed together. I sat down by a big wood fire in an open fireplace in the front room, where he and the other two generals were also sitting. I never spoke a word, and would have been far happier trudging through the snow back to camp, or even as a vidette on a picket post. I felt just as much out of place and uneasy as a mortal would who had been lifted to a seat by the side of the gods on Olympus. Presently supper was announced. The generals all walked into the adjoining room, and Stuart told me to come in. After they had sat down at the table, Stuart observed that I was not there and sent for me. I was still sitting by the fire. I obeyed his summons like a good soldier, and took my place among the *dil majores*. I was pretty hungry, but did not enjoy my supper. I would have preferred fasting or eating with the couriers. I know I never spoke a word to any one—I don't think I raised my eyes from off my plate while I was at the table.

Now, while I felt so much oppressed by the presence of men of such high rank, there was nothing in their deportment that produced it. It was the same way the next morning. Stuart had to send after me to come in to breakfast. I went pretty much in the same dutiful spirit that Gibbon says that he broke his marriage engagement: "I sighed as a lover and obeyed as a son." But now my courage rose; I actually got into conversation with Joe Johnston, whom I would have regarded it as a great privilege the day before to view through a long-range telescope. The generals talked of Judah P. Benjamin's (who was then Secretary of War) breach of courtesy to Stonewall Jackson that had caused Jackson to send in his resignation. They were all on Jackson's side. There was nothing going on about Centreville to indicate the evacuation that took place three weeks after that. Stuart let me have a horse to ride back to camp. As soon as I got there, Col. Jones sent for me to come to his tent. I went, and he offered me the place of adjutant of the regiment. I had had no more expectation of such a thing than of being translated on Elijah's chariot to the skies. Of course, I accepted it. I was never half as much frightened in any fight I was in as I was on the first dress parade I conducted. But I was not permitted to hold the position long. About two months after that, when we had marched to meet McClellan at Yorktown, my regiment reorganized under the new act of the Confederate Congress. Fitz Lee was elected colonel in place of Jones. This was the result of an attempt to mix democracy with military discipline. Fitz Lee did not reappoint me as adjutant, and so I lost my first commission on the spot where Cornwallis lost his sword. This was at the time an unrecognized favor. If I had been retained as adjutant, I would probably have never been anything else. So at the close of the first year of the war I was, in point of rank, just where I had begun. Well, it did not break my heart. When the army was retiring from Centreville, Stuart's cavalry was the rear guard, and I had attracted his favorable notice by several expeditions I had led to the rear of the enemy. So Stuart told me to come to his headquarters and act as a scout for him. A scout is not a spy who goes in disguise, but a soldier in arms and uniform, who goes among as enemy's lines to get information about them. Among the survivors of the Army of the Potomac there are many legends afloat, and religiously believed to be true, of a mysterious person—a sort of Flying Dutchman or Wandering Jew—prowling among their camps in the daytime in the garb of a beggar or with a pilgrim's staff, and leading cavalry raids upon them at night. In popular imagination, I have been identified with that mythical character.

On the day after Mr. Lincoln's assassination, Secretary Stanton telegraphed to Gen. Hancock, then in command at Winchester, Va., that I had been seen at the theatre in Washington on that fatal night. Fortunately, I could prove an alibi by Hancock himself, as I was at that very time negotiating a truce with him. I recently heard an officer of the United States army tell a story of his being with the guard for a wagon train, and my passing him with my command on the pike, all of us dressed as Federal soldiers, and cutting the train out from behind him. I laughed at it, like everybody who heard it, and did not try to unsettle his faith. To have corrected it would have been as cruel as to dispel the illusion of childhood that the story of "Little Red Riding Hood" is literally true, or to doubt the real presence of Santa Claus. It was all pure fiction about our being dressed in blue uniforms, or riding with him. I did capture the wagon train at the time and place mentioned, Oct. 26, 1863, at the Chestnut Fork, near Warrenton, Va., but we never even saw the guard. They had got sleepy, and gone on to camp, and left me to take care of their wagons—which I did. The quartermaster in charge of them, Capt. Stone, who was made prisoner, called to pay his respects to me a few days ago. I can now very well understand how the legendary heroes of Greece were created. I always wore the Confederate uniform, with the insignia of my rank. So did my men. So any success I may have had, either as an individual scout or partisan commander, cannot be accounted for on the theory that it was accomplished through disguise. The hundreds of prisoners I took are witnesses to the contrary.

FAUQUIER COUNTY, VA., FEB. 4, 1863.

GENERAL:—I arrived in this neighborhood about one week ago. Since then I have been, despite the bad weather, quite actively engaged with the enemy. The result up to this time has been the capture of twenty-eight Yankee cavalry together with all their horses, arms, etc. The evidence of parole I forward with this. I have also paroled a number of deserters. Col. Sir Percy Wyndham, with over two hundred cavalry, came up to Middleburg last week to punish me, as he said, for my raids on his picket line. I had a slight skirmish with him, in which my loss was three men, captured by the falling of their horses; the enemy's loss, one man and three horses captured. He set a very nice trap a few days ago to catch me in. I went into it, but, contrary to the Colonel's expectations, brought the trap off with me, killing one, capturing twelve; the balance running. The extent of the annoyance I have been to the Yankees may be judged of by the fact that, baffled in their attempts to capture me, they threaten to retaliate on citizens for my acts.

I forward to you some correspondence I have had on the subject. The most of the infantry has left Fairfax and gone towards Fredericksburg. In Fairfax there are five or six regiments of cavalry; there are about three hundred at Dranesville. They are so isolated from the rest of the command, that nothing would be easier than their capture. I have harassed them so much that they do not keep their pickets over half a mile from camp. There is no artillery there. I start on another trip day after to-morrow.

I am, most respectfully, yours, etc.,

JOHN S. MOSBY.

MAJ.-GEN. J. E. B. STUART.

HEADQUARTERS CAVALRY DIVISION, FEB. 8, 1863.

Respectfully forwarded as additional proof of the prowess, daring, and efficiency of Mosby (without commission) and his band of a dozen chosen spirits.

J. E. B. STUART,
MAJOR-GENERAL COMMANDING.

HEADQUARTERS, FEB. 11, 1863.

Respectfully forwarded to the Adjutant and Inspector-General as evidence of merit of Capt. Mosby.

R. E. LEE,
GENERAL.

Chapter III.

After the battle of Fredericksburg, in December, 1862, there was a lull in the storm of war. The men on the outposts along the Rappahannock had a sort of truce to hostilities, and began swapping tobacco and coffee, just as the soldiers of Wellington and Soult, on the eve of a great battle, filled their canteens from the same stream. At that time, Stuart determined to make a Christmas raid about Dumfries, which was on Hooker's line of communication with Washington. I went with him. He got many prisoners, and wagons loaded with bonbons and all the good things of the festive season. It made us happy, but almost broke the sutlers' hearts. A regiment of Pennsylvania cavalry left their camp on the Occoquan, and their Christmas turkeys, and came out to look for us. They had better have stayed at home; for all the good they did was to lead Stuart's cavalry into their camp as they ran through it. After leaving Dumfries, Stuart asked me to take Beattie and go on ahead. The road ran through a dense forest, and there was danger of an ambuscade, of which every soldier has a horror who has read of Braddock's defeat. Beattie and I went forward at a gallop, until we met a large body of cavalry. As no support was in sight, several officers made a dash at us, and at the same time opened such a fire as to show that peace on earth and good will to men, which the angels and morning stars had sung on that day over 1800 years ago, was no part of their creed. The very fact that we did not run away ought to have warned them that somebody was behind us. When the whole body had got within a short distance of us, Stuart, who had heard the firing, came thundering up with the 1st Virginia cavalry. All the fun was over with the Pennsylvanians then. There was no more merry Christmas for them. Wade Hampton was riding by the side of Stuart. He went into the fight and fought like a common (or, rather, an uncommon) trooper. The combat was short and sharp, and soon became a rout; the Federal cavalry ran right through their camp, and gave a last look at their turkeys as they passed. But alas! they were "grease, but living grease no more" for them. There was probably some method in their madness in running through their camp. They calculated, with good reason, that the temptation would stop the pursuit.

A few days ago I read, in a book giving the history of the telegraph in the war, the dispatch sent to Washington by the operator near there: "The 17th Pennsylvania cavalry just passed here, furiously charging to the rear." When we got to Burke's Station, on the Orange and Alexandria Railroad, while his command was closing up, Stuart put his own operator in charge of the instrument, and listened to a telegraphic conversation between the general commanding at Fairfax Court-House and the authorities at Washington. In order to bewilder and puzzle them, he sent several messages, which put them on a false scent. Just before leaving, he sent a message to Quartermaster-General Meigs, complaining of the inferior quality of the mules recently furnished by him. The wire was then cut. Having learned by the telegraph that Fairfax Court-House was held by a brigade of infantry, Stuart marched around north of it, and went into Loudoun—a land flowing with plenty. He made his headquarters at Col. Rogers's, near Dover, and rested until the next day. On the morning he left, I went to his room, and asked him to let me stay behind for a few days with a squad of men. I thought I could do something with them. He readily assented. I got nine men—including, of course, Beattie—who volunteered to go with me. This was the beginning of my career as a partisan. The work I accomplished in two or three days with this squad induced him to let me have a larger force to try my fortune. I took my men down into Fairfax, and in two days captured twenty cavalrymen, with their horses, arms, and equipments. I had the good luck, by mere chance, to come across a forester named John Underwood, who knew every rabbit-path in the county. He was a brave soldier, as well as a good guide. His death a few months afterward, at the hands of a deserter from our own army, was one of the greatest losses I sustained in the war. I dismounted to capture one of the picket posts, who could be seen by the light of their fire in the woods. We walked up within a few yards of it. The men, never suspecting danger, were absorbed in a game of euchre. I halted, and looked on for a minute or two, for I hated to spoil their sport. At last I fired a shot, to let them know that their relief had come. Nobody was hurt; but one fellow was so much frightened that he nearly jumped over the tops of the trees.

They submitted gracefully to the fate of war. I made them lie down by a fence, and left a mounted man to stand guard over them while I went to capture another post about two miles off. These were Vermont cavalry, and being from the land of steady habits did not indulge in cards like their New York friends, whom I had just left in the fence corner. I found them all sound asleep in a house, except the sentinel. Their horses were tied to the trees around it. The night was clear and crisp and cold. As we came from the direction of their camp, we were mistaken for the patrol until we got upon them. The challenge of the sentinel was answered by an order to charge, and it was all over with the boys from the Green Mountains. Their surprise was so great that they forgot that they had only pistols and carbines. If they had used them, being in a house, they might have driven us off. They made no resistance. The next day I started back to rejoin Stuart, who was near Fredericksburg. I found him in his tent, and when I reported what I had done, he expressed great delight. So he agreed to let me go back with fifteen men and try my luck again. I went and never returned. I was not permitted to keep the men long. Fitz Lee complained of his men being with me, and so I had to send them back to him. But while I had them I kept things lively and humming. I made many raids on the cavalry outposts, capturing men, arms, and horses. Old men and boys had joined my band. Some had run the gauntlet of Yankee pickets, and others swam the Potomac to get to me. Most men love the excitement of fighting, but abhor the drudgery of camps. I mounted, armed and equipped my command at the expense of the United States government. There was a Confederate hospital in Middleburg, where a good many wounded Confederate soldiers had been left during our Maryland campaign a few months before. These were now convalescent. I utilized them. They would go down to Fairfax on a raid with me, and then return to the hospital. When the Federal cavalry came in pursuit, they never suspected that the cripples they saw lying on their couches or hobbling about on crutches were the men who created the panic at night in their camps. At last I got one of the cripples killed, and that somewhat abated their ardor.

There are many comic as well as tragic elements that fill up the drama of war. One night I went down to Fairfax to take a cavalry picket. When I got near the post I stopped at the house of one Ben Hatton. I had heard that he had visited the picket post that day to give some information to them about me. I gave him the choice of Castle Thunder or guiding me through the pines to the rear of the picket.

Ben did not hesitate to go with me. Like the Vicar of Bray, he was in favor of the party in power. There was a deep snow on the ground, and when we got in sight of the picket fire, I halted and dismounted my men. As Ben had done all I wanted of him, and was a non-combatant, I did not want to expose him to the risk of getting shot, and so I left him with a man named Gall (generally called "Coonskin," from the cap he wore), and Jimmie, an Irishman, to guard our horses, which we left in the pines. With the other men, I went to make the attack on foot. The snow being soft, we made no noise, and had them all prisoners almost before they got their eyes open. But just then a fusilade was opened in the rear, where our horses were. Leaving a part of my men to bring on the prisoners, we mounted the captured horses and dashed back to the place where I had dismounted, to meet what I supposed was an attempt of the enemy to make a reprisal on me. When I got there I found Ben Hatton lying in a snow-bank, shot through the thigh, but Jimmy and Coonskin had vanished. All that Ben knew was that he had been shot; he said that the Yankees had attacked their party, but whether they had carried off Jimmie and Coonskin, or Jimmie and Coonskin had carried them, he couldn't tell. What made the mystery greater was that all our horses were standing just as we left them, including the two belonging to the missing men. With our prisoners and spoil, we started home, Ben Hatton riding behind one of the men. Ben had lost a good deal of blood, but he managed to hold on. When we got into the road we met a body of Wyndham's cavalry coming up to cut us off. They stopped and opened fire on us. I knew this was a good sign, and that they were not coming to close quarters in the dark. We went on by them. By daybreak I was twenty miles away. As soon as it was daylight, Wyndham set out full speed up the pike to catch me. He might as well have been chasing the silver-footed antelope,

> *That gracefully and gayly springs,*
> *As o'er the marble courts of kings.*

I was at a safe distance before he started. He got to Middleburg during the day, with his horses all jaded and blown. He learned there that I had passed through about the dawn of day. He returned to camp with the most of his com-mand leading their broken-down horses. In fact, his pursuit had done him more damage than my attack. He was an English officer, trained in the cavalry schools of Europe; but he did not understand such business. This affair was rather hard on Ben Hatton. He was the only man that got a hurt; and that was all he got. As it was only a flesh wound, it healed quickly; but, even if he had died from it, fame would have denied her requiem to his name. His going with me had been as purely involuntary as if he had been carried out with a halter round his neck to be hanged. I left him at his house, coiled up in bed, within a few hundred yards of the Yankee pickets. He was too close to the enemy for me to give him any surgical assistance; and he had to keep his wound a profound secret in the neighborhood, for fear the Yankees would hear of it and how he got it. If they had ever found it out, Ben's wife would have been made a widow. In a day or so, Coonskin and Jimmie came in, but by different directions. We had given them up for lost. They trudged on foot through the snow all the way up from Fairfax. Neither one knew that Ben Hatton had been shot. Each one supposed that all the others were prisoners, and he the only one left to tell the tale of the disaster. Both firmly believed that they had been attacked by the enemy, and, after fighting as long as Sir John Falstaff did by Shrewsbury clock, had been forced to yield; but they could not account for all our horses being where we left them. The mistakes of the night had been more ludicrous than any of the incidents of Goldsmith's immortal comedy, "She Stoops to Conquer." By a comparison of the statements of the three, I found out that the true facts were these: In order to keep themselves warm, they had walked around the horses a good deal and got separated. Coonskin saw Jimmie and Ben Hatton moving about in the shadow of a tree, and took them to be Yankees. He immediately opened on them, and drew blood at the first fire. Hatton yelled and fell. Jimmie, taking it for granted that Coonskin was a Yankee, returned his fire; and so they were dodging and shooting at each other from behind trees, until they saw us come dashing up. As we had left them on foot a short while before, it never occurred to them that we were coming back on the captured horses. After fighting each other by mistake and wounding Ben Hatton, they had run away from us. It was an agreeable surprise to them to find that I had their horses. Ben Hatton will die in the belief that the Yankees shot him; for I never told him any better. I regret that historical truth forbids my concluding this comedy according to the rules of the drama—with a marriage.

FAUQUIER COUNTY, VA., FEB. 28, 1863.

GENERAL:—I have the honor to report, that at four o'clock on the morning of the 26th instant I attacked and routed, on the Ox road, in Fairfax, about two miles from Germantown, a cavalry outpost, consisting of a lieutenant and fifty men. The enemy's loss was one lieutenant and three men killed, and five captured; number of wounded not known; also thirty-nine horses, with all their accoutrements, brought off. There were also three horses killed.

I did not succeed in gaining the rear of the post, as I expected, having been discovered by a vidette when several hundred yards off, who fired, and gave the alarm, which compelled me to charge them in front. In the terror and confusion occasioned by our terrific yells, the most of them saved themselves by taking refuge in a dense thicket, where the darkness effectually concealed them. There was also a reserve of one hundred men half a mile off who might come to the rescue. Already encumbered with prisoners and horses, we were in no condition for fighting. I sustained no loss. The enemy made a small show of fight, but quickly yielded. They were in log houses, with the chinking knocked out, and ought to have held them against a greatly superior force, as they all had carbines.

My men behaved very gallantly, although mostly raw recruits. I had only twenty-seven men with me. I am still receiving additions to my numbers.

If you would let me have some of the dismounted men of the First Cavalry, I would undertake to mount them. I desire some written instructions from you with reference to exportation of products within the enemy's lines. I wish the bearer of this to bring back some ammunition, also some large-size envelopes and blank paroles.

I have failed to mention the fact the enemy pursued me as far as Middleburg, without accomplishing anything, etc. . . .

JNO. S. MOSBY.

—MAJ.-GEN. J. E. B. STUART.

FAIRFAX COURT HOUSE, JAN. 27, 1863.

Sir:—Last night my pickets were driven in by some of Stuart's cavalry, wounding one and capturing nine. I then started with some two hundred men in pursuit.

Some twenty-seven miles beyond my pickets at Middleburg, I came up with them, and after a short skirmish, captured twenty-four of them. I have just returned.

P. WYNDHAM.

CAPT. CARROLL H. PORTER,
ASSISTANT ADJUTANT-GENERAL.

Chapter IV.

It was the latter part of January, 1863, when I crossed the Rappahannock into Northern Virginia, which from that time until the close of the war was the theatre on which I conducted partisan operations. The country had been abandoned to the occupation of the Federal army the year before, when Johnston retired from Centreville, and had never been held by us afterward, except during the short time when the Confederate army was passing through in Gen. Lee's first campaign into Maryland. I told Stuart that I would, by incessant attacks, compel the enemy either greatly to contract his lines or to reinforce them; either of which would be of great advantage to the Southern cause. The means supplied me were hardly adequate to the end I proposed, but I thought that zeal and celerity of movement would go far to compensate for the deficiency of my numbers. There was a great stake to be won, and I resolved to play a bold game to win it. I think that Stuart was the only man in the army of Northern Virginia, except two or three who accompanied me and knew me well, who expected that I would accomplish anything. Other detachments of cavalry had been sent there at different times that had done little or nothing.

Nearly every one thought that I was starting out on a quixotic enterprise, that would result in doing no harm to the enemy, but simply in getting all of my own men killed or captured. When at last I secured an independent command, for which I had so longed, I was as happy as Columbus when he set forth from the port of Palos with the three little barks Isabella had given him to search for an unknown continent. My faith was strong, and I never for a moment had a feeling of discouragement or doubted my ability to reap a rich harvest from what I knew was still an ungleaned field. I stopped an hour or so at Warrenton, which has always been a sort of political shrine from which the Delphian Apollo issues his oracles. After the war I made it my home, and it is generally supposed that I resided there before the war; the fact is that I never was in that section of Virginia until I went there as a soldier. The Union soldiers knew just as much about the country as I did.

I recall vividly to mind the looks of surprise and the ominous shaking of the heads of the augurs when I told them that I proposed going farther North to begin the war again along the Potomac. Their criticism on my command was pretty much the same as that pronounced on the English mission to Cabul some years ago—that it was too small for an army and too large for an embassy.

When I bade my friends at the Warren-Green Hotel "good-by," I had their best wishes for my success, but nothing more. They all thought that I was going on the foolhardy enterprise of an Arctic voyager in search of the North Pole. My idea was to make the Piedmont region of the country lying between the Rappahannock and Potomac Rivers the base of my operations. This embraces the upper portion of the counties of Fauquier and Loudoun. It is a rich, pastoral country, which afforded subsistence for my command, while the Blue Ridge was a safe point to which to retreat if hard pressed by the superior numbers that could be sent against us. It was inhabited by a highly refined and cultivated population, who were thoroughly devoted to the Southern cause. Although that region was the Flanders of the war, and harried worse than any of which history furnishes an example since the desolation of the Palatinates by Louis XIV,[1] yet the stubborn faith of the people never wavered. Amid fire and sword they remained true to the last, and supported me through all the trials of the war. While the country afforded an abundance of subsistence, it was open and scant of forests, with no natural defensive advantages for repelling hostile incursions. There was no such shelter there as Marion had in the swamps of the Pedee, to which he retreated. It was always my policy to avoid fighting at home as much as possible, for the plain reason that it would have encouraged an overwhelming force to come again, and that the services of my own command would have been neutralized by the force sent against it. Even if I defeated them, they would return with treble numbers. On the contrary, it was safer for me, and greater results could be secured, by being the aggressor and striking the enemy at unguarded points. I could thus compel him to guard a hundred points, while I could select any one of them for attack. If I could do so, I generally slipped over when my territory was invaded and imitated Scipio by carrying the war into the enemy's camps.

I have seen it stated in the reports of some Federal officers that they would throw down the gage of battle to me in my own country and that I would not accept it. I was not in the habit of doing what they wanted me to do. Events

---

[1][*Telegram.*]   Kernstown, Va., Nov. 26, 1864.

Sheridan to Halleck:—"I will soon commence work on Mosby. Heretofore I have made no attempt to break him up, as I would have employed ten men to his one, and for the reason that I have made a scapegoat of him for the destruction of private rights. Now there is going to be an intense hatred of him in that portion of the valley which is nearly a desert. I will soon commence on Loudoun County, and let them know there is a God in Israel. Mosby has annoyed me considerably; but the people are beginning to see that he does not injure me a great deal, but causes a loss to them of all that they have spent their lives in accumulating. Those people who live in the vicinity of Harper's Ferry are the most villanous in this valley, and have not yet been hurt much. If the railroad is interfered with, I will make some of them poor. Those who live at home in peace and plenty want the duello part of this war to go on; but when they have to bear the burden by loss of property and comforts, they will cry for peace." When Sheridan started in March, 1865, from Winchester, to join Grant in front of Petersburg, he left my command behind him, more flourishing than it ever had been. The *"intense hatred"* he had hoped to excite in the people of the valley for me, by burning their homes, was only felt for him. They were not willing that I should be a scapegoat to bear another's sins.

showed that my judgment was correct. After I had once occupied I never abandoned it, although the wave of invasion several times rolled over it.

News of the surrender, or, rather, the evacuation, of Richmond came to me one morning in April, 1865, at North Fork, in Loudoun County, where my command had assembled to go on a raid. Just two or three days before that I had defeated Colonel Reno, with the Twelfth Pennsylvania Cavalry, at Hamilton, a few miles from there, which was the last fight in which I commanded. Reno afterward enjoyed some notoriety in connection with the Custer massacre. My purpose was to weaken the armies invading Virginia, by harassing their rear. As a line is only as strong as its weakest point, it was necessary for it to be stronger than I was at every point, in order to resist my attacks. It is easy, therefore, to see the great results that may be accomplished by a small body of cavalry moving rapidly from point to point on the communications of an army. To destroy supply trains, to break up the means of conveying intelligence, and thus isolating an army from its base, as well as its different corps from each other, to confuse their plans by capturing dispatches, are the objects of partisan war. It is just as legitimate to fight an enemy in the rear as in front. The only difference is in the danger. Now, to prevent all these things from being done, heavy detachments must be made to guard against them. The military value of a partisan's work is not measured by the amount of property destroyed, or the number of men killed or captured, but by the number he keeps watching. Every soldier withdrawn from the front to guard the rear of an army is so much taken from its fighting strength.

I endeavored, as far as I was able, to diminish this aggressive power of the army of the Potomac, by compelling it to keep a large force on the defensive. I assailed its rear, for there was its most vulnerable point. My men had no camps. If they had gone into camp, they would soon have all been captured. They would scatter for safety, and gather at my call, like the Children of the Mist. A blow would be struck at a weak or unguarded point, and then a quick retreat. The alarm would spread through the sleeping camp, the long roll would be beaten or the bugles would sound to horse, there would be mounting in hot haste and a rapid pursuit. But the partisans generally got off with their prey. Their pursuers were striking at an invisible foe. I often sent small squads at night to attack and run in the pickets along a line of several miles. Of course, these alarms were very annoying, for no human being knows how sweet sleep is but a soldier. I wanted to use and consume the Northern cavalry in hard work. I have often thought that their fierce hostility to me was more on account of the sleep I made them lose than the number we killed and captured. It has always been a wonder with people how I managed to collect my men after dispersing them. The true secret was that it was a fascinating life, and its attractions far more than counterbalanced its hardships and dangers. They had no camp duty to do, which, however necessary, is disgusting to soldiers of high spirit. To put them to such routine work is pretty much like hitching a race-horse to a plow.

Many expeditions were undertaken and traps laid to capture us, but all failed, and my command continued to grow and flourish until the final scene at Appomattox. It had just reached its highest point of efficiency when the time came to surrender. We did not go into a number of traps set to catch us, but somehow we always brought the traps off with us. One stratagem was after the model of the Grecian horse, and would have done credit to Ulysses. They sent a train of wagons up the Little River turnpike from Fairfax, apparently without any guard, thinking that such a bait would surely catch me. But in each wagon were concealed six of the Bucktails, who would, no doubt, have stopped my career, if I had given them a chance. Fortunately, I never saw them, for on that very day I had gone by another route down to Fairfax. When the Bucktails returned, they had the satisfaction of knowing that I had been there in their absence. At that time Hooker's army was in winter quarters on the Rappahannock, with a line of communication with Washington, both by land and water. The troops belonging to the defences at Washington were mostly cantoned in Fairfax, with their advance post at Centreville. West of the Blue Ridge, Milroy occupied Winchester. From my rendezvous east of the ridge I could move on the radius and strike any point on the circumference of the circle which was not too strongly guarded. But if I compelled them to be stronger everywhere than I was, then so much the better. I had done my work. Panics had often occurred in the camp when we were not near; the pickets became so nervous, expecting attacks, that they fired at every noise. It was thought that the honor as well as the safety of the army required that these depredations should no longer be endured, and that something must be done to stop them. Of course, the best way to do it was to exterminate the band, as William of Orange did the Macdonald of Glencoe. A cavalry expedition, under a Major Gilmer, was sent up to Loudoun to do the work. He had conceived the idea that I had my headquarters in Middleburg, and might be caught by surrounding the place in the night-time. He arrived before daybreak, and threw a cordon of pickets around it. At the dawn of day he had the village as completely invested as Metz was by the Germans. He then gradually contracted his lines, and proceeded in person to the hotel where he supposed I was in bed. I was not there; I never had been. Soldiers were sent around to every house with orders to arrest every man they could find. When he drew in his net there was not a single soldier in it. He had, however, caught a number of old men. It was a frosty morning, and he amused himself by making a soldier take them through a squad drill to keep them warm; occasionally he would make them mark time in the street front of the hotel. All this afforded a good deal of fun to the major, but was rather rough on the old men. He thought, or pretended to think, that they were the parties who had attacked his pickets. After a night march of twenty-five miles, he did not like to return to camp without some trophies, so he determined to carry the graybeards with him. He mounted each one behind a trooper, and started off. Now, it so happened that I had notified my men to meet that morning at Rector's Cross Roads, which is about four miles above Middleburg. When I got there I heard that the latter place was occupied by Federal cavalry. With seventeen men I started down the pike to look after them. Of course, with my small force, all that I could expect to do was to cut off some straggling parties who might be marauding about the neighborhood. When I got near Middleburg I learned that they had gone. We entered the town at a gallop. The ladies all immediately crowded around us. There were, of course, no men among them; Major Gilmer had taken them with him. There was, of course, great indignation at the rough usage they had received, and their wives never expected to see them again. And then, to add to the pathos of the scene, were the tears and lamentations of the daughters. There were many as pure and as bright as any pearl that ever shone in Oman's green water. Their beauty had won the hearts of many of my men. To avenge the wrongs of distressed damsels is one of the vows of knighthood; so we spurred on to overtake the Federal cavalry, in hopes that by some accident of war we might be able to liberate the prisoners.

Chapter V.

"Still o'er these scenes my memory wakes,
And fondly broods with miser care!
Time but the impression stronger makes,
As streams their channels deeper wear."   —BURNS.

About five miles below Middleburg is the village of Aldie, where I expected that the Federal cavalry would halt. But when I got within a mile of it I met a citizen, just from the place, who told me the cavalry had passed through. With five or six men I rode forward while the others followed on more slowly. Just as I rose to the top of the hill on the outskirts of the village, I suddenly came upon two Federal cavalrymen ascending from the opposite side. Neither party had been aware of the approach of the other, and our meeting was so unexpected that our horses' heads nearly butted together before we could stop. They surrendered, of course, and were sent to the rear. They said that they had been sent out as videttes. Looking down the hill, I saw before me several mounted men in the road, whom I took to be a part of the rear-guard of Major Gilmer's column. We dashed after them. I was riding a splendid horse—a noble bay—Job's war-horse was a mustang compared to him—who had now got his mettle up and carried me at headlong speed right among them. I had no more control over him than Mazeppa had over the Ukraine steed to which he was bound. I had scarcely started in the charge, before I discovered that there was a body of cavalry dismounted at a mill near the roadside, which I had not before seen. They were preparing to feed their horses. As their pickets had given no alarm, they had no idea that an enemy was near, and were stunned and dazed by the apparition of a body of men who they imagined must have dropped from the clouds upon them. The fact was that we were as much surprised as they were. I was unable to stop my horse when I got to them, but he kept straight on like a streak of lightning. Fortunately, the dismounted troopers were so much startled that it never occurred to them to take a shot at me *in transitu*. They took it for granted that an overwhelming force was on them, and every man was for saving himself. Some took to the Bull Run mountain, which was near by, and others ran into the mill and buried themselves like rats in the wheat bins. The mill was grinding, and some were so much frightened that they jumped into the hoppers and came near being ground up into flour. When we pulled them out there was nothing blue about them.

As I have stated, my horse ran with me past the mill. My men stopped there and went to work, but I kept on. And now another danger loomed up in front of me. Just ahead was the bridge over Little River, and on the opposite bank I saw another body of cavalry looking on in a state of bewildered excitement. They saw the stampede at the mill and a solitary horseman, pistol in hand, riding full speed right into their ranks. They never fired a shot. Just as I got to the bridge I jumped off my horse to save myself from capture; but just at the same moment they wheeled and took to their heels down the pike. They had seen the rest of my men coming up. If I had known that they were going to run I would have stayed on my horse. They went clattering down the pike, with my horse thundering after them. He chased them all the way into the camp. They never drew rein until they got inside their picket lines. I returned on foot to the mill; not a half a dozen shots were fired. All that couldn't get away surrendered. But just then a Federal officer made his appearance at the bridge. He had ridden down the river, and, having just returned, had heard the firing, but did not comprehend the situation. Tom Turner of Maryland, one of the bravest of my men, dashed at him. As Turner was alone, I followed him. I now witnessed a single-handed fight between him and the officer. For want of numbers, it was not so picturesque as the combat, described by Livy, between the Horatii and the Curatii, nor did such momentous issues depend upon it. But the gallantry displayed was equally as great. Before I got up I saw the horse of the Federal officer fall dead upon him, and at the same time Turner seemed about to fall from his horse. The Federal officer, who was Capt. Worthington of the Vermont cavalry, had fired while lying under his horse at Turner and inflicted quite a severe wound. The first thing Turner said to me was that his adversary had first surrendered, which threw him off his guard, and then fired on him. Worthington denied it, and said his shot was fired in fair fight. I called some of the men to get him out from under his horse. He was too much injured by the fall to be taken away, so I paroled and left him with a family there to be cared for. While all this was going on, the men were busy at the mill. They had a good deal of fun pulling the Vermont boys out of the wheat bins. The first one they brought out was so caked with flour that I thought they had the miller. We got the commanding officer, Capt. Huttoon, and nineteen men and twenty-three horses, with their arms and equipments. I lingered behind with one man, and sent the captures back to Middleburg. Now, all the ladies there had been watching and listening as anxiously to hear from us as Andromache and her maids did for the news of the combat between Hector and Achilles. Presently they saw a line of blue coats coming up the pike, with some gray ones mixed among them. Then the last ray of hope departed—they thought we were all prisoners, and that the foe was returning to insult them. One of the most famous of my men—Dick Moran—rode forward as a herald of victory. He had the voice of a fog horn, and proclaimed the glad tidings to the town. While I was still sitting on my horse at the mill, three more of the Vermont men, thinking that all of us had gone, came out from their hiding place. I sent them on after the others. Up to this time I had been under the impression that it was Maj. Gilmer's rear-guard that I had overtaken. I now learned that this was a body of Vermont cavalry that had started that morning several hours after Gilmer had left. They had halted to feed their horses at the mill. As they came up they had seen a body of cavalry turn off toward Centreville. That was all they knew. I then rode down the road to look after my horse that I had lost. I had not gone far before I met the old men that Maj. Gilmer had taken off.

They were all happy at the ludicrous streak of fortune that had brought them deliverance. It seems that Maj. Gilmer knew nothing of the intention of Capt. Huttoon to pay Middleburg a visit that day. When he got below Aldie he saw a considerable body of cavalry coming from the direction of Fairfax. It never occurred to him that they were his own people. He took them for my men, and thought I was trying to surround him. Even if he did think the force he saw was my command, it is hard to understand why he should run away from the very thing that he was in search of. But so he did. Just at the point where he was when he saw the Vermont men the pike crosses the old Braddock road. It is the same on which the British general marched with young George Washington to death and defeat on the Monongahela. Maj. Gilmer turned and started down the Braddock road at about the speed that John Gilpin rode to Edmonton on his wedding day. The ground was soft, and his horses sank knee deep in the mud at every jump. Of course, those broke down first that were carrying two. As he thought he was hard pressed, he kept on fast and furious, taking no heed of those he left on the roadside. It was necessary to sacrifice a part to save the rest. Long before he got to Centreville, about one-half of his horses were sticking in the mud, and all his prisoners had been abandoned. They had to walk home. Maj. Gilmer never came after me again. I heard that he resigned his commission in disgust, and, with Othello, "bade farewell to the big wars that make ambition virtue." There was rejoicing in Middleburg that evening; all ascribed to a special providence the advent of the Vermont cavalry just in time to stampede the New Yorkers, and make them drop their prisoners; and that my horse had run away, and carried me safely through the Vermont squadron. The miller, too, was happy, because I had appeared just in time to save his corn. At night, with song and dance, we celebrated the events, and forgot the dangers of the day.

HEADQUARTERS CAVALRY BRIGADE,
FAIRFAX COURT-HOUSE, VA., MARCH 3, 1863.

SIR:—By order of Col. R. B. Price, I directed, on the night of the 1st instant, a reconnoissance to go in direction of Aldie.

The officer who commanded this reconnoissance was Major

Joseph Gilmer, of the Eighteenth Pennsylvania Cavalry. He had two hundred men. The orders to him were to proceed carefully, and send back couriers through the night with information whether they saw any enemy or not. This last order was disobeyed. They were not to cross Cub Run until daylight, and then try and gain all information possible by flankers and small detached scouting parties.

Major Gilmer went to Middleburg, and, while returning, the videttes of the First Vermont Cavalry noticed a part of his advance and prepared to skirmish. The advance fell back toward Aldie. Major Gilmer, instead of throwing out a party to reconnoitre, turned off with nearly the whole of his command in the direction of Groveton, to gain Centreville. The horses returned exhausted from being run at full speed for miles. A few of Major Gilmer's men left his command and went along the Little River turnpike toward the Vermont detachment. They reported that the men seen were a part of a scouting party under Major Gilmer, and that no enemy were in Aldie. Capt. Huttoon then entered the town, and halted to have the horses fed near a mill. Immediately beyond was a rising ground which hid the guerillas. While the horses were unbridled and feeding, the surprise occurred. As both the officers have been captured, and as the detachment was not under my command, and is not attached to this brigade, I have no means of receiving any official or exact report from them, nor is there any one belonging to that detachment here. All men belonging to this detachment seem to have fought well; the enemy did not pursue them; they fell back in good order.

Major Gilmer, when he returned, was unable to make a report to Lieut.-Col. [John S.] Krepps, who during the time I was confined from sickness, had charge of the camp. I ordered Major Gilmer under arrest early this morning, and have sent to Col. R. B. Price charges, of which the annexed is a copy. Major Gilmer lost but one man, belonging to the Fifth New York Cavalry, who was mortally wounded by the enemy and afterwards robbed. He was away from the command and on this side of Aldie, his horse having given out. The enemy seemed to have been concealed along the line of march and murdered this man, when returning, without provocation.

I have the honor to be, very respectfully, your obedient servant,

ROBT. JOHNSTONE,
Lieut.-Col. Commanding Cavalry Brigade.

CAPT. C. H. POTTER,
ASSISTANT ADJUTANT-GENERAL.

GENERAL ORDERS, WAR DEPARTMENT.
ADJUTANT-GENERAL'S OFFICE.

No. 229. *WASHINGTON, JULY* 23, 1863.

I. Before a General Court Martial, which convened in the city of
Washington, D. C., March 27, 1863, pursuant to General Orders,
No. 20, dated Headquarters Cavalry, Defences of Washington, near
Fort Scott, Virginia, February 2, 1863, and Special Orders, No. 146,
dated February 10, 1863; No. 150, dated February 16, 1863; No.
161, dated March 6, 1863; and No. 164, dated March 21, 1863,
Headquarters Cavalry, Department of Washington, and of which
Colonel E. B. Sawyer, 1st Vermont Cavalry, is President, was
arraigned and tried—

Major Joseph Gilmer, 18th Pennsylvania Cavalry.
Charge I.—"Drunkenness."
Specification—"In this; that *Joseph Gilmer*, a Major of the 18th Penn-
sylvania Cavalry, he then being in the service of the United States, and
while in command of a reconnoitring party, on the second day of
March, 1863, was so intoxicated from the effects of spirituous liquors
as to be incapacitated to perform his duties in an officer-like manner.
This at or near the village of Aldie, in the State of Virginia."
Charge II.—"Cowardice."
Specification—"In this; that *Joseph Gilmer*, a Major in the 18th Pennsylvania Cavalry, he then being in the service of the United States,
upon the second day of March, 1863, did permit and encourage a
detachment of cavalry, in the service of the United States, and under
his command, to fly from a small body of the 1st Vermont Cavalry,
who were mistaken for the enemy, without sending out any person or
persons to ascertain who they were, or what were their numbers; and
that the said cavalry under his command, as above stated, were much
demoralized, and fled many miles through the country in great confusion and disorder. This near Aldie, in the State of Virginia."

To which charges and specifications the accused, Major *Joseph Gilmer*, 18th Pennsylvania Cavalry, pleaded "Not Guilty."

Finding.

The Court, having maturely considered the evidence adduced, finds the accused, Major *Joseph Gilmer*, 18th Pennsylvania Cavalry, as follows:—

Charge I.

Of the *Specification*, "Guilty."

Of the Charge, "Guilty."

Charge II.

Of the *Specification*, "Guilty."

Of the Charge, "Not Guilty."

Sentence.

And the Court does therefore sentence him, Major *Joseph Gilmer*, 18th Pennsylvania Cavalry, *"To be cashiered."*

II. The proceedings of the Court in the above case were disapproved by the Major-General commanding the Department of Washington, on account of fatal defects and irregularities in the record. But the testimony shows that the accused was *drunk* on duty, and brought disgrace upon himself and the service. The President directs that, as recommended by the Department Commander, he be dismissed the service; and Major *Joseph Gilmer*, 18th Pennsylvania Cavalry, accordingly ceases to be an officer in the United States Service since the 20th day of July, 1863.

By order of the Secretary of War:

E. D. TOWNSEND,
ASSISTANT ADJUTANT-GENERAL.

FAIRFAX COURT HOUSE, MARCH 2, 1863.

Sir:—Fifty men of the First Vermont Cavalry, from Companies H and M, under captains Huttoon and Woodward, were surprised in Aldie while feeding their horses by about 15 of the enemy. Both captains captured and about 15 men. They saw no enemy but the attacking party. Major Gilmer has returned with the scouting party that left last night. They were to Middleburg and saw but one rebel. I have anticipated the report of Lieutenant-Colonel Krepps, now in command, which will be forwarded in probably one hour.

ROBT. JOHNSTONE,

LIEUTENANT-COLONEL, COMMANDING CAVALRY BRIGADE.

CAPT. C. H. POTTER,

ASSISTANT ADJUTANT-GENERAL.

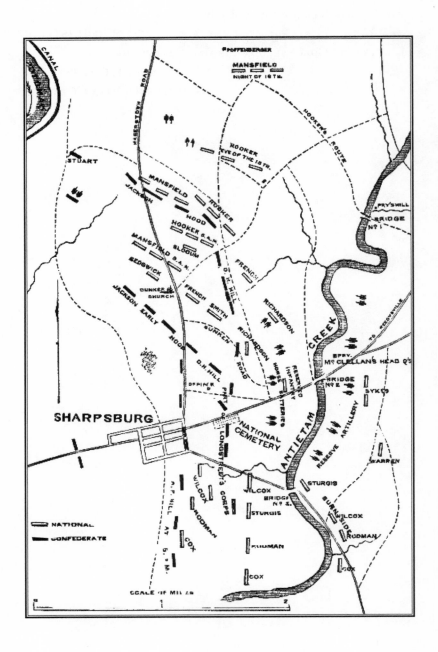

*So brilliant that he could not make a mistake, George McClellan
probably had one of the most promising careers of any officer in the
U.S. Army prior to the war. He overcame many organizational
challenges building the Army of the Potomac into a viable fighting
force.*

*McClellan was a brilliant strategist—on paper. He could move
his Army by sea and river to threaten Richmond, but lose the nerve to
take it. Sadly, he never could wield the sword of his own making. At
Antietam, McClellan got his "second chance" to prove himself a worthy general to President Lincoln. In this almost-won battle, McClellan writes how the plan was his, but the faults were not. Blind to
reality, McClellan counts the outcome by measures of victory that no
longer had any meaning in this new kind of war.*

Excerpt from *McClellan's Own Story*

BY GEORGE MCCLELLAN

Chapter XXXV.

Entering Frederick—The lost despatch—Advance—The battle of South
Mountain—Gen. Scott hails McClellan.

In riding into Frederick I passed through Sumner's corps, which I had not
seen for some time. The men and officers were so enthusiastic as to show
that they had lost none of their old feeling. During the march (from Washington
up) I was much with the regulars, generally encamping with them. I never can
forget their constant enthusiasm; even when I passed through them several
times a day on the march they would jump up (if at a rest) and begin cheering in
a way that regulars are not wont to do. Poor fellows!

Our reception at Frederick was wonderful. Men, women, and children crowded around us, weeping, shouting, and praying; they clung around old Dan's neck and almost suffocated the old fellow, decking him out with flags. The houses were all decorated with flags, and it was a general scene of joy. The secession expedition had been an entire failure in that quarter; they received no recruits of the slightest consequence and no free-will offerings of any kind.

It was soon ascertained that the main body of the enemy's forces had marched out of the city on the two previous days, taking the roads to Boonsborough and Harper's Ferry, thereby rendering it necessary to force the passes through the Catoctin and South Mountain ridges, and gain possession of Boonsborough and Rohrersville, before any relief could be extended to Col. Miles at Harper's Ferry.

On the 13th an order fell into my hands issued by Gen. Lee, which fully disclosed his plans, and I immediately gave orders for a rapid and vigorous forward movement.

The following is a copy of the order referred to:

"HEADQUARTERS, ARMY OF NORTHERN VIRGINIA, SEPT. 9, 1862.
"*SPECIAL ORDERS, NO.* 191.

"The army will resume its march to-morrow, taking the Hagerstown road. Gen. Jackson's command will form the advance, and after passing Middletown, with such portion as he may select, will take the route towards Sharpsburg, cross the Potomac at the most convenient point, and by Friday night take possession of the Baltimore and Ohio Railroad, capture such of the enemy as may be at Martinsburg, and intercept such as may attempt to escape from Harper's Ferry.

"Gen. Longstreet's command will pursue the same road as far as Boonsborough, where it will halt with the reserve, supply, and baggage trains of the army.

"Gen. McLaws, with his own division and that of Gen. R. H. Anderson, will follow Gen. Longstreet; on reaching Middletown he will take the route to Harper's Ferry, and by Friday morning possess himself of the Maryland Heights and endeavor to capture the enemy at Harper's Ferry and vicinity.

"Gen. Walker, with his division, after accomplishing the object in which he is now engaged, will cross the Potomac at Cheek's ford, ascend its right bank to Lovettsville, take possession of Loudon Heights, if practicable, by Friday morning; Keys's ford on his left, and the road between the end of the mountain and the Potomac on his right. He will, as far as practicable, co-operate with Gen. McLaws and Gen. Jackson in intercepting the retreat of the enemy.

"Gen. D. H. Hill's division will form the rear-guard of the army, pursuing the road taken by the main body. The reserve artillery, ordnance and supply-trains, etc., will precede Gen. Hill.

"Gen. Stuart will detach a squadron of cavalry to accompany the commands of Gens. Longstreet, Jackson, and McLaws, and, with the main body of the cavalry, will cover the route of the army and bring up all stragglers that may have been left behind.

"The commands of Gens. Jackson, McLaws, and Walker, after accomplishing the objects for which they have been detached, will join the main body of the army at Boonsborough or Hagerstown.

"Each regiment on the march will habitually carry its axes in the regimental ordnance-wagons, for use of the men at their encampments, to procure wood, etc.

"By command of Gen. R. E. Lee.

"R. H. CHILTON,
"Assist. Adj.-Gen.

"MAJ.-GEN. D. H. HILL,
"Commanding Division."

On the morning of the 13th Gen. Pleasonton was ordered to send Reynolds's brigade and a section of artillery in the direction of Gettysburg, and Rush's regiment towards Jefferson to communicate with Franklin, to whom the 6th U. S. Cavalry and a section of artillery had previously been sent, and to proceed with the remainder of his force in the direction of Middletown in pursuit of the enemy.

After skirmishing with the enemy all the morning, and driving them from several strong positions, he reached Turner's Gap of the South Mountain in the afternoon, and found the enemy in force and apparently determined to defend the pass. He sent back for infantry to

Gen. Burnside, who had been directed to support him, and proceeded to make a reconnoissance of the position.

The South Mountain is at this point about one thousand feet in height, and its general direction is from northeast to southwest. The national road from Frederick to Hagerstown crosses it nearly at right angles through Turner's Gap, a depression which is some four hundred feet in depth.

The mountain on the north side of the turnpike is divided into two crests or ridges by a narrow valley, which, though deep at the pass, becomes a slight depression at about a mile to the north. There are two country roads—one to the right of the turnpike and the other to the left—which give access to the crests overlooking the main road. The one on the left, called the "Old Sharpsburg road," is nearly parallel to, and about half a mile distant from, the turnpike until it reaches the crest of the mountain, when it bends off to the left. The other road, called the "Old Hagerstown road," passes up a ravine in the mountains about a mile from the turnpike, and, bending to the left over and along the first crest, enters the turnpike at the Mountain House near the summit of the pass.

On the night of the 13th the positions of the different corps were as follows:

Reno's corps at Middletown, except Rodman's division at Frederick.

Hooker's corps on the Monocacy, two miles from Frederick.

Sumner's corps near Frederick.

Banks's corps near Frederick.

Sykes's division near Frederick.

Franklin's corps at Buckeystown.

Couch's division at Licksville.

The orders from headquarters for the march on the 14th were as follows:

13th, 11.30 P.M.—Hooker to march at daylight to Middletown.

13th, 11.30 P.M.—Sykes to move at six A.M., after Hooker, on the Middletown and Hagerstown road.

14th, 1 A.M.—Artillery reserve to follow Sykes closely.

13th, 8.45 P.M.—Turner to move at seven A.M.

14th, 9 A.M.—Sumner ordered to take the Shookstown road to Middletown.[1]

13th, 6.45 P.M.—Couch ordered to move to Jefferson with his whole division.

On the 14th Gen. Pleasonton continued his reconnoissance. Gibson's battery and afterwards Benjamin's battery (of Reno's corps) were placed on high ground to the left of the turnpike, and obtained a direct fire on the enemy's position in the Gap.

Gen. Cox's division, which had been ordered up to support Gen. Pleasonton, left its bivouac near Middletown at six A.M. The 1st brigade reached the

---

[1]By letter, dated Boston, May 19, 1884, Gen. F. A. Walker called the attention of Gen. McClellan to a statement made by the Comte de Paris in his *History of the Civil War in America*, attributing delay in the advance from Frederick to Gen. Sumner and the 2d corps. The following reply, which I find among the papers relating to South Mountain, indicates Gen. McClellan's intention to embody its substance in his narrative when he should reach this point in his review:

32 Washington Square, N. Y., May 21, 1884.

My Dear Sir: Yours of the 19th has just reached me.

My attention was never called to the point in question.

Like yourself, I am fully satisfied as to the candor and honesty of the Comte de Paris, but his work is not free from unintentional errors, of which this is an example.

My report shows that at 8.45 P.M. of the 13th the 2d corps was ordered to move at seven A.M. on the 14th by the direct road to Middletown, following Sykes at an hour's interval. Hooker did not move as promptly as ordered, and this delayed Sykes and Sumner. Therefore at nine A.M. I ordered Sumner to take the more circuitous road by Shookstown, that his march might be free from encumbrance.

The 2d corps made its march and arrived on the field as rapidly as circumstances permitted.

I was never dissatisfied with this march of the 2d corps, and never criticised it to any one.

I can imagine the 2d corps and its brave old commander slow in getting *out* of a fight, but they certainly never showed any hesitation or tardiness in getting *into* battle. The promptness and energy with which Sumner moved from Grapevine bridge to the field of Fair Oaks is simply one example of the manner in which that corps always acted while under my command. You may rest assured that no member of the 2d corps has its honor more at heart, or is more proud of its uniformly admirable conduct, whether on the march or in battle, than is the commander under whom it first served.

In my account of Antietam I will take care to correct the error of the comte.

And am always your friend,

Geo. B. McClellan.

Gen. F. A. Walker.

scene of action about 9 A.M., and was sent up the old Sharpsburg road by Gen. Pleasonton to feel the enemy and ascertain if he held the crest on that side in strong force. This was soon found to be the case; and Gen. Cox having arrived with the other brigade, and information having been received from Gen. Reno that the column would be supported by the whole corps, the division was ordered to assault the position. Two 20-pounder Parrotts of Simmons's battery and two sections of McMullan's battery were left in the rear in position near the turnpike, where they did good service during the day against the enemy's batteries in the Gap. Scammon's brigade was deployed, and, well covered by skirmishers, moved up the slope to the left of the road with the object of turning the enemy's right, if possible. It succeeded in gaining the crest and establishing itself there, in spite of the vigorous efforts of the enemy, who was posted behind stone walls and in the edges of timber, and the fire of a battery which poured in canister and case-shot on the regiment on the right of the brigade. Col. Crook's brigade marched in columns at supporting distance. A section of McMullan's battery, under Lieut. Croome (killed while serving one of his guns), was moved up with great difficulty, and opened with canister at very short range on the enemy's infantry, by whom (after having done considerable execution) it was soon silenced and forced to withdraw.

One regiment of Crook's brigade was now deployed on Scammon's left and the other two in his rear, and they several times entered the first line and relieved the regiments in front of them when hard pressed. A section of Sumner's battery was brought up and placed in the open space in the woods, where it did good service during the rest of the day.

The enemy several times attempted to retake the crest, advancing with boldness, but were each time repulsed. They then withdrew their battery to a point more to the right, and formed columns on both our flanks. It was now about noon, and a lull occurred in the contest which lasted about two hours, during which the rest of the corps was coming up. Gen Wilcox's division was the first to arrive. When he reached the base of the mountain Gen. Cox advised him to consult Gen. Pleasonton as to a position. The latter indicated that on the right afterwards taken up by Gen Hooker. Gen. Wilcox was in the act of moving to occupy this ground when he received an order from Gen. Reno to move up the old Sharpsburg road and take a position to its right overlooking the turnpike. Two regiments were detached to support Gen. Cox at his request. One section of Cooke's battery was placed in position near the turn of the road (on the crest), and opened fire on the enemy's batteries across the Gap. The division was proceeding to deploy to the right of the road when the enemy suddenly opened (at one hundred and fifty yards) with a battery which enfiladed the road at this point, drove off Cooke's cannoneers with their limbers and caused a temporary panic in which the guns were nearly lost. But the 79th N. Y. and 17th Mich. promptly rallied, changed front under a heavy fire, and moved out to protect the guns, with which Capt. Cooke had remained. Order was soon restored, and the division formed in line on the right of Cox, and was kept concealed as much as possible under the hillside until the whole line advanced. It was exposed not only to the fire of the battery in front, but also to that of the batteries on the other side of the turnpike, and lost heavily.

Shortly before this time Gens. Burnside and Reno arrived at the base of the mountain, and the former directed the latter to move up the divisions of Gens. Sturgis and Rodman to the crest held by Cox and Wilcox, and to move upon the enemy's position with his whole force as soon as he was informed that Gen. Hooker (who had just been directed to attack on the right) was well advanced up the mountain.

Gen. Reno then went to the front and assumed the direction of affairs, the positions having been explained to him by Gen. Pleasonton. Shortly before this time I arrived at the point occupied by Gen. Burnside, and my headquarters were located there until the conclusion of the action. Gen. Sturgis had left his camp at one P.M., and reached the scene of action about 3.30 P.M. Clark's battery, of his division, was sent to assist Cox's left by order of Gen. Reno, and two regiments (2d Md. and 6th N. H.) were detached by Gen. Reno and sent forward a short distance on the left of the turnpike. His division was formed in rear of Wilcox's, and Rodman's division was divided; Col. Fairchild's brigade being placed on the extreme left, and Col. Harland's, under Gen. Rodman's personal supervision, on the right.

My order to move the whole line forward and take or silence the enemy's batteries in front was executed with enthusiasm. The enemy made a desperate resistance, charging our advancing lines with fierceness, but they were everywhere routed, and fled.

Our chief loss was in Wilcox's division. The enemy's battery was found to be across a gorge and beyond the reach of our infantry; but its position was made untenable, and it was hastily removed and not again put in position near us. But the batteries across the Gap still kept up a fire of shot and shell.

Gen. Wilcox praises very highly the conduct of the 17th Mich. in this advance—a regiment which had been organized scarcely a month, but which charged the advancing enemy in flank in a manner worthy of veteran troops; and also that of the 45th Penn., which bravely met them in front.

Cooke's battery now reopened fire. Sturgis's division was moved to the front of Wilcox's, occupying the new ground gained on the further side of the slope, and his artillery opened on the batteries across the Gap. The enemy made an effort to turn our left about dark, but were repulsed by Fairchild's brigade and Clark's battery.

At about seven o'clock the enemy made another effort to regain the lost ground, attacking along Sturgis's front and part of Cox's. A lively fire was kept up until nearly nine o'clock, several charges being made by the enemy and repulsed with slaughter, and we finally occupied the highest part of the mountain.

Gen. Reno was killed just before sunset, while making a reconnoissance to the front, and the command of the corps devolved upon Gen. Cox. In Gen. Reno the nation lost one of its best general officers. He was a skilful soldier, a brave and honest man.

There was no firing after ten o'clock, and the troops slept on their arms, ready to renew the fight at daylight; but the enemy quietly retired from our front during the night, abandoning their wounded, and leaving their dead in large numbers scattered over the field. While these operations were progressing on the left of the main column, the right, under Gen. Hooker, was actively engaged. His corps left the Monocacy early in the morning, and its advance reached the Catoctin creek about one P.M. Gen. Hooker then went forward to examine the ground.

At about one o'clock Gen. Meade's division was ordered to make a diversion in favor of Reno. The following is the order sent:

SEPT. 14, 1 P.M.

General: Gen. Reno requests that a division of yours may move up on the right (north) of the main road. Gen. McClellan desires you to comply with this request, holding your whole corps in readiness to support the movement, and taking charge of it yourself.

Sumner's and Banks's corps have commenced arriving. Let Gen. McClellan be informed as soon as you commence your movement.

GEORGE D. RUGGLES,

COL., ASST. ADJ.-GEN., AND AIDE-DE-CAMP.

MAJ.-GEN. HOOKER.

Meade's division left Catoctin creek about two o'clock, and turned off to the right from the main road on the old Hagerstown road to Mount Tabor church, where Gen. Hooker was, and deployed a short distance in advance, its right resting about one and a half miles from the turnpike. The enemy fired a few shots from a battery on the mountain-side, but did no considerable damage. Cooper's battery, "B," 1st Penn. Artillery, was placed in position on high ground at about three and a half o'clock, and fired at the enemy on the slope, but soon ceased by order of Gen. Hooker, and the position of our lines prevented any further use of artillery by us on this part of the field. The 1st Mass. Cavalry was sent up the valley to the right to observe the movements, if any, of the enemy in that direction, and one regiment of Meade's division was posted to watch a road coming in the same direction. The other divisions were deployed as they came up—Gen. Hatch's on the left, and Gen. Ricketts's, which arrived at five P.M., in the rear. Gen. Gibbon's brigade was detached from Hatch's division by Gen. Burnside, for the purpose of making a demonstration on the enemy's centre, up the main road, as soon as the movements on the right and left had sufficiently progressed. The 1st Penn. Rifles, of Gen. Seymour's brigade, were sent forward as skirmishers to feel the enemy, and it was found that he was in force. Meade was then directed to advance his division to the right of the road, so as to outflank them, if possible, and then to move forward and attack, while Hatch was directed to take with his division the crest on the left of the old Hagerstown road, Ricketts's division being held in reserve. Seymour's brigade was sent up to the top of the slope, on the right of the ravine through which the road runs, and then moved along the summit parallel to the road, while Col. Gallagher's and Col. Magilton's brigades moved in the same direction along the slope and in the ravine.

The ground was of the most difficult character for the movement of troops, the hillside being very steep and rocky, and obstructed by stone walls and timber. The enemy was very soon encountered, and in a short time the action became general along the whole front of the division. The line advanced steadily up the mountain-side, where the enemy was posted behind trees and rocks, from which he was gradually dislodged. During this advance Col. Gallagher, commanding 3d brigade, was severely wounded, and the command devolved upon Lieut.-Col. Robert Anderson.

Gen. Meade, having reason to believe that the enemy was attempting to outflank him on his right, applied to Gen. Hooker for reinforcements. Gen. Duryea's brigade, of Ricketts's division, was ordered up, but it did not arrive until the close of the action. It was advanced on Seymour's left, but only one regiment could open fire before the enemy retired and darkness intervened.

Gen. Meade speaks highly of Gen. Seymour's skill in handling his brigade on the extreme right, securing by his manoeuvres the great object of the movement—the outflanking of the enemy.

While Gen. Meade was gallantly driving the enemy on the right, Gen. Hatch's division was engaged in a severe contest for the possession of the crest on the left of the ravine. It moved up the mountain in the following order: Two regiments of Gen. Patrick's brigade deployed as skirmishers, with the other two regiments of the same brigade supporting them; Col. Phelps's brigade in line of battalions in mass at deploying distance, Gen. Doubleday's brigade in the same order bringing up the rear. The 21st N. Y. having gone straight up the slope, instead of around to the right as directed, the 2d U. S. Sharpshooters was sent out in its place. Phelps's and Doubleday's brigades were deployed in turn as they reached the woods, which began about half up the mountain. Gen. Patrick with his skirmishers soon drew the fire of the enemy, and found him strongly posted behind a fence which bounded the cleared space on the top of the ridge, having on his front the woods through which our line was advancing, and in his rear a cornfield full of rocky ledges, which afforded good cover to fall back to if dislodged.

Phelps's brigade gallantly advanced, under a hot fire, to close quarters, and, after ten or fifteen minutes of heavy firing on both sides (in which Gen. Hatch was wounded while urging on his men), the fence was carried by a charge, and our line advanced a few yards beyond it, somewhat sheltered by the slope of the hill.

Doubleday's brigade, now under the command of Lieut.-Col. Hoffmann (Col. Wainwright having been wounded), relieved Phelps, and continued firing for an hour and a half; the enemy, behind ledges of rocks some thirty or forty paces in our front, making a stubborn resistance and attempting to charge on the least cessation of our fire. About dusk Col. Christian's brigade of Ricketts's division came up and relieved Doubleday's brigade, which fell back into line behind Phelps's. Christian's brigade continued the action for thirty or forty minutes, when the enemy retired, after having made an attempt to flank us on the left, which was repulsed by the 75th N. Y. and 7th Ind.

The remaining brigade of Ricketts's division (Gen. Hartsuff's) was moved up in the centre, and connected Meade's left with Doubleday's right. We now had possession of the summit of the first ridge, which commanded the turnpike on both sides of the mountain, and the troops were ordered to hold their positions until further orders, and slept on their arms.

Late in the afternoon Gen. Gibbon, with his brigade and one section of Gibbon's battery ("B," 4th Artillery), was ordered to move up the main road on the enemy's centre. He advanced a regiment on each side of the road, preceded by skirmishers, and followed by the other two regiments in double column; the artillery moving on the road until within range of the enemy's guns, which were firing on the column from the gorge.

The brigade advanced steadily, driving the enemy from his positions in the woods and behind stone walls, until they reached a point well up towards the top of the pass, when the enemy, having been reinforced by three regiments, opened a heavy fire on the front and on both flanks. The fight continued until nine o'clock, the enemy being entirely repulsed; and the brigade, after having suffered severely, and having expended all its ammunition, including even the cartridges of the dead and wounded, continued to hold the ground it had so gallantly won until twelve o'clock, when it was relieved by Gen. Gorman's brigade, of Sedgwick's division, Sumner's corps (except the 6th Wis., which remained on the field all night). Gen. Gibbon, in this delicate movement, handled his brigade with as much precision and coolness as if upon parade, and the bravery of his troops could not be excelled.

The 2d corps (Sumner's) and the 12th corps (Williams's) reached their final positions shortly after dark. Gen. Richardson's division was placed near Mount Tabor Church, in a position to support our right, if necessary; the 12th corps and Sedgwick's division bivouacked around Bolivar, in a position to support our centre and left.

Gen. Sykes's division of regulars and the artillery reserve halted for the night at Middletown. Thus on the night of the 14th the whole army was massed in the vicinity of the field of battle, in readiness to renew the action the next day or to move in pursuit of the enemy. At daylight our skirmishers were advanced, and it was found that he had retreated during the night, leaving his dead on the field and his wounded uncared for.

I had reached the front at Middletown about noon, or a little before noon, and while there received the messenger from Harper's Ferry by whom I sent the despatch to Gen. Miles before mentioned. Immediately afterwards I rode forward to a point from which I could see the Gap and the adjacent ground. About the time I started Reno sent back a message desiring that a division might be sent to the rear of the pass. I sent the order to Hooker to move at once. (Burnside had nothing to do with this.) Marcy went with him and remained there most of the day. I rather think that he really deserved most of the credit for directing the movement, but, with his usual modesty, he would say little or nothing about it.

I pushed up Sturgis to support Cox, and hurried up Sumner to be ready as a reserve. Burnside never came as near the battle as my position. Yet it was his command that was in action! He spent the night in the same house that I did. In the course of the evening, when I had prepared the telegram to the President announcing the result of the day, I showed it to Burnside before sending it off, and asked if it was satisfactory to him; he replied that it was altogether so. Long afterwards it seems that he came to the conclusion that I did not give him sufficient credit; but he never said a word to me on the subject.

On the next day I had the honor to receive the following very kind despatch from the President:

"WAR DEPARTMENT,
"WASHINGTON, SEPT. 15, 1862, 2.45 P.M.

"Your despatch of to-day received. God bless you and all with you! Destroy the rebel army, if possible.

"A. LINCOLN.

"To MAJ.-GEN. McCLELLAN."

The following despatch was also received on the 16th:

"WEST POINT, 16TH, 1862.
"(RECEIVED, FREDERICK, 16TH, 1862, 10.40 A.M.)

"To Maj.-Gen. McClellan:
"Bravo, my dear general! Twice more and it's done.

"WINFIELD SCOTT."

Chapter XXXVI.

Antietam—Pursuit from South Mountain—Position of the enemy—The Battle—Burnside's failure—His contradictory statements—Letters of Col. Sackett.

On the night of the battle of South Mountain orders were given to the corps commanders to press forward their pickets at early dawn. This advance revealed the fact that the enemy had left his positions, and an immediate pursuit was ordered; the cavalry, under Gen. Pleasonton, and the three corps under Gens. Summer, Hooker, and Mansfield (the latter of whom had arrived that morning and assumed command of the 12th [Williams's] corps), by the national turnpike and Boonsborough; the corps of Gens. Burnside and Porter (the latter command at that time consisting of but one weak division, Sykes's) by the old Sharpsburg road; and Gen. Franklin to move into Pleasant Valley, occupy Rohrersville by a detachment, and endeavor to relieve Harper's Ferry.

Gens. Burnside and Porter, upon reaching the road from Boonsborough to Rohrersville, were to reinforce Franklin or to move on Sharpsburg, according to circumstances.

Franklin moved towards Brownsville and found there a force of the enemy, much superior in numbers to his own, drawn up in a strong position to receive him.

At this time the cessation of firing at Harper's Ferry indicated the surrender of that place.

The cavalry overtook the enemy's cavalry in Boonsborough, made a dashing charge, killing and wounding a number, and capturing 250 prisoners and 2 guns.

Gen. Richardson's division of the 2d corps, pressing the rear-guard of the enemy with vigor, passed Boonsborough and Keedysville, and came upon the main body of the enemy, occupying in large force a strong position a few miles beyond the latter place.

It had been hoped to engage the enemy on the 15th. Accordingly instructions were given that if the enemy were overtaken on the march they should be attacked at once; if found in heavy force and in position, the corps in advance should be placed in position for attack and await my arrival.

Early in the morning I had directed Burnside to put his corps in motion upon the old Sharpsburg road, but to wait with me for a time until more detailed news came from Franklin. About eight o'clock he begged me to let him go, saying that his corps had been some time in motion, and that if he delayed longer he would have difficulty in overtaking it; so I let him go. At about midday I rode to the point where Reno was killed the day before, and found that Burnside's troops, the 9th corps, had not stirred from its bivouac, and still blocked the road for the regular division. I sent for Burnside for an explanation, but he could not be found. He subsequently gave as an excuse the fatigued and hungry condition of his men.

"HEADQUARTERS, ARMY OF POTOMAC,
"SEPT. 15, 12.30 P.M.

"Gen. Burnside:
"Gen. McClellan desires you to let Gen. Porter's go on past you, if necessary. You will then push your own command on as rapidly as possible. The general also desires to know the reason for your delay in starting this morning.
"Very respectfully, your obedient servant,
"GEO. D. RUGGLES,
"COL. AND A. D. C."

After seeing the ground where Reno fell, and passing over Hooker's battle-ground of the previous day, I went rapidly to the front by the main road, being received by the troops, as I passed them, with the wildest enthusiasm. Near Keedysville I met Sumner, who told me that the enemy were in position in strong force, and took me to a height in front of Keedysville whence a view of the position could be obtained. We were accompanied by a numerous staff and escort; but no sooner had we shown ourselves on the hill than the enemy opened upon us with rifled guns, and, as his firing was very good, the hill was soon cleared of all save Fitz-John Porter and myself. I at once gave orders for the positions of the bivouacs, massing the army so that it could be handled as required. I ordered Burnside to the left. He grumbled that his troops were fatigued, but I started him off anyhow.

The first rapid survey of the enemy's position inclined me to attack his left, but the day was far gone.

He occupied a strong position on the heights, on the west side of Antietam creek, displaying a large force of infantry and cavalry, with numerous batteries of artillery, which opened on our columns as they appeared in sight on the Keedysville road and Sharpsburg turnpike, which fire was returned by Capt. Tidball's light battery, 2d U. S. Artillery, and Pettit's battery, 1st N. Y. Artillery.

The division of Gen. Richardson, following close on the heels of the retreating foe, halted and deployed near Antietam river, on the right of the Sharpsburg road. Gen. Sykes, leading on the division of regulars on the old

Sharpsburg road, came up and deployed to the left of Gen. Richardson, on the left of the road.

Antietam creek, in this vicinity, is crossed by four stone bridges—the upper one on the Keedysville and Williamsport road; the second on the Keedysville and Sharpsburg turnpike, some two and a half miles below; the third about a mile below the second, on the Rohrersville and Sharpsburg road; and the fourth near the mouth of Antietam creek, on the road leading from Harper's Ferry to Sharpsburg, some three miles below the third. The stream is sluggish, with few and difficult fords. After a rapid examination of the position I found that it was too late to attack that day, and at once directed the placing of the batteries in position in the centre, and indicated the bivouacs for the different corps, massing them near and on both sides of the Sharpsburg turnpike. The corps were not all in their positions until the next morning after sunrise.

On the morning of the 16th it was discovered that the enemy had changed the position of his batteries. The masses of his troops, however, were still concealed behind the opposite heights. Their left and centre were upon and in front of the Sharpsburg and Hagerstown turnpike, hidden by woods and irregularities of the ground; their extreme left resting upon a wooded eminence near the cross-roads to the north of J. Miller's farm, their left resting upon the Potomac. Their line extended south, the right resting upon the hills to the south of Sharpsburg, near Snavely's farm.

The bridge over the Antietam near this point was strongly covered by riflemen protected by rifle-pits, stone fences, etc., and enfiladed by artillery. The ground in front of this line consisted of undulating hills, their crests in turn commanded by others in their rear. On all favorable points the enemy's artillery was posted, and their reserves, hidden from view by the hills on which their line of battle was formed could manœuvre unobserved by our army, and from the shortness of their line could rapidly reinforce any point threatened by our attack. Their position, stretching across the angle formed by the Potomac and Antietam, their flanks and rear protected by these streams, was one of the strongest to be found in this region of country, which is well adapted to defensive warfare.

On the right, near Keedysville, on both sides of the Sharpsburg turnpike, were Sumner's and Hooker's corps. In advance, on the right of the turnpike and near the Antietam river, Gen. Richardson's division of Gen. Sumner's corps was posted. Gen. Sykes's division of Gen. Porter's corps was on the left of the turnpike and in line with Gen. Richardson, protecting the bridge No. 2

over the Antietam. The left of the line, opposite to and some distance from bridge No. 3, was occupied by Gen. Burnside's corps.

Before giving Gen. Hooker his orders to make the movement which will presently be described, I rode to the left of the line to satisfy myself that the troops were properly posted there to secure our left flank from any attack made along the left bank of the Antietam, as well as to enable us to carry bridge No. 3.

I rode along the whole front, generally in front of our pickets, accompanied by Hunt, Duane, Colburn, and a couple of orderlies, and went considerably beyond our actual and eventual left. Our small party drew the enemy's fire frequently, and developed the position of most of his batteries. I threw some of the regulars a little more to the left, and observed that our extreme left was not well placed to cover the position against any force approaching from Harper's Ferry by the left bank of the Antietam; also that the ground near "Burnside's bridge" was favorable for defence on our side, and that an attack across it would lead to favorable results. I therefore at once ordered Burnside to move his corps nearer the bridge, occupy the heights in rear, as well as to watch the approach from Harper's Ferry just spoken of. I gave this order at midday; it was near night before it was executed. I also instructed him to examine all the vicinity of the bridge, as he would probably be ordered to attack there next morning.

In front of Gens. Sumner's and Hooker's corps, near Keedysville, and on the ridge of the first line of hills overlooking the Antietam, and between the turnpike and Fry's house on the right of the road, were placed Capts. Taft's, Langner's, Von Kleizer's, and Lieut. Weaver's batteries of 20-pounder Parrott guns; on the crest of the hill in the rear and right of bridge No. 3, Capt. Weed's 3-inch and Lieut. Benjamin's 20-pounder batteries. Gen. Franklin's corps and Gen. Couch's division held a position in Pleasant Valley in front of Brownsville, with a strong force of the enemy in their front. Gen. Morell's division of Porter's corps was *en route* from Boonsborough, and Gen. Humphreys's division of new troops *en route* from Frederick, Md. About daylight on the 16th the enemy opened a heavy fire of artillery on our guns in position, which was promptly returned; their fire was silenced for the time, but was frequently renewed during the day.

It was afternoon before I could move the troops to their positions for attack, being compelled to spend the morning in reconnoitring the new position taken up by the enemy, examining the ground, finding fords, clearing the approaches, and hurrying up the ammunition and supply-trains, which had been delayed by the rapid march of the troops over the few practicable approaches from Frederick. These had been crowded by the masses of infantry, cavalry, and artillery pressing on with the hope of overtaking the enemy before he could form to resist an attack. Many of the troops were out of rations on the previous day, and a good deal of their ammunition had been expended in the severe action of the 14th.

My plan for the impending general engagement was to attack the enemy's left with the corps of Hooker and Mansfield, supported by Sumner's and, if necessary, by Franklin's; and as soon as matters looked favorably there, to move the corps of Burnside against the enemy's extreme right, upon the ridge running to the south and rear of Sharpsburg, and, having carried their position, to press along the crest towards our right; and whenever either of these flank movements should be successful, to advance our centre with all the forces then disposable.

About two P.M. Gen. Hooker, with his corps, consisting of Gens. Ricketts's, Meade's, and Doubleday's divisions, was ordered to cross the Antietam at a ford, and at bridge No. 1, a short distance above, to attack and, if possible, turn the enemy's left. Gen. Sumner was ordered to cross the corps of Gen. Mansfield (the 12th) during the night, and hold his own (the 2d) corps ready to cross early the next morning. On reaching the vicinity of the enemy's left a sharp contest commenced with the Pennsylvania reserves, the advance of Gen. Hooker's corps, near the house of D. Miller. The enemy was driven from the strip of woods where he was first met. The firing lasted until after dark, when Gen. Hooker's corps rested on their arms on ground won from the enemy.

When I returned to the right, and found that Hooker's preparations were not yet complete, I went to hurry them in person. It was perhaps half-past three to four o'clock before Hooker could commence crossing and get fairly in motion up the opposite slopes. I accompanied the movement, at the head of the column, until the top of the ridge was fairly gained, indicated the new direction to be taken, and then returned to headquarters—not to the camp, but to a house further in advance (Fry's house), where I passed the night.

During the night Gen. Mansfield's corps, consisting of Gens. Williams's and Greene's divisions, crossed the Antietam at the same ford and bridge that Gen. Hooker's troops had passed, and bivouacked on the farm of J. Poffenberger, about a mile in rear of Gen. Hooker's position.

At daylight on the 17th the action was commenced by the skirmishers of the Pennsylvania reserves. The whole of Gen. Hooker's corps was soon engaged, and drove the enemy from the open field in front of the first line of woods into a second line of woods beyond, which runs to the eastward of and nearly parallel to the Sharpsburg and Hagerstown turnpike. This contest was obstinate, and as the troops advanced the opposition became more determined and the number of the enemy greater. Gen. Hooker then ordered up the corps of Gen. Mansfield, which moved promptly toward the scene of action.

The first division, Gen. Williams's, was deployed to the right on approaching the enemy; Gen. Crawford's brigade on the right, its right resting on the Hagerstown turnpike; on his left Gen. Gordon's brigade. The second division, Gen. Greene's, joining the left of Gordon's, extended as far as the burnt buildings to the north and east of the white church on the turnpike. During the deployment that gallant veteran, Gen. Mansfield, fell mortally wounded while examining the ground in front of his troops. Gen. Hartsuff, of Hooker's corps, was severely wounded while bravely pressing forward his troops, and was taken from the field.

The command of the 12th corps fell upon Gen. Williams. Five regiments of the first division of this corps were new troops. One brigade of the second division was sent to support Gen. Doubleday.

The 125th Penn. Volunteers were pushed across the turnpike into the woods beyond J. Miller's house, with orders to hold the position as long as possible.

The line of battle of this corps was formed, and it became engaged about seven A.M., the attack being opened by Knapp's (Penn.), Cothran's (N. Y.), and Hampton's (Pittsburgh) batteries. To meet this attack the enemy had pushed a strong column of troops into the open fields in front of the turnpike, while he occupied the woods on the west of the turnpike in strong force. The woods (as was found by subsequent observation) were traversed by outcropping ledges of rock. Several hundred yards to the right and rear was a hill which commanded the debouch of the woods, and in the fields between was a long line of stone fences, continued by breastworks of rails, which covered the enemy's infantry from our musketry. The same woods formed a screen behind which his movements were concealed, and his batteries on the hill and the rifle-works covered from the fire of our artillery in front.

For about two hours the battle raged with varied success, the enemy endeavoring to drive our troops into the second line of wood, and ours in turn to get possession of the line in front.

Our troops ultimately succeeded in forcing the enemy back into the woods near the turnpike, Gen. Greene with his two brigades crossing into the woods to the left of the Dunker church. During this conflict Gen. Crawford, commanding 1st division after Gen. Williams took command of the corps, was wounded and left the field.

Gen. Greene being much exposed and applying for reinforcements, the

13th N. J., 27th Ind., and the 3d Md. were sent to his support with a section of Knapp's battery.

At about nine o'clock A.M. Gen. Sedgwick's division of Gen. Sumner's corps arrived. Crossing the ford previously mentioned, this division marched in three columns to the support of the attack on the enemy's left. On nearing the scene of action the columns were halted, faced to the front, and established by Gen. Sumner in three parallel lines by brigade, facing toward the south and west; Gen. Gorman's brigade in front, Gen. Dana's second, and Gen. Howard's third, with a distance between the lines of some seventy paces. The division was then put in motion and moved upon the field of battle, under fire from the enemy's concealed batteries on the hill beyond the roads. Passing diagonally to the front across the open space, and to the front of the first division of Gen. Williams's corps, this latter division withdrew.

Entering the woods on the west of the turnpike, and driving the enemy before them, the first line was met by a heavy fire of musketry and shell from the enemy's breastworks and the batteries on the hill commanding the exit from the woods. Meantime a heavy column of the enemy had succeeded in crowding back the troops of Gen. Greene's division, and appeared in rear of the left of Sedgwick's division. By command of Gen. Sumner, Gen. Howard faced the third line to the rear preparatory to a change of front to meet the column advancing on the left; but this line, now suffering from a destructive fire both in front and on its left which it was unable to return, gave way towards the right and rear in considerable confusion, and was soon followed by the first and second lines.

Gen. Gorman's brigade, and one regiment of Gen. Dana's, soon rallied and checked the advance of the enemy on the right. The second and third lines now formed on the left of Gen. Gorman's brigade and poured a destructive fire upon the enemy.

During Gen. Sumner's attack he ordered Gen. Williams to support him. Brig.-Gen. Gordon, with a portion of his brigade, moved forward, but when he reached the woods the left of Gen. Sedgwick's division had given way; and finding himself, as the smoke cleared up, opposed to the enemy in force with his small command, he withdrew to the rear of the batteries at the second line of woods. As Gen. Gordon's troops unmasked our batteries on the left they opened with canister; the batteries of Capt. Cothran, 1st N. Y., and "I," 1st Artillery, commanded by Lieut. Woodruff, doing good service. Unable to withstand this deadly fire in front and the musketry-fire from the right, the enemy again sought shelter in the woods and rocks beyond the turnpike.

During this assault Gens. Sedgwick and Dana were seriously wounded and taken from the field. Gen. Sedgwick, though twice wounded and faint from loss of blood, retained command of his division for more than an hour after his first wound, animating his command by his presence.

About the time of Gen. Sedgwick's advance Gen. Hooker, while urging on his command, was severely wounded in the foot and taken from the field, and Gen. Meade was placed in command of his corps. Gen. Howard assumed command after Gen. Sedgwick retired.

The repulse of the enemy offered opportunity to rearrange the lines and reorganize the commands on the right, now more or less in confusion. The batteries of the Pennsylvania reserve, on high ground near J. Poffenberger's house, opened fire and checked several attempts of the enemy to establish batteries in front of our right, to turn that flank and enfilade the lines.

While the conflict was so obstinately raging on the right Gen. French was pushing his division against the enemy still further to the left. This division crossed the Antietam at the same ford as Gen. Sedgwick, and immediately in his rear. Passing over the stream in three columns, the division marched about a mile from the ford, then, facing to the left, moved in three lines towards the enemy: Gen. Max Weber's brigade in front, Col. Dwight Morris's brigade of raw troops—undrilled, and moving for the first time under fire—in the second, and Gen. Kimball's brigade in the third. The division was first assailed by a fire of artillery, but steadily advanced, driving in the enemy's skirmishers, and encountered the infantry in some force at the group of houses on Roulette's farm. Gen. Weber's brigade gallantly advanced with an unwavering front and drove the enemy from their position about the houses.

While Gen. Weber was hotly engaged with the first line of the enemy, Gen. French received orders from Gen. Sumner, his corps commander, to push on with renewed vigor to make a diversion in favor of the attack on the right. Leaving the new troops, who had been thrown into some confusion from their march through cornfields, over fences, etc., to form as a reserve, he ordered the brigade of Gen. Kimball to the front, passing to the left of Gen. Weber. The enemy was pressed back to near the crest of the hill, where he was encountered in greater strength posted in a sunken road forming a natural rifle-pit running in a northwesterly direction. In a cornfield in rear of this road were also strong bodies of the enemy. As the line reached the crest of the hill a galling fire was opened on it from the sunken road and cornfield. Here a terrific fire of musketry burst from both lines, and the battle raged along the whole line with great slaughter.

The enemy attempted to turn the left of the line, but were met by the 7th Va. and 132d Penn. Volunteers and repulsed. Foiled in this, the enemy made a determined assault on the front, but were met by a charge from our lines which drove them back with severe loss, leaving in our hands some 300 prisoners and several stands of colors. The enemy, having been repulsed by the terrible execution of the batteries and the musketry-fire on the extreme right, now attempted to assist the attack on Gen. French's division by assailing him on his right and endeavoring to turn this flank; but this attack was met and checked by the 14th Ind. and 8th O. Volunteers, and by canister from Capt. Tompkins's battery, 1st R. I. Artillery. Having been under an almost continuous fire for nearly four hours, and the ammunition nearly expended, this division now took position immediately below the crest of the heights on which they had so gallantly fought, the enemy making no attempt to regain their lost ground.

On the left of Gen. French, Gen. Richardson's division was hotly engaged. Having crossed the Antietam about 9.30 A.M. at the ford crossed by the other divisions of Sumner's corps, it moved on a line nearly parallel to the Antietam, and formed in a ravine behind the high grounds overlooking Roulette's house; the 2d (Irish) brigade, commanded by Gen. Meagher, on the right; the 3d brigade, commanded by Gen. Caldwell, on his left, and the brigade commanded by Col. Brooks, 53d Penn. Volunteers, in support. As the division moved forward to take its position on the field, the enemy directed a fire of artillery against it, but, owing to the irregularities of the ground, did but little damage.

Meagher's brigade, advancing steadily, soon became engaged with the enemy posted to the left and in front of Roulette's house. It continued to advance under a heavy fire nearly to the crest of the hill overlooking Piper's house, the enemy being posted in a continuation of the sunken road and cornfield before referred to. Here the brave Irish brigade opened upon the enemy a terrific musketry-fire.

All of Gen. Sumner's corps was now engaged—Gen. Sedgwick on the right, Gen. French in the centre, and Gen. Richardson on the left. The Irish brigade sustained its well-earned reputation. After suffering terribly in officers and men, and strewing the ground with their enemies as they drove them back, their ammunition nearly expended, and their commander, Gen. Meagher, disabled by the fall of his horse shot under him, this brigade was ordered to give place to Gen. Caldwell's brigade, which advanced to a short distance in its rear. The lines were passed by the Irish brigade breaking by company to the rear, and Gen. Caldwell's by company to the front, as steadily as on drill. Col. Brooks's brigade now became the second line.

The ground over which Gens. Richardson's and French's divisions were fighting was very irregular, intersected by numerous ravines, hills covered with growing corn, enclosed by stonewalls, behind which the enemy could advance unobserved upon any exposed point of our lines. Taking advantage of this, the enemy attempted to gain the right of Richardson's position in a cornfield near Roulette's house, where the division had become separated from that of Gen. French's. A change of front by the 52d N. Y. and 2d Del. Volunteers, of Col. Brooks's brigade, under Col. Frank, and the attack made by the 53d Penn. Volunteers, sent further to the right by Col. Brooks to close this gap in the line, and the movement of the 132d Penn. and 7th Va. Volunteers, of Gen. French's division, before referred to, drove the enemy from the cornfield and restored the line.

The brigade of Gen. Caldwell, with determined gallantry, pushed the enemy back opposite the left and centre of this division, but, sheltered in the sunken road, they still held our forces on the right of Caldwell in check. Col. Barlow, commanding the 61st and 64th N. Y. regiments, of Caldwell's brigade, seeing a favorable opportunity, advanced the regiments on the left, taking the line in the sunken road in flank, and compelled them to surrender, capturing over 300 prisoners and three stands of colors.

The whole of the brigade, with the 57th and 66th N. Y. regiments, of Col. Brooks's brigade, who had moved these regiments into the first line, now advanced with gallantry, driving the enemy before them in confusion into the cornfield beyond the sunken road. The left of the division was now well advanced, when the enemy, concealed by an intervening ridge, endeavored to turn its left and rear.

Col. Cross, 5th N. H., by a change of front to the left and rear, brought his regiment facing the advancing line. Here a spirited contest arose to gain a commanding height, the two opposing forces moving parallel to each other, giving and receiving fire. The 5th, gaining the advantage, faced to the right and delivered its volley. The enemy staggered, but rallied and advanced desperately at a charge. Being reinforced by the 81st Penn., these regiments met the advance by a countercharge. The enemy fled, leaving many killed, wounded, and prisoners, and the colors of the 4th N. C., in our hands.

Another column of the enemy, advancing under shelter of a stone wall and cornfield, pressed down on the right of the division; but Col. Barlow again advanced the 61st and 64th N. Y. against these troops, and, with the attack of Kimball's brigade on the right, drove them from this position.

Our troops on the left of this part of the line having driven the enemy far back, they, with reinforced numbers, made a determined attack directly in front. To meet this Col. Barlow brought his two regiments to their position in line, and drove the enemy through the cornfield into the orchard beyond, under a heavy fire of musketry, and a fire of canister from two pieces of artillery in the orchard, and a battery further to the right throwing shell and case-shot. This advance gave us possession of Piper's house, the strong point contended for by the enemy at this part of the line, it being a defensible building several hundred yards in advance of the sunken road. The musketry-fire at this point of the line now ceased. Holding Piper's house, Gen. Richardson withdrew the line a little way to the crest of a hill—a more advantageous position. Up to this time the division was without artillery, and in the new position suffered severely from artillery-fire which could not be replied to. A section of Robertson's horse-battery, commanded by Lieut. Vincent, 2d Artillery, now arrived on the ground and did excellent service. Subsequently a battery of brass guns, commanded by Capt. Graham, 1st Artillery, arrived, and was posted on the crest of the hill, and soon silenced the two guns in the orchard. A heavy fire soon ensued between the battery further to the right and our own. Capt. Graham's battery was bravely and skilfully served, but, unable to reach the enemy, who had rifled guns of greater range than our smoothbores, retired by order of Gen. Richardson, to save it from useless sacrifice of men and horses. The brave general was himself mortally wounded while personally directing its fire.

Gen. Hancock was placed in command of the division after the fall of Gen. Richardson. Gen. Meagher's brigade, now commanded by Col. Burke, of the 63d N. Y., having refilled their cartridge-boxes, was again ordered forward, and took position in the centre of the line. The division now occupied one line in close proximity to the enemy, who had taken up a position in the rear of Piper's house. Col. Dwight Morris, with the 14th Conn. and a detachment of the 108th N. Y., of Gen. French's division, was sent by Gen. French to the support of Gen. Richardson's division. This command was now placed in an interval in the line between Gen. Caldwell's and the Irish brigades.

The requirements of the extended line of battle had so engaged the artillery that the application of Gen. Hancock for artillery for the division could not be complied with immediately by the chief of artillery or the corps commanders in his vicinity. Knowing the tried courage of the troops, Gen. Hancock felt confident that he could hold his position, although suffering from the enemy's artillery, but was too weak to attack, as the great length of the line he was obliged to hold prevented him from forming more than one line of battle, and, from his advanced position, this line was already partly enfiladed by the batteries of the enemy on the right, which were protected from our batteries opposite them by the woods at the Dunker church.

Seeing a body of the enemy advancing on some of our troops to the left of his position, Gen. Hancock obtained Hexamer's battery from Gen. Franklin's corps, which assisted materially in frustrating this attack. It also assisted the attack of the 7th Me., of Franklin's corps, which, without other aid, made an attack against the enemy's line, and drove in skirmishers who were annoying our artillery and troops on the right. Lieut. Woodruff, with battery I, 2d Artillery, relieved Capt. Hexamer, whose ammunition was expended. The enemy at one time seemed to be about making an attack in force upon this part of the line, and advanced a long column of infantry towards this division; but on nearing the position, Gen. Pleasonton opening on them with sixteen guns, they halted, gave a desultory fire, and retreated, closing the operations on this portion of the field. I return to the incidents occurring still further to the right.

Between twelve and one P.M. Gen. Franklin's corps arrived on the field of battle, having left their camp near Crampton's Pass at six A.M. leaving Gen. Couch with orders to move with his division to occupy Maryland Heights. Gen. Smith's division led the column, followed by Gen. Slocum's.

It was first intended to keep this corps in reserve on the east side of the Antietam, to operate on either flank or on the centre, as circumstances might require; but on nearing Keedysville the strong opposition on the right, developed by the attacks of Hooker and Sumner, rendered it necessary at once to send this corps to the assistance of the right wing.

On nearing the field, hearing that one of our batteries—A, 4th U. S. Artillery, commanded by Lieut. Thomas, who occupied the same position as Lieut. Woodruff's battery in the morning—was hotly engaged without supports, Gen. Smith sent two regiments to its relief from Gen. Hancock's brigade. On inspecting the ground Gen. Smith ordered the other regiments of Hancock's brigade, with Frank's and Cowen's batteries, 1st N. Y. Artillery, to the threatened position. Lieut. Thomas and Capt. Cothran, commanding batteries, bravely held their positions against the advancing enemy, handling their batteries with skill.

Finding the enemy still advancing, the 3d brigade of Smith's division, commanded by Col. Irvin, 49th Penn. volunteers, was ordered up, and passed through Lieut. Thomas's battery, charged upon the enemy, and drove back the advance until abreast of the Dunker church. As the right of the brigade came opposite the woods it received a destructive fire, which checked the advance and threw the brigade somewhat into confusion. It formed again behind a rise of ground in the open space in advance of the batteries.

Gen. French having reported to Gen. Franklin that his ammunition was nearly expended, that officer ordered Gen. Brooks, with his brigade, to reinforce him. Gen. Brooks formed his brigade on the right of Gen. French, where they remained during the remainder of the day and night, frequently under the fire of the enemy's artillery.

It was soon after the brigade of Col. Irvin had fallen back behind the rise of ground that the 7th Me., by order of Col. Irvin, made the gallant attack already referred to.

The advance of Gen. Franklin's corps was opportune. The attack of the enemy on this position, but for the timely arrival of his corps, must have been disastrous, had it succeeded in piercing the line between Gens. Sedgwick's and French's divisions.

Gen. Franklin ordered two brigades of Gen. Slocum's division, Gen. Newton's and Col. Torbert's, to form in column to assault the woods that had been so hotly contested before by Gens. Sumner and Hooker; Gen. Bartlett's brigade was ordered to form as a reserve. At this time Gen. Sumner, having command on the right, directed further offensive operations to be postponed, as the repulse of this, the only remaining corps available for attack, would peril the safety of the whole army.

Gen. Porter's corps, consisting of Gen. Sykes's division of regulars and volunteers, and Gen. Morell's division of volunteers, occupied a position on the east side of Antietam creek upon the main turnpike leading to Sharpsburg, and directly opposite the centre of the enemy's line. This corps filled the interval between the right wing and Gen. Burnside's command and guarded the main approach from the enemy's position to our trains of supplies.

It was necessary to watch this part of our line with the utmost vigilance, lest the enemy should take advantage of the first exhibition of weakness here to push upon us a vigorous assault for the purpose of piercing our centre and turning our rear, as well as to capture or destroy our supply-trains. Once having penetrated this line, the enemy's passage to our rear could have met with but feeble resistance, as there were no reserves to reinforce or close up the gap.

Towards the middle of the afternoon, proceeding to the right, I found that Sumner's, Hooker's, and Mansfield's corps had met with serious losses. Several general officers had been carried from the field severely wounded, and the aspect of affairs was anything but promising. At the risk of greatly exposing our centre, I ordered two brigades from Porter's corps, the only available troops, to reinforce the right. Six battalions of Sykes's regulars had been thrown across the Antietam bridge on the main road, to attack and drive back the enemy's sharpshooters, who were annoying Pleasonton's horse-batteries in advance of the bridge. Warren's brigade, of Porter's corps, was detached to hold a position on Burnside's right and rear; so that Porter was left at one time with only a portion of Sykes's division and one small brigade of Morell's division (but little over 3,000 men) to hold his important position.

Gen. Sumner expressed the most decided opinion against another attempt during that day to assault the enemy's position in front, as portions of our troops were so much scattered and demoralized. In view of these circumstances, after making changes in the position of some of the troops, I directed the different commanders to hold their positions, and, being satisfied that this could be done without the assistance of the two brigades from the centre, I countermanded the order, which was in course of execution.

Gen Slocum's division replaced a portion of Gen. Sumner's troops, and positions were selected for batteries in front of the woods. The enemy opened several heavy fires of artillery on the position of our troops after this, but our batteries soon silenced them.

On the morning of the 17th Gen. Pleasonton, with his cavalry division and the horse-batteries, under Capts. Robertson, Tidball, and Lieut. Haines, of the 2d Artillery, and Capt. Gibson, 3d Artillery, was ordered to advance on the turnpike towards Sharpsburg, across bridge No. 2, and support the left of Gen. Sumner's line. The bridge being covered by a fire of artillery and sharpshooters, cavalry skirmishers were thrown out, and Capt. Tidball's battery advanced by piece and drove off the sharpshooters with canister sufficiently to establish the batteries above mentioned, which opened on the enemy with effect. The firing was kept up for about two hours, when, the enemy's fire slackening, the batteries were relieved by Randall's and Van Reed's batteries, U. S. Artillery.

About three o'clock Tidball, Robertson, and Haines returned to their positions on the west of Antietam, Capt. Gibson having been placed in position on the east side to guard the approaches to the bridge. These batteries did good service, concentrating their fire on the column of the enemy about to attack Gen. Hancock's position, and compelling it to find shelter behind the hills in rear.

Gen. Sykes's division had been in position since the 15th, exposed to the enemy's artillery and sharpshooters. Gen. Morell had come up on the 16th and relieved Gen. Richardson on the right of Gen. Sykes. Continually under the vigilant watch of the enemy, this corps guarded a vital point.

The position of the batteries under Gen. Pleasonton being one of great exposure, the battalion of the 2d and 10th U. S. Infantry, under Capt. Pollard, 2d Infantry, was sent to his support. Subsequently four battalions of regular infantry, under Capt. Dryer, 4th Infantry, were sent across to assist in driving off the sharpshooters of the enemy.

The battalion of the 2d and 10th Infantry, advancing far-beyond the batteries, compelled the cannoneers of a battery of the enemy to abandon their guns. Few in numbers, and unsupported, they were unable to bring them off. The heavy loss of this small body of men attests their gallantry.

The troops of Gen Burnside held the left of the line opposite bridge No. 3. The attack on the right was to have been supported by an attack on the left. Preparatory to this attack, on the evening of the 16th, Gen. Burnside's corps was moved forward and to the left, and took up a position nearer the bridge.

I visited Gen. Burnside's position on the 16th, and, after pointing out to him the proper dispositions to be made of his troops during the day and night, informed him that he would probably be required to attack the enemy's right on the following morning, and directed him to make careful reconnoissances.

Gen. Burnside's corps, consisting of the divisions of Gens Cox, Wilcox, Rodman, and Sturgis, was posted as follows: Col. Crook's brigade, Cox's division, on the right, Gen. Sturgis's division immediately in rear; on the left was Gen. Rodman's division, with Gen. Scammon's brigade, Cox's division, in support.

Gen. Wilcox's division was held in reserve. The corps bivouacked in position on the night of the 16th.

Early on the morning of the 17th I ordered Gen. Burnside to form his troops and hold them in readiness to assault the bridge in his front, and to await further orders.

At eight o'clock an order was sent to him by Lieut. Wilson, topographical engineers, to carry the bridge, then to gain possession of the heights beyond, and to advance along their crest upon Sharpsburg and its rear.

After some time had elapsed, not hearing from him, I despatched an aide to ascertain what had been done. The aide returned with the information that but little progress had been made. I then sent him back with an order to Gen. Burnside to assault the bridge at once and carry it at all hazards. The aide returned to me a second time with the report that the bridge was still in the possession of the enemy. Whereupon I directed Col. Sackett, inspector-general, to deliver to Gen. Burnside my positive order to push forward his troops without a moment's delay, and, if necessary, to carry the bridge at the point of the bayonet; and I ordered Col. Sackett to remain with Gen. Burnside and see that the order was executed promptly.

After these three hours' delay the bridge was carried at one o'clock by a brilliant charge of the 51st N. Y. and 51st Penn. Volunteers. Other troops were then thrown over and the opposite bank occupied, the enemy retreating to the heights beyond.

A halt was then made by Gen. Burnside's advance until three P.M.; upon hearing which I directed one of my aides, Col. Key, to inform Gen. Burnside that I desired him to push forward his troops with the utmost vigor and carry the enemy's position on the heights; that the movement was vital to our success; that this was a time when we must not stop for loss of life, if a great object could thereby be accomplished; that if, in his judgment, his attack would fail, to inform me so at once, that his troops might be withdrawn and used elsewhere on the field. He replied that he would soon advance, and would go up the hill as far as a battery of the enemy on the left would permit. Upon this report I again immediately sent Col. Key to Gen. Burnside with orders to advance at once, if possible to flank the battery, or storm it and carry the heights; repeating that if he considered the movement impracticable, to inform me, so that his troops might be recalled. The advance was then gallantly resumed, the enemy driven from the guns, the heights handsomely carried, and a portion of the troops even reached the outskirts of Sharpsburg. By this time it was nearly dark, and strong reinforcements just then reaching the enemy from Harper's Ferry attacked Gen. Burnside's troops on their left flank, and forced them to retire to a lower line of hills nearer the bridge.

If this important movement had been consummated two hours earlier, a position would have been secured upon the heights from which our batteries might have enfiladed the greater part of the enemy's line, and turned their right and rear. Our victory might thus have been much more decisive.

The ground held by Burnside beyond the bridge was so strong that he ought to have repulsed the attack and held his own. He never crossed the bridge in person!

The following is the substance of Gen. Burnside's operations, as given in his report:

Col. Crook's brigade was ordered to storm the bridge. This bridge, No. 3, is a stone structure of three arches, with stone parapets. The banks of the stream on the opposite side are precipitous, and command the eastern approaches to the bridge. On the hill-side immediately by the bridge was a stone fence running parallel to the stream. The turns of the roadway as it wound up the hill were covered by rifle-pits and breastworks of rails, etc. These works and the woods that covered the slopes were filled with the enemy's rifle-men, and batteries were in position to enfilade the bridge and its approaches.

Gen. Rodman was ordered to cross the ford below the bridge. From Col. Crook's position it was found impossible to carry the bridge.

Gen. Sturgis was ordered to make a detail from his division for that purpose. He sent forward the 2d Md. and 6th N. H. These regiments made several successive attacks in the most gallant style, but were driven back.

The artillery of the left were ordered to concentrate their fire on the woods above the bridge. Col. Crook brought a section of Capt. Simmons's battery to a position to command the bridge. The 51st N. Y. and 51st Penn. were then ordered to assault the bridge. Taking advantage of a small spur of the hills which ran parallel to the river, they moved towards the bridge. From the crest of this spur they rushed with bayonets fixed and cleared the bridge.

The division followed the storming party; also the brigade of Col. Crook as support. The enemy withdrew to still higher ground some five or six hundred yards beyond, and opened a fire of artillery on the troops in the new positions on the crest of the hill above the bridge.

Gen. Rodman's division succeeded in crossing the ford after a sharp fire of musketry and artillery, and joined on the left of Sturgis; Scammon's brigade crossing as support. Gen. Wilcox's division was ordered across to take position on Gen. Sturgis's right.

These dispositions being completed about three o'clock, the command moved forward, except Sturgis's division left in reserve. Clark's and Darell's batteries accompanied Rodman's division, Cooke's battery with Wilcox's division, and a section of Simmons's battery with Col. Crook's brigade. A section of Simmons's battery, and Muhlenberg's and McMullan's batteries, were in position. The order for the advance was obeyed by the troops with alacrity. Gen. Wilcox's division, with Crook in support, moved up on both sides of the turnpike leading from the bridge to Sharpsburg; Gen. Rodman's division, supported by Scammon's brigade, on the left of Gen. Wilcox. The enemy retreated before the advance of the troops. The 9th N. Y., of Gen. Rodman's division, captured one of the enemy's batteries and held it for some time. As the command was driving the enemy to the main heights on the left of the town, the light division of Gen. A. P. Hill arrived upon the field of battle from Harper's Ferry, and with a heavy artillery-fire made a strong attack on the extreme left. To meet this attack the left division diverged from the line of march intended, and opened a gap between it and the right. To fill up this it was necessary to order the troops from the second line. During these movements Gen. Rodman was mortally wounded. Col. Harland's brigade, of Gen. Rodman's division, was driven back. Col. Scammon's brigade, by a change of front to rear on his right flank, saved the left from being driven completely in. The fresh troops of the enemy pouring in, and the accumulation of artillery against this command, destroyed all hope of its being able to accomplish anything more.

It was now nearly dark. Gen. Sturgis was ordered forward to support the left. Notwithstanding the hard work in the early part of the day, his division moved forward with spirit. With its assistance the enemy were checked and held at bay.

The command was ordered to fall back by Gen. Cox, who commanded on the field the troops engaged in this affair beyond the Antietam.

Night closed the long and desperately contested battle of the 17th. Nearly two hundred thousand men and five hundred pieces of artillery were for fourteen hours engaged in this memorable battle. We had attacked the enemy in a position selected by the experienced engineer then in person directing their operations. We had driven them from their line on one flank, and secured a footing within it on the other. The Army of the Potomac, notwithstanding the moral effect incident to previous reverses, had achieved a victory over an adversary invested with the prestige of recent success. Our soldiers slept that night conquerors on a field won by their valor and covered with the dead and wounded of the enemy.

Thirteen guns, 39 colors, upwards of 15,000 stands of small arms, and more than 6,000 prisoners were the trophies which attest the success of our arms in the battles of South Mountain, Crampton's Gap, and Antietam. Not a single gun or color was lost by our army during these battles.

When I was on the right on the afternoon of the 17th I found the troops a good deal shaken—that is, some of them who had been in the early part of the action. Even Sedgwick's division commenced giving way under a few shots from a battery that suddenly commenced firing from an unexpected position. I had to ride in and rally them myself. Sedgwick had been carried off very severely wounded. The death of Mansfield, the wounding of Hooker, Richardson, and Sedgwick, were irreparable losses in that part of the field. It was this afternoon, when I was on the right, that on the field of battle I gave Hancock a division—that of Richardson, who was mortally wounded.

Early next morning (the 18th) Burnside sent to ask me for a fresh division to enable him to hold his own. I sent word that I could send none until I came myself to see the state of affairs, and in a few minutes rode over there and carefully examined the position. Burnside told me that his men were so demoralized and so badly beaten the day before that were they attacked they would give way. I told him I could see no evidences of that, but that I would *lend* him Morell's division for a short time, though I would probably need it again elsewhere in a few hours. I instructed him to place one brigade on some heights that ran across the valley on our left, in order to cover the left flank, the rest on the heights in rear of the bridge, to cover the retreat of his men, should that prove necessary. The division was accordingly sent to him, and towards evening I learned that he had thrown it across the river and withdrawn his own men, his excuse to me being that he could not trust his men on the other side! The evening before he was at my headquarters, and told some of my aides that his men were badly beaten.

Long afterwards I learned from Col. Grif. Stedman (11th Conn. regiment) that on the night of the 17th he was with his then colonel (Kingsbury), who was mortally wounded and lying in a house on our side of the bridge, close to it. Burnside came by and gave orders for the wounded to be removed still further to the rear, stating that the corps were entirely defeated and demoralized, and that the house in question would soon be occupied by the enemy. As Kingsbury was in no condition to be removed, Stedman determined to remain with him and share his fate. It is needless to say that the house was not occupied by the enemy, and that Burnside was in no condition to know the real state of his command, as he had not been with it. But I have mentioned enough to show what his real opinions and state of mind were on the evening of the 17th and the morning of the 18th. Yet in face of all this he subsequently testified before the

Committee on the Conduct of the War that he had on the morning of the 18th asked me for the reinforcement of a division to enable him to renew the attack, stating at the same time that his men were in superb condition, ready for any work, and that I had committed a great error in not renewing the battle early on the morning of the 18th. The real facts, so far as Burnside was concerned, were as I have given them above. But although his men were not, perhaps, in magnificent condition, they were by no means so demoralized as he represented them to be. I cannot, from my long acquaintance with Burnside, believe that he would deliberately lie, but I think that his weak mind was turned; that he was confused in action; and that subsequently he really did not know what had occurred, and was talked by his staff into any belief they chose.

I have only adverted to the very pernicious effects of Burnside's inexcusable delay in attacking the bridge and the heights in rear. What is certain is that if Porter or Hancock had been in his place the town of Sharpsburg would have been ours, Hill would have been thrown back into the Potomac, and the battle of Antietam would have been very decisive in its results.

[In a monograph prepared by Gen. William B. Franklin, "In Memory of General McClellan," that distinguished soldier thus speaks of the Maryland campaign and its results, and specially of the result of the battle of Antietam:

"Without orders placing him in command other than the verbal request of the President, and without orders of any kind from any one, he started on the Maryland campaign to find the enemy, who had been so foolish as to invade a State which had remained true to the Union. The victories of Turner's and Crampton's gaps of South Mountain, and of Antietam, were the results, the last battle followed by the hurried retreat of Gen. Lee beyond the Potomac. History will some day tell why the Confederate army was not driven into the Potomac instead of across it. It will show that its escape was not due to want of generalship of the commanding general, nor to the absence of necessary orders to subordinates."

At the time of his death Gen. McClellan was about to write a condensed account of the battle of Antietam for the *Century* magazine. He had reviewed the events preceding South Mountain when his pen was arrested. From among the papers found lying on his writing-table, where he had left them four hours before his death, the editor regards the letters of Gen. Sackett, which here follow, as important to be published for the purposes of that history which has not heretofore been written.]

Letters from Gen. Sackett.

"FEB. 20, 1876.

"MY DEAR GENERAL: In reply to your note I will state that, at about nine o'clock on the morning of the battle of Antietam, you told me to mount my horse and to proceed as speedily as possible with orders directing Gen. Burnside to move his troops across the bridge or stream in his front at once, and then to push them forward vigorously, without a moment's delay, to secure the heights beyond.

"You moreover directed me to remain with Gen. Burnside until I saw his troops well under way up the heights in the direction of Sharpsburg, and then to return and report to you.

"I started at once, as fast as my horse could carry me. I found Gen. Burnside on an elevated point (near the position of Lieut. Benjamin's 20-pounder battery) commanding an extensive view of the battle-field. I gave him your orders, which seemed to annoy him somewhat, as he said to me: 'McClellan appears to think I am not trying my best to carry this bridge; you are the third or fourth one who has been to me this morning with similar orders.' I told him I knew you were exceedingly anxious, and regarded his getting across the stream and moving on Sharpsburg with rapidity and vigor at once as of vital importance to a complete success.

"Gen. Burnside ordered assaults to be made on the bridge, which were for a long time unsuccessful. I had been at his headquarters for fully three hours when Col. Key arrived from your headquarters with positive orders to push across the bridge and to move rapidly up the heights; to carry the bridge at the point of the bayonet, if necessary, and not stop for loss of life, as sacrifices must be made in favor of success.

"As soon as Col. Key had gone I suggested to Gen. Burnside, were he to go down near the bridge, his presence among the troops could have the effect to encourage and stimulate the men to renewed efforts. He said he would, and immediately mounted his horse and rode in the direction of the bridge, but soon returned saying the bridge had been carried and the troops were crossing over as rapidly as possible. He likewise mentioned at this time that Col. Henry Kingsbury had been mortally wounded in the assault on the bridge.

"Gen. Burnside at once issued instructions for the move in the direction of Sharpsburg, but for some unaccountable reason things moved slowly and there was a long delay in getting the troops in motion.

"Col. Key again returned with instructions to Gen. Burnside to push forward his troops rapidly and with vigor, to secure the heights, as every moment gained was of the utmost importance to our success.

"I remained with Gen. Burnside until his troops were well, and seemingly successfully, under way up the heights—they having gallantly driven the enemy from the field for fully one-half the distance in the direction of Sharpsburg.

"Seeing this, and everything apparently going well, I returned to headquarters, where I found Gen. Fitz-John Porter, you being away temporarily on a visit to the right of the battle-field. It was at this time past four o'clock in the afternoon.

"It was not long after this that the check and repulse of Gen. Burnside's advance was witnessed.

"Often since that time I have thought what a serious misfortune was the death of the noble and energetic Reno. Had not that chivalric soldier fallen at South Mountain, Antietam certainly would have been in its results a very different affair. It would have been one of the most, if not the most, complete and important battle of the war.

"I am, general, very truly yours,

"D. B. SACKETT,

"INSPECTOR-GEN., U. S. A.

"To GEN. GEO. B. McCLELLAN."

"NEW YORK CITY, MARCH 9, 1876.

"MY DEAR GENERAL: I will state, in respect to a conversation had in my presence between Gen. Burnside and yourself, that late in the evening of the day of the battle of Antietam I was with you in your tent when Gen. Burnside entered. The position occupied, and the condition of his command, became at once the topic of conversation with you two.

"As I understood the matter, Gen. Burnside desired to withdraw his troops to the left bank of the stream, giving as a reason for the move the dispirited condition of his men; stating further that if he remained in his present position and an attack was made by the enemy, he very much feared the result.

"You replied: 'General, your troops must remain where they are and must hold their ground.' Gen. Burnside then said: 'If I am to hold this position at all hazards I must be largely reinforced'—and, if not much mistaken, he mentioned the number of men necessary for the purpose at 5,000.

"You then replied (with emphasis): 'General, I expect you to hold your own, and with the force now under your command.'

"At this point other general officers arrived, and I left the tent and heard nothing more of the conversation.

"Afterward, in looking over Gen. Burnside's testimony before the Committee on the Conduct of the War, I was a good deal surprised to read:

"'I went to Gen. McClellan's tent, and in course of conversation I expressed the same opinion (that the attack might be renewed the next morning at five o'clock), and told him that if I could have 5,000 fresh troops to pass in advance of my line I would be willing to commence the attack on the next morning.'

"This statement brought back to my mind vividly that evening's conversation after Antietam. The conversation between Gen. Burnside and yourself, as I heard it, and Gen. Burnside's testimony before the committee, differ widely.

"I may be mistaken, but it has always appeared to me that the conversation to which I was a witness, and the statement made before the War Committee, must have referred to one and the same matter—the fighting condition of Gen. Burnside's command on the night after the battle of Antietam.

"I am, general, very truly yours,

"D. B. SACKETT,
"INSPECTOR-GEN. U. S. A.

"To GEN. GEO. B. McCLELLAN."

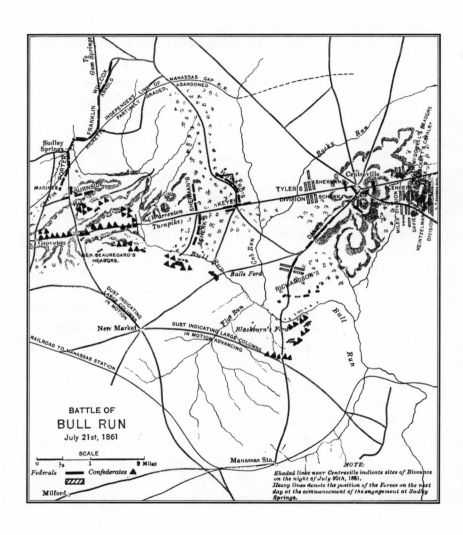

BATTLE OF
BULL RUN
July 21st, 1861

SCALE

0   ½   1   2 Miles

Federals ▬▬▬   *Confederates* ▲

NOTE:
Shaded lines near Centreville indicate sites of Bivouacs
on the night of July 20th, 1861.
Heavy lines denote the position of the Forces on the next
day at the commencement of the engagement at Sudley
Springs.

Probably the best corps commander in the Confederate Army after Stonewall Jackson, James Longstreet was a shrewd judge of battle. While other corps or division commanders were content to obey orders, Longstreet never fought on his part of the line without keeping a larger picture of the battle in his head. With this talent, he delivered the killing stroke without waiting for orders, boldly seizing any opportunity the fortunes of war would throw him. Thankfully for Lee (and later Bragg), Longstreet did the right thing before receiving orders to do it—an important consideration since orders moved no faster than galloping horses in the slow-moving battles of the nineteenth century.

However, there were also times when Longstreet saw the chances for victory slip away because orders couldn't reach the right sub-commanders in time to exploit such fleeting opportunities. Concise in recalling his frustrations and triumphs, Longstreet wastes little ink protecting his reputation, instead honestly pointing out the shortcomings and strengths of both sides in his memoir.

Excerpts from *From Manassas to Appomattox*

BY JAMES LONGSTREET

Chapter IX.

ROBERT E. LEE IN COMMAND.

The Great General's Assignment not at first assuring to the Army—Able as an Engineer but limited as to Field Service—He makes the Acquaintance of his Lieutenants—Calls a Council—Gains Confidence by saying

Nothing—"A Little Humor now and then"—Lee plans a Simultaneous Attack on McClellan's Front and Rear—J. E. B. Stuart's Daring Reconnoissance around the Union Army.

The assignment of General Lee to command the army of Northern Virginia was far from reconciling the troops to the loss of our beloved chief, Joseph E. Johnston, with whom the army had been closely connected since its earliest active life. All hearts had learned to lean upon him with confidence, and to love him dearly. General Lee's experience in active field work was limited to his West Virginia campaign against General Rosecrans, which was not successful. His services on our coast defences were known as able, and those who knew him in Mexico as one of the principal engineers of General Scott's column, marching for the capture of the capital of that great republic, knew that as military engineer he was especially distinguished; but officers of the line are not apt to look to the staff in choosing leaders of soldiers, either in tactics or strategy. There were, therefore, some misgivings as to the power and skill for field service of the new commander. The change was accepted, however, as a happy relief from the existing halting policy of the late temporary commander.

During the first week of his authority he called his general officers to meet him on the Nine Miles road for a general talk. This novelty was not reassuring, as experience had told that secrecy in war was an essential element of success; that public discussion and secrecy were incompatible. As he disclosed nothing, those of serious thought became hopeful, and followed his wise example. The brigadiers talked freely, but only of the parts of the line occupied by their brigades; and the meeting finally took a playful turn. General Toombs's brigade was before some formidable works under construction by General Franklin. He suggested an elevation a few hundred yards in his rear, as a better defensive line and more comfortable position for his men; a very good military point. This seemed strange in General Toombs, however, as he was known to have frequent talks with his troops, complaining of West Point men holding the army from battle, digging and throwing up lines of sand instead of showing lines of battle, where all could have fair fight.

Referring to his suggestion to retire and construct a new line, General D. H. Hill, who behind the austere presence of a major-general had a fund of dry humor, said,—

"I think it may be better to advance General Toombs's brigade, till he can bring Franklin's working parties under the fire of his short-range arms, so that the working parties may be broken up."

General Whiting, who was apprehensive of bayous and parallels, complained of sickness in his command, and asked a change of position from the unfair Fair Oaks. Though of brilliant, highly cultivated mind, the dark side of the picture was always more imposing with him. Several of the major-generals failed to join us till the conference was about to disperse. All rode back to their camps little wiser than when they went, except that they found General Lee's object was to learn of the temper of those of his officers whom he did not know, and of the condition and tone among their troops. He ordered his engineers over the line occupied by the army, to rearrange its defensive construction, and to put working parties on all points needing reinforcing. Whiting's division was broken up. Three of the brigades were ordered to A. P. Hill's division. He was permitted to choose two brigades that were to constitute his own command. Besides his own, he selected Hood's brigade. With these two he was ordered by way of Lynchburg to report to General Jackson, in the Valley district.

General Lee was seen almost daily riding over his lines, making suggestions to working parties and encouraging their efforts to put sand-banks between their persons and the enemy's batteries, and they were beginning to appreciate the value of such adjuncts. Above all, they soon began to look eagerly for his daily rides, his pleasing yet commanding presence, and the energy he displayed in speeding their labors.

The day after the conference on the Nine Miles road, availing myself of General Lee's invitation to free interchange of ideas, I rode over to his headquarters, and renewed my suggestion of a move against General McClellan's right flank, which rested behind Beaver Dam Creek. The strength of the position was explained, and mention made that, in consequence of that strong ground, a move somewhat similar, ordered by General Johnston for the 28th of May, was abandoned. At the same time he was assured that a march of an hour could turn the head of the creek and dislodge the force behind it. He received me pleasantly and gave a patient hearing to the suggestions, without indicating approval or disapproval. A few days after he wrote General Jackson:*

"HEAD-QUARTERS, NEAR RICHMOND, VA.,
"JUNE 11, 1862.

"Brigadier-General Thomas J. Jackson,
"*Commanding Valley District:*
"GENERAL,—Your recent successes have been the cause of the liveliest joy in this army as well as in the country. The admiration excited by your skill and boldness has been constantly mingled with solicitude for your situation. The practicability of reinforcing you has been the subject of earnest consideration. It has been determined to do so at the expense of weakening this army. Brigadier-General Lawton, with six regiments from Georgia, is on the way to you, and Brigadier-General Whiting, with eight veteran regiments, leaves here to-day. The object is to enable you to crush the forces opposed to you. Leave your enfeebled troops to watch the country and guard the passes covered by your cavalry and artillery, and with your main body, including Ewell's division and Lawton's and Whiting's commands, move rapidly to Ashland by rail or otherwise, as you may find most advantageous, and sweep down between the Chickahominy and Pamunkey, cutting up the enemy's communications, etc., while this army attacks General McClellan in front. He will thus, I think, be forced to come out of his intrenchments, where he is strongly posted on the Chickahominy, and apparently preparing to move by gradual approaches on Richmond. Keep me advised of your movements, and, if practicable, precede your troops, that we may confer and arrange for simultaneous attack.
"I am, with great respect, your obedient servant,

"R. E. LEE, *GENERAL.*"

The brigades under Generals Lawton and Whiting were transported as above ordered.

As indicated in his letter to General Jackson, General Lee's plan was a

---

*Rebellion Record, vol. xii. part iii. p. 910.

simultaneous attack on General McClellan's army front and rear. Following his instructions for General Jackson, on the same day he ordered his cavalry, under General Stuart, upon a forced reconnoissance around General McClellan's army to learn if the ground behind his army was open.

These plans and the promptness with which they were conceived and put in operation ought to be a sufficient refutation of the silly report that the Confederacy had any idea of withdrawing from their capital,—a report which, notwithstanding its unreasonable nature, was given a degree of credence in some quarters.*

Upon nearing Richmond, after leaving Yorktown, General Johnston's first thought had been to stand on the table-lands between the Pamunkey and the Chickahominy Rivers, on the flank of McClellan's march for Richmond, and force him into battle. He selected ground with that view and posted his army, where it remained some eight days, giving general and engineer officers opportunity to ride over and learn the topographical features of the surroundings. A prominent point was Beaver Dam Creek, which was so noted by the officers. When Johnston proposed to recross the Chickahominy and make battle on the 28th of May, in anticipation of McDowell's approach, the strong ground at Beaver Dam Creek again came under discussion and was common talk between the generals, so that the position and its approaches became a familiar subject. Then Stuart's famous ride had correlative relation to the same, and drew us to careful study of the grounds.

For the execution of his orders General Stuart took twelve hundred cavalry and a section of Stuart's horse artillery. The command was composed of parts

---

*Of interest in this connection is a letter to the author from General D. H. Hill:

"FAYETTEVILLE, ARK., February 4, 1879.

"General James Longstreet:

"MY DEAR GENERAL,—I never heard of the proposed abandonment of Richmond at the time General Lee took command. I had charge of one of the four divisions with which the retreat from Yorktown was effected, and was called several times into General Lee's most important councils. I never heard any officer suggest such a course in these councils or in private conversations.

"I feel sure that General Johnston always intended to fight the invading force, and so far as I know no officer of rank entertained any other view.

"I remember very well that some days before the council on the Nine Miles road (when yourself, A. P. Hill, and myself were present) that you suggested the plan of attacking McClellan's right flank, and that I expressed my preference for an attack on the other flank. This shows that there was no thought of retreat.

"Very truly yours,
"D. H. Hill."

of the First, Fourth, and Ninth Virginia Cavalry. The Fourth, having no field officer on duty with it, was distributed for the expedition between the First, Colonel Fitzhugh Lee, and the Ninth, Colonel W. H. F. Lee commanding; also two squadrons of the Jeff Davis Legion, Lieutenant-Colonel W. T. Martin commanding. The section of artillery was under First Lieutenant James Breathed.

On the night of the 12th of June he gathered his squadrons beyond the Chickahominy, and the next day marched by the road west of the Richmond, Fredericksburg, and Potomac Railroad towards Louisa Court-House, to produce the impression, should the march be discovered, that he was going to join General Jackson. After a march of fifteen miles, he bivouacked in the pine forests of Hanover, near the South Anna Bridge, without light or sound of bugle, and, throwing aside the cares of the day and thoughts of the morrow, sunk to repose such as the soldier knows how to enjoy. An hour before daylight he was up in readiness to move as soon as the first light of morning revealed the line of march. Up to that moment no one of the expedition, except the commander, knew the direction or the purpose of the march. He called his principal officers about him and told of the object of the ride, and impressed the necessity for secrecy, prompt and intelligent attention to orders. At the mute signal the twelve hundred men swung into their saddles and took the road leading to the right and rear of McClellan's army. At Hanover Court-House a small force of the enemy's cavalry was discovered, but they retired towards their camp, out of the line of Stuart's ride. At Hawes's Shop a picket was driven off and several vedettes captured. They proved to be of the Fifth United States Cavalry, General Lee's old regiment. Between Hawes's Shop and Old Church the advance-guard, well to the front, reported the presence of the enemy, apparently in some force. The column pressed forward, expecting a fierce encounter of Southern volunteers with United States regulars, but the latter was a single troop and retreated beyond Totopotomy Creek to Old Church, where there was a camp of four companies of the Fifth Cavalry under Captain Royal, which made a brave stand. Captain Latane led the first squadron, and Captain Royal received the first shock, and furiously the combat went on, both leaders falling, Latane dead and Royal severely wounded. The enemy fled and scattered through the woods. A number of prisoners were taken, including several officers, and there were captured horses, arms, equipments, and four guidons. In the enemy's camp, near Old Church, several officers and privates were captured, a number of horses and arms taken, and the stores and tents were burned. Here it became a question whether to attempt to return by way of Hanover Court-House or to press on and try to make a circuit around the entire army, and take the chance of fording or swimming the Chickahominy beyond the enemy's extreme left. Stuart decided that the bolder ride "was the quintessence of prudence."*

Arriving opposite Garlick's, on the Pamunkey,—one of the enemy's supply stations,—a squadron was sent out and burned two transports with army stores and a number of wagons. Near Tunstall's Station a wagon-train was discovered guarded by five companies of cavalry, which manifested a determination to stand and defend it, but they abandoned it and rode away, leaving the train in possession of Stuart, who burned it, and, night coming on, the country was brilliantly lighted up by its flames. After resting a few hours at Talleysville, the ride was resumed, and the party reached the Chickahominy at Forges Bridge at daylight. The stream was not fordable, but, by exercise of great energy and industry, a rude foot-bridge was laid. That part of the command near it dismounted and walked over, swimming their horses. In a few hours the bridge was made strong and the artillery and other mount were passed safely over to the Richmond side, and resumed the march for their old camp-grounds.

This was one of the most graceful and daring ride known to military history, and revealed valuable fact concerning the situation of the Union forces, their operations, communications, etc. When congratulated upon his success, General Stuart replied, with a lurking twinkle in his eye, that he had left a general behind him. Asked as to the identity of the unfortunate person, he said, with his joyful laugh, "General Consternation."

Chapter XIV.

SECOND BATTLE OF MANASSAS (BULL RUN).

Battle opened by the Federals on Jackson's Right, followed by Kearny—Longstreet's Reconnoissance—Stuart, the Cavalry Leader, sleeps on the Field of Battle—Pope thought at the Close of the 29th that the Confederates were retreating—Second Day—Fitz-John Porter struck in Flank—Longstreet takes a Hand in the Fight late in the Day—Lee under Fire—The Federal Retreat to Centreville—That Point turned—Pope again dislodged—"Stonewall" Jackson's Appearance and Peculiarities—Killing of "Fighting Phil" Kearny—Losses—Review of the Campaign.

---

*Official account, Rebellion Record, vol. xi. part i. p. 1036.

General Pope at daylight sent orders to General Sigel's corps, with Reynolds's division, to attack as soon as it was light enough to see, and bring the enemy to a stand if possible. At the same time orders were sent to Heintzelman and Reno for their corps to hurry along the turnpike and join on the right of Sigel. The batteries opened in an irregular combat on the left, centre, and right a little after eight o'clock, and drew from Jackson a monotonous but resolute response. And thus early upon the 29th of August was begun the second battle upon this classic and fateful field.

I marched at daylight and filed to the left at Gainesville at nine o'clock. As the head of the column approached Gainesville the fire of artillery became more lively, and its volume swelled to proportions indicating near approach to battle. The men involuntarily quickened step, filed down the turnpike, and in twenty minutes came upon the battle as it began to press upon Jackson's right, their left battery partially turning his right. His battle, as before stated, stood upon its original line of the unfinished railroad.

As my columns approached, the batteries of the leading brigades were thrown forward to ground of superior sweep. This display and the deploy of the infantry were so threatening to the enemy's left batteries that he thought prudent to change the front of that end of his line more to his left and rear. Hood's two brigades were deployed across the turnpike at right angles, supported by the brigade under Evans. A battery advanced on their right to good position and put in some clever work, which caused the enemy to rectify all that end of his line. Kemper deployed two of his brigades, supported by the third, on the right of Hood. The three brigades under Wilcox were posted in rear of Hood and Evans, and in close supporting distance. On Hood's left and near Jackson's right was open field, of commanding position. This was selected by Colonel Walton, of the Washington Artillery, for his battalion, and he brought it bounding into position as soon as called. The division under D. R. Jones was deployed in the order of the others, but was broken off to the rear, across the Manassas Gap Railroad, to guard against forces of the enemy reported in the direction of Manassas Junction and Bristoe. As formed, my line made an obtuse angle forward of Jackson's, till it approached Manassas Gap Railroad, where D. R. Jones's division was broken in echelon to the rear. At twelve o'clock we were formed for battle.

About eleven o'clock, Hooker's division filed to the right from the turnpike, to reinforce the Federal right under Kearny, who, with Sigel's corps and Reynolds's division, were engaged in a desultory affair against Jackson's left, chiefly of artillery.

R. H. Anderson's division marched at daylight along the Warrenton turn-pike for Gainesville.

When I reported my troops in order for battle, General Lee was inclined to engage as soon as practicable, but did not order. All troops that he could hope to have were up except R. H. Anderson's division, which was near enough to come in when the battle was in progress. I asked him to be allowed to make a reconnoissance of the enemy's ground, and along his left. After an hour's work, mounted and afoot, under the August sun, I returned and reported adversely as to attack, especially in view of the easy approach of the troops reported at Manassas against my right in the event of severe contention. We knew of Ricketts's division in that quarter, and of a considerable force at Manassas Junction, which indicated one corps.

At two o'clock Kearny made an earnest opening against Jackson's left, but no information of battle reached us on the right. He made severe battle by his division, and with some success, but was checked by Jackson's movements to meet him. General Stevens supported his battle, but his numbers were not equal to the occasion. General Sigel joined in the affair, and part of General Hooker's division, making a gallant fight, but little progress. General Grover's brigade made a gallant charge, but a single brigade was a trifle, and it met with only partial success, and was obliged to retire with heavy loss of killed and wounded,—four hundred and eighty-four.

At one time the enemy broke through the line, cutting off the extreme left brigade, and gained position on the railroad cut; but Jackson and A. P. Hill reinforced against that attack, and were in time to push it back and recover the lost ground.

Their attacks were too much in detail to hold even the ground gained, but they held firmly to the battle and their line until after night, when they withdrew to await orders for the next day.

Though this fight opened at two o'clock, and was fiercely contested till near night, no account of it came from headquarters to my command, nor did General Jackson think to send word of it. General Lee, not entirely satisfied with the report of my reconnoissance, was thinking of sending some of the engineers for more critical survey of his right front, when his chief of cavalry sent to inform him of the approach of a formidable column of infantry and artillery threatening his right. Wilcox's division was changed to supporting position of our right, under Jones, and I rode to look at this new force, its strength, and the ground of its approach. It was the column of McDowell's and Porter's corps, marching under the joint order. Porter's corps in advance deployed Morell's division, and ordered Butterfield's brigade, preceded by a regiment of skirmishers, to advance on their right, Sykes's division to support Morell. As this was in process of execution, McDowell, whose corps was in rear, rode to the front and objected to the plan and attack so far from the main force.

A few shots were exchanged, when all became quiet again. We saw nothing of McDowell's corps, and our cavalry had not been able to get far enough towards their rear to know of its presence or force. He afterwards drew off from Porter's column and marched by the Sudley Springs road to join the main force on the turnpike. I rode back and reported to General Lee that the column was hardly strong enough to mean aggressive work from that quarter, and at the same time reported a dust along the New Market road which seemed to indicate movement of other troops from Manassas.

General Stuart rode up, making similar report, and asked for orders. As our chief was not ready with his orders at the moment, Stuart was asked to wait. The latter threw himself on the grass, put a large stone under his head, asked the general to have him called when his orders were ready for him, and went sound asleep.

Our chief now returned to his first plan of attack by his right down the turnpike. Though more than anxious to meet his wishes, and anticipating his orders, I suggested, as the day was far spent, that a reconnoissance in force be made at nightfall to the immediate front of the enemy, and if an opening was found for an entering wedge, that we have all things in readiness at daylight for a good day's work. After a moment's hesitation he assented, and orders were given for the advance at early twilight.

This gave General Stuart half an hour *siesta*. When called, he sprang to his feet, received his orders, swung into his saddle, and at a lope, singing, "If you want to have a good time, jine the cavalry," his banjo-player, Sweeny, on the jump behind him, rode to his troopers.

Wilcox was recalled and ordered to march in support of Hood and Evans when they advanced on the reconnoissance. It so happened that our advance had been anticipated by an order to move from the enemy's side against us. They attacked along the turnpike by King's division about sunset.

To the Confederates, who had been searching for an opportunity during the greater part of the day, and were about to march through the approaching darkness to find it, this was an agreeable surprise. Relieved of that irksome toil, and ready for work, they jumped at the presence, to welcome in countercharge the enemy's coming. A fierce struggle of thirty minutes gave them advantage which they followed through the dark to the base of the high ground held by bayonets and batteries innumerable as compared with their limited ranks. Their task accomplished, they were halted at nine o'clock to await the morrow. One cannon, a number of flags, and a few prisoners were taken.

Generals Wilcox and Hood were ordered to carefully examine the position of the enemy and report of the feasibility of attack at daylight. They came to corps headquarters a little before twelve o'clock, and made separate reports, both against attack, with minute items of their conclusions. Hood was ordered to have the carriage of the captured gun cut up and left, and both were ordered to withdraw their commands to their first positions.

Meanwhile, General Pope had sent orders to General Porter, dated 4:30 P.M., to attack upon my right flank, but the order was not received until it was too late for battle, and the force was not strong enough, and a fight at that hour might have been more unfortunate than the fights by detail on their right. If it had been sent to General McDowell before he left, the two corps, if he could have been induced to go in, might have given serious trouble. The field on their left was favorable for tactics, but on Porter's front it was rough, and R. H. Anderson's division was in striking distance of their left, if that effort had been made.

Anderson marched in the dark as far as Hood's front before reporting for position, and was ordered back to Gainesville.

The 4.30 order was issued under the impression that my troops, or the greater part of them, were still at Thoroughfare Gap, and General Pope said, in his official report,—

> "I believe, in fact I am positive, that at five o'clock in the afternoon of the 29th, General Porter had in his front no considerable body of the enemy. I believed then, as I am very sure now, that it was easily practicable for him to have turned the right flank of Jackson and to have fallen upon his rear; that if he had done so, we should have gained a decisive victory over the army under Jackson before he could have been joined by any of the forces of Longstreet."*

---

*Rebellion Record, vol. xii. part ii. p. 40. General Pope.

After night, Porter's column marched by its right to follow the route of McDowell.

The morning of the 30th broke fair, and for the Federal commander bright with anticipations for the day. He wired the Washington authorities of success, that "the enemy was retreating to the mountains," and told of his preparations for pursuit. It seems that he took my reconnoissance for a fight, and my withdrawal for retreat, also interpreting reports from the right as very favorable. He reported,—

"General Hooker estimated the loss of the enemy as at least two to one, and General Kearny as at least three to one."

He construed the operations of the night of the 29th and the reports of the morning of the 30th as indications of retreat of the Confederates. Prisoners captured during the night, paroled and returning to him, so reported on the morning of the 30th, and his general officers had impressions of the Confederate left that confirmed the other accounts, and convinced him that we were in retreat.

The forces threatening our right the day before having marched around towards the turnpike, D. R. Jones's division was advanced to position near Kemper's right. Colonel S. D. Lee's artillery battalion was advanced to relieve the Washington Artillery, making our line complete, in battle front.

About one o'clock in the afternoon, General Pope ordered attack against Jackson's front by the corps under General Porter, supported by King's division, Heintzelman and Reno to move forward and attack Jackson's left, to turn it and strike down against the flank, Ricketts's division in support of it; but Ricketts was recalled and put near the turnpike, to support that part of Porter's field.

During the early part of this severe battle not a gun was fired by my troops, except occasional shots from S. D. Lee's batteries of reserve artillery, and less frequent shots from one or two of my other batteries.

Developments appearing unfavorable for a general engagement, General Lee had settled upon a move by Sudley Springs, to cross Bull Run during the night and try to again reach Pope's rear, this time with his army.

About three P.M. I rode to the front to prepare to make a diversion a little before dark, to cover the plan proposed for our night march. As I rode, batteries resting on the sides of the turnpike thought that battle was at hand, and called their officers and men to stand to their guns and horses. Passing by and beyond my lines, a message came from General Jackson reporting his lines heavily pressed, and asking to be reinforced. Riding forward a few rods to an open, which gave a view of Jackson's field, I came in sight of Porter's battle, pil-ing up against Jackson's right, centre, and left. At the same time an order came from General Lee for a division to be sent General Jackson. Porter's masses were in almost direct line from the point at which I stood, and in enfilade fire. It was evident that they could not stand fifteen minutes under the fire of batteries planted at that point, while a division marching back and across the field to aid Jackson could not reach him in an hour, more time probably than he could stand under the heavy weights then bearing down upon him. Boldness was prudence! Prompt work by the wing and batteries could relieve the battle. Reinforcements might not be in time, so I called for my nearest batteries. Ready, anticipating call, they sprang to their places and drove at speed, saw the opportunity before it could be pointed out, and went into action. The first fire was by Chapman's battery, followed in rolling practice by Boyce's and Reilly's. Almost immediately the wounded began to drop off from Porter's ranks; the number seemed to increase with every shot; the masses began to waver, swing-ing back and forth, showing signs of discomfiture along the left and left centre.

In ten or fifteen minutes it crumbled into disorder and turned towards the rear. Although the batteries seemed to hasten the movements of the discomfited, the fire was less effective upon broken ranks, which gave them courage, and they made brave efforts to rally; but as the new lines formed they had to breast against Jackson's standing line, and make a new and favorable target for the batteries, which again drove them to disruption and retreat. Not satisfied, they made a third effort to rally and fight the battle through, but by that time they had fallen back far enough to open the field to the fire of S. D. Lee's artillery battalion. As the line began to take shape, this fearful fire was added to that under which they had tried so ineffectually to fight. The combination tore the line to pieces, and as it broke the third time the charge was ordered. The heavy fumes of gunpowder hanging about our ranks, as stimulating as sparkling wine, charged the atmo-sphere with the light and splendor of battle. Time was culminating under a flow-ing tide. The noble horses took the spirit of the riders sitting lightly in their saddles. As orders were given, the staff, their limbs already closed to the horses' flanks, pressed their spurs, but the electric current overleaped their speedy strides, and twenty-five thousand braves moved in line as by a single impulse. My old horse, appreciating the importance of corps headquarters, envious of the spread of his comrades as they measured the green, yet anxious to maintain his *rôle*, moved up and down his limited space in lofty bounds, resolved to cover in the air the space allotted his more fortunate comrades on the plain.

Leaving the broken ranks for Jackson, our fight was made against the lines near my front. As the plain along Hood's front was more favorable for the tread of soldiers, he was ordered, as the column of direction, to push for the plateau at the Henry House, in order to cut off retreat at the crossings by Young's Branch. Wilcox was called to support and cover Hood's left, but he lost sight of two of his brigades,—Featherston's and Pryor's,—and only gave the aid of his single brigade. Kemper and Jones were pushed on with Hood's right, Evans in Hood's direct support. The batteries were advanced as rapidly as fields were opened to them, Stribling's, J. B. Richardson's, Eshleman's, and Rogers's having fairest field for progress.

At the first sound of the charge, General Lee sent to revoke his call in favor of Jackson, asked me to push the battle, ordered R. H. Anderson's division up, and rode himself to join me.

In the fulness of the battle, General Toombs rode up on his iron-gray under sweat and spur, his hat off, and asked for his command. He was told that a courier was about to start with an order for the division commander, and would guide him. He asked to be the bearer of the order, received it, and with the guide rode to find his post in the battle. The meeting of the brigade and its commander was more than joyful.

Jackson failed to pull up even on the left, which gave opportunity for some of the enemy's batteries to turn their fire across the right wing in enfilade, as we advanced, and the enemy strongly reinforced against us from troops drawn from Jackson's front, but we being on the jump, the fire of the batteries was not effective. It was severely threatening upon General Lee, however, who would ride under it, notwithstanding appeals to avoid it, until I thought to ride through a ravine, and thus throw a traverse between him and the fire. He sent orders to Jackson to advance and drive off or capture the batteries standing in his front and firing across our line, but it was not in season to relieve us. Hood's aggressive force was well spent when his troops approached the Chinn House, but R. H. Anderson was up and put in to reinforce and relieve his battle.

General Pope drew Ricketts's division from his right to brace his left, then Reno's command to aid in checking our march, but its progress, furiously resisted, was steady, though much delayed. Piatt's brigade was also put against us. This made time for Porter to gather his forces. His regulars of Sykes's division, particularly, made desperate resistance, that could only be overcome by our overreaching lines threatening their rear.

When the last guns were fired the thickening twilight concealed the lines of friend and foe, so that the danger of friend firing against friend became imminent. The hill of the Henry House was reached in good time, but darkness coming on earlier because of thickening clouds hovering over us, and a gentle fall of rain closely following, the plateau was shut off from view, and its ascent only found by groping through the darkening rainfall. As long as the enemy held the plateau, he covered the line of retreat by the turnpike and the bridge at Young's Branch. As he retired, heavy darkness gave safe-conduct to such of his columns as could find their way through the weird mists.

Captain William H. Powell, of the Fourth Regular Infantry, wrote of his experience,—

"As we filed from the battle-field into the turnpike leading over the stone bridge, we came upon a group of mounted officers, one of whom wore a peculiar style of hat which had been seen on the field that day, and which had been the occasion of a great deal of comment in the ranks. As we passed these officers, the one with the peculiar hat called out in a loud voice,—

" 'What troops are those?'

" 'The regulars,' answered somebody.

" 'Second Division, Fifth Corps,' replied another.

" 'God bless them! they saved the army,' added the officer.

"Subsequently we learned that he was General Irvin McDowell."

"As we neared the bridge we came upon confusion. Men singly and in detachments were mingled with sutlers' wagons, artillery caissons, supply wagons, and ambulances, each striving to get ahead of the other. Vehicles rushed through organized bodies and broke the columns into fragments. Little detachments gathered by the road-side after crossing the bridge, crying out to members of their regiments as a guide to scattered comrades. And what a night it was! Dark, gloomy, and beclouded by the volumes of smoke which had risen from the battle-field.*

At six o'clock, General Pope received report of the Sixth Corps, that had marched from Alexandria under General Franklin to the vicinity of Centreville, and ordered the several commands to concentrate about that hamlet during the

---

*Battles and Leaders of the Civil War.

night. The Second Corps from the Army of the Potomac under General Sumner also joined him at Centreville.

But for the dropping off of two of Wilcox's brigades from close connection with the right wing, and the deflection of Drayton's brigade, which was taken off by some unauthorized and unknown person from my right to the support of cavalry, it is possible that my working column could have gained the plateau of the Henry House before it was dark. Or if Jackson had been fresh enough to pull up even with us, he could have retained the commands under Reno and Sykes's regulars in his front, which could have given us safe sweep to the plateau, an hour before sundown, and in sight of great possibilities.

By morning of the 31st everything off the turnpike was nasty and soggy. Stuart's cavalry, followed by Pryor's brigade, were ordered across the Run at Stone Bridge as a diversion, while we were trying another move to reach the enemy's rear. The Confederates had worked all of the winter before, fortifying this new position, just taken by Pope at Centreville. Direct pursuit by the turnpike against these fortifications would therefore be fruitless.

General Jackson was called to head-quarters early in the morning. Upon receiving General Lee's orders to cross Bull Run at Sudley's and march by Little River turnpike to intercept the enemy's march, he said, "Good!" and away he went, without another word, or even a smile.

Though the suggestion of a smile always hung about his features, it was commonly said that it never fully developed, with a single exception, during his military career, though some claim there were other occasions on which it ripened, and those very near him say that he always smiled at the mention of the names of the Federal leaders whom he was accustomed to encounter over in the Valley behind the Blue Ridge. Standing, he was a graceful figure, five feet ten inches in height, with brown wavy hair, full beard, and regular features. At first glance his gentle expression repelled the idea of his severe piety, the full beard concealing the lower features, which had they been revealed would have marked the character of the man who claimed "his first duty to God, and his next to Jackson and General Lee." Mounted, his figure was not so imposing as that of the bold dragoon, Charley May, on Black Tom. He had a habit of raising his right hand, riding or sitting, which some of his followers were wont to construe into invocation for Divine aid, but they do not claim to know whether the prayers were for the slain, or for the success of other fields. The fact is, he received a shot in that hand at the First Bull Run, which left the hand under partial paralysis and the circulation through it imperfect. To relieve the pressure and assist the circulation he sometimes raised his arm.

I was ordered to look after the dead and those whose misfortune it was to be wounded, till Jackson could have time to stretch out on his new march, then to follow him, leaving the work to details and to General D. H. Hill's division, just coming in from Richmond.

After giving orders for the day, General Lee rode out towards Centreville for personal observation, halted, and dismounted at a point which seemed safe from danger or observation. Suddenly alarm was given of "The enemy's cavalry!" The group dispersed in hot haste to have the heels of their animals under them. The rush and confusion frightened the general's horse, so that he pulled him violently to the ground, severely spraining his right wrist, besides breaking some of the bones of the hand.

On reaching his head-quarters, Jackson ordered the assembly sounded, mounted his horse, and marched for the Sudley Springs crossing. He cleared the way in time for my column to reach that point at dark, the head of his own column tapping Little River turnpike. The march was over a single-track country road, bad enough on the south side of the river, much worn through a post-oak forest over quicksand subsoil on the north side. If Jackson had been followed by an enemy whose march he wished to baffle, his gun-carriages could not have made deeper cuts through the mud and quicksand.

Stuart was ordered over to the Little River turnpike, and advanced to the vicinity of Ox Hill and Fairfax Court-House. He made some interesting captures and reports of movements by the enemy. He slept near their lines, north of the turnpike, east of Chantilly.

The Little River and Warrenton turnpikes converge and join as they near Fairfax Court-House. At vulnerable points on the latter, General Pope posted parts of his command to cover his rearward march. At Ox Hill (Chantilly) were stationed. Heintzelman's and Reno's corps, the divisions of Hooker, Kearny, Stevens, and Reno.

Early on the 1st of September the Confederates resumed their march. Jackson reached Ox Hill late in the afternoon, and deployed by inversion,—A. P. Hill's division on his right, Ewell's under Lawton next, his own under Stuart on his left, on the right of the road. On the left of the road were Stuart's cavalry and the artillery. Two of Hill's brigades were thrown out to find the enemy, and were soon met by his advance in search of Jackson, which made a furious attack, driving back the Confederate brigades in some disorder. Stevens, appreciating the crisis as momentous, thought it necessary to follow the opportunity by aggressive battle, in order to hold Jackson away from the Warrenton turnpike. Kearny, always ready to second any courageous move, joined in the daring battle. At the critical moment the rain and thunder-storm burst with great violence upon the combatants, the high wind beating the storm in the faces of the Confederates. So firm was the unexpected battle that part of Jackson's line yielded to the onslaught. At one moment his artillery seemed in danger. Stevens was killed when the storm of battle, as well as that of the elements, began to quiet down. Stuart's cavalry drew near Jackson's left during the progress of the battle. As I rode up and met General Jackson, I remarked upon the number of his men going to the rear:

"General, your men don't appear to work well to-day."

"No," he replied, "but I hope it will prove a victory in the morning."

His troops were relieved as mine came up, to give them a respite till morning. While my reliefs were going around, General Philip Kearny rode to the line in search of his division. Finding himself in the presence of Confederates, he wheeled his horse and put spurs, preferring the danger of musket-balls to humiliating surrender. Several challenges called, but not heeded, were followed by the ring of half a dozen muskets, when he fell mortally hurt, and so perished one of the most gallant and dashing of the Union generals.

"SEPTEMBER 2, 1862.

"Major-General John Pope,
"United States Army:
"Sir,—The body of General Philip Kearny was brought from the field last night, and he was reported dead. I send it forward under a flag of truce, thinking the possession of his remains may be a consolation to his family.
"I am, sir, respectfully, your obedient servant,

"R. E. LEE,
"GENERAL."*

The rain so concealed the fight in its last struggles that the troops escaped before we were aware that it had been abandoned.

---

*Rebellion Record.

As both Federal division commanders fell, the accounts fail to do justice to their fight. Stevens in his short career gave evidence of courage, judgment, skill, and genius not far below his illustrious antagonist.

During the fight Stuart had parties out seeking information, and early on the second had his troopers in the saddle in pursuit. The army, ready to move, awaited reports of the cavalry, which came from time to time, as they followed on the line of retreat. From Fairfax Court-House came the report that the enemy's rear had passed in rapid retreat quite out of reach, approaching the fortifications of Alexandria and Washington City. Arms were ordered stacked, and a good rest was given the troops. Stuart's cavalry pursued and engaged the retreating army.

In the afternoon the First Corps started on the march *via* Dranesville for Leesburg and the Potomac River, followed on the third by the Second.

The results to the Confederates of the several engagements about Manassas Plains were seven thousand prisoners, two thousand of the enemy's wounded, thirty pieces of artillery, many thousand small-arms picked up from the field, and many colors, besides the captures made at Manassas Junction by General Jackson.*

A fair estimate of forces engaged:

Federal army, aggregate 63,000
Confederates 53,500

Losses between Rappahannock River and Washington:

Federals, aggregate 15,000
Confederates 10,000

The figures are given in round numbers, as the safest approximate estimate, but the records now accessible give accurate details of losses in each command about the same as these.

And so it came to pass that from Cedar Run and Bull Run we had the term *All Run*. It is due to the gallant Sumner and his brave corps, however, to say that they so covered the last as to save disgraceful retreat.

A cursory review of the campaign reveals the pleasure ride of General Fitzhugh Lee by Louisa Court-House as most unseasonable. He lost the fruits

*Rebellion Record, vol. xii. part ii. p. 558. General Lee's report.

of our summer's work, and lost the Southern cause. Proud Troy was laid in ashes. His orders were to meet his commander on the afternoon of the 17th, on the plank-road near Raccoon Ford, and upon this appointment was based General Lee's order of march for the 18th. If the march had been made as appointed, General Lee would have encountered the army of General Pope upon weak ground from Robertson River to near Raccoon Ford of the Rapidan, and thus our march would have been so expedited that we could have reached Alexandria and Washington before the landing of the first detachment of the Army of the Potomac at Alexandria on the 24th. The artillery and infantry were called to amend the delinquency by severe marches and battles.

It would have been possible to make good the lost time, but the despatch lost in the Stuart escapade was handed to General Pope that morning (the 18th), and gave him notice of our plans and orders. The delay thus brought about gave time for him to quit his weaker ground and retire to strong defensive heights behind the Rappahannock River, where he held us in check five days.

Referring to the solid move proposed before opening the campaign by the upper Rapidan to strike Pope's right, it may be said that it was not so dependent upon the cavalry that was marching behind us. That used by Jackson in his battle of the 9th was enough for immediate use. Jackson could have passed the upper Rapidan on the 16th, and followed by the right wing in time to strike Pope's right on the 17th in solid phalanx, *when time was mightier than cannonballs.* After losing eight days between Orange Court-House and the Rappahannock, we found at last that we must adopt the move by our left to get around the strong ground of the Rappahannock, *and the move must now be made by detachments, not so approved of the usages of war.* I was west of the Rappahannock when the command should have been at Washington City.

The conduct of General Pope's army after his receipt of the captured despatch was good, especially his plans and orders for the 27th and 28th. The error was his failure to ride with his working columns on the 28th, to look after and conduct their operations. He left them in the hands of the officer who lost the first battle of Manassas. His orders of the 28th for General McDowell to change direction and march for Centreville were received at 3.15 P.M. Had they been promptly executed, the commands, King's division, Sigel's corps, and Reynolds's division, should have found Jackson by four o'clock. As it was, only the brigades of Gibbon and Doubleday were found passing by Jackson's position after sunset, when he advanced against them in battle. He reported it "sanguinary." With the entire division of King and that of Reynolds, with Sigel's corps, it is possible that Pope's campaign would have brought other important results. On the 29th he was still away from the active part of his field, and in consequence failed to have correct advice of the time of my arrival, and quite ignored the column under R. H. Anderson approaching on the Warrenton turnpike. On the 30th he was misled by reports of his officers and others to believe that the Confederates were in retreat, and planned his movements upon false premises.

Jackson's march to Bristoe and Manassas Junction was hazardous, or seemed so, but in view of his peculiar talent for such work (the captured despatch of General Pope giving information of his affairs), and Lee's skill, it seemed the only way open for progressive manœuvre. The strength of the move lay in the time it gave us to make issue before all of the Army of the Potomac could unite with the army under General Pope. His game of hide-and-seek about Bull Run, Centreville, and Manassas Plains was grand, but marred in completeness by the failure of General A. P. Hill to meet his orders for the afternoon of the 28th. As a leader he was fine; as a wheel-horse, he was not always just to himself. He was fond of the picturesque.

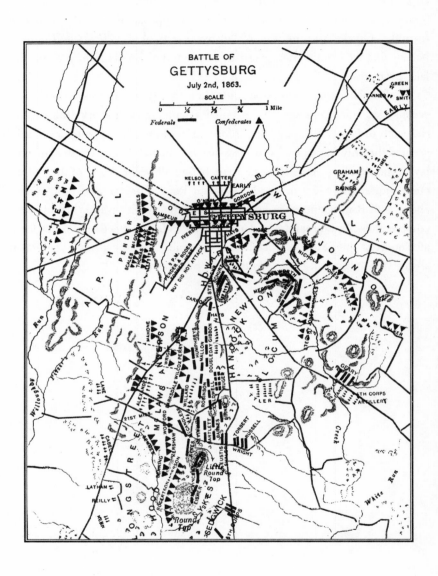

Abner Doubleday.

His name does not stand as tall as Grant, Sherman, Lee, or Jackson if we disregard his mythic connection to the birth of baseball.

There were other generals who did a better job commanding a division—and others who did worse. Doubleday was one of many average generals who performed the scut work of battle at division and brigade level. They could not be well to the rear, instead having to be close enough to the action in order to command.

Such was Doubleday's view of the third day of Gettysburg, when his regiments poured flanking fire on Pickett's Charge as it hit the Union line to his right. His description of battle shows where orders written in ink are translated into actions written in blood. It's "take that fence line" versus "hold at all costs."

Excerpt from *Chancellorsville and Gettysburg*

BY ABNER DOUBLEDAY

Chapter VI.

The battle of the third day—Johnson's division driven out.

At dawn on the 3d the enemy opened on us with artillery, but the firing had no definite purpose, and after some hours it gradually slackened.

The principal interest early in the day necessarily centred on the right, where Johnson's position not only endangered the safety of the army, but compromised our retreat. It was therefore essential to drive him out as soon as possible. To this end batteries were established during the night on all the prominent points in that vicinity. Geary had returned with his division about midnight, and was not a little astonished to find the rebels established in the works he had left. He determined to contest possession with them at daylight. In the meantime he joined Greene and formed part of his line perpendicular to our main line of battle, and part fronting the enemy.

On the other hand, Ewell, having obtained a foothold, swore he would not be driven out, and hastened to reinforce Johnson with Daniels's and O'Neill's brigades from Rodes's division.

As soon as objects could be discerned in the early gray of the morning our artillery opened fire. As Johnson, on account of the steep declivities and other obstacles, had not been able to bring any artillery with him, he could not reply. It would not do to remain quiet under this fire, and he determined to charge, in hopes of winning a better position on higher ground. His men—the old Stonewall brigade leading—rushed bravely forward, but were as gallantly met by Kane's brigade of Geary's division and a close and severe struggle ensued for four hours among the trees and rocks. Ruger's division of the Twelfth Corps came up and formed on the rebel left, taking them in flank and threatening them in reverse. Indeed, as the rest of our line were not engaged, there was plenty of support for Geary. Troops were sent him, including Shaler's brigade, which took the front, and was soon warmly engaged in re-establishing the line.

At about 11 A.M., finding the contest hopeless, and his retreat threatened by a force sent down to Rock Creek, Johnson yielded slowly and reluctantly to a charge made by Geary's division, gave up the position and withdrew to Rock Creek, where he remained until night.

Our line was once more intact. All that the enemy had gained by dogged determination and desperate bravery was lost from a lack of co-ordination, caused perhaps by the great difficulty of communicating orders over this long concave line where every route was swept by our fire.

Lee had now attacked both flanks of the Army of the Potomac without having been able to establish himself permanently on either. Notwithstanding the repulse of the previous day he was very desirous of turning the left, for once well posted there he could secure his own retreat while interposing between Meade and Washington. He rode over with Longstreet to that end of the line to see what could be done. General Wofford, who commanded a brigade of McLaws's division, writes in a recent letter to General Crawford, United States Army, as follows: "Lee and Longstreet came to my brigade Friday morning before, the artillery opened fire. I told him that the afternoon before, I nearly reached the crest. He asked if I could not go there now. I replied, "No, General, I think not." He said quickly, "Why not?" "Because," I said, "General, the enemy have had all night to intrench and reinforce. I had been pursuing a broken enemy and the situation was now very different."

Having failed at each extremity, it only remained to Lee to retreat, or attack the centre. Such high expectations had been formed in the Southern States in regard to his conquest of the North that he determined to make another effort. He still had Pickett's division, the flower of Virginia, which had not been engaged, and which was full of enthusiasm. He resolved to launch them against our centre, supported on either flank by the advance of the main portion of the army. He had hoped that Johnson's division would have been able to maintain its position on the right, so that the Union centre could be assailed in front and rear at the same time, but Johnson having been driven out, it was necessary to trust to Pickett alone, or abandon the whole enterprise and return to Virginia.

Everything was quiet up to 1 P.M., as the enemy were massing their batteries and concentrating their forces preparatory to the grand charge—the supreme effort—which was to determine the fate of the campaign, and to settle the point whether freedom or slavery was to rule the Northern States.

It seems to me there was some lack of judgment in the preparations. Heth's division, now under Pettigrew, which had been so severely handled on the first day, and which was composed in a great measure of new troops, was designated to support Pickett's left and join in the attack at close quarters. Wilcox, too, who one would think had been pretty well fought out the day before, in his desperate enterprise of attempting to crown the crest, was directed to support the right flank of the attack. Wright's brigade was formed in rear, and Pender's division on the left of Pettigrew, but there was a long distance between Wilcox and Longstreet's forces on the right.

At 1 P.M., a signal gun was fired and one hundred and fifteen guns opened against Hancock's command, consisting of the First Corps under Newton, the Second Corps under Gibbon, the Third Corps under Birney, and against the Eleventh Corps under Howard. The object of this heavy artillery fire was to break up our lines and prepare the way for Pickett's charge. The exigencies of the battle had caused the First Corps to be divided, Wadsworth's division being on the right at Culps Hill, Robinson on Gibbon's right, and my own division intervening between Caldwell on the left and Gibbon on the right. The convex shape of our line did not give us as much space as that of the enemy, but General Hunt, Chief of Artillery, promptly posted eighty guns along the crest— as many as it would hold—to answer the fire, and the batteries on both sides suffered severely in the two hours' cannonade. Not less than eleven caissons were blown up and destroyed; one quite near me. When the smoke went up from these explosions rebel yells of exultation could be heard along a line of several miles. At 3 P.M. General Hunt ordered our artillery fire to cease, in order to cool the guns, and to preserve some rounds for the contest at close quarters, which he foresaw would soon take place.

My own men did not suffer a great deal from this cannonade, as I sheltered them as much as possible under the crest of the hill, and behind rocks, trees, and stone fences.

The cessation of our fire gave the enemy the idea they had silenced our batteries, and Pickett at once moved forward, to break the left centre of the Union line and occupy the crest of the ridge.[1] The other forces on his right and left were expected to move up and enlarge the opening thus made, so that finally, the two wings of the Union Army would be permanently separated, and flung off by this entering wedge in eccentric directions.

This great column of attack, it was supposed, numbered about seventeen thousand men, but southern writers have a peculiar arithmetic by which they always cipher down their forces to nothing. Even on the left, on the preceding day, when our troops in front of Little Round Top were assailed by a line a mile and a half long, they figure it almost out of existence. The force that now advanced would have been larger still had it not been for a spirited attack by Kilpatrick against the left of Longstreet's corps, detaining some troops there which otherwise might have co-operated in the grand assault against our centre.

It necessarily took the rebels some time to form and cross the intervening space, and Hunt took advantage of the opportunity to withdraw the batteries that had been most injured, sending others in their place from the reserve artillery, which had not been engaged. He also replenished the ammunition boxes, and stood ready to receive the foe as he came forward—first with solid shot, next with shell, and lastly, when he came to close quarters, with canister.

General Meade's headquarters was in the centre of this cannonade, and as the balls were flying very thickly there, and killing the horses of his staff, he found it necessary temporarily to abandon the place. Where nothing is to be gained by exposure it is sound sense to shelter men and officers as much as possible. He rode over to Power's Hill, made his headquarters with General

---

[1]The attack was so important, so momentous, and so contrary to Longstreet's judgment, that when Pickett asked for orders to advance he gave no reply, and Pickett said proudly, "I shall go forward, sir!"

Slocum, and when the firing ceased rode back again. During his absence the charge took place. He has stated that it was his intention to throw the Fifth and Sixth Corps on the flanks of the attacking force, but no orders to this effect were issued, and it is questionable whether such an arrangement would have been a good one. It would have disgarnished the left, where Longstreet was still strong in numbers, and in forming perpendicular to our line of battle the two corps would necessarily have exposed their own outer flanks to attack. Indeed, the rebels had provided for just such a contingency, by posting Wilcox's brigade and Perry's brigade under Colonel Lang on the right, and Pender's division, now under Trimble, on the left, both in rear of the charging column under Pickett and Pettigrew. Owing to a mistake or misunderstanding, this disposition, however, did not turn out well for the enemy. It was not intended by Providence that the Northern States should pass under the iron rule of the slave power, and on this occasion every plan made by Lee was thwarted in the most unexpected manner.

The distance to be traversed by Pickett's column was about a mile and a half from the woods where they started, to the crest of the ridge they desired to attain. They suffered severely from our artillery, which opened on them with solid shot as soon as they came in sight; when half way across the plain they were vigorously shelled; double canisters were reserved for their nearer approach.

At first the direction of their march appeared to be directly toward my division. When within five hundred yards of us, however, Pickett halted and changed direction obliquely about forty-five degrees, so that the attack passed me and struck Gibbon's division on my right. Just here one of those providential circumstances occurred which favored us so much, for Wilcox and Lang, who guarded Pickett's right flank, did not follow his oblique movement, but kept on straight to the front, so that soon there was a wide interval between their troops and the main body, leaving Pickett's right fully uncovered.

The rebels came on magnificently. As fast as the shot and shell tore through their lines they closed up the gaps and pressed forward. When they reached the Emmetsburg road the canister began to make fearful chasms in their ranks. They also suffered severely from a battery on Little Round Top, which enfiladed their line. One shell killed and wounded ten men. Gibbon had directed his command to reserve their fire until the enemy were near enough to make it very effective. Pickett's advance dashed up to the fence occupied by the skirmishers of the Second Corps, near the Emmetsburg road, and drove them back; then the musketry blazed forth with deadly effect, and Pettigrew's men began to waver on the left and fall behind; for the nature of the ground was such that they were more exposed than other portions of the line. They were much shaken by the artillery fire, and that of Hays' division sent them back in masses.[2]

Before the first line of rebels reached a second fence and stone wall, behind which our main body was posted, it was obliged to pass a demi-brigade under Colonel Theodore B. Gates, of the Twentieth New York State Militia, and a Vermont brigade under General Stannard, both belonging to my command. When Pickett's right became exposed in consequence of the divergence of Wilcox's command, Stannard seized the opportunity to make a flank attack, and while his left regiment, the Fourteenth, poured in a heavy oblique fire, he changed front with his two right regiments, the Thirteenth and Sixteenth, which brought them perpendicular to the rebel line of march. In cases of this kind, when struck directly on the flank, troops are more or less unable to defend themselves, and Kemper's brigade crowded in toward the centre in order to avoid Stannard's energetic and deadly attack.

They were closely followed up by Gates' command, who continued to fire into them at close range. This caused many to surrender, others to retreat outright, and others simply to crowd together. Simultaneously with Stannard's attack, the Eighth Ohio, which was on picket, overlapping the rebel left, closed in on that flank with great effect. Nevertheless, the next brigade—that of Armistead—united to Garnett's brigade, pressed on, and in spite of death-dealing bolts on all sides, Pickett determined to break Gibbon's line and capture his guns.

Although Webb's front was the focus of the concentrated artillery fire, and he had already lost fifty men and some valuable officers, his line remained firm and unshaken. It devolved upon him now to meet the great charge which was to decide the fate of the day. It would have been difficult to find a man better fitted for such an emergency. He was nerved to great deeds by the memory of his ancestors, who in former days had rendered distinguished services to the Republic, and felt that the results of the whole war might depend upon his

---

[2]The front line of Hays' division, which received this charge, was composed of the Twelfth New Jersey, Fourteenth Connecticut, and First Delaware. The second line was composed of the One Hundred and Eleventh, One Hundred and Twenty-fifth, One Hundred and Twenty-sixth, and Thirty-ninth New York.

holding of the position. His men were equally resolute. Cushing's battery, A, Fourth United States Artillery, which had been posted on the crest, and Brown's Rhode Island Battery on his left, were both practically destroyed by the cannonade. The horses were prostrated, every officer but one was struck, and Cushing had but one serviceable gun left.

As Pickett's advance came very close to the first line, young Cushing, mortally wounded in both thighs, ran his last serviceable gun down to the fence, and said: *"Webb, I will give them one more shot!"* At the moment of the last discharge he called out, *"Good-by!"* and fell dead at the post of duty.

Webb sent for fresh batteries to replace the two that were disabled, and Wheeler's First New York Independent Battery came up just before the attack, and took the place of Cushing's battery on the left.

Armistead pressed forward, leaped the stone wall, waving his sword with his hat on it, followed by about a hundred of his men, several of whom carried battle-flags. He shouted, "Give them the cold steel, boys!" and laid his hands upon a gun. The battery for a few minutes was in his possession, and the rebel flag flew triumphantly over our line. But Webb was at the front, very near Armistead, animating and encouraging his men. He led the Seventy-second Pennsylvania regiment against the enemy, and posted a line of wounded men in rear to drive back or shoot every man that deserted his duty. A portion of the Seventy-first Pennsylvania, behind a stone wall on the right, threw in a deadly flanking fire, while a great part of the Sixty-ninth Pennsylvania and the remainder of the Seventy-first made stern resistance from a copse of trees on the left, near where the enemy had broken the line, and where our men were shot with the rebel muskets touching their breasts.

Then came a splendid charge of two regiments, led by Colonel Hall, which passed completely through Webb's line, and engaged the enemy in a hand-to-hand conflict.[3] Armistead was shot down by the side of the gun he had taken. Dying in the effort to extend the area of slavery over the free States, he may have felt that he had been engaged in an unjust cause; for he said to one of our officers who leaned over him: "Tell Hancock I have wronged him and have wronged my country."

Both Gibbon and Webb were wounded, and the loss in officers and men

---

[3]Colonel Norman J. Hall, commanding a brigade in Hancock's corps, who rendered this great service, was one of the garrison who defended Fort Sumter at the beginning of the war. At that time he was the Second Lieutenant of my company.

was very heavy; two rebel brigadier-generals were killed, and more prisoners were taken than twice Webb's brigade; 6 battle-flags, and 1,463 muskets were also gathered in.[4]

My command being a little to the left, I witnessed this scene, and, after it was over, sent out stretcher-bearers attached to the ambulance train, and had numbers of wounded Confederates brought in and cared for. I was told that there was one man among these whose conversation seemed to indicate that he was a general officer. I sent to ascertain his rank, but he replied: "Tell General Doubleday in a few minutes I shall be where there is no rank." He expired soon after, and I never learned his name.

The rebels did not seem to appreciate my humanity in sending out to bring in their wounded, for they opened a savage fire against the stretcher-bearers. One shell burst among us, a piece of it knocked me over on my horse's neck, and wounded Lieutenant Cowdry of my staff.

When Pickett—the great leader—looked around the top of the ridge he had temporarily gained, he saw it was impossible to hold the position. Troops were rushing in on him from all sides. The Second Corps were engaged in a furious assault on his front. His men were fighting with clubbed muskets, and even banner staves were intertwined in a fierce and hopeless struggle. My division of the First Corps were on his right flank, giving deadly blows there, and the Third Corps were closing up to attack. Pettigrew's forces on his left had given way, and a heavy skirmish line began to accumulate on that flank. He saw his men surrendering in masses, and, with a heart full of anguish, ordered a retreat. Death had been busy on all sides, and few indeed now remained of that magnificent column which had advanced so proudly, led by the Ney of the rebel army, and these few fell back in disorder, and without organization, behind Wright's brigade, which had been sent forward to cover the retreat. At first, however, when struck by Stannard on the flank, and when Pickett's charge was spent, they rallied in a little slashing, where a grove had been cut down by our troops to leave an opening for our artillery. There two regiments of Rowley's brigade of my division, the One Hundred and Fifty-first Pennsylvania and the Twentieth New York State Militia, under Colonel Theodore B. Gates, of the latter reg-

---

[4]The spirit of the men was remarkable. Lieutenant Woodruff, of the First United States Artillery, whose battery had been very efficient in repelling the enemy's charge, was leaning against a tree, mortally wounded, when his second in command came to see if he could be of any service. The dying officer told him to go back to his guns, as the fighting there was more important than his own fate.

iment, made a gallant charge, and drove them out. Pettigrew's division, it is said, lost 2,000 prisoners and 15 battle-flags on the left.

While this severe contest was going on in front of Webb, Wilcox deployed his command and opened a feeble fire against Caldwell's division on my left. Stannard repeated the manoeuvre which had been so successful against Kemper's brigade by detaching the Fourteenth and Sixteenth Vermont to take Wilcox in flank. Wilcox thus attacked on his right, while a long row of batteries tore the front of his line to pieces with canister, could gain no foothold. He found himself exposed to a tremendous cross fire, and was obliged to retreat, but a great portion of his command were brought in as prisoners by Stannard[5] and battle-flags were gathered in sheaves.

A portion of Longstreet's corps, Benning's, Robertson's, and Law's brigades, advanced against the two Round Tops to prevent reinforcements from being sent from that vicinity to meet Pickett's charge. Kilpatrick interfered with this programme, however, for about 2 P.M. he made his appearance on our left with Farnsworth's brigade and Merritt's brigade of regulars, accompanied by Graham's and Elder's batteries of the regular army, to attack the rebel right, with a view to reach their ammunition trains, which were in that vicinity. The rebels say his men came on yelling like demons. Having driven back the skirmishers who guarded that flank, Merritt deployed on the left and soon became engaged there with Anderson's Georgia brigade, which was supported by two batteries. On the right Farnsworth, with the First Vermont regiment of his brigade, leaped a fence, and advanced until he came to a second stone fence, where he was checked by an attack on his right flank from the Fourth Alabama regiment of Law's brigade, which came back for that purpose from a demonstration it was making against Round Top. Farnsworth then turned and leaping another fence in a storm of shot and shell, made a gallant attempt to capture Backman's battery, but was unable to do so, as it was promptly supported by the Ninth Georgia regiment of Anderson's brigade. Farnsworth was killed in this charge, and the First Vermont found itself enclosed in a field, with high fences on all sides, behind which masses of infantry were constantly rising up and firing. The regiment was all broken up and forced to retire in detachments. Kilpatrick after fighting some time longer without making much progress, fell

---

[5] As Stannard's brigade were new troops, and had been stationed near Washington, the men had dubbed them *The Paper Collar Brigade*, because some of them were seen wearing paper collars, but after this fight the term was never again applied to them.

back on account of the constant reinforcements that were augmenting the force opposed to him. Although he had not succeeded in capturing the ammunition train, he had made a valuable diversion on the left, which doubtless prevented the enemy from assailing Round Top with vigor, or detaching a force to aid Pickett.

The Confederate General Benning states that the prompt action of General Law in posting the artillery in the road and the Seventh and Ninth Georgia regiments on each side, was all that saved the train from capture. "There was nothing else to save it." He also says two-thirds of Pickett's command were killed, wounded, or captured. Every brigade commander and every field officer except one fell. Lee and Longstreet had seen from the edge of the woods, with great exultation, the blue flag of Virginia waving over the crest occupied by the Union troops. It seemed the harbinger of great success to Lee. He thought the Union army was conquered at last. The long struggle was over, and peace would soon come, accompanied by the acknowledgment of the independence of the Southern Confederacy. It was but a passing dream; the flag receded, and soon the plain was covered with fugitives making their way to the rear. Then, anticipating an immediate pursuit, he used every effort to rally men and officers, and made strenuous efforts to get his artillery in position to be effective.

The Confederate General A. R. Wright criticises this attack and very justly says, "The difficulty was not so much in reaching Cemetery Ridge or taking it. My brigade did so on the afternoon of the 2d, but the trouble was to hold it, for the whole Federal army was massed in a sort of horse shoe, and could rapidly reinforce the point to any extent; while the long enveloping Confederate line could not support promptly enough." This agrees with what I have said in relation to the convex and concave orders of battle.

General Gibbon had sent Lieutenant Haskell of his staff to Power's Hill to notify General Meade that the charge was coming. As Meade approached his old headquarters he heard firing on the crest above, and went up to ascertain the cause. He found the charge had been repulsed and ejaculated "Thank God!"

When Lee learned that Johnson had yielded his position on the right, and therefore could not co-operate with Pickett's advance, he sent Stuart's cavalry around to accomplish the same object by attacking the right and rear of our army. Howard saw the rebel cavalry moving off in that direction, and David McM. Gregg, whose division was near White's Creek where it crosses the Baltimore pike, received orders about noon to guard Slocum's right and rear.

Custer had already been contending with his brigade against portions of the enemy's force in that direction, when Gregg sent forward McIntosh's brigade to relieve him, and followed soon after with J. Irvin Gregg's brigade. Custer was under orders to join Kilpatrick's command, to which he belonged, but the exigencies of the battle soon forced Gregg to detain him. McIntosh, having taken the place of Custer, pushed forward to develop the enemy's line, which he found very strongly posted, the artillery being on a commanding ridge which overlooked the whole country, and covered by dismounted cavalry in woods, buildings, and behind fences below. McIntosh became warmly engaged and sent back for Randol's battery to act against the rebel guns on the crest, and drive the enemy out of the buildings. The guns above were silenced by Pennington's and Randol's batteries, and the force below driven out of the houses by Lieutenant Chester's section of the latter. The buildings and fences were then occupied by our troops. The enemy attempted to regain them by a charge against McIntosh's right flank, but were repulsed. In the meantime Gregg came up with the other brigade, and assumed command of the field. The battle now became warm, for W. H. F. Lee's brigade, under Chambliss, advanced to support the skirmish line, and the First New Jersey, being out of ammunition, was charged and routed by the First Virginia. The Seventh Michigan, a new regiment which came up to support it, was also driven in; for the enemy's dismounted line reinforced the First Virginia. The latter regiment, which had held on with desperate tenacity, although attacked on both flanks, was at last compelled to fall back by an attack made by part of the Fifth Michigan. The contending forces were now pretty well exhausted when, to the dismay of our men, a fresh brigade under Wade Hampton, which Stuart had kept in reserve, made its appearance, and new and desperate exertions were required to stem its progress. There was little time to act, but every sabre that could be brought forward was used. As Hampton came on, our artillery under Pennington and Randol made terrible gaps in his ranks. Chester's section kept firing canister until the rebels were within fifty yards of him. The enemy were temporarily stopped by a desperate charge on their flank, made by only sixteen men of the Third Pennsylvania Cavalry, under Captains Treichel and Rogers, accompanied by Captain Newhall of McIntosh's staff. This little band of heroes were nearly all disabled or killed, but they succeeded in delaying the enemy, already shattered by the canister from Chester's guns, until Custer was able to bring up the First Michigan and lead them to the charge, shouting "Come on, you wolverines!" Every available sabre was thrown in. General McIntosh and his staff and orderlies charged into the *mêlée* as individuals. Hampton and Fitz

Lee headed the enemy, and Custer our troops. Lieutenant Colonel W. Brooke-Rawle, the historian of the conflict, who was present, says, "For minutes, which seemed like hours, amid the clashing of the sabres, the rattle of the small arms, the frenzied imprecations, the demands to surrender, the undaunted replies, and the appeals for mercy, the Confederate column stood its ground." A fresh squadron was brought up under Captain Hart of the First New Jersey, and the enemy at last gave way and retired. Both sides still confronted each other, but the battle was over, for Pickett's charge had failed, and there was no longer any object in continuing the contest.

Stuart was undoubtedly baffled and the object of his expedition frustrated; yet he stated in his official report that he was in a position to intercept the Union retreat in case Pickett had been successful. At night he retreated to regain his communications with Ewell's left.

This battle being off of the official maps has hardly been alluded to in the various histories which have been written; but its results were important and deserve to be commemorated.

When Pickett's charge was repulsed, and the whole plain covered with fugitives, we all expected that Wellington's command at Waterloo of *"Up, guards, and at them!"* would be repeated, and that a grand counter-charge would be made. But General Meade had made no arrangements to give a return thrust. It seems to me he should have posted the Sixth and part of the Twelfth Corps in rear of Gibbon's division the moment Pickett's infantry were seen emerging from the woods, a mile and a half off. If they broke through our centre these corps would have been there to receive them, and if they failed to pierce our line and retreated, the two corps could have followed them up promptly before they had time to rally and reorganize. An advance by Sykes would have kept Longstreet in position. In all probability we would have cut the enemy's army in two, and captured the long line of batteries opposite us, which were but slightly guarded. Hancock, lying wounded in an ambulance, wrote to Meade, recommending that this be done. Meade, it is true, recognized in some sort the good effects of a counter-blow; but to be effective the movement should have been prepared beforehand. It was too late to commence making preparations for an advance when some time had elapsed and when Lee had rallied his troops and had made all his arrangements to resist an assault. It was ascertained afterward that he had twenty rounds of ammunition left per gun, but it was not evenly distributed and some batteries in front had fired away all their cartridges. A counter-charge under such circumstances is considered almost imperative in war, for the beaten army, running and dismayed, cannot, in the nature of things, resist with much spirit; whereas the pursuers, highly elated by their success, and with the prospect of ending the contest, fight with more energy and bravery. Rodes says the Union forces were so long in occupying the town and in coming forward after the repulse of the enemy that it was generally thought they had retreated. Meade rode leisurely over to the Fifth Corps on the left, and told Sykes to send out and see if the enemy in his front was firm and holding on to their position. A brigade preceded by skirmishers was accordingly sent forward, but as Longstreet's troops were well fortified, they resisted the advance, and Meade—finding some hours had elapsed and that Lee had closed up his lines and was fortifying against him—gave up all idea of a counter-attack.

Chapter VII.

General retreat of the enemy—criticisms of distinguished confederate officers.

Lee was greatly dispirited at Pickett's failure, but worked with untiring energy to repair the disaster.

There was an interval of full a mile between Hill and Longstreet, and the plain was swarming with fugitives making their way back in disorder. He hastened to get ready to resist the counter-charge, which he thought was inevitable, and to plant batteries behind which the fugitives could rally. He also made great personal exertions to reassure and reassemble the detachments that came in. He did not for a moment imagine that Meade would fail to take advantage of this golden opportunity to crush the Army of Virginia and end the war.

The most distinguished rebel officers admit the great danger they were in at this time, and express their surprise that they were not followed up.

The fact is, Meade had no idea of leaving the ridge. I conversed the next morning with a corps commander who had just left him. He said: "Meade says he thinks he can hold out for part of another day here, if they attack him."

This language satisfied me that Meade would not go forward if he could avoid it, and would not impede in any way the rebel retreat across the Potomac. Lee began to make preparations at once and started his trains on the morning of the 4th. By night Rodee's division, which followed them, was in bivouac two miles west of Fairfield. It was a difficult task to retreat burdened with 4,000 prisoners, and a train fifteen miles long, in the presence of a victorious enemy, but it was successfully accomplished as regards his main body. The roads, too, were bad and much cut up by the rain.

While standing on Little Round Top Meade was annoyed at the fire of a rebel battery posted on an eminence beyond the wheat-field, about a thousand yards distant. He inquired what troops those were stationed along the stone fence which bounded the hither side of the wheat-field. Upon ascertaining that it was Crawford's division of the Fifth Corps, he directed that they be sent forward to clear the woods in front of rebel skirmishers, who were very annoying, and to drive away the battery, *but not to get into a fight that would bring on a general engagement.* As Crawford unmasked from the stone fence the battery opened fire on his right. He sent Colonel Ent's regiment, deployed as skirmishers, against the guns, which retired as Ent approached. McCandless, who went forward with his brigade, moved too far to the right, and Crawford ordered him to change front and advance toward Round Top. He did so and struck a rebel brigade in flank which was behind a temporary breastwork of rails, sods, etc. When this brigade saw a Union force apparently approaching from their own lines to attack them in flank, they retreated in confusion, after a short resistance, and this disorder extended during the retreat to a reserve brigade posted on the low ground in their rear. Their flight did not cease until they reached Horner's woods, half a mile distant, where they immediately intrenched themselves. These brigades belonged to Hood's division, then under Law.

Longstreet says, "When this (Pickett's) charge failed, I expected that, of course, the enemy would throw himself against our shattered ranks and try to crush us. I sent my staff officers to the rear to assist in rallying the troops, and hurried to our line of batteries as the only support that I could give them." . . . "I knew if the army was to be saved these batteries must check the enemy." . . . "For unaccountable reasons the enemy did not pursue his advantage."

Longstreet always spoke of his own men as invincible, and stated that on the 2d they did the best three hours' fighting that ever was done, but Crawford's[6] attack seemed to show that they too were shaken by the defeat of Pickett's grand charge.

In regard to the great benefit we would have derived from a pursuit, it may not be out of place to give the opinion of a few more prominent Confederate officers.

---

[6]Crawford was also one of those who took a prominent part in the defence of Fort Sumner, at the beginning of the war. We each commanded detachments of artillery on that occasion.

Colonel Alexander, Chief of Longstreet's artillery, says in a communication to the "Southern Historical Papers:"

I have always believed that the enemy here lost the greatest opportunity they ever had of routing Lee's army by a prompt offensive. They occupied a line shaped somewhat like a horseshoe. I suppose the greatest diameter of this horseshoe was not more than one mile, and the ground within was entirely sheltered from our observation and fire, with communications by signals all over it, and they could concentrate their whole force at any point and in a very short time without our knowledge. Our line was an enveloping semi-circle, over four miles in development, and communication from flank to flank, even by courier, was difficult, the country being well cleared and exposed to the enemy's view and fire, the roads all running at right angles to our lines, and, some of them at least, broad turnpikes where the enemy's guns could rake for two miles. It is necessary now to add any statement as to the superiority of the Federal force, or the exhausted and shattered condition of the Confederates for a space of at least a mile in their very centre, to show that a great opportunity was thrown away? I think General Lee himself was quite apprehensive the enemy would *riposte,* and that it was that apprehension which brought him alone out to my guns, where he could observe all the indications.

General Trimble, who commanded a division of Hill's corps, which supported Pickett in his advance, says, "By all the rules of warfare the Federal troops should (as I expected they would) have marched against our shattered columns and sought to cover our army with an overwhelming defeat."

Colonel Simms, who commanded Semmes's Georgia brigade in the fight with Crawford just referred to, writes to the latter, "There was much confusion in our army so far as my observation extended, and I think we would have made but feeble resistance, if you had pressed on, on the evening of the 3d."

General Meade, however, overcome by the great responsibilities of his position, still clung to the ridge, and fearful of a possible disaster would not take the risk of making an advance. And yet if he could have succeeded in crushing Lee's army then and there, he would have saved two years of war with its immense loss of life and countless evils. He might at least have thrown in Sedgwick's corps, which had not been actively engaged in the battle, for even if it was repulsed the blows it gave would leave the enemy little inclination to again assail the heights.

At 6.30 P.M. the firing ceased on the part of the enemy, and although they retained their position the next day, the battle of Gettysburg was virtually at an end.

The town was still full of our wounded, and many of our surgeons, with rare courage, remained there to take charge of them, for it required some nerve to run the risk of being sent to Libby prison when the fight was over, a catastrophe which has often happened to our medical officers. Among the rest, the chief surgeons of the First Corps, Doctor Theodore Heard and Doctor Thomas H. Bache, refused to leave their patients, and in consequence of the hasty retreat of the enemy were fortunately not carried off.

After the battle Meade had not the slightest desire to recommence the struggle. It is a military maxim that to a flying enemy must be given a wall of steel or a bridge of gold. In the present instance it was unmistakably the bridge of gold that was presented. It was hard to convince him that Lee was actually gone, and at first he thought it might be a device to draw the Union army from its strong position on the heights.

Our cavalry were sent out on the 4th to ascertain where the enemy were, and what they were doing. General Birney threw forward a reconnoitering party and opened fire with a battery on a column making their way toward Fairfield, but he was checked at once and directed *on no account to bring on a battle*. On the 5th, as it was certain the enemy were retreating, Sedgwick received orders to follow up the rear of the rebel column. He marched eight miles to Fairfield Pass. There Early, who was in command of the rear guard, was endeavoring to save the trains, which were heaped up in great confusion. Sedgwick, after a distant cannonade, reported the position too strong to be forced. It was a plain, two miles wide, surrounded by hills, and it would not have been difficult to take it, but Sedgwick knew Meade favored the "bridge of gold" policy, and was not disposed to thwart the wishes of his chief. In my opinion Sedgwick should have made an energetic attack, and Meade should have supported it with his whole army, for our cavalry were making great havoc in the enemy's trains in rear; and if Lee, instead of turning on Kilpatrick, had been forced to form line against Meade, the cavalry, which was between him and his convoys of ammunition, in all probability might have captured the latter and ended the war. Stuart, it is true, was following up Kilpatrick, but he took an indirect route and was nearly a day behind. I do not see why the force which was now promptly detached from the garrisons of Washington and Baltimore and sent to Harper's Ferry could not have formed on the Virginia side of the Potomac opposite Williamsport, and with the co-operation of General Meade have cut off the ammunition of which Lee stood so much in need. As the river had risen and an expedition sent out by General French from Frederick had destroyed the bridge at Falling Waters, everything seemed to favor such a plan. The moment it was ascertained that Lee was cut off from Richmond and short of ammunition the whole North would have turned out and made a second Saratoga of it. As it was, he had but few rounds for his cannon, and our artillery could have opened a destructive fire on him from a distance without exposing our infantry. It was worth the effort and there was little or no danger in attempting it. Meade had Sedgwick's fresh corps and was reinforced by a division of 11,000 men under General W. F. Smith (Baldy Smith). French's division of 4,000 at Frederick, and troops from Washington and Baltimore were also available to assist in striking the final blow. The Twelfth Corps was also available, as Slocum volunteered to join in the pursuit. Meade, however, delayed moving at all until Lee had reached Hagerstown and then took a route that was almost twice as long as that adopted by the enemy. Lee marched day and night to avoid pursuit, and when the river rose and his bridge was gone, so that he was unable to cross, he gained six days in which to choose a position, fortify it, and renew his supply of ammunition before Meade made his appearance.

In consequence of repeated orders from President Lincoln to attack the enemy, Meade went forward and confronted Lee on the 12th. He spent that day and the next in making reconnoissances and resolved to attack on the 14th; but Lee left during the night, and by 8 A.M. the entire army of the enemy were once more on Virginia soil.

The Union loss in this campaign is estimated by the Count of Paris, who is an impartial observer, at 2,884 killed, 13,709 wounded, and 6,648 missing; total, 23,186.

The rebel loss he puts at 2,665 killed, 12,599 wounded, 7,464 missing; total, 22,728.

Among the killed in the battle on the rebel side were Generals Armistead, Barksdale, Garnett, Pender, and Semmes; and Pettigrew during the retreat.

Among the wounded were Generals G. T. Anderson, Hampton, Jenkins, J. M. Jones, Kemper, and Scales.

Archer was captured on the first day.

Among the killed on the Union side were Major General Reynolds and Brigadier-Generals Vincent, Weed, Zook, and Farnsworth.

Among the wounded were Major-Generals Sickles (losing a leg), Hancock, Doubleday, Gibbon, Barlow, Warren, and Butterfield, and Brigadier-Generals Graham, Stannard, Paul (losing both eyes), Barnes, Brooke, and Webb.

The staff officer is defined by a cliché—he's the guy in the rear head-quarters who reaps the glory of battle without having to fight it. That is not the picture drawn by G. Moxley Sorrel, a staff officer serving the HQ of James Longstreet's corps. Recounting his experience at Chickamauga and The Wilderness, Sorrel shows how staff work is interwoven in the action and how exercising initiative can win a fight without waiting for orders to attack. Staff officers are more than messengers. Sometimes a commander may delegate to one of his staff the hurried command of several brigades when a fleeting oppor-tunity must be exploited. Sorrel does his share of such work and does not gloss over the dangers faced by staff who sometimes must wade into the action.

Excerpts from *Recollections of a Confederate Staff Officer*

BY G. MOXLEY SORREL

Chapter XXV

BATTLE OF CHICKAMAUGA, SEPTEMBER 20, 1863.

Arrival at Catoosa—Riding to General Bragg—The meeting—Order of battle—Polk the right wing, Longstreet the left—Attack to begin on right—Delayed some hours—Left wing takes it up victoriously—Attack on right checked—Thomas reinforces his right against Longstreet's assaults—Cannot stand and retreats toward Chattanooga—A great victory for the Confederates—Pursuit next day expected—Bragg says no—Army marches to positions in front of Chattanooga—A barren result—Lieutenant-General Polk—Sketch.

It was about three o'clock in the afternoon of September 19 that our rickety train pulled up, with jerks and bangs, at the little railway landing, called Catoosa Platform. Longstreet and some of his personal staff, Colonels Sorrel and Manning, were in this train and immediately took horse. The remainder of the staff, with most of the horses, were on a train two or three hours later. The Lieutenant-General and part of his staff at once started to find General Bragg.

That General should surely have had guides to meet and conduct us to the conference on which so much depended. A sharp action had taken place during the day and it would appear that if Bragg wanted to see anybody, Longstreet was the man. But we were left to shift for ourselves, and wandered by various roads and across small streams through the growing darkness of the Georgia forest in the direction of the Confederate General's bivouac. At one point in our hunt for him we narrowly escaped capture, being almost in the very center of a strong picket of the enemy before our danger was discovered. A sharp right-about gallop, unhurt by the pickets' hasty and surprised fire, soon put us in safety, and another road was taken for Bragg, about whom by this time some hard words were passing.

But all things have an end, even a friendly hunt for an army commander, and between 10 and 11 o'clock that night we rode into the camp of Gen. Braxton Bragg. He was asleep in his ambulance, and when aroused immediately entered into private conference with Longstreet. It lasted about an hour, and in that time the plan of battle for next day was definitely settled, and then we all took to the leafy ground under the tall oaks and hickories for some sleep against the work before us.

An hour was quite enough to settle the plan and details, since nothing could be simpler than the operation proposed for Rosecrans's destruction.

Bragg's army was already occupying favorable ground and but little preliminary movement was positively necessary. The enemy's force was not far off in our immediate front, seemingly easy to attack. Bragg's army was, however, strange to say, rather deficient in artillery, and its want was felt the next day. Our own batteries, under Alexander, had not yet detrained. Bragg made a good disposition of his separate divisions and commands, dividing his army into two wings, the right under Lieutenant-General Polk and the left under Lieutenant-General Longstreet. There was consequently thrown under the latter three of Hood's brigades and two of McLaws's (under Hood), and Stuart's and Preston's divisions (under Buckner), and a division of B. R. Johnson's, and Hindman's with artillery. The order for the day was simple in the extreme.

There was no question about all the troops being in position by daylight, and at that hour the attack was to be opened by General Polk on the extreme right and followed up vigorously by the lines to the left, until the entire front of Bragg's fine army should be engaged and charging the enemy, exposed to an attack so furious it was not believed he could sustain it, and he could not. It will be shown how he was partially saved after the roughest handling he had had since Bull Run. The right wing was formed of Breckinridge's and Cleburne's divisions under D. H. Hill, Walker's and Biddell's divisions under Walker, and Cheatham's division, besides artillery.

Longstreet's front had Wheeler's cavalry on his extreme left, then Hindman, Hood's corps, Stuart, and Preston in the order named, and they were ready for their work at daylight on the 20th, the other commands in close support. Unhappily, a most serious delay occurred on the right, by which Polk's attack was retarded until near 10 o'clock, a loss of at least four previous hours. Lieutenant-General Hill's command was on Polk's extreme right and should have begun the attack. Orders sent during the night by General Polk failed to reach him. On our part we waited with the utmost impatience for the guns, but no sound came until 10 o'clock. Then Polk's attack was made, but does not appear to have achieved a decided success. The enemy were able to hold their ground against most of the right wing commands.

When it came, as it quickly did, to the left wing to put in its work there was another tale. The ground was in parts difficult in front of us, but never was a more determined, dashing attack made, never a more stubborn resistance. But our men would not be denied. The fighting lasted nearly all day. Finally everything broke before us, and the enemy's right was in full flight. It was a panic-stricken host that fled. Our Virginia contingent was always to the front and seemed to fire their western comrades with emulation of the grand example of the Army of Northern Virginia.

Unhappily, amid shouts of victory, General Hood was shot down at the head of his seasoned veterans. His leg was taken off on the field, the operation being well borne. But we were forced into a temporary halt.

Reinforcements were pouring fresh and ready against our front. The attack of the right wing having partly broken down, the enemy in front of Polk was not held to their own, but were in large numbers free for a masterly movement by that fine soldier, Gen. George Thomas. He was a Virginian, and it is said started to join his Southern friends at the beginning, but was finally won over to the Northern side.

He was one of the ablest of their soldiers, perhaps none equaled him, and I heartily wish he had been anywhere but at Chickamauga. Thomas pressed rapid columns to relieve his overwhelmed right and was in time to make a good stand, but it was unavailing, although costing more blood and time. His defenses were finally broken down, about dark, by our incessant hammering, and it was right-about-face and hasty retreat to Chattanooga.

This was just as darkness spread its mantle over the fields and forests, and simultaneously there sprang up on that bloodstained battle-ground camp fires innumerable, and the wildest Confederate cheers and yells for victory that ever stirred the hearts of warriors—and such warriors as had that day borne the battle-flags forward. It was one of the greatest of the many Confederate successes.

That night was passed in caring for the wounded, burying the dead, and cooking rations, for in all that host there was probably only one who did not believe that "pursuit" would be the word early next day, and that was the commander-in-chief. It is thought by some that General Bragg did not know a victory had been gained. He does not appear to have been closely present on the battlefield, nor for that matter was Rosecrans. A unique instance of a great battle being fought out of the immediate presence of the respective commanders. The next morning Bragg asked Longstreet for suggestions. "Move instantly against Rosecrans's rear to destroy him," was the instant reply. "Should we fail, we can put him in retreat, and then clear East Tennessee of Burnside and the Union forces."

Apparently, Bragg adopted this view, and gave orders to march out at 4 P.M. The right wing marched about eight miles, ours next day at daylight. We were halted at the Chickamauga Red House Ford, I think it was, and then directed to march to Chattanooga. At the close of the battle we could have strolled into that town; now it was vigorously defended. This was the fruit of the great battle; the pitiable end of the glorious victory that was ours. The spoils were 8,000 prisoners, 36 pieces of artillery, 15,000 small arms, and 25 stands of colors.

It was a lasting regret that I had no more than a passing glimpse during these operations of the distinguished soldier, Lieut.-Gen. Leonidas Polk, second in command of Bragg's army.

A pure and lofty character, nothing but the most self-sacrificing, patriotic convictions, and the almost peremptory wishes of the Executive had led him to lay down his great Episcopal station and duties and take to arms. His training at West Point had well prepared him for the stern efforts in the field awaiting Southern men. Throughout his army career he was never without a desire to put by his sword and take up again his dearly loved people, his Bishop's staff, for prayer and strength and consolation in their many trials and sufferings. But the President, holding him in the highest esteem and confidence, insisted on retaining him in the armies of the Confederacy. He could not but yield. Of commanding presence and most winning address, he served with distinction and renown. While suffering at the hands of Bragg treatment unjust and harsh, he on the other hand had won to himself the abiding affection and confidence of all officers and men whom he commanded.

On June 1, 1864, near Marietta, Georgia, that noble life ended. In the distance lay the hills of the Etowah; on the right, Kenesaw reared its lofty heights. The Generals—Johnston, Hardee, and Polk—had together walked off to observe a portion of the enemy's lines, some distance away. Soon after they slowly separated.

Dr. W. M. Polk, the General's son, eminent in his profession, and author of his interesting biography, simply relates what then happened (Vol. II, p. 349):

General Polk walked to the crest of the hill, and, entirely exposed, turned himself around as if to take a farewell view. Folding his arms across his breast, he stood intently gazing on the scene below. While thus he stood, a cannon shot crashed his breast, and opening a wide door, let free that indomitable spirit. He fell upon his back with his feet to the foe. Amid the shot and shell now poured upon the hill, his faithful escort gathered up the body and bore it to the foot of the hill. There in a sheltered ravine his sorrow-stricken comrades silent and in tears, gathered around his mangled corpse.

Chapter XXVI

CHATTANOOGA—INCIDENTS

The Western army—Its general appearance—Feeling toward Bragg—President Davis's visit—An incident in battle—General W. W. Mackall, chief of Bragg's staff—Losses—A captured saber—General Forrest—General Benning and Longstreet—Vizitelly's battle-picture—Quartermaster Mitchell dead—Manning wounded—President Davis's escort—The Austrian captain's brilliant uniform.

We were therefore marched back to what was called the siege of Chattanooga, finding the enemy there in fine spirits after the indulgent reprieve granted him; strengthening his works, perfecting his communications with the rear, and pouring in men from the East, who, following our own movements, were necessarily late in arriving by the outer line. Bragg put his army in position across Missionary Creek (subject to perilous overflow) and occupied Lookout Mountain with his left and Missionary Ridge with his right, and here I shall leave the army while jotting down some observations and incidents since we left Virginia.

The personal appearance of Bragg's army was, of course, matter of interest to us of Virginia. The men were a fine-looking lot, strong, lean, long-limbed fighters. The Western tunic was much worn by both officers and men. It is an excellent garment, and its use could be extended with much advantage. The army gave one the feeling of a very loose organization. There were indeed corps, so called, but not that compact, shoulder-to-shoulder make-up of Lee's army. There a First Corps man would so speak of himself, just as a Third Georgia Regiment man would speak of the regiment to which he belonged. The artillery, which seemed to me not as strong as should be, looked a bit primitive. The battalion unit was not often met with; but, on the contrary, many single independent batteries, nominally attached to infantry commands, but on the day of the battle wandering loose, hunting for their supports. The subsistence and quartermaster's departments were well supplied with food and forage, but weak in transportation.

The tone of the army among its higher officers toward the commander was the worst conceivable. Bragg was the subject of hatred and contempt, and it was almost openly so expressed. His great officers gave him no confidence as a general-in-chief. The army was thus left a helpless machine, and its great disaster in November at Missionary Ridge and Lookout Mountain could easily be foreseen with Bragg retained in command.

Mr. Davis made his celebrated visit to the camp to see and hear for himself. It is difficult, even now, to recall and realize that unprecedented scene. The President, with the commander-in-chief, and the great officers of the army, assembled to hear the opinion of the General's fitness for command. In the presence of Bragg and his corps commander he asked of each his opinion, and his reasons if adverse. This was eye to eye with the President, the commander-in-chief, and the generals. There was no lack of candor in answer to such challenge with men like Longstreet, Cheatham, Hill, Cleburne, and Stewart. Some very plain language was used in answer, but it seems that one and all were quite agreed as to Bragg's unfitness for command of that army. These opinions were received by the President and his general without comment, and Mr. Davis got more than he came for.

An incident of the day of battle will indicate some differences between the Eastern and Western armies in the reception of orders. While Thomas was heavily reinforcing his right, a column of fours was seen marching across Gen. A. P. Stewart's front. If attacked, its destruction was certain. I pointed out the opportunity to General Stewart, his position being admirable for the purpose. His answer was that he was there by orders and could not move until he got others. I explained that I was chief of staff to Longstreet and felt myself competent to give such an order as coming from my chief, and that this was customary in our Virginia service. General Stewart, however, courteously insisted that he could not accept them unless assured the orders came direct from Longstreet. Valuable time was being lost, but I determined to have a whack at those quick-moving blue masses. Asking General Stewart to get ready, that I hoped soon to find Longstreet, I was off, and luckily did find him after an eager chase. Longstreet's thunderous tones need not be described when, in the first words of explanation, he sent me back with orders to Stewart to fall on the reinforcing column with all his power. Stewart was ready and pushed forward handsomely. In a few minutes, with little or no loss to himself, he had broken up Thomas's men and taken many prisoners. This was quite late in the afternoon, twilight coming on.

My brother-in-law, General W. W. Mackall, was serving with Bragg as chief of staff, although his rank and attainments qualified him for higher duties. But the Executive at Richmond was not favorably disposed toward him, and the best that could be had for service must content him. It seems that he and Bragg had been long friends, having served together in the old Army. I was glad to come up with him, and delighted his soul by a gift of a five-pound bale of Virginia Killikinick smoking tobacco, in place of the vile stuff he was blowing off.

The numbers on both sides, and the casualties, are generally accepted as follows: Rosecrans's strength, 60,867; Bragg's strength, 60,366. Rosecrans's losses, 16,550; Bragg's losses, 17,800.

It was during the battle that I became the possessor of a handsomely mounted saber. In a part of the field near us there was a sudden sharp, deadly scrimmage between some of our mounted men and the enemy, a small force on each side. It was soon over, and Hardy, one of my couriers, a stout, ready Georgian, came to me with a beautiful saber, evidently a presentation to the lieutenant-colonel whose name was engraved on it. My fellow made me a gift of the handsome blade, and I wore it until peace came. What became of the lieutenant-colonel I could never ascertain.

> *"His sword it is rust,*
> *His bones they are dust,*
> *His soul is with the Saints I trust."*

The good sword was treasured until a few years ago, when the ladies of the Confederate Museum at Richmond asked me to put it among their collection, and there it hangs to-day, I hope for many years.

It was on the 20th that I had my look at the celebrated Forrest. Truly a most powerful, impressive figure of a great cavalryman. He was yet to become still greater, as one of the first commanders of the South, and subsequent studies of his life and career only expand this admiration into deeper feelings for the great soldier.

Dr. John Wyeth's interesting biography of Forrest, published only in the past few years, is most fascinating, and has gone far to place him as one of the greatest leaders of the Civil War. During the battle a queer scene between Longstreet and the valiant old brigadier, Benning, commanding one of Hood's brigades, illustrates Longstreet's grim calm in action, and the excitability of "Old Rock," as his men called him. A sudden counter-stroke of the enemy had smashed his brigade and they were badly scattered. Benning thought that they were "all gone." Seizing an artillery horse that was galloping by, harness flying, he threw himself on the terrified animal and found Longstreet. "General," said the brigadier, "I am ruined; my brigade was suddenly attacked and every man killed; not one is to be found. Please give orders where I can do some fighting." Longstreet saw the excitement and quickly cooled it. "Nonsense, General, you are not so badly hurt. Look about you. I know you will find at least one man, and with him on his feet report your brigade to me, and you two shall have a place in the fighting-line."

Benning saw it, took the hint, hunted up his men, who were not so badly mauled after all, and with a respectable body was soon ready for work.

Vizitelly, the English artist, had started from Richmond with us, to sketch and draw for the campaign; something stopped him on the way, drink, probably. At all events, he arrived very sheep-faced, long after the battle. He took me aside with: "Colonel, I am in an awful mess. I must send drawings and a picture of this great battle to my paper somehow. Cannot you help me?" We were at the time not very far from a little field that had a scene during the fighting which struck me, even then, as somewhat picturesque. The open field crowned with thick woods at one side, through which frowned half a dozen Federal guns and a brigade of ours moving up in beautiful order to capture it. I said as much as this to Vizitelly, and sent him to look at the spot. He returned, on fire with his artist's fancies. and shut himself up for several days. Then he emerged with drawings, and much letter-press of what he had *actually* seen; and principally a very large drawing beautifully finished of the so-called "Little scene." But heavens! all resemblance had ceased. Instead of the slight affair, three solid lines of infantry were moving across a great stretch of ground against hundreds of guns that were devastating our troops in fire and smoke. In the central portion there was the wounding and fall of a great officer and the closing in of the soldiers to protect him. "What think you?" said the proud Vizitelly. "Splendid, but nothing like it took place." "No matter, it might have happened, and besides all battle-pictures are drawn with such freedom." "Who is the general just falling?" "That, sir, is General Hood, drawn the instant of being shot." "But, my good Vizitelly, Hood was not within a mile of that little field I gave you." "No matter, he was shot, no one will deny that; and I must have a great interesting center for my picture. You fellows are altogether too particular. This goes by first underground chance, and you will see it in the *London Illustrated News*." And so I did in the quiet sitting-room of a Northern friend later on.

He is not the only one of artistic imagination for battle-pictures.

At Chicakamauga we lost our quartermaster, Major Mitchell, of Virginia, a valuable officer. A sudden attack of diphtheria carried him off like a stroke of lightning. Major Erasmus Taylor, of Orange Court House, Virginia, was immediately appointed in his place, and served with us efficiently until the close of the war.

Lieutenant-Colonel Manning, of our staff, was slightly wounded in the battle of the 20th. A fragment of shell pierced his scalp, causing much loss of blood, but otherwise no great damage. He was soon about his ordnance duties as good as ever.

When President Davis came to Bragg's army on his visit of conciliation and support to his general, there was a universal turnout to give the Executive our best reception. At all headquarters the least shabby uniforms were looked up and our best belongings for horse and man were brought out. Mr. Davis had a really fine escort to the top of Lookout Mountain and back to quarters. At First Corps headquarters we still had the pleasure of Captain Fitzgerald Ross with us, a companionable and honorable officer and gentleman. On this occasion we thought it time for Ross to show the quality of his Austrian corps, and most reluctantly he consented to ride with us in full uniform. It was a beauty and a wonder! Sky-blue tunic and trousers, fitting skin-tight to the body and legs, loaded down with the richest gold braid and ornaments. Tiny boots, tasseled and varnished, incased the Captain's shapely Hussar legs. And then the pelisse hanging from the left shoulder!—it would be the envy of any woman. The color, still sky-blue, of the finest cloth, lined with buff satin, gold braided and richly furred. A smart, richly plumed Hungarian busby, with handsomely mounted curved saber and gold cords, completed the costume of this brilliant representative of his corps d'élite.

We gave Ross our plaudits and thanks for his fine appearance, and only on returning was there any annoyance. The large cortege about the President parted and some of us found ourselves riding with Ross under Maj.-Gen. John C. Breckinridge. Our route lay through one of his divisions camped in the noble primeval forests. The men were scattered all about attending to their personal matters, cooking, cleaning arms, mending, and, as it seemed, many stripped to the waist examining very closely their shirts and undergarments.

Without going into particulars, all soldiers in the field must be careful in this respect. Long-worn clothing had a way of "gathering" things, and it was what had to be done in all our armies. But when the scattered troops saw the brilliant apparition of Captain Ross riding with their General there was a shout and a rush to him. Such was the rough admiration exhibited that harm might have come to him but for Breckinridge. He motioned the men back, said the Captain was his guest, and, "When you fellows get to his army on a visit you will find him treating you more civilly; so get back to your bivouacs and make yourselves clean."

There was a good-natured cheer for Breckinridge, Ross, the President, and all the rest of us, and we got back to camp with much cheerful chaff for poor Ross and his gay uniform.

Chapter XXX

BATTLE OF THE WILDERNESS, MAY 6, 1864.

General Grant in command of all the Union forces—Takes station with Army of the Potomac—His career—His successes—Later kind feelings of Southern people toward him—His dinner party at Savannah—His plan of campaign—The policy of attrition—Grant moves his army—The Wilderness—Disparity of numbers—Courier service an example of our economy in men—Kershaw promoted major-general, commanding McLaws's division—Sketch—Lee decides to strike—Grant on the march—They meet on May 5th—An indecisive partial contest—Early on May 6 Longstreet comes up—Finds situation serious—Hancock's successful attack on Third Corps—It is checked—Our flank attack on Hancock's left—He is rolled up and sent back—General Lee wants to lead troops—Longstreet wounded and Jenkins killed by fire of our own men—Major-General Wadsworth, U.S.A., killed—Attack resumed later—Not successful—Night ends long day's fighting.

The Army of Northern Virginia was now to deal with a new force—a general with the great prestige of repeated victories in the West, and of undeniable ability. Lieutenant-General U.S. Grant had been made Commander-in-Chief of all the Federal armies in the field, and realizing the extraordinary achievements of Lee's army, left the scene of his operations, and retaining Meade in command of the Army of the Potomac, took his station by that army for the supreme direction of military affairs. Grant's career was wonderful; were it not a fact, it would be thought a fairy tale. A West Point graduate of mediocrity, serving well in Mexico, but so given over to drink that his retirement from the Army may be said to have been compulsory. This was followed by hard-working attempts to make a living for his family, in humble occupations, until the stirring events of 1861 brought him forward, as they did every one who had enjoyed the opportunity of a soldier's education. Obtaining command of an Illinois regiment, his field service began, and was followed up with much success; until, placed in command of important armies in Tennessee and Kentucky, he was able to break up the Confederate plans, and finally, by his crushing defeat of Bragg at

Missionary Ridge, prepared the way for Hood's destruction at Franklin and Nashville, and Sherman's "march to the sea."

Now came his work in Virginia, which is to be touched on, and then his Presidency for two terms. During much of this time he was said to be intemperate, but if true it made no difference in the results accomplished. Mr. Lincoln was thought to be looking up Grant's brand of whiskey for some of his other generals. This General's character made him very dear to his friends. He was always true and helpful to them, and possessed a certain directness and simplicity of action that was in itself most attractive.

General Grant's conduct toward our leader in the closing scenes at Appomattox and his vigorous defense of Lee when threatened by unprincipled and powerful Northern politicians are not likely to be forgotten by the Southern people. With the passing of time his fame as a great commander appears to be growing, and will probably still grow after careful study of his campaigns. Only once did I have the opportunity of meeting this remarkable man. It was during the "third term" plans of the Republican party that his friends were carrying him on visits to various parts of the country. He was in Savannah with Sheridan and others for a few days and was entertained at a handsome dinner-party, of some dozen or more leading gentlemen of the city, by General Henry R. Jackson, a wealthy and prominent Democratic citizen. He was himself a marked personality—a lawyer of eminence; had been Minister to Austria under Buchanan; was to be Minister to Mexico under Cleveland; was a poet and an orator, besides of the highest character, attainments, and social attractions. The dinner was a great success, served lavishly in the old Southern fashion, with various courses of wine, which the rough Sheridan brusquely put aside. "He wanted champagne, must have it at once." And he *did* have it from start to finish.

Grant was in excellent form, looked well and talked well; his glass was not touched. Fresh from his tour around the world he had much to say. He had been deeply interested in Japan and talked incisively of that wonderful country, really a monologue of a full hour, the table intent and absorbed in the fresh observations that fell from him. Then it became time for his departure to meet a public appointment, and we rose to bow him out. Resuming our seats and attention to the old Madeiras, we agreed that for a silent man Grant was about the most interesting one we had recently found. His talk was clean-cut, simple, direct, and clear.

The General-in-Chief made his headquarters near Culpeper. The Army of the Potomac was about 130,000 strong in aggregate, and consisted of Hancock's

Second Corps, Warren's Fifth, and Sedgwick's Sixth; besides Burnside's Ninth, held apart near Rappahannock railroad bridge. Lee's army lay west of the Rapidan, R. H. Anderson's division facing Madison Court House; the Second and Third Corps (Ewell's and Hill's), two divisions of the First, and Alexander's artillery were at Mechanicsville; Pickett's division of the First was south of the James. Our strength is stated by Colonel Taylor to have been 63,998.

We were at no loss to understand Grant's intention. The Northern papers, as well as himself, had boldly and brutally announced the purpose of "attrition"—that is, the Federals could stand the loss of four or five men to the Confederates' one, and threw nice strategy into the background. It was known that we were almost past recruiting our thin ranks, and the small figures of the army as it now stood; while the double numbers of the Federals could be reproduced from the immense resources in population, not to speak of their foreign field of supplies under inducement of liberal bounties.

Grant started his march the night of May 3d, via Germanna and Elys Fords, Wilson's and Gregg's cavalry leading. Burnside was also ordered to him.

The Wilderness was a wild, tangled forest of stunted trees, with in places impassable undergrowth, lying between Fredericksburg and Orange Court House, probably sixteen or seventeen miles square. Some farm clearings and a shanty or two for a few poor inhabitants might occasionally be seen. Two principal roads penetrated this repulsive district, the Orange Plank Road and the turnpike. The ground generally lay flat and level.

And now was to begin the last and greatest of the campaigns of the Army of Northern Virginia. The campaign of *attrition* on one side met and foiled by the fine flower of the ablest strategy on the other. It was Grant's stubborn perseverance, indifferent to the loss of life, against Lee's clear insight and incessant watchfulness. Our army always ready, ever fighting, was to hold the Federal forces from the Wilderness to the final break at Petersburg, from May to March, ten months of supreme effort, most exhaustive to a commander. Marshall Marmont says, "The attacking general has, to a large extent, command of the mind of his defensive opponents." It is doubtless true, but Lee often gave his mind necessary relief and chanced success by a sudden initiative against Grant. The latter would unexpectedly find part of his army attacked with swift energy and would get something for his mind to work on besides the control of Lee's.

Referring to the disparity of numbers, we did in truth want men. A little detail will show how we had to economize them. Until recently there had been small cavalry details at general headquarters and with corps and division chiefs.

These, however, were all sent back to serve with the regimental colors, and the courier service they had been doing taken up by assignments of men from the infantry ranks who could keep themselves mounted.

Six were allowed for corps headquarters, four for divisions, and two for brigades. Being picked men, the service was well performed; but the time was not far off when these able men had again to take up their muskets by their colors. Disabled fellows who could ride but did no marching were put at the important courier duties and did well! The enemy said we were robbing the cradle and the grave, and it was more or less true.

Maj.-Gen. J. B. Kershaw, a lawyer from South Carolina, was one of the most distinguished and efficient officers of the Virginia army. His service had been long and uninterrupted. Coming out with a fine South Carolina regiment among the first to be sent to Virginia, his abilities soon made him its colonel. He served long in that rank, his steady courage and military aptitude invariably showing handsomely in the arduous service of his regiment.

It was one of those forming the South Carolina Brigade of McLaws's division. Longstreet was quick to perceive Kershaw's merit and recommended him for promotion. It was sometime coming. But when he was brigadier-general and placed in command of the brigade he maintained his high reputation fully. In 1864 he was promoted to be major-general, and continuing his service with Longstreet's corps, his conduct and abilities were conspicuous until the very end of hostilities. General Kershaw was of most attractive appearance, soldierly and handsome, of medium size, well set up, light hair and moustache, with clean-cut, high-bred features.

Grant's movement was soon made known to Lee, and the latter prepared to strike. It was his way, he waited not for the blow; better give it, was a large part of his strategy. It was thought Grant could best be met by a stroke as he marched. The Second and Third Corps were ordered forward by the Plank Road. Our own two divisions, Field's and Kershaw's, the latter commanding in McLaws's place, and Alexander's batteries were near Gordonsville and ordered to move by the Plank Road to Parker's Store. The route was changed at General Longstreet's request, and he found a good guide in James Robinson, well known to our Quartermaster Taylor, who lived at Orange Court House. We were at Richard's shop at 5 p. m. on May 5th, Rosser's cavalry then being engaged at that point with part of Sheridan's; the latter moving off when we came up. The march had been twenty-eight miles, and there orders from the Commanding General were received for changing direction so as to unite with other troops on the Plank Road. Directions conforming were issued to resume march at midnight.

Both armies being now in quick motion, the collision was soon to come; indeed, had already come with Heth's and Wilcox's divisions, ending late that night after fierce battle. I make no attempt at detail of all Confederate and Union movements, but the great battle of the Wilderness is now to be fought and the important part in it taken by the First Army Corps briefly sketched.

Strange to say, the two divisions of our Third Corps, Heth's and Wilcox's, after their severe battle made no attempt at defensive field work or trenching when firing ceased that night. In explanation, it is said they expected to be withdrawn and consequently did no work nor replenished their ammunition. But Hancock, accomplished general that he was, suffered himself to fall into no such pit. He had his men at work all night strengthening his position, and was thus enjoying the soldier's high feeling of confidence; and then with the sun he let fly at the troops in front of him, apparently inviting attack with no ground defenses whatever. It was distressing to realize such failure in the field work, and the result came near a great disaster.

Longstreet had moved at 1 a.m., the march being difficult and slow in the dense forest by side tracks and deep furrowed roadways. At daylight he was on the Plank Road and in close touch with Lee when Hancock struck the two unprepared divisions. The situation when we came on the scene, that of May 6th, was appalling. Fugitives from the broken lines of the Third Corps were pouring back in disorder and it looked as if things were past mending. But not so to James Longstreet; never did his great qualities as a tenacious, fighting soldier shine forth in better light. He instantly took charge of the battle, and threw his two divisions across the Plank Road, Kershaw on the right, Field on the left. None but seasoned soldiers like the First Corps could have done even that much. I have always thought that in its entire splendid history the simple act of forming line in that dense undergrowth, under heavy fire and with the Third Corps men pushing to the rear through the ranks, was perhaps its greatest performance for steadiness and inflexible courage and discipline. Hill's men were prompt to collect and reform in our rear and soon were ready for better work. General Lee was under great excitement immediately on the left. He wanted to lead some of our troops into action, but the Texas brigade was about him and swore they would do nothing unless he retired. A confident message from Longstreet through Colonel Venable that his line would be restored within an hour also helped him to regain his calm; and then at it we went in earnest, on both sides of the road. Hancock's success had loosened his ranks somewhat, which helped us when we fell on him. It was a hard shock of battle by six of our brigades, three on each side of the road. No artillery came into play, the ground not being fit for it. The enemy's advance was checked, then wavered, and finally relinquished; our troops pushing forward into the recovered lines. Longstreet had redeemed his promise to his commander. Meantime sharp work had also been going on at the left by Lieutenant-General Ewell—the never sleeping Ewell—and the prospects were bright.

R. H. Anderson, with Hill's corps, had come up and reported to Longstreet, who posted part of it on the right. Latrobe, of our staff, had received painful wounds in the thigh and hand, in this fight, while pushing the men forward. It had taken several hours to achieve this and a slight pause in the activities of the armies occurred. Gen. M. L. Smith, an engineer from General Headquarters, had reported to Longstreet and examined the situation on our right, where he discovered the enemy's left somewhat exposed and inviting attack; and now came our turn. General Longstreet, calling me, said: "Colonel, there is a fine chance of a great attack by our right. If you will quickly get into those woods, some brigades will be found much scattered from the fight. Collect them and take charge. Form a good line and then move, your right pushed forward and turning as much as possible to the left. Hit hard when you start, but don't start until you have everything ready. I shall be waiting for your gun fire, and be on hand with fresh troops for further advance."

No greater opportunity could be given to an aspiring young staff officer, and I was quickly at work. The brigades of Anderson, Mahone, and Wofford were lined up in fair order and in touch with each other. It was difficult to assemble them in that horrid Wilderness, but in an hour we were ready. The word was given, and then with heavy firing and ringing yells we were upon Hancock's exposed left, the brigades being ably commanded by their respective officers. It was rolled back line after line. I was well mounted, and despite the tangled growth could keep with our troops in conspicuous sight of them, riding most of the charge with Mahone's men and the Eighteenth Virginia. Some correspondence will be found in the Appendix about it. A stand was attempted by a reserve line of Hancock's, but it was swept off its feet in the tumultuous rush of our troops, and finally we struck the Plank Road lower down. On the other side of it was Wadsworth's corps in disorder. (I had last seen him under flag of truce at Fredericksburg.) Though the old General was doing all possible to fight it, his men would not stay. A volley from our pursuing troops brought down the gallant New Yorker, killing both rider and horse.

There was still some life left in the General, and every care was given him by our surgeon. Before they could get to him, however, some of his valuables—watch, sword, glasses, etc.—had disappeared among the troops. One of the men came up with, "Here, Colonel, here's his map." It was a good general map of Virginia, and of use afterwards. We were then so disorganized by the chase through the woods that a halt was necessary to reform, and I hastened back to General Longstreet to press for fresh troops. There was no need with him. He had heard our guns, knew what was up, and was already marching, happy at the success, to finish it with the eager men at his heels.

There was quite a party of mounted officers and men riding with him—Generals Kershaw and Jenkins, the staff, and orderlies. Jenkins, always enthusiastic, had thrown his arm about my shoulder, with, "Sorrel, it was splendid; we shall smash them now." And turning back I was riding by Longstreet's side, my horse's head at his crupper, when firing broke out from our own men on the roadside in the dense tangle.

The Lieutenant-General was struck. He was a heavy man, with a very firm seat in the saddle, but he was actually lifted straight up and came down hard. Then the lead-torn coat, the orifice close to the right shoulder pointed to the passage of the heavy bullet of those days. His staff immediately dismounted him, at foot of a branching tree, bleeding profusely.

The shot had entered near the throat and he was almost choked with blood. Doctor Cullen, his medical director, was quickly on the spot. Even then the battle was in the leader's mind, and he sent word to Major-General Field to go straight on. He directed me to hasten to General Lee, report what had been accomplished, and urge him to continue the movement he was engaged on; the troops being all ready, success would surely follow, and Grant, he firmly believed, be driven back across the Rapidan. I rode immediately to General Lee, and did not again see my chief until his return to duty in October. The fatal firing that brought him down also killed General Jenkins, Captain Foley and several orderlies. Jenkins was a loss to the army—brave, ardent, experienced and highly trained, there was much to expect of him.

The firing began among some of the Virginia troops that had rushed the attack. Our detour was such that it was quite possible to expect the capture of prisoners, and when Longstreet's party was seen, followed by Jenkins's brigade and part of Kershaw's command, in the shaded light of the dense tangle, a shot or two went off, then more, and finally a strong fusilade. The officers of our party acted splendidly in the effort to avert confusion and stop the deadly firing. General Kershaw was conspicuous about it, and our signal officer, Captain

J. H. Manning, deliberately, calmly rode through the fire up to the Virginians, holding up his hands and making signs that we were friends. This happened between twelve and one o'clock. My report to General Lee was, as instructed, immediate. I found him greatly concerned by the wounding of Longstreet and his loss to the army. He was most minute in his inquiries and was pleased to praise the handling of the flank attack. Longstreet's message was given, but the General was not in sufficient touch with the actual position of the troops to proceed with it as our fallen chief would have been able to do; at least, I received that impression, because activity came to a stop for the moment. A new attack with stronger forces was settled on. It was to be made direct on the enemy's works, lower down the Plank Road, in the hope of dislodging him.

But meantime the foe was not idle. He had used the intervening hours in strengthening his position and making really formidable works across the road. When the Confederate troops assaulted them late in the afternoon they met with a costly repulse, and with this the principal operations on our part of the field ceased for the day; it was coming on dark.

William Tecumseh Sherman stands second only to Grant as a military savior of the Union. Grant's brilliant understudy is now on his own, commanding the Union Army after taking Atlanta. Sherman found himself in a situation where obedience to the rules of war threatened to rob him of his victory. Quickly sizing up his situation, Sherman plans to break those rules. Setting up his "March to the Sea," Sherman shows how professionals practice logistics while amateurs rely on tactics.

Excerpt from *Memoirs of General W. T. Sherman*

BY WILLIAM T. SHERMAN

Chapter XX.

Atlanta and After—Pursuit of Hood.

SEPTEMBER AND OCTOBER, 1864.

By the middle of September, matters and things had settled down in Atlanta, so that we felt perfectly at home. The telegraph and railroads were repaired, and we had uninterrupted communication to the rear. The trains arrived with regularity and dispatch, and brought us ample supplies. General Wheeler had been driven out of Middle Tennessee, escaping south across the Tennessee River at Bainbridge; and things looked as though we were to have a period of repose.

One day, two citizens, Messrs. Hill and Foster, came into our lines at Decatur, and were sent to my headquarters. They represented themselves as former members of Congress, and particular friends of my brother John Sherman; that Mr. Hill had a son killed in the rebel army as it fell back before us somewhere near Cassville, and they wanted to obtain the body, having learned from a comrade where it was buried. I gave them permission to go by rail to the rear, with a note to the commanding officer, General John E. Smith, at Cartersville, requiring him to furnish them an escort and an ambulance for the purpose. I invited them to take dinner with our mess, and we naturally ran into a general conversation about politics and the devastation and ruin caused by the war. They had seen a part of the country over which the army had passed, and could easily apply its measure of desolation to the remainder of the State, if necessity should compel us to go ahead.

Mr. Hill resided at Madison, on the main road to Augusta, and seemed to realize fully the danger; said that further resistance on the part of the South was madness, that he hoped Governor Brown, of Georgia, would so proclaim it, and withdraw his people from the rebellion, in pursuance of what was known as the policy of "separate State action." I told him, if he saw Governor Brown, to describe to him fully what he had seen, and to say that if he remained inert, I would be compelled to go ahead, devastating the State in its whole length and breadth; that there was no adequate force to stop us, etc.; but if he would issue his proclamation withdrawing his State troops from the armies of the Confederacy, I would spare the State, and in our passage across it confine the troops to the main roads, and would, moreover, pay for all the corn and food we needed. I also told Mr. Hill that he might, in my name, invite Governor Brown to visit Atlanta; that I would give him a safeguard, and that if he wanted to make a speech, I would guarantee him as full and respectable an audience as any he had ever spoken to. I believe that Mr. Hill, after reaching his home at Madison, went to Milledgeville, the capital of the State, and delivered the message to Governor Brown. I had also sent similar messages by Judge Wright of Rome, Georgia, and by Mr. King, of Marietta. On the 15th of September I telegraphed to General Halleck as follows:

> My report is done, and will be forwarded as soon as I get in a few more of the subordinate reports. I am awaiting a courier from General Grant. All well; the troops are in good, healthy camps, and supplies are coming forward finely. Governor Brown has disbanded his militia, to gather the corn and sorghum of the State. I have reason to believe that he and Stephens want to visit me, and have sent them a

hearty invitation. I will exchange two thousand prisoners with Hood, but no more.

Governor Brown's action at that time is fully explained by the following letter, since made public, which was then only known to us in part by hearsay:

EXECUTIVE DEPARTMENT,
MILLEDGEVILLE, GEORGIA, *SEPTEMBER* 10, 1864.

General J. B. Hood, *commanding Army of Tennessee.*
General: As the militia of the State were called out for the defense of Atlanta during the campaign against it, which has terminated by the fall of the city into the hands of the enemy, and as many of these left their homes without preparation (expecting to be gone but a few weeks), who have remained in service over three months (most of the time in the trenches), justice requires that they be permitted, while the enemy are preparing for the winter campaign, to return to their homes, and look for a time after important interests, and prepare themselves for such service as may be required when another campaign commences against other important points in the State. I therefore hereby withdraw said organization from your command. . . .

JOSEPH C. BROWN.

This militia had composed a division under command of Major General Gustavus W. Smith, and were thus dispersed to their homes, to gather the corn and sorghum, then ripe and ready for the harvesters.

On the 17th I received by telegraph from President Lincoln this dispatch:

WASHINGTON, D. C., *SEPTEMBER* 17, 1864—10 A.M.

Major-General Sherman:
I feel great interest in the subjects of your dispatch, mentioning corn and sorghum, and the contemplated visit to you.

A. LINCOLN, *PRESIDENT OF THE UNITED STATES.*

I replied at once:

HEADQUARTERS MILITARY DIVISION OF THE MISSISSIPPI,
IN THE FIELD, ATLANTA, GEORGIA, *SEPTEMBER 17*, 1864.

President Lincoln, *Washington, D. C.*:

I will keep the department fully advised of all developments connected with the subject in which you feel interested.

Mr. Wright, former member of Congress from Rome, Georgia, and Mr. King, of Marietta, are now going between Governor Brown and myself. I have said to them that some of the people of Georgia are engaged in rebellion, begun in error and perpetuated in pride, but that Georgia can now save herself from the devastations of war preparing for her, only by withdrawing her quota out of the Confederate Army, and aiding me to expel Hood from the borders of the State; in which event, instead of desolating the land as we progress, I will keep our men to the high-roads and commons, and pay for the corn and meat we need and take.

I am fully conscious of the delicate nature of such assertions, but it would be a magnificent stroke of policy if we could, without surrendering principle or a foot of ground, arouse the latent enmity of Georgia against Davis.

The people do not hesitate to say that Mr. Stephens was and is a Union man at heart; and they say that Davis will not trust him or let him have a share in his Government.

W. T. SHERMAN, *MAJOR-GENERAL.*

I have not the least doubt that Governor Brown, at that time, seriously entertained the proposition; but he hardly felt ready to act, and simply gave a furlough to the militia, and called a special session of the Legislature, to meet at Milledgeville, to take into consideration the critical condition of affairs in the State.

On the 20th of September Colonel Horace Porter arrived from General Grant, at City Point, bringing me the letter of September 12th, asking my general views as to what should next be done. He staid several days at Atlanta, and on his return carried back to Washington my full reports of the past campaign, and my letter of September 20th to General Grant in answer to his of the 12th.

About this time we detected signs of activity on the part of the enemy. On the 21st Hood shifted his army across from the Macon road, at Lovejoy's, to the West Point road, at Palmetto Station, and his cavalry appeared on the west side of the Chattahoochee, toward Powder Springs; thus, as it were, stepping aside, and opening wide the door for us to enter Central Georgia. I inferred, however, that his real purpose was to assume the offensive against our railroads, and on the 24th a heavy force of cavalry from Mississippi, under General Forrest, made its appearance at Athens, Alabama, and captured its garrison.

General Newton's division (of the Fourth Corps), and Corse's (of the Seventeenth), were sent back by rail, the former to Chattanooga, and the latter to Rome. On the 25th I telegraphed to General Halleck:

> Hood seems to be moving, as it were, to the Alabama line, leaving open the road to Macon, as also to Augusta; but his cavalry is busy on all our roads. A force, number estimated as high as eight thousand, are reported to have captured Athens, Alabama; and a regiment of three hundred and fifty men sent to its relief. I have sent Newton's division up to Chattanooga in cars, and will send another division to Rome. If I were sure that Savannah would soon be in our possession, I should be tempted to march for Milledgeville and Augusta; but I must first secure what I have. Jeff. Davis is at Macon.
>
> W. T. SHERMAN, *MAJOR-GENERAL.*

On the next day I telegraphed further that Jeff Davis was with Hood at Palmetto Station. One of our spies was there at the time, who came in the next night, and reported to me the substance of his speech to the soldiers. It was a repetition of those he had made at Columbia, South Carolina, and Macon, Georgia, on his way out, which I had seen in the newspapers. Davis seemed to be perfectly upset by the fall of Atlanta, and to have lost all sense and reason. He denounced General Jos. Johnston and Governor Brown as little better than traitors; attributed to them personally the many misfortunes which had befallen their cause, and informed the soldiers that now the tables were to be turned; that General Forrest was already on our roads in Middle Tennessee; and that Hood's army would soon be there. He asserted that the Yankee army would have to retreat or starve, and that the retreat would prove more disastrous than was that of Napoleon from Moscow. He promised his Tennessee and Kentucky soldiers that their feet should soon tread their "native soil," etc., etc. He made no concealment of these vainglorious boasts, and thus gave us the full key to his future designs. To be forewarned was to be forearmed, and I think we took full advantage of the occasion.

On the 26th I received this dispatch:

CITY POINT, VIRGINIA, *SEPTEMBER* 26, 1864—10 A.M.

Major-General Sherman, *Atlanta*:

It will be better to drive Forrest out of Middle Tennessee as a first step, and do any thing else you may feel your force sufficient for. When a movement is made on any part of the sea-coast, I will advise you. If Hood goes to the Alabama line, will it not be impossible for him to subsist his army?

U. S. GRANT, *LIEUTENANT-GENERAL.*

Answer:

HEADQUARTERS MILITARY DIVISION OF THE MISSISSIPPI, IN THE FIELD, ATLANTA, GEORGIA, *SEPTEMBER* 26, 1864.

General: I have your dispatch of to-day. I have already sent one division (Newton's) to Chattanooga, and another (Corse's) to Rome.

Our armies are much reduced, and if I send back any more, I will not be able to threaten Georgia much. There are men enough to the rear to whip Forrest, but they are necessarily scattered to defend the roads.

Can you expedite the sending to Nashville of the recruits that are in Indiana and Ohio? They could occupy the forts.

Hood is now on the West Point road, twenty-four miles south of this, and draws his supplies by that road. Jefferson Davis is there to-day, and superhuman efforts will be made to break my road.

Forrest is now lieutenant-general, and commands all the enemy's cavalry.

W. T. SHERMAN, *MAJOR-GENERAL.*

General Grant first thought I was in error in supposing that Jeff Davis was at Macon and Palmetto, but on the 27th I received a printed copy of his speech made at Macon on the 22d, which was so significant that I ordered it to be telegraphed entire as far as Louisville, to be sent thence by mail to Washington, and on the same day received this dispatch:

WASHINGTON, D.C., SEPTEMBER 27, 1864—9 A.M.

Major-General Sherman, *Atlanta:*
You say Jeff Davis is on a visit to General Hood. I judge that Brown and Stephens are the objects of his visit.

> A. LINCOLN, *PRESIDENT OF THE UNITED STATES.*

To which I replied:

HEADQUARTERS MILITARY DIVISION OF THE MISSISSIPPI,
IN THE FIELD, ATLANTA, GEORGIA, SEPTEMBER 28, 1864.

President Lincoln, *Washington, D.C.:*
I have positive knowledge that Mr. Davis made a speech at Macon, on the 22d, which I mailed to General Halleck yesterday. It was bitter against General Jos. Johnston and Governor Brown. The militia are on furlough. Brown is at Milledgeville, trying to get a Legislature to meet next month, but he is afraid to act unless in concert with other Governors. Judge Wright, of Rome, has been here, and Messrs. Hill and Nelson, former members of Congress, are here now, and will go to meet Wright at Rome, and then go back to Madison and Milledgeville.

Great efforts are being made to reënforce Hood's army, and to break up my railroads, and I should have at once a good reserve force at Nashville. It would have a bad effect, if I were forced to send back any considerable part of my army to guard roads, so as to weaken me to an extent that I could not act offensively if the occasion calls for it.

> W. T. SHERMAN, *MAJOR-GENERAL*

All this time Hood and I were carrying on the foregoing correspondence relating to the exchange of prisoners, the removal of the people from Atlanta, and the relief of our prisoners of war at Andersonville. Notwithstanding the severity of their imprisonment, some of these men escaped from Andersonville, and got to me at Atlanta. They described their sad condition: more than twenty-five thousand prisoners confined in a stockade designed for only ten thousand; debarred the privilege of gathering wood out of which to make huts; deprived of sufficient healthy food, and the little stream that ran through their prison-pen poisoned and polluted by the offal from their cooking and butchering houses above. On the 22d of September I wrote to General Hood, describing the condition of our men at Andersonville, purposely refraining from casting odium on him or his associates for the treatment of these men, but asking his consent for me to procure from our generous friends at the North the articles of clothing and comfort which they wanted, viz., under-clothing, soap, combs, scissors, etc.—all needed to keep them in health—and to send these stores with a train, and an officer to issue them. General Hood, on the 24th, promptly consented, and I telegraphed to my friend Mr. James E. Yeatman, Vice-President of the Sanitary Commission at St. Louis, to send us all the under-clothing and soap he could spare, specifying twelve hundred fine-tooth combs, and four hundred pairs of shears to cut hair. These articles indicate the plague that most afflicted our prisoners at Andersonville.

Mr. Yeatman promptly responded to my request, expressed the articles, but they did not reach Andersonville in time, for the prisoners were soon after removed; these supplies did, however, finally overtake them at Jacksonville, Florida, just before the war closed.

On the 28th I received from General Grant two dispatches:

CITY POINT, VIRGINIA, SEPTEMBER 27, 1864—8:30 A.M.

Major-General Sherman:
It is evident, from the tone of the Richmond press and from other sources of information, that the enemy intend making a desperate effort to drive you from where you are. I have directed all new troops from the West, and from the East too, if necessary, in case none are ready in the West, to be sent to you. If General Burbridge is not too far on his way to Abingdon, I think he had better be recalled and his surplus troops sent into Tennessee.

U. S. GRANT, *LIEUTENANT-GENERAL*.

CITY POINT, VIRGINIA, SEPTEMBER 27, 1864—10:30 A.M.

Major-General Sherman:
I have directed all recruits and new troops from all the Western States to be sent to Nashville, to receive their further orders from you. I was

mistaken about Jeff Davis being in Richmond on Thursday last. He was then on his way to Macon.

U. S. GRANT, *LIEUTENANT-GENERAL.*

Forrest having already made his appearance in Middle Tennessee, and Hood evidently edging off in that direction, satisfied me that the general movement against our roads had begun. I therefore determined to send General Thomas back to Chattanooga, with another division (Morgan's, of the Fourteenth Corps), to meet the danger in Tennessee. General Thomas went up on the 29th, and Morgan's division followed the same day, also by rail. And I telegraphed to General Halleck:

> I take it for granted that Forrest will cut our road, but think we can prevent him from making a serious lodgment. His cavalry will travel a hundred miles where ours will ten. I have sent two divisions up to Chattanooga and one to Rome, and General Thomas started to-day to drive Forrest out of Tennessee. Our roads should be watched from the rear, and I am glad that General Grant has ordered reserves to Nashville. I prefer for the future to make the movement on Milledgeville, Millen, and Savannah. Hood now rests twenty-four miles south, on the Chattahoochee, with his right on the West Point road. He is removing the iron of the Macon road. I can whip his infantry, but his cavalry is to be feared.

There was great difficulty in obtaining correct information about Hood's movements from Palmetto Station. I could not get spies to penetrate his camps, but on the 1st of October I was satisfied that the bulk of his infantry was at and across the Chattahoochee River, near Campbellton, and that his cavalry was on the west side, at Powder Springs. On that day I telegraphed to General Grant:

> Hood is evidently across the Chattahoochee, below Sweetwater. If he tries to get on our road, this side of the Etowah, I shall attack him; but if he goes to the Selma & Talladega road, why will it not do to leave Tennessee to the forces which Thomas has, and the reserves soon to come to Nashville, and for me to destroy Atlanta and march across Georgia to Savannah or Charleston, breaking roads and doing irreparable damage? We cannot remain on the defensive.

The Selma & Talladega road herein referred to was an unfinished railroad from Selma, Alabama, through Talladega, to Blue Mountain, a terminus sixty-five miles southwest of Rome and about fifteen miles southeast of Gadsden, where the rebel army could be supplied from the direction of Montgomery and Mobile, and from which point Hood could easily threaten Middle Tennessee. My first impression was, that Hood would make for that point; but by the 3d of October the indications were that he would strike our railroad nearer us, viz, about Kingston or Marietta.

Orders were at once made for the Twentieth Corps (Slocum's) to hold Atlanta and the bridges of the Chattahoochee, and the other corps were put in motion for Marietta.

The army had undergone many changes since the capture of Atlanta. General Schofield had gone to the rear, leaving General J. D. Cox in command of the Army of the Ohio (Twenty-third Corps). General Thomas, also, had been dispatched to Chattanooga, with Newton's division of the Fourth Corps and Morgan's of the Fourteenth Corps, leaving General D. S. Stanley, the senior major-general of the two corps of his Army of the Cumberland, remaining and available for this movement, viz., the Fourth and Fourteenth, commanded by himself and Major-General Jeff. C. Davis; and after General Dodge was wounded, his corps (the Sixteenth) had been broken up, and its two divisions were added to the Fifteenth and Seventeenth Corps, constituting the Army of the Tennessee, commanded by Major General O. O. Howard. Generals Logan and Blair had gone home to assist in the political canvass, leaving their corps, viz., the Fifteenth and Seventeenth, under the command of Major-Generals Osterhaus and T. E. G. Ransom.

These five corps were very much reduced in strength, by detachments and by discharges, so that for the purpose of fighting Hood I had only about sixty thousand infantry and artillery, with two small divisions of cavalry (Kilpatrick's and Garrard's). General Elliott was the chief of cavalry to the Army of the Cumberland, and was the senior officer of that arm of service present for duty with me.

We had strong railroad guards at Marietta and Kenesaw, Allatoona, Etowah Bridge, Kingston, Rome, Resaca, Dalton, Ringgold, and Chattanooga. All the important bridges were likewise protected by good block-houses, admirably constructed, and capable of a strong defense against cavalry or infantry; and at nearly all the regular railroad stations we had smaller detachments intrenched. I had little fear of the enemy's cavalry damaging our roads seriously, for they rarely made a break which could not be repaired in a few days; but it was absolutely necessary to keep General Hood's infantry off our main route of communication and supply. Forrest had with him in Middle Tennessee about eight thousand cavalry, and Hood's army was estimated at from thirty-five to forty thousand men, infantry and artillery, including Wheeler's cavalry, then about three thousand strong.

We crossed the Chattahoochee River during the 3d and 4th of October, rendezvoused at the old battle-field of Smyrna Camp, and the next day reached Marietta and Kenesaw. The telegraph-wires had been cut above Marietta, and learning that heavy masses of infantry, artillery, and cavalry, had been seen from Kenesaw (marching north), I inferred that Allatoona was their objective point; and on the 4th of October I signaled from Vining's Station to Kenesaw, and from Kenesaw to Allatoona, over the heads of the enemy, a message for General Corse, at Rome, to hurry back to the assistance of the garrison at Allatoona. Allatoona was held by a small brigade, commanded by Lieutenant-Colonel Tourtellotte, my present aide-de-camp. He had two small redoubts on either side of the railroad, overlooking the village of Allatoona, and the warehouses, in which were stored over a million rations of bread.

Reaching Kenesaw Mountain about 8 A.M. of October 5th (a beautiful day), I had a superb view of the vast panorama to the north and west. To the southwest, about Dallas, could be seen the smoke of camp-fires, indicating the presence of a large force of the enemy, and the whole line of railroad from Big Shanty up to Allatoona (full fifteen miles) was marked by the fires of the burning railroad. We could plainly see the smoke of battle about Allatoona, and hear the faint reverberation of the cannon.

From Kenesaw I ordered the Twenty-third Corps (General Cox) to march due west on the Burnt Hickory road, and to burn houses or piles of brush as it progressed, to indicate the head of column, hoping to interpose this corps between Hood's main army at Dallas and the detachment then assailing Allatoona. The rest of the army was directed straight for Allatoona, northwest, distant eighteen miles. The signal-officer on Kenesaw reported that since daylight he had failed to obtain any answer to his call for Allatoona; but, while I was with him, he caught a faint glimpse of the tell-tale flag through an embrasure, and after much time he made out these letters—"C.," "R.," "S.," "E.," "H.," "E.," "R.," and translated the message—"Corse is here." It was a source of great relief, for it gave me the first assurance that General Corse had received his orders, and that the place was adequately garrisoned.

I watched with painful suspense the indications of the battle raging there, and was dreadfully impatient at the slow progress of the relieving column, whose advance was marked by the smokes which were made according to orders, but about 2 P.M. I noticed with satisfaction that the smoke of battle about Allatoona grew less and less, and ceased altogether about 4 P.M. For a time I attributed this result to the effect of General Cox's march, but later in the afternoon the signal-flag announced the welcome tidings that the attack had been fairly repulsed, but that General Corse was wounded. The next day my aide, Colonel Dayton, received this characteristic dispatch:

ALLATOONA, GEORGIA, *OCTOBER* 6, 1864—2 P.M.

Captain L. M. Dayton, *Aide-de-Camp*:
I am short a cheek-bone and an ear, but am able to whip all h—l yet! My losses are very heavy. A force moving from Stilesboro' to Kingston gives me some anxiety. Tell me where Sherman is.
JOHN M. CORSE, *BRIGADIER-GENERAL.*

Inasmuch as the enemy had retreated southwest, and would probably next appear at Rome, I answered General Corse with orders to get back to Rome with his troops as quickly as possible.

General Corse's report of this fight at Allatoona is very full and graphic. It is dated Rome, October 27, 1864; recites the fact that he received his orders by signal to go to the assistance of Allatoona on the 4th, when he telegraphed to Kingston for cars, and a train of thirty empty cars was started for him, but about ten of them got off the track and caused delay. By 7 P.M. he had at Rome a train of twenty cars, which he loaded up with Colonel Rowett's brigade, and part of the Twelfth Illinois Infantry; started at 8 P.M., reached Allatoona (distant thirty-five miles) at 1 A.M. of the 5th, and sent the train back for more men; but the road was in bad order, and no more men came in time. He found Colonel Tourtel-lotte's garrison composed of eight hundred and ninety men; his re-enforcement was one thousand and fifty-four: total for the defense, nineteen hundred and forty-four. The outposts were already engaged, and as soon as daylight came he drew back the men from the village to the ridge on which the redoubts were built.

The enemy was composed of French's division of three brigades, variously reported from four to five thousand strong. This force gradually surrounded the place by 8 A.M., when General French sent in by flag of truce this note:

AROUND ALLATOONA, *OCTOBER* 5, 1864.

Commanding Officer, United States Forces, Allatoona:
I have placed the forces under my command in such positions that you are surrounded, and to avoid a needless effusion of blood I call on you to surrender your forces at once, and unconditionally.

Five minutes will be allowed you to decide. Should you accede to this, you will be treated in the most honorable manner as prisoners of war.

I have the honor to be, very respectfully yours,

S. G. FRENCH,
MAJOR-GENERAL COMMANDING FORCES
CONFEDERATE STATES.

General Corse answered immediately:

Headquarters Fourth Division Fifteenth Corps,
Allatoona, Georgia, 8:30 A.M., *October* 5, 1864.

MAJOR-GENERAL S. G. FRENCH, *CONFEDERATE STATES, ETC.:*
Your communication demanding surrender of my command I acknowledge receipt of, and respectfully reply that we are prepared for the "needless effusion of blood" whenever it is agreeable to you.

I am, very respectfully, your obedient servant,

JOHN M. CORSE,
BRIGADIER-GENERAL COMMANDING FORCES UNITED STATES.

Of course the attack began at once, coming from front, flank, and rear. There were two small redoubts, with slight parapets and ditches one on each side of the deep railroad-cut. These redoubts had been located by Colonel Poe, United States Engineers, at the time of our advance on Kenesaw, the previous June. Each redoubt overlooked the storehouses close by the railroad, and each could aid the other defensively by catching in flank the attacking force of the other. Our troops at first endeavored to hold some ground outside the redoubts, but were soon driven inside, when the enemy made repeated assaults, but were always driven back. About 11 A.M., Colonel Redfield, of the Thirty-ninth Iowa, was killed, and Colonel Rowett was wounded, but never ceased to fight and encourage his men.

Colonel Tourtellotte was shot through the hips, but continued to command. General Corse was at 1 P.M., shot across the face, the ball cutting his ear, which stunned him, but he continued to encourage his men and to give orders. The enemy (about 1.30 P.M. made a last and desperate effort to carry one of the redoubts, but was badly cut to pieces by the artillery and infantry fire from the other, when he began to draw off, leaving his dead and wounded on the ground.

Before finally withdrawing, General French converged a heavy fire of his cannon on the block-house at Allatoona Creek, about two miles from the depot, set it on fire, and captured its garrison, consisting of four officers and eighty-five men. By 4 P.M. he was in full retreat south, on the Dallas road, and got by before the head of General Cox's column had reached it; still several ambulances and stragglers were picked up by this command on that road. General Corse reported two hundred and thirty-one rebel dead, four hundred and eleven prisoners, three regimental colors, and eight hundred muskets captured.

Among the prisoners was a Brigadier-General Young, who thought that French's aggregate loss would reach two thousand. Colonel Tourtellotte says that, for days after General Corse had returned to Rome, his men found and buried at least a hundred more dead rebels, who had doubtless been wounded, and died in the woods near Allatoona. I know that when I reached Allatoona, on the 9th, I saw a good many dead men, which had been collected for burial.

Corse's entire loss, officially reported, was:

GARRISON.	KILLED.	WOUNDED.	MISSING.	TOTAL.
Officers	6	23	6	35
Men	136	330	206	672
Total	142	353	212	707

I esteemed this defense of Allatoona so handsome and important, that I made it the subject of a general order, viz., No. 86, of October 7, 1864:

> The general commanding avails himself of the opportunity, in the handsome defense made of Allatoona, to illustrate the most important principle in war, that fortified posts should be defended to the last, regardless of the relative numbers of the party attacking and attacked. . . . The thanks of this army are due and are hereby accorded to General Corse, Colonel Tourtellotte, Colonel Rowett, officers, and men, for their determined and gallant defense of Allatoona, and it is

made an example to illustrate the importance of preparing in time, and meeting the danger, when present, boldly, manfully, and well.

Commanders and garrisons of the posts along our railroad are hereby instructed that they must hold their posts to the last minute, sure that the time gained is valuable and necessary to their comrades at the front.

BY ORDER OF MAJOR-GENERAL W. T. SHERMAN,

L. M. DAYTON, *AIDE-DE-CAMP.*

The rebels had struck our railroad a heavy blow, burning every tie, bending the rails for eight miles, from Big Shanty to above Acworth, so that the estimate for repairs called for thirty-five thousand new ties, and six miles of iron. Ten thousand men were distributed along the break to replace the ties, and to prepare the road-bed, while the regular repair-party, under Colonel W. W. Wright, came down from Chattanooga with iron, spikes, etc., and in about seven days the road was all right again. It was by such acts of extraordinary energy that we discouraged our adversaries, for the rebel soldiers felt that it was a waste of labor for them to march hurriedly, on wide circuits, day and night, to burn a bridge and tear up a mile or so of track, when they knew that we could lay it back so quickly. They supposed that we had men and money without limit, and that we always kept on hand, distributed along the road, duplicates of every bridge and culvert of any importance.

A good story is told of one who was on Kenesaw Mountain during our advance in the previous June or July. A group of rebels lay in the shade of a tree, one hot day, overlooking our camps about Big Shanty. One soldier remarked to his fellows:

"Well, the Yanks will have to git up and git now, for I heard General Johnston himself say that General Wheeler had blown up *the tunnel* near Dalton, and that the Yanks would have to retreat, because they could get no more rations."

"Oh, hell!" said a listener, "don't you know that old Sherman carries a *duplicate* tunnel along?"

After the war was over, General Johnston inquired of me who was our chief railroad-engineer. When I told him that it was Colonel W. W. Wright, a civilian, he was much surprised, said that our feats of bridge-building and repairs of roads had excited his admiration; and he instanced the occasion at Kenesaw in June, when an officer from Wheeler's cavalry had reported to him in person that he had come from General Wheeler, who had made a bad break in our road about Tilton Station, which he said would take at least a fort-night to repair, and, while they were talking, a train was seen coming down the road, which had passed that very break, and had reached me at Big Shanty as soon as the fleet horseman had reached him (General Johnston) at Marietta!

I doubt whether the history of war can furnish more examples of skill and bravery than attended the defense of the railroad from Nashville to Atlanta during the year 1864.

In person I reached Allatoona on the 9th of October, still in doubt as to Hood's immediate intentions. Our cavalry could do little against his infantry in the rough and wooded country about Dallas, which masked the enemy's movements; but General Corse, at Rome, with Spencer's First Alabama Cavalry and a mounted regiment of Illinois Infantry, could feel the country south of Rome about Cedartown and Villa Rica; and reported the enemy to be in force at both places. On the 9th I telegraphed to General Thomas, at Nashville, as follows:

I came up here to relieve our road. The Twentieth Corps remains at Atlanta. Hood reached the road and broke it up between Big Shanty and Acworth. He attacked Allatoona, but was repulsed. We have plenty of bread and meat, but forage is scarce. I want to destroy all the road below Chattanooga, including Atlanta, and to make for the sea-coast. We cannot defend this long line of road.

And on the same day I telegraphed to General Grant, at City Point:

It will be a physical impossibility to protect the roads, now that Hood, Forrest, Wheeler, and the whole batch of devils, are turned loose without home or habitation. I think Hood's movements indicate a diversion to the end of the Selma & Talladega road, at Blue Mountain, about sixty miles southwest of Rome, from which he will threaten Kingston, Bridgeport, and Decatur, Alabama. I propose that we break up the railroad from Chattanooga forward, and that we strike out with our wagons for Milledgeville, Millen, and Savannah. Until we can repopulate Georgia, it is useless for us to occupy it; but the utter destruction of its roads, houses, and people, will cripple their military resources. By attempting to hold the roads, we will lose a thousand men each month, and will gain no result. I can make this march, and make Georgia howl! We have on hand over eight thousand head of cattle and three million rations of bread, but no corn. We can find plenty of forage in the interior of the State.

Meantime the rebel General Forrest had made a bold circuit in Middle Tennessee, avoiding all fortified points, and breaking up the railroad at several places; but, as usual, he did his work so hastily and carelessly that our engineers soon repaired the damage—then, retreating before General Rousseau, he left the State of Tennessee, crossing the river near Florence, Alabama, and got off unharmed.

On the 10th of October the enemy appeared south of the Etowah River at Rome, when I ordered all the armies to march to Kingston, rode myself to Cartersville with the Twenty-third Corps (General Cox), and telegraphed from there to General Thomas at Nashville:

> It looks to me as though Hood was bound for Tuscumbia. He is now crossing the Coosa River below Rome, looking west. Let me know if you can hold him with your forces now in Tennessee and the expected reënforcements, as, in that event, you know what I propose to do.
> I will be at Kingston to-morrow. I think Rome is strong enough to resist any attack, and the rivers are all high. If he turns up by Summerville, I will get in behind him.

And on the same day to General Grant, at City Point:

> Hood is now crossing the Coosa, twelve miles below Rome, bound west. If he passes over to the Mobile & Ohio Railroad, had I not better execute the plan of my letter sent you by Colonel Porter, and leave General Thomas, with the troops now in Tennessee, to defend the State? He will have an ample force when the reënforcements ordered reach Nashville.

I found General John E. Smith at Cartersville, and on the 11th rode on to Kingston, where I had telegraphic communications in all directions.

From General Corse, at Rome, I learned that Hood's army had disappeared, but in what direction he was still in doubt; and I was so strongly convinced of the wisdom of my proposition to change the whole tactics of the campaign, to leave Hood to General Thomas, and to march across Georgia for Savannah or Charleston, that I again telegraphed to General Grant:

> We cannot now remain on the defensive. With twenty-five thousand infantry and the bold cavalry he has, Hood can constantly break my road. I would infinitely prefer to make a wreck of the road and of the country from Chattanooga to Atlanta, including the latter city; send back all my wounded and unserviceable men, and with my effective army move through Georgia, smashing things to the sea. Hood may turn into Tennessee and Kentucky, but I believe he will be forced to follow me. Instead of being on the defensive, I will be on the offensive. Instead of my guessing at what he means to do, he will have to guess at my plans. The difference in war would be fully twenty-five per cent. I can make Savannah, Charleston, or the mouth of the Chattahoochee (Appalachicola). Answer quick, as I know we will not have the telegraph long.

I received no answer to this at the time, and the next day went on to Rome, where the news came that Hood had made his appearance at Resaca, and had demanded the surrender of the place, which was commanded by Colonel Weaver, reënforced by Brevet Brigadier-General Raum. General Hood had evidently marched with rapidity up the Chattooga Valley, by Summerville, Lafayette, Ship's Gap, and Snake-Creek Gap, and had with him his whole army, except a small force left behind to watch Rome. I ordered Resaca to be further reënforced by rail from Kingston, and ordered General Cox to make a bold reconnaissance down the Coosa Valley, which captured and brought into Rome some cavalrymen and a couple of field-guns, with their horses and men. At first I thought of interposing my whole army in the Chattooga Valley, so as to prevent Hood's escape south; but I saw at a glance that he did not mean to fight, and in that event, after damaging the road all he could, he would be likely to retreat eastward by Spring Place, which I did not want him to do; and, hearing from General Raum that he still held Resaca safe, and that General Edward McCook had also got there with some cavalry reënforcements, I turned all the heads of columns for Resaca, viz., General Cox's, from Rome; General Stanley's, from McGuire's; and General Howard's, from Kingston. We all reached Resaca during that night, and the next morning (13th) learned that Hood's whole army had passed up the valley toward Dalton, burning the railroad and doing all the damage possible.

On the 12th he had demanded the surrender of Resaca in the following letter:

HEADQUARTERS ARMY OF TENNESSEE,
IN THE FIELD, *OCTOBER* 12, 1864.

To the Officer commanding the United States Forces at Resaca, Georgia.

SIR: I demand the immediate and unconditional surrender of the post and garrison under your command, and, should this be acceded to, all white officers and soldiers will be parolled in a few days. If the place is carried by assault, no prisoners will be taken. Most respectfully, your obedient servant,

J. B. HOOD, *GENERAL.*

To this Colonel Weaver, then in command, replied:

HEADQUARTERS SECOND BRIGADE, THIRD DIVISION,
FIFTEENTH CORPS, RESACA, GEORGIA, *OCTOBER* 12, 1864.

To General J. B. Hood:

Your communication of this date just received. In reply, I have to state that I am somewhat surprised at the concluding paragraph, to the effect that, if the place is carried by assault, no prisoners will be taken. In my opinion I can hold this post. If you want it, come and take it.

I am, general, very respectfully, your most obedient servant,
CLARK R. WEAVER, *COMMANDING OFFICER.*

This brigade was very small, and as Hood's investment extended only from the Oostenaula, below the town, to the Connesauga above, he left open the approach from the south, which enabled General Raum and the cavalry of Generals McCook and Watkins to reënforce from Kingston. In fact, Hood, admonished by his losses at Allatoona, did not attempt an assault at all, but limited his attack to the above threat, and to some skirmishing, giving his attention chiefly to the destruction of the railroad, which he accomplished all the way up to Tunnel Hill, nearly twenty miles, capturing *en route* the regiment of black troops at Dalton (Johnson's Forty-fourth United States colored). On the 14th, I turned General Howard through Snake-Creek Gap, and sent General Stanley around by Tilton, with orders to cross the mountain to the west, so as to capture, if possible, the force left by the enemy in Snake-Creek Gap. We found this gap very badly obstructed by fallen timber, but got through that night, and the next day the main army was at Villanow. On the morning of the 16th, the leading division of General Howard's column, commanded by General Charles R. Woods, carried Ship's Gap, taking prisoners part of the Twenty-fourth South Carolina Regiment, which had been left there to hold us in check.

The best information there obtained located Hood's army at Lafayette, near which place I hoped to catch him and force him to battle; but, by the time we had got enough troops across the mountain at Ship's Gap, Hood had escaped down the valley of the Chattooga, and all we could do was to follow him as closely as possible. From Ship's Gap I dispatched couriers to Chattanooga, and received word back that General Schofield was there, endeavoring to coöperate with me but Hood had broken up the telegraph, and thus had prevented quick communication. General Schofield did not reach me till the army had got down to Gaylesville, about the 21st of October.

It was at Ship's Gap that a courier brought me the cipher message from General Halleck which intimated that the authorities in Washington were willing I should undertake the march across Georgia to the sea. The translated dispatch named "Horse-i-bar Sound" as the point where the fleet would await my arrival. After much time I construed it to mean, "Ossabaw Sound," below Savannah, which was correct.

On the 16th I telegraphed to General Thomas, at Nashville:

Send me Morgan's and Newton's old divisions. Reëstablish the road, and I will follow Hood wherever he may go. I think he will move to Blue Mountain. We can maintain our men and animals on the country.

General Thomas's reply was:

Nashville, *October* 17, 1864—10:30 a.m.

Major-General Sherman:
Your dispatch from Ship's Gap, 5 p.m. of the 16th, just received. Schofield, whom I placed in command of the two divisions (Wagner's and Morgan's), was to move up Lookout Valley this a.m. to intercept

Hood, should he be marching for Bridgeport. I will order him to join you with the two divisions, and will reconstruct the road as soon as possible. Will also reorganize the guards for posts and block-houses. . . . Mower and Wilson have arrived, and are on their way to join you. I hope you will adopt Grant's idea of turning Wilson loose, rather than undertake the plan of a march with the whole force through Georgia to the sea, inasmuch as General Grant cannot coöperate with you as at first arranged.

GEORGE H. THOMAS, *MAJOR-GENERAL*.

So it is clear that at that date neither General Grant nor General Thomas heartily favored my proposed plan of campaign. On the same day, I wrote to General Schofield at Chattanooga:

Hood is not at Dear Head Cove. We occupy Ship's Gap and Lafayette. Hood is moving south *via* Summerville, Alpine, and Gadsden. If he enters Tennessee, it will be to the west of Huntsville, but I think he has given up all such idea. I want the road repaired to Atlanta; the sick and wounded men sent north of the Tennessee; my army recomposed; and I will then make the interior of Georgia feel the weight of war. It is folly for us to be moving our armies on the reports of scouts and citizens. We must maintain the offensive. Your first move on Trenton and Valley Head was right—the move to defend Caperton's Ferry is wrong. Notify General Thomas of these my views. We must follow Hood till he is beyond the reach of mischief, and then resume the offensive.

The correspondence between me and the authorities at Washington, as well as with the several army commanders, given at length in the report of the Committee on the Conduct of the War, is full on all these points.

After striking our road at Dalton, Hood was compelled to go on to Chattanooga and Bridgeport, or to pass around by Decatur and abandon altogether his attempt to make us let go our hold of Atlanta by attacking our communications. It was clear to me that he had no intention to meet us in open battle, and the lightness and celerity of his army convinced me that I could not possibly catch him on a sternchase. We therefore quietly followed him down the Chattooga Valley to the neighborhood of Gadsden, but halted the main armies near the Coosa River, at the mouth of the Chattooga, drawing our supplies of corn and meat from the farms of that comparatively rich valley and of the neighborhood.

General Slocum, in Atlanta, had likewise sent out, under strong escort, large trains of wagons to the east, and brought back corn, bacon, and all kinds of provisions, so that Hood's efforts to cut off our supplies only reacted on his own people. So long as the railroads were in good order, our supplies came full and regular from the North; but when the enemy broke our railroads we were perfectly justified in stripping the inhabitants of all they had. I remember well the appeal of a very respectable farmer against our men driving away his fine flock of sheep. I explained to him that General Hood had broken our railroad; that we were a strong, hungry crowd, and needed plenty of food; that Uncle Sam was deeply interested in our continued health and would soon repair these roads, but meantime we must eat; we preferred Illinois beef, but mutton would have to answer. Poor fellow! I don't believe he was convinced of the wisdom or wit of my explanation. Very soon after reaching Lafayette we organized a line of supply from Chattanooga to Ringgold by rail, and thence by wagons to our camps about Gaylesville. Meantime, also, Hood had reached the neighborhood of Gadsden, and drew his supplies from the railroad at Blue Mountain.

On the 19th of October I telegraphed to General Halleck, at Washington:

Hood has retreated rapidly by all the roads leading south. Our advance columns are now at Alpine and Melville Post-Office. I shall pursue him as far as Gaylesville. The enemy will not venture toward Tennessee except around by Decatur. I propose to send the Fourth Corps back to General Thomas, and leave him, with that corps, the garrisons, and new troops, to defend the line of the Tennessee River; and with the rest I will push into the heart of Georgia and come out at Savannah, destroying all the railroads of the State. The break in our railroad at Big Shanty is almost repaired, and that about Dalton should be done in ten days. We find abundance of forage in the country.

On the same day I telegraphed to General L. C. Easton, chief-quartermaster, who had been absent on a visit to Missouri, but had got back to Chattanooga:

Go in person to superintend the repairs of the railroad, and make all orders in my name that will expedite its completion. I want it finished, to bring back from Atlanta to Chattanooga the sick and wounded men and surplus stores. On the 1st of November I want nothing in front of Chattanooga except what we can use as food and clothing and haul in our wagons. There is plenty of corn in the country, and we only want forage for the posts. I allow ten days for all this to be done, by which time I expect to be at or near Atlanta.

I telegraphed also to General Amos Beckwith, chief-commissary in Atlanta, who was acting as chief-quartermaster during the absence of General Easton:

Hood will escape me. I want to prepare for my big raid. On the 1st of November I want nothing in Atlanta but what is necessary for war. Send all trash to the rear at once, and have on hand thirty days' food and but little forage. I propose to abandon Atlanta, and the railroad back to Chattanooga, to sally forth to ruin Georgia and bring up on the seashore. Make all dispositions accordingly. I will go down the Coosa until I am sure that Hood has gone to Blue Mountain.

On the 21st of October I reached Gaylesville, had my bivouac in an open field back of the village, and remained there till the 28th. During that time General Schofield arrived, with the two divisions of Generals Wagner (formerly Newton's) and Morgan, which were returned to their respective corps (the Fourth and Fourteenth), and General Schofield resumed his own command of the Army of the Ohio, then on the Coosa River, near Cedar Bluff. General Joseph A. Mower also arrived, and was assigned to command a division in the Seventeenth Corps; and General J. H. Wilson came, having been sent from Virginia by General Grant, for the purpose of commanding all my cavalry. I first intended to organize this cavalry into a corps of three small divisions, to be commanded by General Wilson; but the horses were well run down, and, at Wilson's instance, I concluded to retain only one division of four thousand five hundred men, with selected horses, under General Kilpatrick, and to send General Wilson back with all the rest to Nashville, to be reorganized and to act under General Thomas in the defense of Tennessee. Orders to this effect were made on the 24th of October.

General Grant, in designating General Wilson to command my cavalry, predicted that he would, by his personal activity, increase the effect of that arm "fifty per cent.," and he advised that he should be sent south, to accomplish all that I had proposed to do with the main army; but I had not so much faith in cavalry as he had, and preferred to adhere to my original intention of going myself with a competent force.

About this time I learned that General Beauregard had reached Hood's army at Gadsden; that, without assuming direct command of that army, he had authority from the Confederate Government to direct all its movements, and to call to his assistance the whole strength of the South. His orders, on assuming command, were full of alarm and desperation, dated—

HEADQUARTERS MILITARY DIVISION OF THE WEST,
OCTOBER 17, 1864.

In assuming command, at this critical juncture, of the Military Division of the West, I appeal to my countrymen, of all classes and sections, for their generous support. In assigning me to this responsible position, the President of the Confederate States has extended to me the assurance of his earnest support. The Executives of your States meet me with similar expressions of their devotion to our cause. The noble army in the field, composed of brave men and gallant officers, are strangers to me, but I know they will do all that patriots can achieve. . . .

The army of Sherman still defiantly holds Atlanta. He can and must be driven from it. It is only for the good people of Georgia and surrounding States to speak the word, and the work is done. We have abundant provisions. There are men enough in the country, liable to and able for service, to accomplish the result. . . .

My countrymen, respond to this call as you have done in days that are past, and, with the blessing of a kind and overruling Providence, the enemy shall be driven from your soil. The security of your wives and daughters from the insults and outrages of a brutal foe shall be established soon, and be followed by a permanent and honorable peace. The claims of home and country, wife and children, uniting with the demands of honor and patriotism, summon us to the field. We cannot, dare not, will not fail to respond. Full of hope and confidence, I come to join you in your struggles, sharing your privations, and, with your brave and true men, to strike the blow that shall bring success to our arms, triumph to our cause, and peace to our country!

G. T. BEAUREGARD, *GENERAL.*

Notwithstanding this somewhat boastful order or appeal, General Beauregard did not actually accompany General Hood on his disastrous march to Nashville, but took post at Corinth, Mississippi, to control the movement of his supplies and to watch me.

At Gaylesville the pursuit of Hood by the army under my immediate command may be said to have ceased. During this pursuit, the Fifteenth Corps was commanded by its senior major-general present, P. J. Osterhaus, in the absence of General John A. Logan; and the Seventeenth Corps was commanded by Brigadier-General T. E. G. Ransom, the senior officer present, in the absence of General Frank P. Blair.

General Ransom was a young, most gallant, and promising officer, son of the Colonel Ransom who was killed at Chapultepec, in the Mexican War. He had served with the Army of the Tennessee in 1862 and 1863, at Vicksburg, where he was severely wounded. He was not well at the time we started from Atlanta, but he insisted on going along with his command. His symptoms became more aggravated on the march, and when we were encamped near Gaylesville, I visited him in company with Surgeon John Moore, United States Army, who said that the case was one of typhoid fever, which would likely prove fatal. A few days after, viz., the 28th, he was being carried on a litter toward Rome; and as I rode from Gaylesville to Rome, I passed him by the way, stopped, and spoke with him, but did not then suppose he was so near his end. The next day, however, his escort reached Rome, bearing his dead body. The officer in charge reported that, shortly after I had passed, his symptoms became so much worse that they stopped at a farm-house by the road-side, where he died that evening. His body was at once sent to Chicago for burial, and a monument has been ordered by the Society of the Army of the Tennessee to be erected in his memory.

On the 26th of October I learned that Hood's whole army had made its appearance about Decatur, Alabama, and at once caused a strong reconnoissance to be made down the Coosa to near Gadsden, which revealed the truth that the enemy was gone, except a small force of cavalry, commanded by General Wheeler, which had been left to watch us. I then finally resolved on my future course, which was to leave Hood to be encountered by General Thomas, while I should carry into full effect the long-contemplated project of marching for the sea-coast, and thence to operate toward Richmond. But it was all-important to me and to our cause that General Thomas should have an ample force, equal to any and every emergency.

He then had at Nashville about eight or ten thousand new troops, and as many more civil employés of the Quartermaster's Department, which were not suited for the field, but would be most useful in manning the excellent forts that already covered Nashville. At Chattanooga, he had General Steedman's division, about five thousand men, besides garrisons for Chattanooga, Bridgeport, and Stevenson; at Murfreesboro' he also had General Rousseau's division, which was full five thousand strong, independent of the necessary garrisons for the railroad. At Decatur and Huntsville, Alabama, was the infantry division of General R. S. Granger, estimated at four thousand; and near Florence, Alabama, watching the crossings of the Tennessee, were General Edward Hatch's division of cavalry, four thousand; General Croxton's brigade, twenty-five hundred; and Colonel Capron's brigade, twelve hundred; besides which, General J. H. Wilson had collected in Nashville about ten thousand dismounted cavalry, for which he was rapidly collecting the necessary horses for a remount. All these aggregated about forty-five thousand men. General A. J. Smith at that time was in Missouri, with the two divisions of the Sixteenth Corps which had been diverted to that quarter to assist General Rosecrans in driving the rebel General Price out of Missouri. This object had been accomplished, and these troops, numbering from eight to ten thousand, had been ordered to Nashville. To these I proposed at first to add only the Fourth Corps (General Stanley), fifteen thousand; and that corps was ordered from Gaylesville to march to Chattanooga, and thence report for orders to General Thomas; but subsequently, on the 30th of October, at Rome, Georgia, learning from General Thomas that the new troops promised by General Grant were coming forward very slowly, I concluded to further reënforce him by General Schofield's corps (Twenty-third), twelve thousand, which corps accordingly marched for Resaca, and there took the cars for Chattanooga. I then knew that General Thomas would have an ample force with which to encounter General Hood anywhere in the open field, besides garrisons to secure the railroad to his rear and as far forward as Chattanooga. And, moreover, I was more than convinced that he would have ample time for preparation; for, on that very day, General R. S. Granger had telegraphed me from Decatur, Alabama:

I omitted to mention another reason why Hood will go to Tuscumbia before crossing the Tennessee River. He was evidently out of supplies. His men were all grumbling; the first thing the prisoners asked for was something to eat. Hood could not get any thing if he should cross this side of Rogersville.

I knew that the country about Decatur and Tuscumbia, Alabama, was bare of provisions, and inferred that General Hood would have to draw his supplies, not only of food, but of stores, clothing, and ammunition, from Mobile, Montgomery, and Selma, Alabama, by the railroad around by Meridian and Corinth, Mississippi, which we had most effectually disabled the previous winter.

General Hood did not make a serious attack on Decatur, but hung around it from October 26th to the 30th, when he drew off and marched for a point on the south side of the Tennessee River, opposite Florence, where he was compelled to remain nearly a month, to collect the necessary supplies for his contemplated invasion of Tennessee and Kentucky.

The Fourth Corps (Stanley) had already reached Chattanooga, and had been transported by rail to Pulaski, Tennessee; and General Thomas ordered General Schofield, with the Twenty-third Corps, to Columbia, Tennessee, a place intermediate between Hood (then on the Tennessee River, opposite Florence) and Forrest, opposite Johnsonville.

On the 31st of October General Croxton, of the cavalry, reported that the enemy had crossed the Tennessee River four miles above Florence, and that he had endeavored to stop him, but without success. Still, I was convinced that Hood's army was in no condition to march for Nashville, and that a good deal of further delay might reasonably be counted on. I also rested with much confidence on the fact that the Tennessee River below Muscle Shoals was strongly patrolled by gunboats, and that the reach of the river above Muscle Shoals, from Decatur as high up as our railroad at Bridgeport, was also guarded by gunboats, so that Hood, to cross over, would be compelled to select a point inaccessible to these gunboats. He actually did choose such a place, at the old railroad-piers, four miles above Florence, Alabama, which is below Muscle Shoals and above Colbert Shoals.

On the 31st of October Forrest made his appearance on the Tennessee River opposite Johnsonville (whence a new railroad led to Nashville), and with his cavalry and field-pieces actually crippled and captured two gunboats with five of our transports, a feat of arms which, I confess, excited my admiration.

There is no doubt that the month of October closed to us looking decidedly squally; but, somehow, I was sustained in the belief that in a very few days the tide would turn.

On the 1st of November I telegraphed very fully to General Grant, at City Point, who must have been disturbed by the wild rumors that filled the country, and on the 2d of November received (at Rome) this dispatch:

CITY POINT, *NOVEMBER* 1, 1864—6 P.M.

Major-General Sherman:

Do you not think it advisable, now that Hood has gone so far north, to entirely ruin him before starting on your proposed campaign? With Hood's army destroyed, you can go where you please with impunity. I believed and still believe, if you had started south while Hood was in the neighborhood of you, he would have been forced to go after you. Now that he is far away he might look upon the chase as useless, and he will go in one direction while you are pushing in the other. If you can see a chance of destroying Hood's army, attend to that first, and make your other move secondary.

U. S. GRANT, *LIEUTENANT-GENERAL*.

My answer is dated—

ROME, GEORGIA, *NOVEMBER* 2, 1864.

Lieutenant-General U. S. Grant, City Point, *Virginia*:

Your dispatch is received. If I could hope to overhaul Hood, I would turn against him with my whole force; then he would retreat to the southwest, drawing me as a decoy away from Georgia, which is his chief object. If he ventures north of the Tennessee River, I may turn in that direction, and endeavor to get below him on his line of retreat; but thus far he has not gone above the Tennessee River. General Thomas will have a force strong enough to prevent his reaching any country in which we have an interest; and he has orders, if Hood turns to follow me, to push for Selma, Alabama. No single army can catch Hood, and I am convinced the best results will follow from our defeating Jeff. Davis's cherished plan of making me leave Georgia by manœuvring. Thus far I have confined my efforts to thwart this plan, and have reduced baggage so that I can pick up and start in any direction; but I regard the pursuit of Hood as useless. Still, if he attempts to invade Middle Tennessee, I will hold Decatur, and be prepared to move in that direction; but, unless I let go of Atlanta, my force will not be equal to his.

W. T. SHERMAN, *MAJOR-GENERAL*.

By this date, under the intelligent and energetic action of Colonel W. W. Wright, and with the labor of fifteen hundred men, the railroad break of fifteen miles about Dalton was repaired so far as to admit of the passage of cars, and I transferred my headquarters to Kingston as more central; and from that place, on the same day (November 2d), again telegraphed to General Grant.

KINGSTON, GEORGIA, *NOVEMBER* 2, 1864.

Lieutenant-General U.S. Grant, *City Point, Virginia*:
If I turn back, the whole effect of my campaign will be lost. By my movements I have thrown Beauregard (Hood) well to the west, and Thomas will have ample time and sufficient troops to hold him until the reinforcements from Missouri reach him. We have now ample supplies at Chattannooga and Atlanta, and can stand a month's interruption to our communications. I do not believe the Confederate army can reach our railroad-lines except by cavalry-raids, and Wilson will have cavalry enough to checkmate them. I am clearly of opinion that the best results will follow my contemplated movement through Georgia.
W. T. SHERMAN, MAJOR-GENERAL.

That same day I received, in answer to the Rome dispatch, the following:

CITY POINT, VIRGINIA, *NOVEMBER* 2, 1864—11:30 A.M.

Major-General Sherman:
Your dispatch of 9 A.M. yesterday is just received. I dispatched you the same date, advising that Hood's army, now that it had worked so far north, ought to be looked upon now as the "object." With the force, however, that you have left with General Thomas, he must be able to take care of Hood and destroy him.

I do not see that you can withdraw from where you are to follow Hood, without giving up all we have gained in territory. I say, then, go on as you propose.
U. S. GRANT, LIEUTENANT-GENERAL.

This was the first time that General Grant ordered the "march to the sea," and, although many of his warm friends and admirers insist that he was the author and projector of that march, and that I simply executed his plans, General Grant has never, in my opinion, thought so or said so. The truth is fully given in an original letter of President Lincoln, which I received at Savannah, Georgia, and have at this instant before me, every word of which is in his own familiar handwriting. It is dated—

WASHINGTON, DECEMBER 26, 1864.

When you were about leaving Atlanta for the Atlantic coast, I was anxious, if not fearful; but; feeling that you were the better judge, and remembering "nothing risked, nothing gained," I did not interfere. Now, the undertaking being a success, the honor is all yours; for I believe none of us went further than to acquiesce; and, taking the work of General Thomas into account, as it should be taken, it is indeed a great success. Not only does it afford the obvious and immediate military advantages, but, in showing to the world that your army could be divided, putting the stronger part to an important new service, and yet leaving enough to vanquish the old opposing force of the whole, Hood's army, it brings those who sat in darkness to see a great light. But what next? I suppose it will be safer if I leave General Grant and yourself to decide.

A. LINCOLN.

Of course, this judgment, made after the event, was extremely flattering and was all I ever expected, a recognition of the truth and of its importance. I have often been asked, by well-meaning friends, when the thought of that march first entered my mind. I knew that an army which had penetrated Georgia as far as Atlanta could not turn back. It must go ahead, but when, how, and where, depended on many considerations. As soon as Hood had shifted across from Lovejoy's to Palmetto, I saw the move in my "mind's eye;" and, after Jeff. Davis's speech at Palmetto, of September 26th, I was more positive in my conviction, but was in doubt as to the time and manner. When General Hood first struck our railroad above Marietta, we were not ready, and I was forced to watch his movements further, till he had "carromed" off to the west of Decatur. Then I was perfectly convinced, and had no longer a shadow of doubt. The only possible question was as to Thomas's strength and ability to meet Hood in the open field. I did not suppose that General Hood, though rash, would venture to attack fortified places like Allatoona, Resaca, Decatur, and Nashville;

but he did so, and in so doing he played into our hands perfectly.

On the 2d of November I was at Kingston, Georgia, and my four corps—the Fifteenth, Seventeenth, Fourteenth, and Twentieth—with one division of cavalry, were strung from Rome to Atlanta. Our railroads and telegraph had been repaired, and I deliberately prepared for the march to Savannah, distant three hundred miles from Atlanta. All the sick and wounded men had been sent back by rail to Chattanooga; all our wagon-trains had been carefully overhauled and loaded, so as to be ready to start on an hour's notice, and there was no serious enemy in our front.

General Hood remained still at Florence, Alabama, occupying both banks of the Tennessee River, busy in collecting shoes and clothing for his men, and the necessary ammunition and stores with which to invade Tennessee, most of which had to come from Mobile, Selma, and Montgomery, Alabama, over railroads that were still broken. Beauregard was at Corinth, hastening forward these necessary preparations.

General Thomas was at Nashville, with Wilson's dismounted cavalry and a mass of new troops and quartermaster's employés amply sufficient to defend the place. The Fourth and Twenty-third Corps, under Generals Stanley and Schofield, were posted at Pulaski, Tennessee, and the cavalry of Hatch, Croxton, and Capron, were about Florence, watching Hood. Smith's (A. J.) two divisions of the Sixteenth Corps were still in Missouri, but were reported as ready to embark at Lexington for the Cumberland River and Nashville. Of course, General Thomas saw that on him would likely fall the real blow, and was naturally anxious. He still kept Granger's division at Decatur, Rousseau's at Murfreesboro', and Steedman's at Chattanooga, with strong railroad guards at all the essential points intermediate, confident that by means of this very railroad he could make his concentration sooner than Hood could possibly march up from Florence.

Meantime, General F. P. Blair had rejoined his corps (Seventeenth), and we were receiving at Kingston recruits and returned furlough-men, distributing them to their proper companies. Paymasters had come down to pay off our men before their departure to a new sphere of action, and commissioners were also on hand from the several States to take the vote of our men in the presidential election then agitating the country.

On the 6th of November, at Kingston, I wrote and telegraphed to General Grant, reviewing the whole situation, gave him my full plan of action, stated that I was ready to march as soon as the election was over, and appointed November 10th as the day for starting. On the 8th I received this dispatch.

CITY POINT, VIRGINIA, *NOVEMBER 7,* 1864—10:30 P.M.

Major-General Sherman:

Your dispatch of this evening received. I see no present reason for changing your plan. Should any arise, you will see it, or if I do I will inform you. I think every thing here is favorable now. Great good fortune attend you! I believe you will be eminently successful, and, at worst, can only make a march less fruitful of results than hoped for.

U. S. GRANT, *LIEUTENANT-GENERAL.*

Meantime trains of cars were whirling by, carrying to the rear an immense amount of stores which had accumulated at Atlanta, and at the other stations along the railroad; and General Steedman had come down to Kingston, to take charge of the final evacuation and withdrawal of the several garrisons below Chattanooga.

On the 10th of November the movement may be said to have fairly begun. All the troops designed for the campaign were ordered to march for Atlanta, and General Corse, before evacuating his post at Rome, was ordered to burn all the mills, factories, etc., etc., that could be useful to the enemy, should he undertake to pursue us, or resume military possession of the country. This was done on the night of the 10th, and next day Corse reached Kingston. On the 11th General Thomas and I interchanged full dispatches. He had heard of the arrival of General A. J. Smith's two divisions at Paducah, which would surely reach Nashville much sooner than General Hood could possibly do from Florence, so that he was perfectly satisfied with his share of the army.

On the 12th, with a full staff, I started from Kingston for Atlanta; and about noon of that day we reached Cartersville, and sat on the edge of a porch to rest, when the telegraph operator, Mr. Van Valkenburg, or Eddy, got the wire down from the poles to his lap, in which he held a small pocket instrument. Calling "Chattanooga," he received this message from General Thomas, dated—

NASHVILLE, *NOVEMBER 12,* 1864—8:30 A.M.

Major-General Sherman:

Your dispatch of twelve o'clock last night is received. I have no fears that Beauregard can do us any harm now, and, if he attempts to follow you. I will follow him as far as possible. If he does not follow you, I will then thoroughly organize my troops, and believe I shall have men enough to ruin him unless he gets out of the way very rapidly.

The country of Middle Alabama, I learn, is teeming with supplies this year, which will be greatly to our advantage. I have no additional news to report from the direction of Florence.

I am now convinced that the greater part of Beauregard's army is near Florence and Tuscumbia, and that you will have at least a clear road before you for several days, and that your success will fully equal your expectations.

GEORGE H. THOMAS, *MAJOR-GENERAL*.

I answered simply: "Dispatch received—all right." About that instant of time, some of our men burnt a bridge, which severed the telegraph-wire, and all communication with the rear ceased thenceforth.

As we rode on toward Atlanta that night, I remember the railroad trains going to the rear with a furious speed; the engineers and the few men about the trains waving us an affectionate adieu. It surely was a strange event—two hostile armies marching in opposite directions, each in the full belief that it was achieving a final and conclusive result in a great war; and I was strongly inspired with the feeling that the movement on our part was a direct attack upon the rebel army and the rebel capital at Richmond, though a full thousand miles of hostile country intervened, and that, for better or worse, it would end the war.

Sometimes after the last shot is fired, the war does not end.

John Hood gives no quarter to history in his memoir, refighting the Atlanta campaign that Sherman had won. On paper, Hood can give Sherman a good thrashing, especially when it came to haggling over the terms of a humanitarian truce. Obviously, barbaric Yankees are not the equal of noble Southerners, who fight their wars according to the rules, so scribbled Hood. By winning his war of words, Hood proves that ink is cheaper than blood. But write as he might, Hood could not retake Atlanta, nor change the inevitable outcome.

To paraphrase Sherman, memoirs are hell.

Excerpt from *Advance and Retreat*

BY JOHN BELL HOOD

Chapter XIII.

Atlanta untenable—losses during the siege compared with those of Sherman, and with those of Johnston from Dalton to Atlanta.

Having stated that our position at Atlanta was untenable, I shall now undertake to give proof of the correctness of my opinion, by demonstrating in what manner Sherman might have captured the city in less than one-third of the time he actually devoted to that end, notwithstanding the idle assertion of General Johnston that he could have held Atlanta "forever"; also to demonstrate that had I ventured to remain longer than fifteen days within the trenches around the city, Sherman could have finally forced me to surrender, or have put my Army to rout in its attempt to escape; and, lastly, that he could have attained his object with one-fourth the loss he sustained during a siege of forty-six days, provided he had availed himself of the natural advantages afforded him.

The Federal commander chose well his crossing of the Chattahoochee, as he approached Atlanta, and the move of McPherson and Schofield upon the Augusta road was ably conceived and executed. Thomas, however, should not have formed line of battle along the lower part of Peach Tree creek with a view to cross the creek, as he endangered the safety of his Corps when he placed it in the angle, formed by this stream and the Chattahoochee, and thus isolated himself from Schofield and McPherson. His right should have rested in the vicinity of, and have covered, the ford nearest the mouth of Peach Tree creek, with a line of skirmishers extending to the Chattahoochee, and batteries in position at proper intervals in rear of this line, and likewise on the north side of the river, so as to thoroughly command the approaches to the railway bridge. His right being established at this ford, his left should have been thrown back north of Decatur, and his entire line strongly entrenched. From this position of perfect safety; he could have made constant demonstrations against the city, whilst McPherson and Schofield destroyed the road to Augusta. At the same time, by use of the batteries near the mouth of Peach Tree creek, and of those on the north bank of the river, near the railway bridge, he could have easily thrown a division across the creek, and have established a strong tête-de-pont on the south bank of the river. I would thus have been forced to form line of battle facing Peach Tree, with no possible chance of successfully assaulting the enemy at any point. His right and rear would have been covered by a deep and muddy stream; his front protected not only by breastworks, but also by one of the branches of Peach Tree creek. I could not have attacked either his left or McPherson and Schofield, without marching out of Atlanta, and exposing our left flank to Thomas. I would have been compelled to abide quietly the destruction of one of our principal roads, without the ability to strike a blow in its defence.

After my loss of the Augusta road, McPherson and Schofield should have marched by the right flank down Peach Tree, in rear of Thomas's line, until their right rested on the Chattahoochee, and then have halted. General Sherman having his Army thus massed, and well in hand, in rear of Peach Tree creek, should have thrown across the Chatahoochee a sufficient number of pontoon bridges to allow the easy and rapid passage of his troops; have sent two corps of Thomas's Army across and down the Chattahoochee, on the northwest side, to a favorable crossing just below Camp creek or one of the deep ravines or creeks, heading in the direction of East Point, and running toward the river upon the southwest side; have laid pontoons, crossed over, and strongly entrenched. Whilst this move was in progress, the main body should have made heavy demonstrations along the line of Peach Tree to the

Augusta road, which diversion would have held my Army in position on the north side of Atlanta.

The two corps below Camp creek having their line and outposts established sufficiently in advance to allow full space for the massing of the Army, Thomas should have left the division in the *tête-de-pont* protected by ditch and abatis, whilst another division, with dismounted cavalry, occupied his position on Peach Tree creek with cavalry on their left, and a few batteries to support their line; then have marched, at dusk, with the remainder of his Army to join the two corps below Camp creek, followed by Schofield and McPherson.

The transportation of the Federal Army having been previously parked on the north side of the Chattahoochee, General Sherman could with entire safety have massed his Army in the space of one night on the southeast side of the river, below this creek, as the two divisions left on Peach Tree had a secure place of refuge in the *tête-de-pont* in the event I had moved out in that direction.

These preparations completed, he should on the morning of the morrow have ordered the divisions and cavalry, along this stream, to make demonstrations against the city whilst Thomas pushed forward in the direction of East Point—changing front forward on his left—and formed line of battle with his left flank resting as high up on Camp creek* as it would afford protection against its being turned, and his right extending to or across the West Point Railway; have instructed Schofield and McPherson to move rapidly, as they had done upon Decatur and the Augusta road, to deploy on Thomas's right along the south bank of South river and east side of Shoal creek, with their right thrown back southeast of Decatur, and to entrench the whole line.

Such would have been the position of the Federal Army within twenty-four hours after it left Peach Tree creek, and within ten days after its first crossing of the Chattahoochee, subsequent to the operations about Kennesaw Mountain, provided it had moved with the rapidity usual with the Confederate Armies. Even had forty-eight hours been required to perfect this movement, Sherman could have so manœuvered as to have held the main body of my troops on Peach Tree until he was willing I should become apprised of his real purpose. In other words, he could without difficulty have entrenched south of Atlanta, before I could have received the necessary information to warrant a change of position from the north to the south side of the city. Moreover, had

---

*See Federals massed just below Camp creek, map, page 167.

I divined at an early instant his contemplated move, his position in rear of Peach Tree, and that of the two corps on Camp creek would—by demonstrations on the north and south sides of the city, with an Army double our own—have rendered it an easy matter to him to gain possession of Atlanta, in spite of every effort on my part.

General Sherman knew as well as I did, that every available man in the Confederacy had been sent either to General Lee, in Virginia, or to General Johnston, in the mountains; that, consequently, he had nothing to fear from the direction of Macon, and that one division would have sufficed to protect his rear, south of the city. When Grant marched round Pemberton at Vicksburg, and placed his rear in front of General Johnston, commanding an Army of twenty-five or thirty thousand men at Jackson, Mississippi, he executed successfully not only one of the boldest, but one of the grandest movements of the war. It will rank with one of the many similar moves of the immortal Jackson, and receive the tribute due to the talent and boldness which planned and achieved it. It was, however, fortunate for General Grant that a "Stonewall" was not at Jackson, Mississippi. No especial daring on the part of General Sherman would have been required to carry out the operations I have designated, since he had no enemy to fear in his rear. General Grant was reported, at this period, to have said that the Confederacy was but a shell.

As I have just remarked, I could not have received in time sufficiently reliable information to justify a change from the north to the south side of Atlanta, and to attack the Federals before they had thoroughly entrenched; it would have been equally impossible to assault later, with hope of success, his line, protected in front by works and abatis, on the left by Camp creek, and on the right by being thrown back and entrenched southeast of Decatur.

This position of the enemy would have necessitated the immediate abandonment of Atlanta or have shut up our Army in the pocket, or *cul de sac*, formed by the Chattahoochee river and Peach Tree creek, and finally have forced us to surrender. Had I attempted to extricate the Army, it would have been almost impossible to have pierced the enemy's works south, and utterly impossible, by reason of the proximity of the Federals, to have laid pontoons and crossed Peach Tree creek—as I would have done when Sherman was at the distance of Jonesboro', but from which I was hindered by the presence of the prisoners at Andersonville.

Sherman had simply to advance his right flank, in order to form a junction with the troops, near Decatur, and thus completely hem in our Army. This plan for the speedy capture of Atlanta could have been executed with an insignificant loss, as it would have been achieved mainly by manœuvre. In view of the impaired *morale* of the Army at the close of the Dalton-Atlanta campaign; the numerical inferiority of our forces; the fact, previously mentioned, that all available troops in the Confederacy, east of the Mississippi, had been sent either to the Army of Northern Virginia or to the Army of Tennessee, with the exception of small forces guarding the seaboard; in view of the proximity of the Chattahoochee river, which flows within five miles of Atlanta, along the foot of the general slope from the mountains of Georgia to the plains, forming with Peach Tree creek a complete *cul de sac*, in which Atlanta is situated; the advantages to be derived from Camp or any other creek in that vicinity, or from the deep ravines running to the river from the southwest side, behind which the Federal Army could have been rapidly deployed forward into line, with no enemy to fear from the rear; in which position Sherman could have readily supplied his Army from the nearest point on the railway north of the river, and have quietly awaited my surrender; in view, then, of the above enumerated sources of weakness and danger, I do not hesitate to challenge the military world to refute my assertions, not only as to the feasibility of the plan I have demonstrated, but also as to the untenability of Atlanta.

How long, I venture to inquire, is it probable that Sherman, after the capture of Jonesboro', would have tarried before occupying the identical position I have designated? The extraordinary haste I made to evacuate Atlanta, after the Federals gained possession of Jonesboro', on the Macon road, fifteen miles below the line from Camp creek to and along South river and Shoal creek, is proof of the great dread I entertained of a speedy occupation of this line. In lieu thereof, Sherman, during or immediately after the destruction of the Augusta road, threw Thomas across Peach Tree creek, into the *cul de sac* aforementioned, separated him from McPherson and Schofield, and subjected him to an assault by the main body of our Army, which should have resulted in the rout and capture of the greater portion of his Army. This move was, moreover, unnecessary, as it was impossible for him to invest Atlanta, approaching it from the north. He therefore consumed forty-six days in the achievement of results which might have been accomplished within a fortnight.

I have, from Dr. A. J. Foard, medical director of the Army, a statement of the total number of killed and wounded from July 18th to September 1st; in other words, from the day I assumed command to the evacuation of Atlanta. As I have already asserted, the number of men wounded in an Army which is standing its ground, and fighting, or is advancing, and driving the enemy, should not constitute an actual loss, and should only in part be comprised in the sum total of losses, since almost all the slightly wounded, proud of their scars, soon return to ranks. Therefore the only correct method of ascertaining the entire loss, during a siege or a campaign, is to deduct the number of effectives at the close of the siege, or campaign, from the number of effectives at the beginning of operations, after adding to the total strength the number of reinforcements, and deducting therefrom the number of troops permanently detached. This calculation should embrace the sick, and those who die from natural causes; losses under this head are, however, rarely of consequence during active operations. It is, as a generality, only when troops are lying in bivouac, or in quarters, that the ravages of disease are to be feared. Therefore, the fairness of this method can in no degree be affected by this minor fact.

Upon this broad and equitable basis, I herewith submit the official return of Colonel A. P. Mason, assistant adjutant general of the Army of Tennessee, showing its strength at different periods whilst under my command. As I desire to compare my strength and losses with Sherman's and Johnston's, I present, at the same time, Dr. Foard's official report of the killed and wounded; General Sherman's returns, showing his effective strength and estimate of losses; and the official statement of General Johnston's adjutant general, exhibiting the strength of the Army of Tennessee at different periods, during the campaign from Dalton to Atlanta.

STRENGTH OF THE ARMY OF TENNESSEE, ON THE 31ST OF JULY, 1864; 20TH SEPTEMBER, 1864; 6TH NOVEMBER, 1864; AND 10TH DECEMBER, 1864.

	JULY 31ST, 1864.				
	PRESENT.			ABSENT.	
	Effective.	Total.	Aggregate.	Total.	Aggregate.
Infantry	30,451	39,414	43,448	93,759	101,715
Cavalry	10,269	15,904	17,313	26,354	28,363
Artillery	3,775	4,610	4,840	6,317	6,606
Total Army	44,495	59,928	65,601	126,430	136,684

SEPTEMBER 20TH, 1864.

| | PRESENT. | | | ABSENT. | |
	Effective.	Total.	Aggregate.	Total.	Aggregate.
Infantry	27,094	36,301	39,962	81,824	89,030
Cavalry	10,543	15,978	17,416	27,005	29,215
Artillery	2,766	3,408	3,570	4,628	4,845
Total Army	40,403	55,687	60,948	113,457	123,090

NOVEMBER 6TH, 1864.

| | PRESENT. | | | ABSENT. | |
	Effective.	Total.	Aggregate.	Total.	Aggregate.
Infantry	25,889	34,559	38,119	79,997	87,016
Cavalry	2,306	3,258	3,532	4,778	5,148
Artillery	2,405	2,913	3,068	4,018	4,203
Total Army	30,600	40,730	44,719	88,793	96,367

DECEMBER 10TH, 1864.

| | PRESENT. | | | ABSENT. | |
	Effective.	Total.	Aggregate.	Total.	Aggregate.
Infantry	18,342	27,222	29,826	71,329	77,631
Cavalry	2,306	3,258	3,532	4,778	5,148
Artillery	2,405	2,913	3,068	4,018	4,203
*Total Army	23,053	33,393	36,426	80,125	86,982

"Respectfully submitted,

"A. P. MASON,

"LIEUTENANT COLONEL, A.A.G."

---

*It should be remembered that, in all estimates of the strength of Armies, the number of *effectives* is alone to be considered; therefore, the first column, in the foregoing return, is that to which reference should be made. Also, that of the forty thousand four hundred and three (40,403) effectives reported present for duty on the 20th September, forty-five hundred (4500) cavalry were absent with Wheeler, in Tennessee. This latter circumstance accounts for my statement, subsequently, that we had thirty-five thousand (35,000) effectives during the campaign to the Alabama line. It should, in addition, be observed that Wheeler's cavalry, ten thousand five hundred and forty-three (10,543) in number, as borne upon Colonel Mason's return, on the 20th September, was left in Georgia when we crossed the Tennessee, and was replaced by Forrest's cavalry, numbering altogether two thousand three hundred and six (2306) effectives. This large detachment will account for the reduction in the strength of our Army, at Palmetto and Florence, as will be seen later in my narrative of the campaign to the Alabama line, and thereafter into Tennessee.

"COLUMBUS, GEORGIA, *APRIL 3D, 1866.*

"Consolidated summaries in the Armies of Tennessee and Mississippi during the campaign commencing May 7th, 1864, at Dalton, Georgia, and ending after the engagement with the enemy at Jonesboro' and the evacuation of Atlanta, furnished for the information of General J. E. Johnston.

"CONSOLIDATED SUMMARY OF CASUALTIES OF THE ARMIES OF TENNESSEE AND MISSISSIPPI IN THE SERIES OF ENGAGEMENTS AROUND AND FROM DALTON, GEORGIA, TO THE ETOWAH RIVER, FOR THE PERIOD COMMENCING MAY THE 7TH, AND ENDING MAY 20TH, 1864:

CORPS.	KILLED.	WOUNDED.	TOTAL.
Hardee's	119	859	978
Hood's	283	1,564	1,847
Polk's Army, Mississippi	42	405	447
	444	2,828	3,372

"CONSOLIDATED SUMMARY OF CASUALTIES OF THE ARMIES OF TENNESSEE AND MISSISSIPPI IN THE SERIES OF ENGAGEMENTS AROUND NEW HOPE CHURCH, NEAR MARIETTA, GEORGIA:

CORPS.	KILLED.	WOUNDED.	TOTAL.
Hardee's	173	1,048	1,221
Hood's	103	679	782
Polk's Army, Mississippi	33	194	227
	309	1,921	2,230

"CONSOLIDATED SUMMARY OF CASUALTIES OF THE ARMIES OF TENNESSEE AND MISSISSIPPI IN THE SERIES OF ENGAGEMENTS AROUND MARIETTA, GEORGIA, FROM JUNE 4TH TO JULY 4TH, 1864:

CORPS.	KILLED.	WOUNDED.	TOTAL.
Hardee's	200	1,433	1,633
Hood's	140	1,121	1,261
Polk's Army, Mississippi	128	926	1,054
	468	3,480	3,948

"CONSOLIDATION OF THE ABOVE THREE REPORTS IS AS FOLLOWS:			
	KILLED.	WOUNDED.	TOTAL.
Dalton to Etowah river	444	2,828	3,272
New Hope Church	309	1,921	2,230
Around Marietta	468	3,480	3,948
	1,221	8,229	9,450

"CONSOLIDATED SUMMARY OF CASUALTIES OF THE ARMY OF TENNESSEE (ARMY OF MISSISSIPPI BEING MERGED INTO IT) IN THE SERIES OF ENGAGEMENTS AROUND ATLANTA, GEORGIA, COMMENCING JULY 4TH, AND ENDING JULY 31ST, 1864:

CORPS.	KILLED.	WOUNDED.	TOTAL.
Hardee's	523	2,774	3,297
Lee's	351	2,408	2,759
Stewart's	436	2,141	2,577
Wheeler's Cavalry	29	156	185
Engineers	2	21	23
	1,341	7,500	8,841

"CONSOLIDATED SUMMARY OF CASUALTIES IN ARMY OF TENNESSEE IN ENGAGEMENTS AROUND ATLANTA AND JONESBORO', FROM AUGUST 1ST TO SEPTEMBER 1ST, 1864:

CORPS.	KILLED.	WOUNDED.	TOTAL.
Hardee's	141	1,018	1,159
Lee's	248	1,631	1,879
Stewart's	93	574	667
	482	3,223	3,705

"CONSOLIDATION OF WHICH TWO REPORTS IS AS FOLLOWS:			
	KILLED.	WOUNDED.	TOTAL.
Around Atlanta, July 4th to July 31st, 1864	1,341	7,500	8,841
Atlanta and Jonesboro', Aug. 1st to Sept. 1st, 1864	482	3,223	3,705
	1,823	10,723	12,546

"I certify that the above reports are from the returns made to my office, and are in my opinion correct.

"(SIGNED) A. J. FOARD."

"MEDICAL DIRECTOR, LATE ARMY OF TENNESSEE."

"Note.—The Atlanta-Dalton campaign began on May 7th, and ended on the 1st of September, 1864, and the above reports are exact copies of those made to the Commanding General during its progress, and in the order in which they here appear.

"General Johnston commanded from the commencement of the campaign until the 18th of July, when he was relieved from duty, and General Hood assigned to the command of the Army. Hence the casualties of battle which occurred in the Army between the 4th and the 18th of July belong to the period of General Johnston's command, and are as follows: Killed. sixty-seven (67); wounded, four hundred and fifty-five (455); total, five hundred and twenty-two (522). These figures, added to the total of casualties as reported up to July 4th, viz., killed, twelve hundred and twenty-one (1221), wounded, eight thousand two hundred and twenty-nine (8229), total, nine thousand four hundred and fifty (9450), gives the entire losses (killed and wounded) in battle for the whole Army, while under the command of General Johnston, as follows, viz: killed, twelve hundred and eighty-eight (1288); wounded, eight thousand six hundred and eighty-four (8684); total, nine thousand nine hundred and seventy-two (9972). A deduction of the same, viz., killed, sixty-seven (67), wounded, four hundred and fifty-five (455), total, five hundred and twenty-two (522), from the total of casualties reported from July 4th to September 1st, viz., killed, eighteen hundred and twenty-three (1823), wounded, ten thousand seven hundred and twenty-three (10,723), total, twelve thousand five hundred and forty-six (12,546), gives of killed seventeen hundred and fifty-six (1756), wounded, ten thousand two hundred and sixty-seven (10,267); total, twelve thousand and twenty-three (12,023), as the entire losses in killed and wounded during that period of the campaign when the Army was commanded by General Hood, viz., from July the 18th to September 1st, 1864, when it ended, and the Army was then prepared for the campaign into Tennessee.

"(SIGNED) A. J. FOARD,
"MEDICAL DIRECTOR LATE ARMY OF TENNESSEE."

"On recapitulating the entire losses of each Army during the entire campaign, from May to September, inclusive, we have, in the Union Army, as per table appended:*

Killed 4,423
Wounded 22,822
Missing 4,442
Aggregate loss . . . . 31,687."

"Headquarters Military Division of the Mississippi,

"In the Field, Atlanta, Georgia, *September 15th, 1864.*

"Prisoners and deserters taken by 'Army in the Field,' Military Division of the Mississippi, during May, June, July, and August, 1864:†

Commands.	Prisoners.		Deserters.		
	Officers.	Men.	Officers.	Men.	Aggregate.
Army of the Cumberland	121	3,838	21	1,543	5,523
Army of the Tennessee	133	2,591	5	576	3,305
Army of the Ohio	16	781	1	292	1,090
Total	270	7,210	27	2,411	9,918

"Sherman's Forces.‡

"Recapitulation—Atlanta Campaign.

Arm.	June 1.	July 1.	August 1.	Sept 1.
Infantry	94,310	88,066	75,659	67,674
Cavalry	12,908	12,039	10,517	9,394
Artillery	5,601	5,945	5,499	4,690
Aggregate	112,819	106,050	91,675	81,758

---

*Sherman's Memoirs, page 132, vol. II.
†Sherman's Memoirs, vol, II. page 134.
‡Sherman's Memoirs, vol. II, page 136.

"NEAR GREENSBORO," NORTH CAROLINA,
"MAY 1, 1865.

"1. The 'effective strength' of the Army of Tennessee, as shown by the tri-monthly return of the 1st of May, 1864, was:*

Infantry. . . . . 37,652 } 40,464
Artillery . . . . 2,812 }
Cavalry 2,392

"This was the entire strength of the Army 'at and near Dalton' at that date.

"2. The movement from Dalton began on the 12th May. On that day Loring's Division, Army of Mississippi, and Cantry's Division, joined at Resaca, with about eight thousand (8000) effectives. French's Division, same Army, joined near Kingston several days later (about four thousand (4000) effectives). Quarles's brigade from Mobile (about twenty-two hundred (2200) effectives) joined at New Hope Church on the 26th. The cavalry of the Mississippi Army, which joined near Adairsville, was estimated at three thousand nine hundred (3900) effectives; and Martin's Cavalry Division, which joined near Resaca, at three thousand five hundred (3500). These were the only reinforcements received while General Johnston had command of the Army.

"3. There was no return (filed) of the Army made after May 1st, until June 10th. The return of June 10th gave, as effectives:

Infantry. . . . . 44,860 } 48,732
Artillery . . . . 3,872 }
Cavalry 10,516

"4. The next return was made on the 1st of July.

Effectives: Infantry. . . . . 39,197 } 42,666
          Artillery. . . . . 3,469 }
          Cavalry 10,023

"On the 3d of July, at Vining's Station, the Fifth and Forty-seventh Georgia Regiments (about six hundred (600) effectives) left the Army for Savannah, under Brigadier General J. K. Jackson.

"5. The next and last return made under General Johnston was on the 10th of July.

---

*Johnston's narrative, pages 574, 575.

Effectives: Infantry............................ 36,901⎱
            Artillery............................. 3,755⎰ 40,656

            Cavalry.............................. 9,971

                    (Exclusive of escorts serving with infantry.)

"This was the estimated force turned over by General Johnston to General Hood.

"6. The report was made under General Johnston, and signed by General Hood. On the 18th of July the command was turned over to General Hood. The first return thereafter was that of August 1st, after the engagements of Peach Tree creek, on the 21st, and around Atlanta, on the 22d and 28th July.

"7. The foregoing figures are taken from the official records kept by me as assistant adjutant general of the Army.

                    "(SIGNED) KINLOCH FALCONER,

                    "ASSISTANT ADJUTANT GENERAL."

I here reiterate that it is impossible General Johnston should have turned over to me fifty thousand six hundred and twenty-seven (50,627) effectives on the 18th of July (as shown in Colonel Falconer's report), for the reason that he had this number in full on the 10th of that month. When, according to this same report, we suffered a loss, over and above the killed and wounded, of four thousand and seventy-three (4073) men who abandoned their colors, and went either to their homes or to the enemy just prior to the retreat across the Chattahoochee river, it is not reasonable to assume that no desertions occurred from the 10th of July—the date of his last return—to the 18th, when a change of commanders took place in the face of the enemy, and under extraordinary circumstances. The supposition that many deserted during this interval is but just and natural. I am, therefore, confident that I am over-liberal in the estimate given—forty-eight thousand seven hundred and fifty (48,750) effectives—in my official report of the effective strength of the Army of Tennessee, when I assumed command. However, I will, in this instance grant, for the sake of argument, that my force on the 18th of July was fifty thousand six hundred and twenty-seven (50,627) effectives.

On the 20th of September, when stragglers had been gathered up, the effective strength of the Confederate Army, according to Colonel Mason's report, was forty thousand four hundred and three (40,403). This number, subtracted from fifty thousand six hundred and twenty-seven (50,627)—less thirty-one hundred

(3100) permanently detached to Macon and Mobile, about the beginning of the siege—shows a loss of seven thousand one hundred and twenty-four (7124), to which should be added two thousand prisoners returned to the ranks by exchange, soon after the fall of Atlanta, and before Colonel Mason made up his return on the 20th of September. These prisoners were overlooked by myself and my chief of staff at the time I made my official report, and increase the total loss, from all causes, to nine thousand one hundred and twenty-four (9124).

Whilst Dr. Foard's report of the killed and wounded is correct, the above estimate is beyond doubt equally accurate, since I received no reinforcements, during the siege, which were not sent back soon after their arrival, with the exception of about two hundred and fifty men of Gholsen's brigade (which small force I have not taken into account), as the following letter from General Shoupe will indicate:

"RICHMOND, *MARCH 10TH, 1865.*

"GENERAL HOOD:—You ask to what extent your Army was strengthened at Atlanta by the return of detailed men, and by dismounted cavalry ordered to you by General Bragg. I have the honor to state that so far as the detailed men are concerned, it was found necessary to return them to the arsenals and shops in rear, and that they were, as I believe, all so returned before the evacuation of Atlanta. Roddy's cavalry, upon the very day it reached Atlanta, was ordered back to Alabama. Gholsen's brigade remained at Atlanta until its evacuation. It was, however, very small—not numbering more than two hundred and fifty (250) men, and was in most miserable condition. So that the reinforcements, in truth, amounted to nothing.

"I have the honor to be very respectfully, etc.,

"F. A. SHOUPE,

"BRIGADIER GENERAL AND CHIEF OF STAFF AT ATLANTA."

Although the number of killed and wounded in the Army of Tennessee proper, during the siege, amounted to twelve thousand and twenty-three (12,023), the actual loss was nine thousand one hundred and twenty-four (9124); thus proving that near three thousand wounded returned to the ranks.

I shall now sum up the loss of the enemy during that same period.

*General Sherman reports his loss in killed, wounded, and missing, around Atlanta during July, August and September, to have been fifteen thousand and thirty-three (15,033). His actual loss during the siege must assuredly have been in excess of this number. In accordance with his recapitulation,† he had on the 1st of July an Army of one hundred and six thousand and seventy (106,070); on the 1st of August, ninety-one thousand six hundred and seventy-five (91,675); and on the 1st of September, eighty-one thousand seven hundred and fifty-eight (81,758), demonstrating an actual loss of twenty-four thousand three hundred and twelve (24,312) men within two months. This number, less the troops discharged or permanently detached, must be the real loss he sustained. I have not been able to glean from his statements the decrease of his Army from this latter source. I find, however, the following recorded in Shoupe's Diary on the 17th of August:

> Enemy's pickets called to ours, and stated that a Kentucky Division, twenty-two hundred (2200) strong, was going out of service, and that neither Old Abe nor Uncle Jeff would get them in service again.

Taking his own statements as a basis of calculation, and assuming the correctness of the report by the picket relative to the discharge of twenty-two hundred (2200) Kentuckians thirteen days prior to the fall of Atlanta, his actual losses (provided he did not during the siege receive reinforcements, of which I can find no mention in his Memoirs), prove to have been twenty-four thousand three hundred and twelve (24,312), plus nineteen hundred and two (1902) killed and wounded early in September, minus twenty-two hundred (2200) discharged; showing an actual loss of twenty-four thousand and fourteen (24,014) effectives against my loss of nine thousand one hundred and twenty-four (9124), although every aggressive movement of importance was initiated by the Confederates.

On the other hand, and according to my opponent's statement,‡ General Sherman had, after Blair's Corps joined him near Rome, a force of one hundred and twelve thousand eight hundred and nineteen (112,819) effectives to oppose General Johnston; and at the close of his victorious march from Dalton to

---

*Sherman's Memoirs, vol. II, page 133.
†Sherman's Memoirs, vol. II, page 136.
‡Sherman's Memoirs, vol. II, page 136.

Atlanta, one hundred and six thousand and seventy (106,070) effectives, which subtracted from the total number one hundred and twelve thousand eight hundred and nineteen (112, 819) in the field, at the beginning of the campaign, demonstrates an actual loss of only six thousand seven hundred and forty-nine (6749) against General Johnston's loss of twenty-five thousand (25,000) men.

This comparison of losses under opposite modes of handling troops, evinces the truth of the principle for which I contend: that losses are always comparatively small in an Army which drives before it the enemy day after day, as in the instance of the Federal Army during the Dalton-Atlanta campaign; or in an Army which holds its ground, as in the instance of the siege of Atlanta when the Federal loss was greatly in excess of our own, by reason of the enthusiasm and self-reliance of the Northern troops having, in the sudden check given to their sweeping career of victory, been somewhat counteracted by depression, consequent desertion, and the tardy return of absentees.

Chapter XIV.

Correspondence with Sherman—citations on the rules of war.

About the time I exchanged with General Sherman the two thousand (2000) prisoners above mentioned, the following correspondence passed between us, in relation to his treatment of the non-combatants of Atlanta:

"HEADQUARTERS MILITARY DIVISION OF THE MISSISSIPPI,
"IN THE FIELD, ATLANTA, GEORGIA, *SEPTEMBER 7TH, 1864.*

"General Hood, *Commanding Confederate Army.*
"General:—I have deemed it to the interest of the United States that the citizens now residing in Atlanta should remove, those who prefer it to go South, and the rest North. For the latter I can provide food and transportation to points of their election in Tennessee, Kentucky, or further North. For the former I can provide transportation by cars as far as Rough and Ready, and also wagons; but, that their removal may be made with as little discomfort as possible, it will be necessary for you to help the families from Rough and Ready to the cars at Love-

joy's. If you consent, I will undertake to remove all the families in Atlanta who prefer to go South to Rough and Ready, with all their moveable effects, viz., clothing, trunks, reasonable furniture, bedding, etc., with their servants, white and black, with the proviso that no force shall be used toward the blacks, one way or another. If they want to go with their masters or mistresses, they may do so; otherwise they will be sent away unless they be men, when they may be employed by our quarter-master.

Atlanta is no place for families or non-combatants, and I have no desire to send them North if you will assist in conveying them South. If this proposition meets your views, I will consent to a truce in the neighborhood of Rough and Ready, stipulating that any wagons, horses, animals, or persons sent there for the purposes herein stated, shall in no manner be harmed or molested; you in your turn agreeing that any cars, wagons, or carriages, persons or animals sent to the same point, shall not be interfered with. Each of us might send a guard of, say one hundred (100) men, to maintain order; and limit the truce to, say, two days after a certain time appointed.

"I have authorized the Mayor to choose two citizens to convey to you this letter, with such documents as the Mayor may forward in explanation and shall await your reply.

"I have the honor to be your obedient servant,

"W. T. SHERMAN,

"MAJOR GENERAL COMMANDING."

"HEADQUARTERS ARMY OF TENNESSEE,
"OFFICE CHIEF OF STAFF, *SEPTEMBER 9TH, 1864.*

"Major General W. T. Sherman, *Commanding United States Forces in Georgia.*
"General:—Your letter of yesterday's date, borne by James M. Ball and James R. Crew, citizens of Atlanta, is received. You say therein, 'I deem it to be to the interest of the United States that the citizens now residing in Atlanta should remove,' etc.

"I do not consider that I have any alternative in this matter. I therefore accept your proposition to declare a truce of two days, or such time as may be necessary to accomplish the purpose mentioned, and shall render all assistance in my power to expedite the transportation of citizens in this direction. I suggest that a staff officer be appointed by you to superintend the removal from the city to Rough and Ready, while I appoint a like officer to control their removal further South; that a guard of one hundred men be sent by either party as you propose, to maintain order at the place, and that the removal begin on Monday next.

"And now, sir, permit me to say that the unprecedented measure you propose transcends, in studied and ingenious cruelty, all acts ever before brought to my attention in the dark history of war.

"In the name of God and humanity, I protest, believing that you will find that you are expelling from their homes and firesides the wives and children of a brave people.

"I am, General, very respectfully, your obedient servant,

"J. B. HOOD, *GENERAL*."

"HEADQUARTERS MILITARY DIVISION OF THE MISSISSIPPI,
"IN THE FIELD, ATLANTA, GEORGIA, *SEPTEMBER 10TH, 1864.*

"General J. B. Hood, *Commanding Army of Tennessee, Confederate Army.*
"General:—I have the honor to acknowledge the receipt of your letter of this date, at the hands of Messrs. Ball and Crew, consenting to the arrangements I had proposed to facilitate the removal South of the people of Atlanta, who prefer to go in that direction. I enclose you a copy of my orders, which will, I am satisfied, accomplish my purpose perfectly.

"You style the measures proposed 'unprecedented,' and appeal to the dark history of war for a parallel, as an act of 'studied and ingenious cruelty.' It is not unprecedented; for General Johnston himself very wisely and properly removed the families all the way from Dalton down, and I see no reason why Atlanta should be excepted. Nor is it necessary to appeal to the dark history of war, when recent and modern examples are so handy. You yourself burned dwelling houses along your parapet, and I have seen to-day fifty houses that you have rendered uninhabitable because they stood in the way of your forts and men. You defended Atlanta on a line so close to town that every cannon shot and many musket shots from our line of investment, that overshot their mark, went into the habitations of women and children. General Hardee did the same at Jonesboro', and General Johnston did the same, last summer, at Jackson, Mississippi. I have not accused you of heartless cruelty, but merely instance these cases of very recent occurrence, and could go on and enumerate hundreds of others, and challenge any fair man to judge which of us has the heart of pity for the families of a 'brave people.'

"I say it is kindness to these families of Atlanta to remove them now, at once, from scenes that women and children should not be exposed to, and the 'brave people' should scorn to commit their wives and children to the rude barbarians who thus, as you say, violate the laws of war, as illustrated in the pages of its dark history.

"In the name of common sense, I ask you not to appeal to a just God in such a sacrilegious manner. You who, in the midst of peace and prosperity, have plunged a nation into war—dark and cruel war— who dared and badgered us to battle, insulted our flag, seized our arsenals and forts that were left in the honorable custody of peaceful ordnance sergeants, seized and made 'prisoners of war' the very garrisons sent to protect your people against negroes and Indians, long before any overt act was committed by the (to you) hated Lincoln Government; tried to force Kentucky and Missouri into rebellion, spite of themselves; falsified the vote of Louisiana; turned loose your privateers to plunder unarmed ships; expelled Union families by the thousands, burned their houses, and declared, by an act of your Congress, the confiscation of all debts due Northern men for goods had and received! Talk thus to the marines, but not to me, who have seen these things, and who will this day make as much sacrifice for the peace and honor of the South as the best born Southerner among you! If we must be enemies, let us be men, and fight it out as we propose to do and not deal in such hypocritical appeals to God and humanity. God will judge us in due time, and he will pronounce whether it be more humane to fight with a town full of women and the families of a brave people at our back, or to remove them in time to places of safety among their own friends and people.

"I am, very respectfully, your obedient servant,

W. T. SHERMAN,
"MAJOR GENERAL COMMANDING."

"HEADQUARTERS ARMY OF TENNESSEE,
"*SEPTEMBER 12TH, 1864.*

"Major General W. T. Sherman, *Commanding Military Division of the Mississippi.*

"General:—I have the honor to acknowledge the receipt of your letter of the 9th inst., with its inclosure in reference to the women, children, and others, whom you have thought proper to expel from their homes in the city of Atlanta. Had you seen proper to let the matter rest there, I would gladly have allowed your letter to close this correspondence, and, without your expressing it in words, would have been willing to believe that, while 'the interests of the United States,' in your opinion, compelled you to an act of barbarous cruelty, you regretted the necessity, and we would have dropped the subject; but you have chosen to indulge in statements which I feel compelled to notice, at least so far as to signify my dissent, and not allow silence in regard to them to be construed as acquiescence.

"I see nothing in your communication which induces me to modify the language of condemnation with which I characterized your order. It but strengthens me in the opinion that it stands 'pre-eminent in the dark history of war for studied and ingenious cruelty.' Your original order was stripped of all pretences; you announced the edict for the sole reason that it was to the interest of the United States. This alone you offered to us and the civilized world as an all-sufficient reason for disregarding the laws of God and man. 'You say that General Johnston himself very wisely and properly removed the families all the way from Dalton down.' It is due to that gallant soldier and gentleman to say that no act of his distinguished career gives the least color to your unfounded aspersions upon his conduct. He depopulated no villages, nor towns, nor cities, either friendly or hostile. He offered and extended friendly aid to his unfortunate fellow-citizens who desired to flee from your fraternal embraces. You are equally unfortunate in your attempt to find a justification for this act of cruelty, either in the defence of Jonesboro', by General Hardee, or of Atlanta, by myself. General Hardee defended his position in front of Jonesboro' at the expense of injury to the houses; an ordinary, proper, and justifiable act of war. I defended Atlanta at the same risk and cost. If there was any fault in either case, it was your own, in not giving notice, especially in the case of Atlanta, of your purpose to shell the town, which is usual in war among civilized nations. No inhabitant was expelled from his home and fireside by the orders of General Hardee or myself, and therefore your recent order can find no support from the conduct of either of us. I feel no other emotion other than pain in reading that portion of your letter which attempts to justify your shelling Atlanta, without notice, under pretence that I defended Atlanta upon a line so close to town that every cannon shot, and many musket balls from your line of investment, that overshot their mark, went into the habitations of women and children. I made no complaint of your firing into Atlanta in any way you thought proper. I make none now, but there are a hundred thousand witnesses that you fired into the habitations of women and children for weeks, firing far above and miles beyond my line of defence. I have too good an opinion, founded both upon observation and experience, of the skill of your artillerists, to credit the insinuation that they for several weeks unintentionally fired too high for my modest fieldworks, and slaughtered women and children by accident and want of skill.

"The residue of your letter is rather discussion. It opens a wide field for the discussion of questions which I do not feel are committed to me. I am only a General of one of the Armies of the Confederate States, charged with military operations in the field, under the direction of my superior officers, and I am not called upon to discuss with you the causes of the present war, or the political questions which led to or resulted from it. These grave and important questions have been committed to far abler hands than mine, and I shall only refer to them so far as to repel any unjust conclusion which might be drawn from my silence. You charge my country with 'daring and badgering you to battle.' The truth is, we sent commissioners to you, respectfully offering a peaceful separation, before the first gun was fired on either side. You say we insulted your flag. The truth is, we fired upon it, and those who fought under it, when you came to our doors upon the mission of subjugation. You say we seized upon your forts and arsenals, and made prisoners of the garrisons sent to protect us against Indians and negroes. The truth is, we, by force of arms, drove out insolent intruders and took possession of our own forts and arsenals, to resist your claims to do minion over masters, slaves, and Indians, all of *whom* are to this day, with a unanimity unexampled in the history of the world, warring against your attempts to become their masters. You say that we tried to force Kentucky and Missouri into rebellion in spite of themselves. The truth is, my Government, from the beginning of this struggle to this hour, has again and again offered, before the whole world, to leave it to the unbiassed will of these States, and all others, to determine for themselves whether they will cast their destiny with your Government or ours; and your Government has resisted this fundamental principle of free institutions with the bayonet and labors daily, by force and fraud, to fasten its hateful tyranny upon the unfortunate freemen of these States. You say we falsified the vote of Louisiana. The truth is, Louisiana not only separated herself from your Government by nearly a unanimous vote of her people, but has vindicated the act upon every battle-field from Gettysburg to the Sabine, and has exhibited an heroic devotion to her decision, which challenges the admiration and respect of every man capable of feeling sympathy for the oppressed or admiration for heroic valor. You say that we turned loose pirates to plunder your unarmed ships. The truth is, when you robbed us of our part of the Navy, we built and bought a few vessels, hoisted the flag of our country, and swept the seas, in defiance of your Navy, around the whole circumference of the globe. You say we have expelled Union families by thousands. The truth is, not a single family has been expelled from the Confederate States, that I am aware of; but, on the contrary, the moderation of our Government towards traitors has been a fruitful theme of denunciation by its enemies and well meaning friends of our cause. You say my Government, by acts of Congress, has confiscated 'all debts due Northern men for goods sold and delivered.' The truth is, our Congress gave due and ample time to your merchants and traders to depart from our shores with their ships, goods, and effects, and only sequestrated the property of our enemies in retaliation for their acts—declaring us traitors, and confiscating our property wherever their power extended, either in their country or our own. Such are your accusations, and such are the facts known of all men to be true.

"You order into exile the whole population of a city; drive men, women, and children from their homes at the point of the bayonet, under the plea that it is to the interest of your Government, and on the claim that it is an act of 'kindness to these families of Atlanta.' Butler only banished from New Orleans the registered enemies of his Government, and acknowledged that he did it as a punishment. You issue a sweeping edict, covering all the inhabitants of a city, and add insult to the injury heaped upon the defenceless by assuming that you have done them a kindness. This you follow by the assertion that you 'will make as much sacrifice for the peace and honor of the South as the best born Southerner.' And, because I characterize what you call a kindness as being real cruelty, you presume to sit in judgment between me and my God; and you decide that my earnest prayer to the Almighty Father to save our women and children from what you call kindness, is a 'sacrilegious, hypocritical appeal.'

"You came into our country with your Army, avowedly for the purpose of subjugating free white men, women, and children, and not only intend to rule over them, but you make negroes your allies, and desire to place over us an inferior race, which we have raised from barbarism to its present position, which is the highest ever attained by that race, in any country, in all time. I must, therefore, decline to accept your statements in reference to your kindness toward the people of Atlanta, and your willingness to sacrifice everything for the peace and honor of the South, and refuse to be governed by your decision in regard to matters between myself, my country, and my God.

"You say, 'let us fight it out like men.' To this my reply is—for myself, and I believe for all the true men, ay, and women and children, in my country—we will fight you to the death! Better die a thousand deaths than submit to live under you or your Government and your negro allies!

"Having answered the points forced upon me by your letter of the 9th of September, I close this correspondence with you; and, notwithstanding your comments upon my appeal to God in the cause of humanity, I again humbly and reverently invoke his Almighty aid in defence of justice and right.

"Respectfully, your obedient servant,

"J. B. HOOD, *GENERAL*."

"Headquarters Military Division of the Mississippi,
"Atlanta, Ga., *September, 14th, 1864.*

"General J. B. Hood, *Commanding Army of Tennessee.*

"General:—Yours of September 12th is received, and has been carefully perused. I agree with you that this discussion by two soldiers is out of place, and profitless; but you must admit that you began the controversy by characterizing an official act of mine in unfair and improper terms. I reiterate my former answer, and to the only new matter contained in your rejoinder add: We have no 'negro allies' in this Army; not a single negro soldier left Chattanooga with this Army, or is with it now. There are a few guarding Chattanooga, which General Stedman sent at one time to drive Wheeler out of Dalton.

"I was not bound by the laws of war to give notice of the shelling of Atlanta, a 'fortified town, with magazines, arsenals, foundries, and public stores;' you were bound to take notice. See the books.

"This is the conclusion of our correspondence, which I did not begin, and terminate with satisfaction.

"I am, with respect, your obedient servant,

"W. T. SHERMAN,
"Major General Commanding."

I preferred here to close the discussion, and, therefore, made no reply to his last communication inviting me to "see the books."

I will at present, however, consider this subject, and cite a few authorities upon the above disputed points, in order to show that General Sherman's conduct, in this instance, was in violation of the laws which should govern nations in time of war.

Atlanta could not properly be designated a regularly fortified city. It was simply protected by temporary breastworks, of the same character as those used by Johnston and Sherman, during the preceding campaign. The fortifications consisted of a ditch, with a log to act as protection to the heads of the men whilst firing, and of brushwood, when it could be obtained, thrown out in front as an obstruction to a rapid advance of the enemy. A large portion of the line, which passed through open fields, was devoid of this latter safeguard. Moreover, only a few of the heavy guns and batteries were covered by embankments with embrasures.

Fortifications, it is well known, are divided into two classes: temporary, and permanent. Those I have described, around Atlanta, come under the head of the first class. The latter are constructed of the best material, iron, and stone, with parapet, deep and wide ditch and glacis, similar to the fortifications on Governor's Island, and those of Fortress Monroe. In the construction of permanent works, every exertion is made to render them as strong and durable as possible.

It might be supposed, from General Sherman's Memoirs, that Atlanta was not only a thoroughly fortified town, but was provisioned to endure a siege of a year or more, after all communication was cut off; that it possessed arsenals and machine shops as extensive as those in Richmond and Macon—an illusion created, probably, by a dilapidated foundry, near the Augusta road, which had been in use prior to the war. General Sherman, therefore, cannot assert, in order to justify certain acts, that Atlanta was a regularly fortified town. And whereas I marched out at night, allowing him the following day to enter the city, unopposed, as he himself acknowledges, and whereas no provocation was given by the authorities, civil or military, he can in no manner claim that extreme war measures were a necessity.

It has been argued that Wellington sanctioned extreme measures against the Basques, at the time he was opposed to Marshal Soult, at Bayonne, in 1814. Wellington perceived that, by pillage and cruel treatment, his Spanish allies, under Mina and Morilla, were arousing the Basques to arms, and at once ordered the Spanish troops to abstain from such odious conduct. He was, unfortunately, too late in his discovery; the appetite for plunder had become so inordinate that his proclamation was disregarded by his allies, and he was subsequently forced to threaten extreme measures, in order to check the partisan warfare which initiated the cruelties and horrors he deplored. This is the unquestionable interpretation of the subjoined passage: "A sullen obedience followed, but the plundering system was soon renewed, and this, with the mischief already done, was enough to arouse the inhabitants of *Bedary*, as well as those of the Val-de-Baigorre, into action. They commenced and continued a partisan warfare until Lord Wellington, incensed by their activity, issued a proclamation calling upon them to take arms openly, and join Soult, or stay peaceably at home, declaring that he would otherwise burn their villages and hang all the inhabitants."*

The inhabitants of Atlanta gave no such cause for action on the part of General Sherman, nor was the safety of the Federal Army in any manner

*Peninsular War, B. XXIII, chap. 3.

involved. Nevertheless he ordered women and children, the infirm and the sick, in fact the entire population to go either North or South.

The subjoined appeal of the Mayor and Councilmen of Atlanta was powerless to alter the determination of the Federal commander:

"ATLANTA, GEORGIA, *SEPTEMBER 11TH, 1864.*

"Major General W. T. Sherman.

"Sir:—We, the undersigned, Mayor and two of the Council for the city of Atlanta, for the time being the only legal organ of the people of the said city, to express their wants and wishes, ask leave most earnestly but respectfully to petition you to reconsider the order requiring them to leave Atlanta.

"At first view, it struck us that the measure would involve extraordinary hardship and loss, but since we have seen the practical execution of it, so far as it has progressed, and the individual condition of the people, and heard their statements as to the inconveniences, loss, and suffering attending it, we are satisfied that the amount of it will involve in the aggregate consequences appalling and heart-rending.

"Many poor women are in advanced state of pregnancy, others now having young children, and whose husbands, for the greater part, are either in the Army, prisoners, or dead.

"Some say: 'I have such a one sick at my house; who will wait on them when I am gone?' Others say: 'What are we to do? We have no house to go to, and no means to buy, build, or rent any; no parents, relatives, or friends to go to.' Another says: 'I will try and take this or that article of property, but such and such things I must leave behind, though I need them much.' We reply to them: 'General Sherman will carry your property to Rough and Ready, and General Hood will take it thence on.' And they will reply to that: 'But I want to leave the railroad at such a place, and cannot get conveyance from there on.'

"We only refer to a few facts, to try to illustrate in part how this measure will operate in practice. As you advanced, the people north of this fell back, and before your arrival here, a large portion of the people had retired South; so that the country south of this is already crowded, and without houses enough to accommodate the people, and we are informed that many are now staying in churches and other out-buildings.

"This being so, how is it possible for the people still here (mostly women and children) to find any shelter? And how can they live through the Winter in the woods—no shelter or subsistence, in the midst of strangers who know them not, and without the power to assist them much, if they were willing to do so.

"This is but a feeble picture of the consequences of this measure. You know the woe, the horrors, and the sufferings cannot be described by words; imagination can only conceive it, and we ask you to take these things into consideration.

"We know your mind and time are constantly occupied with the duties of your command, which almost deters us from asking your attention to this matter, but thought it might be that you had not considered this subject in all of its awful consequences, and that on more reflection you, we hope, would not make this people an exception to all mankind; for we know of no such instance ever having occurred— surely never in the United States—and what has this *helpless* people done, that they should be driven from their homes, to wander strangers, and outcasts, and exiles, and to subsist on charity?

"We do not know as yet the number of people still here; of those who are here, we are satisfied a respectable number, if allowed to remain at home, could subsist for several months without assistance, and a respectable number for a much longer time, and who might not need assistance at any time.

"In conclusion, we most earnestly and solemnly petition you to reconsider this order, or modify it, and suffer this unfortunate people to remain at home, and enjoy what little means they have.

"Respectfully submitted,

> "JAMES M. CALHOUN, *MAYOR*.
> "E. E. RAWSON, *COUNCILMAN*.
> "S. C. WELLS, *COUNCILMAN*."

I shall now cite a few authorities upon the rights of war, to ascertain in how far the course pursued toward the inhabitants of Atlanta is in accordance with those laws which are now universally recognized.

Halleck, Vattel, and Grotius establish the following rules:*

---

*Grotius, B. III, chap. 12, sec. 8. (The italics are the author's.)

"* * * It is a just remark made by some theologians, that all *Christian* princes and rulers who wish to be found *such* in the sight of God, as well as that of men, will deem it a duty to interpose their authority to prevent or suppress all *unnecessary* violence in the taking of terms, for acts of rigor can never be carried to an extreme without involving great numbers of the innocent in ruin; and practices of that kind, beside being no way conducive to the termination of war, are totally repugnant to every principle of Christianity and justice."

"Women, children, feeble old men, and sick persons, come under the description of enemies; and we have certain rights over them, inasmuch as they belong to the nation with whom we are at war, and as, between nation and nation, all rights and pretensions affect the body of society, together with all its members. But these are enemies who make no resistance; and consequently we have no right to maltreat their persons, or use any violence against them. ***This is so plain a maxim of justice and humanity that at present every nation, in the least degree civilized, acquiesces in it."* * * *

"Since women and children are subjects of the State, and members of the Nation, they are to be ranked in the class of enemies. But it does not thence follow that we are justifiable in treating them like men who bear arms, or are capable of bearing them."†

"At present war is carried on by regular troops; the people, the peasants, the citizens, take no part in it, and generally have nothing to fear from the sword of the enemy. Provided the inhabitants submit to him who is master of the country, pay the contributions imposed, and refrain from all hostilities, they live in as perfect safety as if they were friends; they continue in possession of what belongs to them; the country people come freely to the camp to sell their provisions, and are protected as far as possible from the calamities of war."‡

"Since the object of a just war is to repress injustice and violence, and forcibly to compel him who is deaf to the voice of justice, we have a right to put in practice, against the enemy, every measure that is necessary in order to weaken him and disable him from resisting us and

---

*Vattel, B. III, chap. 8, sec. 145.

†Vattel, B. III, chap. 5, sec. 72.

‡Vattel, B. III, chap. 8, sec. 147. Incorporated by Halleck, Law of War, chap. 18, sec. 3.

supporting his injustice; and we may choose such methods as are the most efficacious and best calculated to attain the end in view, provided they be not of an odious kind, nor unjustifiable in themselves, and prohibited by the laws of nature."*

"The lawfulness of the end does not give a real right to anything further than barely the means necessary to the attainment of that end. Whatever we do beyond that is reprobated by the law of nature, is faulty and condemnable at the tribunal of conscience. Hence it is that the right to such, or such acts of hostility, varies according to circumstances. What is just and perfectly innocent in war in one particular situation, is not always so on other occasions. Right goes hand-in-hand with necessity and the exigencies of the case, but never exceeds them."†

"All these classes (old men, women and children, the clergy, magistrates, and other civil officers), which, by general usage or the municipal laws of the belligerent State, are exempt from military duty, are no subject to the general rights of a belligerent over the enemy's person. To these are added, by modern usage, all persons who are not organized or called into military service, though capable of its duties, but who are left to pursue their usual pacific avocations. All these are regarded as *non-combatants.*"‡

General Sherman admits, in his Memoirs, that he burned stores and dwellings; that "the heart of the city was in flames all night;" that he telegraphed to Grant he had "made a wreck of Atlanta,"§ which he afterwards termed "the ruined city." The following quotations will show whether or not he was justified in this destruction of property:

"And with respect to things, the case is the same as with respect to persons—things belonging to the enemy, continue such wherever they are. But we are not hence to conclude, any more than in the case of persons, that we everywhere possess a right to treat these things as things belonging to the enemy."‖

---

*Vattel, B. III, chap. 8, sec. 138.
†Vattel, B. III, chap. 8, sec. 137.
‡Halleck, Laws of War, chap. 16, sec. 2.
§Sherman's Memoirs, vol. II, page 154.
‖ Vattel, B. III, chap. 5, sec. 74.

"The wanton destruction of public monuments, temples, tombs, statues, paintings, etc., is absolutely condemned, even by the voluntary law of nations, as never being conducive to the lawful object of war. The pillage and destruction of towns, the devastation of the open country, ravaging, setting fire to houses, are measures no less odious and detestable on every occasion where they are evidently put in practice without absolute necessity or, at least, very cogent reasons. But as the perpetrators of such outrageous deeds might attempt to palliate them, under pretext of deservedly punishing the enemy, be it here observed that the natural and voluntary law of nations does not allow us to inflict such punishments, except for enormous offences against the law of nations."*

When General Lee entered Pennsylvania with his Army, he gave strict orders to destroy no property, and to pay for all provisions obtained from the enemy. Marshal Soult was likewise magnanimous in his conduct, after he had been not only compelled to storm the defences of Oporto, but to fight from street to street, in order to finally force a surrender. Napier states that the French found some of their comrades who had been taken prisoners, "fastened upright and living, but with their eyes burst, their tongues torn out, and their other members mutilated and gashed." This ghastly sight notwithstanding, many of the French soldiers and officers endeavored, at the risk of their lives, to check the vengeance of their comrades, Soult did not, even after this fearful resistance and these examples of barbarous cruelty, send off the women and children, the infirm and the sick, and then burn their homes; on the contrary,† "Recovering and restoring a part of the plunder, he caused the inhabitants remaining in town to be treated with respect; he invited, by proclamation, all those who had fled to return, and he demanded no contribution; but restraining with a firm hand the violence of his men, he contrived, from the captured public property, to support the Army and even to succor the poorest and most distressed of the population."

Although it is customary, previous to a general assault of a fortified town of which the demand for surrender has been rejected, that the commanding offi-

---

*Vattel, B. III, chap. 9, sec. 173. Incorporated by Halleck. Laws of War, chap. 19, sec. 24.
†Napier, Peninsular War, B. VI, chaps. 4 and 7.

cer give warning (on account of the extraordinary sacrifice of life, to which his troops must necessarily be subjected) that he will not be responsible for the lives of the captured, as did Lieutenant General Lee in my name at Resaca. No officer should allow his soldiers to burn and pillage after victory has been secured.

"Hold"

It takes an entire chapter for Lew Wallace, a Union general better known as the author of Ben-Hur, *to describe the ordeal of this single word. Wallace gives a vivid hour-by-hour description of the holding action his division fought at Monocacy Junction against Jubal Early during his raid on Washington. The odds were not in Wallace's favor—a division minus one brigade against Early's depleted corps of several divisions. Understanding the bigger strategic picture, Wallace crafts his battle plan to cover the two roads leading out of Monocacy to Baltimore and Washington. Whichever half of Wallace's line Early hits hard will reveal his objective.*

A general on a battlefield is like a god, Jeff Shaara once wrote, but Wallace shows how un-godlike a general can be, suffering strokes of bad luck beyond his control. God can do anything; generals can't.

Excerpt from *An Autobiography*

BY LEW WALLACE

LXXIII

The doctor's horse—Available troops—Their disposition—The two bridges—General Ricketts—The twenty-four-pounder howitzer—The fight in the cornfield—Colonel Clendenin.

The horse that had fallen to me had been, as I afterwards learned, the favorite servant of a physician in Frederick City; and now, besides age and a constitutional tendency to slowness, a lost shoe furnished him an excuse for a half-limp. So it was a trifle before midnight when we dismounted in front of headquarters at the Junction.

Colonel Catlin was very glad to see us, having been uneasy lest I should be detained too long in Frederick. By his scouts he had been kept well informed of the movements of the enemy. He took me into the meagrely furnished room, lighted by a single candle, and in reply to a question gave me a list of troops then at the Junction, the arrivals from Baltimore during the day. I am able to restore the list by aid of official reports, and I give it with a sense of gratitude, and a keen desire to perpetuate far as in me lies the memory of organizations that offered themselves, without a murmur, to the extreme sacrifices demanded of them next day.

The One Hundred and Sixth New York, Captain Edward Paine commanding; the One Hundred and Fifty-first New York, Colonel William Emerson commanding; the Fourteenth New Jersey, Lieutenant-Colonel C. K. Hall commanding; the Eighty-seventh Pennsylvania, Lieutenant-Colonel J. A. Stahel commanding.

These composed the First Brigade of the Third Division of the Sixth Army Corps, under Colonel William S. Truex. And when the Tenth Vermont, Colonel Henry, then marching from Frederick, arrived, the First Brigade would be present in its entirety.

I asked Colonel Catlin about the strength of the regiments, and remember his answer.

"Speaking without returns," he said, "I saw them get off the cars and move to bivouac down by the creek, and judge them to average five hundred men each, some more, some less."

"Two thousand! That is good. How about General Ricketts."

"Colonel Truex told me the general would be up on the first troop-train. He looks for it about one o'clock to-night."

I ordered Colonel Ross to be on hand at the coming of the train, and called for pen and ink. Every one offered me a pencil. I had to send to the block-house for the other articles, including the loan of a couple of candles. Finally I took seat at the table, and dictated the following order:

"HEADQUARTERS, MONOCACY JUNCTION,
"JULY 8, 1864.

"*General Ricketts*:
General,—I am instructed by the general commanding to direct you to move your whole command to the left of the railroad, with your front

to the Monocacy, with a view of guarding the approaches on the Washington road.

"You will establish your picket-line as you may deem best suited to attain this object, connecting on your right with the line of Brigadier-General E. B. Tyler. The men will move to the position indicated at once; your pickets will then be established. You will provide your command with three days' rations.

"No citizen within your lines will be permitted to leave them without a written pass from your headquarters. Citizens will only be admitted to give information touching the movements of the enemy.

"You will make to these headquarters a morning field-return of your command. You will also report by regiments the number of rounds of ammunition per man in your division. You will report the means of transportation in your command.

"MAX. WOODHULL, AIDE-DE-CAMP."[1]

To General Tyler I sent an order similar in effect, only he was directed to encamp his men on the right of the railroad, and establish his pickets connecting with those of General Ricketts on his left.

In these two orders the reader must see my dispositions for the battle which it was not to be doubted would be of early occurrence in the morning. Taken in connection with the conversation with General Tyler while we were making ready to vacate Frederick, it ought not to be difficult to comprehend them.

That is to say, all north of the railroad belonged to General Tyler; it being his to hold the stone bridge and the Baltimore turnpike, by which such of us as came out alive might retreat; while south of the railroad was to be assigned to General Ricketts, upon whom I thought the stress of the fighting would fall. The raw men to Tyler; the veterans to Ricketts.

It is to be added now, that before news of the arrival of General Ricketts reached me, I had resolved to take position at Monocacy Junction, and stay there with the twenty-five hundred men drawn from my own department. The resolution is to be seen in my promises to President Garrett; and the danger to Washington, when confirmed, but hardened the determination. To stay without reference to the odds against me, and do all possible to hamper and hinder

---

[1.] *War Records*, series 1, vol. li., part i., p. 1175.

the march of the Confederates, and force a showing of their purpose and strength—such was my resolution.

These preparations off my hands, I made a pillow of my folded coat, stretched myself upon the floor, and tried to sleep, but could not. The length of the line to be defended—fully three miles if the sinuosities of the river were followed—and the meagerness of the defenders, would not out of mind. Nor could I cover up the desperation of the work—how hopeless it was of victory. The sputtering candles upon the tables were not plainer to me, when I looked at them, than that the venture upon which I was launched could have but one result, if what was reported of Early's army were but half true.

There are two other points to plague me. The first will not be new to officers who, under trying circumstances, have felt their spirits flinch under the goad of responsibility. To what extent did my right as commander go in the exposure of the men under me? Was there not a limit to my authority? And what weight was I morally bound to give the admitted fact, that the venture proposed was desperate as respects both life and victory? Suffice it that I settled the point in a manner to my own satisfaction, at least, by the old argument that the obligations of duty were not apportionable; or if so, they were heavier upon the officer than his men.

The next point lingered longest with me, and, I am bound to confess, had a sharper sting than the other. The risk of battle taken, if I lost, as seemed inevitable, the chief of staff in Washington, having at last the excuse for which he had been so long lying in wait, would not spare me. No, not though his safety was within the scope of my effort, as well as that of the city in which he was housed.

I tried in thought of the matter to be philosophical; but it ought not to be strange to anybody if I could not sleep; nay, if, knowing myself so at his mercy, I gnashed my teeth.

In the midst of these unpleasantnesses, Colonel Ross, answering the challenge of the orderly, appeared in the door, and behind him a stranger. I arose, and was introduced to Brigadier-General James Ricketts, chief of the Third Division of the old justly famous Sixth Army Corps.

He was slightly above the average height of men, a little inclined to corpulency, quick and bluff in manner and speech, Celtic in feature and complexion, and at the moment serious. Beyond the usual hand-shake, there was no ceremony between us, no asking after health or news, no gossip, no apologies.

"It is true, then, that Jubal Early is here?" he asked.

"Yes, at Frederick City. His camp-fires are in sight."

"How many men has he?"

"That is variously reported. Sigel put it at twenty to thirty thousand. I know nothing personally beyond the fact that yesterday, just west of the town, my people whipped his advance-guard under Bradley Johnson."

"Hum!" said Ricketts, taking a moment to digest the answer. Then abruptly, "What are you going to do?"

"I came here to fight."

"How many men have you?"

"Twenty-five hundred of my own department. There are said to be five or six hundred stragglers from General Sigel, but I have refused to recognize or ration them."

Ricketts studied me a moment, then burst out, "Twenty-five hundred against thirty thousand."

"How many have you?" I asked.

"About five thousand."

"Seven thousand five hundred," I said. "That's first rate."

"It is fight, you say. Well"—the old soldier was thinking fast—"what for?"

"Objects?"

"Yes."

"I have three objects. I want first to make him tell us where he is going, whether to Baltimore or Washington."

"That's good. But how?"

"There are two turnpikes here within two miles of each other, one to Baltimore, the other to Washington. The one he makes his main fight for will, I take it, expose his object. I am already convinced he means Washington."

"Think so? How far is it from here to Washington?"

"About sixty miles."

"Two marches," said Ricketts, reflectively.

"Yes—forced marches. Leaving Frederick in the morning, he could, there being no interruption, reach the city by day after to-morrow in the evening."

"He has the reputation of being a good soldier." Ricketts observed.

"That he will now lose."

"How so?"

"He should be in Washington now."

"Impossible!"

"Not at all," I replied. "He had only to cross the Potomac at Edwards Ferry below Harper's Ferry. No power on earth could then have saved the city from him. As it is, he has fooled away his time and chances, and an opportunity which, if now lost by him, the Confederacy can never hope for again."

Ricketts laughed, but composing himself, resumed, "You had three objects, I believe you said."

"Yes, you have the first one. As to the second—it is strange, and argues ability, that Early should have been able to march an army from the vicinity of Richmond, drive Hunter out of his road, put Sigel to sleep on Maryland Heights, and turn up here, only two marches from Washington, with none of our people—no, not one—to tell within ten thousand what his strength is, so effectively has he curtained his columns behind his cavalry. And now there is nobody between Early and Washington but us. Our duty is plain. It is to push the curtain aside, and make him show us what all he has."

Ricketts brought his hand down upon the table, and swore a round soldier's oath in emphasis of his, "That's so—that's so!"

And I went on. "You have my second object, and I will pass to the third, which I think the most important of the three. If we can maintain ourselves here, and by hook or crook get thirty-six or forty hours on Early, that, added to the two days of forced marching required of him, will give General Grant ample time to get a corps or two into Washington and make it safe. General Grant is the only hope, and he must have notice and time."

"But Halleck, what is he doing?"

"Defending Harper's Ferry."

Ricketts looked at me curiously, and said, "I don't understand you."

"Instead of strengthening me here, he has sent batteries and thousands of men to the old Ferry, and they are on Maryland Heights now, of no more account in the defence of Washington than so many stones. I have been here three days, and he has not so much as wired me a word of intelligence respecting the enemy, or in the way of encouragement."

Then I told Ricketts of the invitation I had received to go to Harper's Ferry and join the useless army on Maryland Heights.

"What! And give Early a clear road to Washington! Never—never! We'll stay here. Give me your orders."

I saw then he was aroused, and thoroughly in sympathy with me, and said, with a feeling I could not have hidden had I wanted to: "General Ricketts, I knew you would stay with me, and, in proof of it, here is an order drawn in advance of your arrival. Read it, and you will see my opinion of you."

Taking the order from the table, I delivered it to him; and when he had finished the reading, he put it in a pocket, and, giving me his hand, said, "You expect the fight in the morning?"

"Yes, in the morning."

"Very well. I should be in my position before day-break. Let one of your officers come and show it to me."

"Colonel Ross will go with you," I answered. "He knows the ground." And to Ross I said: "The position is across the pike behind the wooden bridge." Turning again to Ricketts, I added: "I put you across the Washington pike because it is the post of honor. There the enemy will do his best fighting."

Again we shook hands and separated; and when Ricketts was gone, I lay down and slept never more soundly.

While our slender breakfast was getting ready in the morning, I walked out to the bluff by the railroad bridge. Everywhere I read the promise of a beautiful summer day. There was not a speck in the sky, and the departing night had left a coolness in the air delicious and most refreshing. Behind me little columns of smoke were slowly rising; the same indications across the river told where our pickets were in post and wide awake; beyond them, in the direction of Frederick, a denser smoke lay along the earth in the form of a pallid cloud hanging not higher than a tree-top, and it spoke of the enemy; and everywhere friends and foes alike were at coffee or making it. The smell of new mown hay from the yellowing stubble-fields was lost in the sooty perfume of the many fires.

Breakfast over, with my staff I rode to General Ricketts, and found him down in the low land of the little creek not far from the mill, and together we went to get a look at his men in position. In the posting, Colonel Ross had shown excellent judgment. It was, in fact, so satisfactory to General Ricketts, when viewed at daylight, that he left it unchanged—a circumstance which did not surprise me, to whom the colonel had given too many proofs of his soldierly qualities for surprise.

In the *negligée* of general rest, the regiments were in two lines extending north and south, with an interval of seventy or eighty yards between them, the railroad in the centre, their left in deployment over a hill, their right in a depression. Below, and not far away, the gray-stained, roofed, wooden bridge spanned the river. As we passed along, Ricketts would say, "There is such a regiment; and this such another"; now it was a New Jersey, now a New York, now a Vermont. At the conclusion of the informal inspection, we continued our ride to a point well forward of the first line on the summit of the hill from which the valley spread in smiling landscape clear to the mountains in the west.

With my glass I swept the country in the direction of the city, searching for signs of the enemy. Directly I caught sight of a dark line beginning to stretch itself out on the Buckeystown road.

"They are moving," I said to Ricketts.

"Which way?"

"This way," I answered, and passed the glass to him. In a few seconds he gave me the glass back, saying:

"Two miles and more. We can reach them easily."

Turning to one of his officers. "Ride," he said, "and tell Captain—What is his name?"

"Alexander," I returned.

"Tell Captain Alexander to open fire." Then to me, "There's something in having the first shot."

"Those we see are cavalry," I said.

Presently another column appeared on the Washington pike leading directly to the wooden bridge.

"A regiment on the pike," I said.

Ricketts took a deliberate look at the second apparition, and then remarked: "Yes, two regiments, as regiments on both sides now go. They are too few to mean a serious, straight attack. The other column is sheering round to our left. Is there a ford in that direction?"

"There is one about a mile below the bridge here. But it is held by six squadrons of Illinois cavalry."

After watching the developments for a time, I broke off: "We must get a welcome ready for the fellows coming at us. Look beyond the bridge a little to the left, and you will see two companies of Ohio men deploying as skirmishers. There is not enough of them. Please reinforce them with a company. And send another company to the bridge—and have the officer in charge get kindling ready to touch off in an instant. It may be necessary to burn the bridge. He will hold it till I send him word."

An orderly galloped down the hill with Ricketts' directions. About that time the report of a gun broke the impending silence, the first of the battle, one of Alexander's.

Now Ricketts was an old artillerist.

"A Parrott!" he exclaimed. "Have you nothing better?"

"Yes, a twenty-four-pounder howitzer."

"That will do. Let them have it!"

Evidently my prejudice against the three-inch rifled gun was well seconded.

Soon an officer came up the hill at a furious pace. Pulling rein in front of me, and saluting, he said: "I am Captain Wiegel, General Tyler's assistant adjutant-general. He sends me to report to you, and say that, with your permission, I will take charge of the howitzer in the work by the block-house."

"Do you know how to service it?"

"Perfectly."

"You are the man I want. Go and get to work."

The captain departed as he came. Soon afterwards two companies broke from Ricketts' forward line, and went to the front on the double-quick. Who they were I did not know, but I watched them. One halted at the mouth of the bridge; the other continued on, never stopping until merged in the array of skirmishers across the pike. Simultaneously the vedettes rode in, followed by the pickets. They were the last troops to avail themselves of the bridge, the last that ever crossed it.

Meantime the regiments moving against us, though under Alexander's fire, at a certain distance halted and deployed, executing the fanlike movement with a rapidity and regularity simply beautiful. While deploying, they advanced to the attack yelping after their style.

"Old soldiers!" said Ricketts.

"Yes," I said. "But see what comes now!"

As I spoke, up the pike there tore forward through clouds of dust groups of laboring horses dragging bright brass guns and clumsy caissons. The riders plied their whips viciously.

"How many guns?" asked Ricketts.

"Sixteen."

"But you must be counting caissons as well."

"No, guns; all brass pieces."

He whistled low, and said, much like a father sending his love and regrets after a lost son, "If I had my old battery here!"

Here the howitzer, opening upon the racers, took up its cry; a very loud note it was, an immense pounding sound singularly laden with encouragement to us. Alexander, with his three guns— the other three were with Tyler—and Wiegel, by the block-house, lost not a minute, so fair was the target. Then shortly the skirmishers joined in with their practice, ours firing from cover, and sending their *vis-à-vis* to the ground crawling forward like snakes.

I saw Wiegel's first shell burst above the gunners on the pike. Before the little bunched-up white cloud left by the missile had disappeared, before the howitzer could be reloaded, the pike was cleared. And such a skurrying! The groups divided, some going to the right of the road, some to the left. I could see the drivers using their whips mercilessly, the horses plunging, the riders tossing in their seats like rag puppets. Under other circumstances the sight had been amusing; but I knew better than to laugh. It was experience, not fear or panic, governing the gunners. The survivors of unnumbered fights, they were seeking the best positions from which to deal us their thunder. In a space incredibly brief they were all out of view, and widely apart behind barns and out-houses, under shelter of haystacks or hidden in clumps of bushes. I could see none of them, search as I might.

"There!" said Ricketts. "Did you hear that?"

"What?"

"Some sharp-shooter is after us. He is getting the range."

"Where is he?"

"Over there by the red barn."

I turned my glass in that direction without success. While looking for the fellow—why I do not know—a ball zipped by between us.

Doubtless we both had the same idea at the same instant. If we stayed there, invisible riflemen would get one of us. We wheeled, and rode farther up the hill. And while in the act, over our heads, making light of the air through which it sped, there went a shell in flight towards the mansion-house in the perspective across meadows in the southeast.

"Whose house is that?" asked Ricketts, drawing rein.

"A Mr. Thomas's."

"Well, were I near him I should advise him to take to the woods. It will be an uncomfortable habitation before the day is done."

As we were going over the crest of the hill, I stopped and looked back, attracted by a sudden increase of viciousness in the exchange between the skirmishers.

"Look at that," I said.

"What is it?" Ricketts asked, drawing rein.

"That clump of half-grown trees towards the river. You see it?"

"Yes."

"It is directly in front of the right of our skirmishers, and the enemy is filling it with men. If they turn our flank, I shall have to burn the bridge."

Ricketts observed intently, but presently exclaimed: "It's all right! Our fellows see the game. The weeds hide a lot of them crawling to the right, and they will get there in time."

Thereupon we sat silent. Out of the little grove a score or more men in gray broke yelping; but "ours," meeting them with a sharp, spattering fire, sent them to cover, where, if they had been killed, they could not have crouched closer.

"Good!" I said. "The old bridge has another chance for life."

While I spoke, two, three, five guns from as many different positions across the river opened fire. A minute, and still others joined in. By the white smoke clouds we could count them—eighteen in all.

"There—listen—from up the river," I said.

Under the near-by cannonading, in the intervals between guns and exploding shells, we caught detonations lower in tone but not so frequent.

"What does that mean?" Ricketts asked.

"It means the enemy is trying to get the stone bridge on the Baltimore pike some two miles above this. He is engaging Tyler."

"What of that bridge?"

"If Tyler loses it," I replied, "we are cut off."

Ricketts became thoughtful.

"Is there no other way of getting us out?"

"None, except we take to the Washington pike."

"Who is Tyler?"

"A man of intelligence, and brave. He has been in the war from the beginning, and understands the need of the bridge to us clearly as we do. I rely upon him."

We continued on over the hill.

TEN O'CLOCK

Behind the summit, well down the north face, we came upon the two brigades of Ricketts' division fronted westwardly, and lying down. Parts of the lines were without cover. With a splendid contempt for the shells streaming above them, and the sharp explosions so nerve-racking to young soldiers, the whole command seemed in mid-enjoyment of a morning nap. There I separated from Ricketts.

"If at any time you wish to communicate with me," I told him, "a messenger will find me on the height yonder, just beyond the block-house. From that point I can overlook your whole field; and, besides, Tyler's left joins you there."

After that I rode first to the mill, near which the surgeons of the division had established a field-hospital, intending, as I was told, to use the building for shelter of the wounded. The place appeared well selected for the purpose, its one inconvenience being that it was under fire.

Some doors had been unhinged and laid lengthwise on trestles, forming a table about which the operators stood in a little group. Most of them were in their shirt-sleeves, and they were all perfectly composed. A few were smoking. While I sat surveying the scene, a man was brought in bloody and screaming. In a moment he lay stripped. A jagged fragment of a shell had torn a furrow across his breast. I could see his lungs clipped and exposed. No need of probing. The chief gave the wound one look, and followed it with a silent wave of the hand; whereupon the under-assistants lifted the doomed subject and bore him away to die slowly and in agony. As I turned to escape the spectacle—from the piercing cries there was no escape—it came to me what some may think a horrible thought: why should not a surgeon, seeing death inevitable, be required to speed the end?

Seeing others wounded coming in, I called my officers, and rode away, and as we started a cannonading broke out in the south. The halt was instantaneous.

"What is that?" asked Ross.

"The enemy has reached one of the fords below the wooden bridge," I answered.

"What can Clendenin do against artillery?" young Woodhull inquired.

"Nothing but get out of the way. In other words, the enemy will get his feet wet crossing the river; all the same, he is now making to our side of it, bringing Ricketts the real tug of the day. Let us ride now, and find a position from which we can watch him."

The road we took from the mill to gain the height above the block-house led across a stretch in plain view of the able gunners giving us such worry from the other side of the river. Hardly had we begun the sloping rise when they saw the party and turned all their guns upon it—how many we had not time to count. The noise overhead became deafening, and the whiz of flying iron incessant. Up all around us sprang little gushes of gravel and yellow dust.

There was not an instant I did not look to see a horse, possibly a horse and rider, go down. I thought to make haste, and plied spurs to quicken my steed. I beat him with the flat of my sabre in vain. He could not be brought to discern his danger or ours. Walk he would. Finally I called to my men: "Go ahead! As you love your lives, gallop on!"

They looked everywhere but at me.

"Do you hear? Go ahead!" I again yelled to them. "Don't you see they are making a target of the crowd?"

Not a man showed a sign of hurry. They would have died first. So at a slow walk, as horses move, we rode through the most searching artillery-fire I ever encountered—a confusing fire—and that no one of the party was hit appears to me even at this long, belated hour miraculous.

TEN-THIRTY O'CLOCK

The height which I had chosen for a stand-point, at last safely gained, was under fire like all the rest of the field. Below us, on the brink of the river-bluff, Captain Wiegel and his squad of gunners stood by the twenty-four-pounder, and he was not wasting his ammunition. The piece, and the half-finished work encircling it, were a centre of attention with the eager enemy. Lines of fire from a dozen or more points terminated there. Following the flight of a shell, I observed a regiment lying down directly behind Wiegel's position. Every missile that passed him overshot reached the regiment. I sent to inquire whose command it was and what it was doing there.

"Colonel Landstreet's Baltimore regiment, in reserve by order of General Tyler, and supporting Captain Wiegel," was the answer.

The colonel's idea of "supporting a battery" was to locate himself directly in its rear. He was, of course, shifted to one side, but not until he had lost some of his men.

Not to offer too much of an attraction to the enemy, I had our horses led out of his sight, after which there was leisure to think of the situation. The valley west of the Monocacy and the low grounds on our side of the river, up far as the Thomas mansion, were in plain view, except as it was obstructed by the swiftly vanishing clouds incessantly flecking the air. Up at the stone bridge in the north the guns were still at work, a notice after their kind that Tyler,

Gilpin, and Low were holding their own, and their hundred-day men rapidly veteranizing. Giving attention then southward beyond Ricketts, I was struck by a portentous silence there, a silence heavy with meaning; insomuch that a messenger was not required to come and tell me of the fords lost to us and of Confederates across and forming for attack.

And Clendenin—where was he? A common soldier with a putty heart could find in the conditions of the field plenty of excuses for taking to the Washington pike and abandoning me. Was he of that kind? I sent a man serving as orderly with a hastily dictated note requesting the colonel, if he had not already done so, to fall back through Urbana in the direction of New Market on the railroad, and do his utmost to keep the enemy from getting in my rear.[2]

It may be well believed that at this period of the affair I kept an eye closely on my watch. Was I not fighting for time?

When the slow-going minute-hand reached.

ELEVEN O'CLOCK

I felt a thrill of gratification. Four hours gained! Four hours, and Early still in Frederick, not one step nearer his great prize than when the dawn delivered the steeples of the town from the envelope of night! Should I give notice to the authorities in Washington, and to General Grant at City Point, of what was going on? Not yet, I said to myself—not yet. For if asked, I could not have told to which city my antagonist was going, or how many men he had. Looking towards Frederick, I could see the smoke of camp-fires and wagons in park, and artillery, and a cloud of soldiers ominously suggestive of yet another army corps. Nevertheless, the revelations were as yet too indefinite for committal to the wires; besides which it remained to see what Ricketts and his sturdy regiments could do. I had come to have an immense confidence in him and them. How many hours additional might they not win for the Cause? Away down in my heart I was conscious of the fluttering of a hope which I was not sanguine enough to put into words.

What with anxiety and excitement my tongue had become very dry; but having put a lemon in my pocket in the morning, I was finding relief sucking it, when Colonel Catlin, near by, asked, "Are not those skirmishers I see yonder?"

---

[2]In good time the courier returned to tell me Clendenin was then in Urbana covering the road to New Market. He had anticipated my suggestion.

"Where?"

"There, just south of the cornfield?"

I brought my glass to bear, and as promptly called Woodhull and Ross to my side, and each wrote at my dictation:

"GENERAL RICKETTS,—A line of skirmishers is advancing from the south beyond the cornfield at your left. I suggest you change front in that direction, and advance to the cornfield fence, concealing your men behind it. They will be enfiladed, but that can't be helped.

"LEW WALLACE."

"Make haste," I said to the orderly, giving him one of the duplicates and retaining the other.

Within five minutes the brigades were on their feet; within another five minutes one of them was lying down behind the fence, while the other moved leisurely to take position on its left. The manœuvring brought both bodies into view from the west side of the river, and the gunners there were in nowise loath to profit by the advantage offered. This, of course, called Alexander and Wiegel into action.

The cannonading and the noise of bursting shells were furious—I had almost said infernal. Sympathy for the brave men under the iron rain racked me like a sharp pain; but, as said, the conditions were beyond help. The furrow had been begun; it was fast reddening under the plough; not for that, however, could I then cry stop.

Presently my attention was claimed by another sight. The cornfield of which I have spoken as on Ricketts' left—his front now—was wide. How many acres it contained I cannot say; but the crop was in mid-growth, luxuriantly green and high as a man's waist. At the fence of the farther side the skirmishers disappeared; in their place there now came a line extending the length of the field, and more. Clearing the fence, the new-comers halted in the corn to regain their alignment, then advanced. I could see guidons, and several flags with pale-blue crosses on red fields, and white stars in the crosses, signifying regiments.

"They are cavalry," I said.

"That's good!" Ross replied.

"Why so?"

"Horsemen afoot are easy for infantry.'

"But they may be mounted infantry."

"I don't know any difference. A horse always spoils a good soldier."

I could not help retorting, "I haven't observed that a horse had done you any hurt."

Gaps had to be made in the fence for the passage of mounted officers. These, once through, galloped to their places. Then at a signal—a bugle-call probably—the array having attained its proper front, it started forward slowly at first; suddenly, after the passage of a space, arms were shifted, and, taking to the double-quick, the men raised their battle-cry, which, sounding across the field and intervening distance, rose to me on the height, sharper, shriller, and more like the composite yelping of wolves than I had ever heard it. And when to these were presently superadded a tempestuous tossing of guidons, waving of banners, and a furious trampling of the young corn that flew before them like splashed billows, the demonstration was more than exciting—it was really fearful; and, watching it, I understood as never before the old Vandal philosophy which taught that the sublimest inspiration of courage lay in the terrible.

A brave spectacle it was indeed; yet, as Marshal Roberts said of the charge of the Six Hundred, it was not war. I could not understand it; and whatever of admiration I felt as a beholder was lost in amazement, all because of one extraordinary feature—not a man engaged in it took time or thought it necessary to stop, though for an instant, and fire a shot! Through my glasses I could easily make out officers mounted and waving their swords, and, as I thought, cheering the line forward. What did they mean? One of them there must have been the chief; what did he mean? Did he know of what was before him? Or was he of the Southerners who, still sceptical of the courage of the North, imagined that all to be done now was to set up the yell, wave the flags, and go with a rush, and win?

My eyes dropped involuntarily to the fence—it was of rough rails—towards which the charge was coming. On the hither side of it, in the corners, I saw indistinctly what looked like daubs of blue pigment in spots darker for the shade covering them. I knew them to be soldiers—our soldiers. They lay ever so still, reminding me of hunters in a broad runway, the deer in sight and speeding down upon them. Here and there I could see men half-risen peering through the spaces between the rails—they were company officers. Behind them other figures in uniforms were standing by horses; and in them I recognized field-officers. One man was in his saddle—Ricketts. He drew all my attention. Everybody in his vicinity seemed waiting on him; and presently, like the rest, I was doing the same, waiting for the word that would call the daubs of blue pigment into life and deadly action. The bristling, noisy wave was drawing nigh and nigher. How close would he permit it to come? The word was his; was it not time to give it? He sat the horse like a block of wood, calm, indifferent. I could not see that he was even watchful. There was a noticeable fever in my blood which I tried to cool sucking more vigorously at the lemon, and saying to myself, "He knows his men, and what they can be relied upon to do."

We thus in observation were almost breathlessly silent, and for a reason: not only did our fortunes depend upon what was about to take place; we were witnessing a rare incident which might not come to us again though we lived a hundred years. And in our minds there was a flutter of questions: "What will be the effect of the fire? Will it hush the howling? Will it stop the rush?" I felt my flesh creep, imagining the annihilation that must follow its delivery.

I heard no command given; however, up rose the figures behind the fence, up as one man. I saw the gleaming of the burnished gun-barrels as they were laid upon the upper rails. The aim taken was with deadliest intent—never more coolly. I could form no correct judgment of the distance, probably a hundred and twenty-five or thirty yards, then a ragged eruption of fire, and for an instant smoke interfered with the view.

"My God!" cried Woodhull. "They are all killed!"

With return of fair vision, we looked for the line. It had disappeared. Not a man of it was to be seen, only the green of the trodden corn, some horses galloping about riderless, and a few mounted officers bravely facing the unexpected storm.

"No," I said, in reply to Woodhull, "they are not all killed. Give the fellows unhurt time to crawl along the furrows back to the fence, and you will see."

There was a cheer, no doubt by whom given. Then succeeded a firing at will. More saddles emptied, other horses rushing madly about. And ere long the thitherward fence was darkened with climbers, under whom whole sections of the rails went down, so little did the fugitives stand upon the order of their going. A few minutes more and not a living thing could be discovered in the field. Even the masterless horses were gone; while the wounded, crouching close to avoid the pitiless rain of bullets in the air above them, lay under the corn hidden as by a mantle. And they and the dead—how many were there of them?[3]

So far victory. I sent an orderly to Ricketts with congratulations, and then consulted my watch.

HIGH NOON

Five hours from my very able antagonist, General Early! I counted them, beginning at seven o'clock, not once but many times, much as I fancy a miser counts his gold pieces.

I had leisure then to look about me.

In the mean time fighting had been going on up at the stone bridge. That General Tyler had not ordered Colonel Landstreet to his support argued well. Nevertheless, I sent Colonel Ross to see, and report upon the affair.

In my immediate front, across the river, skirmishing continued as in the morning, and the batteries there still maintained their fire, replied to by Alexander and Wiegel. I doubt if there was a nook or corner far up as the Thomas mansion, and beyond it even, that went free of search by shells thrown with singular skill.

---

[3]A few years ago, during President McKinley's administration, General John B. Gordon and I accidentally met in the reception-room of the White House and were introduced to each other. He was then United States Senator. We took seats upon a sofa, and talked of the battle of Monocacy.

Among other things, General Gordon said he had long wished to know me, and in explanation stated that I was the only person who had whipped him during the war. I replied differing with him, and argued that while it was true I had accomplished the purpose for which the fight was made, still the possession of the field remained to him. "In that sense," he insisted, "you are right; but you snatched Washington out of our hands—there was the defeat." And he continued, "The duty of driving you off the road fell to me; and I did it, but not until you had repulsed several attacks, and crippled us so seriously we could not begin pushing our army forward until next morning about ten o'clock."

In course of the conversation I remarked: "The strangest thing of the whole battle was the conduct of the officer who made the first attack upon General Ricketts. Did he imagine he could stampede veterans of the old Sixth Army Corps by a rush without fire?"

"Ah, that's the very point," Gordon replied. "We did not know of the presence on the field of any portion of the Sixth Corps. They told us in Frederick you had only hundred-day men, a class of soldiers we had often met and cleaned out without firing a shot—exactly as General——attempted."

I found General Gordon remarkably frank and communicative, and a most delightful conversationalist. He took away with him my profoundest respect.

The circumstance of liveliest concern to me, however, was that, often as I turned my eyes to the roads trending southwardly from Frederick, they fell upon reinforcing columns of Confederates in steady march to the fords below the wooden bridge.

LXXIV

The deserting engineer—The disabled howitzer—Burning of the wooden bridge—The telegram to Grant—The cowardly brigade—The skirmishers on the iron bridge—Lieutenant Davis—The beginning of the retreat.

I tried to estimate the strength of the forces in motion before me, but could not. Enough that they were as three to our one, and that when they came to stand upon our side of the river in order of battle all the advantages of the position which had been our strength would fail us utterly. It was ugly thinking of the odds; nevertheless, what I beheld settled at least one of the three objects for which I was making the struggle—General Early meant to possess himself of the pike Ricketts was defending, the undermeaning of which was Washington. Should I not say so to Generals Halleck and Grant? I again decided not yet. By burning the wooden bridge, and holding on till five or six o'clock, it would not be in General Early's power to move his main body before the next day. In other words, time then took first place in my purpose—twenty, or even twelve hours added to the two marches yet required of my doughty enemy would be ample for General Grant to land his interfering corps in the city. I resolved to hold on.

To General Ricketts I then sent word that, in the absence of ambulances, I had determined upon a train of cars to receive and carry off such of the wounded as could be moved; the train, I informed him, was in waiting behind the first hill east of the railroad bridge. Therewith I suggested having his wounded taken thither while the lull in the fight permitted.

Within half an hour afterwards an officer came to me and reported that he had been to look for the train, and it was gone; the engineer, frightened by shells flying over the hill, had run away, taking every car with him.

It took me some time to recover from this blow. Indeed, could hands have been laid upon him, I think yet I could have stood quietly by and seen the cowardly wretch hanged. But there was no remedy. The hurt and the maimed must lie where they fell—in that respect like the dead. My keenest pang, I remember, was in the reflection that when the retreat took place—it looked more probable to me then than at any previous time—the unfortunates, few or many, must look to the enemy for care and relief, and that he, hampered by like sufferers of his own, might find his mercy too greatly strained.

One o'Clock

At this hour all of the action going on was in my front across the river and up at the stone bridge. From the latter place nothing could be heard but the dropping fire of skirmishers; while here the air continued riven with shells.

Colonel Bliss, the corps commissary, came up from his storehouse near headquarters bringing a sackful of crackers and sardines, and, the lull permitting, we lunched. The colonel reminded me of a case of wine received by him the evening before from Baltimore bearing my address, a present from some friend possessed of the blessed gift of gentle remembrance. I disposed of his suggestion that we tap it then by thoughtlessly telling him to keep it for supper.

In the same interval of comparative calm, Colonel Ross reached me from up the river. He had found General Tyler in active oversight of his attenuated line. Off Crum's ford, about a mile above us, the enemy were assembled as if to attack; but the bluff was steep, and could be easily held by the two or three companies who had the locality in charge. Colonel A. L. Brown, he said, had his hands more than full, having the stone bridge and another ford beyond it to keep with but seven companies of his own regiment (the One Hundred and Forty-ninth Ohio) and Captain Lieb's mounted infantry. Ross said he had found the colonel with his command posted on the crest of a ridge on the Frederick side of the river. Attacked by a largely superior force, Brown had succeeded in repelling several charges supported by artillery, and was in good spirits. His hundred-day men were behaving splendidly.

So then, summing up, at one o'clock, notwithstanding the attacks received, we were exactly as in the morning, only there were now to our score against General Early *six hours*. The officers of my staff, with the exception of Colonel Ross, who was characteristically grave, were inclined to be jolly; a mood not possible for me to second because of a point that would not out of mind—the enemy was taking a great deal of time down at the ford. Either he was waiting for more men, or he had already so many that the ordering them for battle was troublesome. Profiting by the sad outcome of his first drive at Ricketts, he was of mind now to make a certainty of the second. With that idea I kept my glass in service, sweeping the whole southern section of approach.

Two o'Clock

About two o'clock I noticed mounted men whom I took to be officers riding leisurely along the farther side of the cornfield going east. Occasionally they stopped as if to survey our position. I spoke to the officers with me.

"There will not be much more delay. Yonder, I take it, is the man in chief command reconnoitering us."

Within five minutes the strangers disappeared. Presently I caught sight of flags and the gleam of muskets; then I made out an advancing line of battle with the river on its left. It halted, and while I was wondering at the halt, another body swung by companies left into line of its right; then another—and another—until the prolonged front outreached Ricketts' left, offering a dangerous lap.

The call on us for action was immediate.

I sent Colonel Catlin at speed to Ricketts, warning him, and suggesting that he put his whole command into one line; so only could he equalize the fronts.

At the same time an orderly hurried to Wiegel asking if he could not bring his howitzer to bear upon the Confederates in mid-manœuvre. The man returned to me on the run.

"The gun is disabled," he said.

"Disabled? How?"

"A green fellow serving it forgot the cartridge, and rammed a shell down first."

The effect upon me may be imagined. The howitzer alone was worth all Alexander's six rifles.

"Bring the horses," I said. "We must ride now."

I went first to Captain Wiegel, whom I found trying to inject powder into the vent of the piece—a makeshift requiring patience, and, in view of the practice of the enemy upon his little earthwork, enough of nerve to make a dozen Marlboroughs.

"Up-end the gun," I called to him.

"I've tried that; it won't do."

Considering the howitzer lost to us—lost, too, when it could have done us infinite good—I continued on to the wooden bridge.

I stopped once to observe what was to be seen of Ricketts' readiness for the tempest before him. His Second Brigade appeared moving into place on the left of his First. The enfilading from the guns across the river was terrible. It swept his whole formation from flank to flank. I had a doubt if there could have been a more vigorous practice of artillery. Actually shells seemed to be in flight from every direction, and the horrible hissing and screeching they made in going were more dreadful to the imagination than were their explosions in fact. Then I heard infantry firing, and from the sound knew that this time the enemy was indulging no foolishness. I could not see him, but judged he had opened his fire five or six hundred yards away, and was keeping it up while advancing. As yet the men of the Sixth were not replying. They were waiting to make sure; in their grim silence I somehow took on another store of faith and confidence.

As said, I was going to the wooden bridge. My object was to release the guard taking care of it, that they might join their regiments, then never in such need of every available man, and I could see but one way of relieving them.

"Have you a match?" I asked the captain of one of the two companies there. "All right, apply it now."

He stooped to a pile of dry grass and kindling heaped against the inner face of the long-seasoned pine weather-boarding of the bridge. Just then I had a thought:

The skirmishers! My God, what will become of them?" I shouted.

Ross rode through the old structure to its farther exit, and returned to tell me: "They are too far off to be reached. They will retreat at sight of the smoke."

At first a guilty sense touched me. The appearances of the thing looked so like a wilful desertion. Nevertheless, I reflected rapidly and with a clear head. The men were engaged. To have recalled them then would have been to endanger the bridge, possession of which by the enemy, certain to follow fast on their heels, would have been to admit him to the flank and rear of Ricketts' thousands on the hill. Hard, very hard, but the exigencies demanded loss of the few rather than of the many—or, rather, that the few must be left to take their chances with the foe in front or the river at their back. And thinking of the objects of the fight, my will grew hard as iron.

By that time the fire was blazing.

"All right, let it burn," I said to the captain of the guard, "and do you take your men with speed to your regiments."

They moved off on the run. I lingered awhile to see that the flames did their work reliably. A great smoke began to fill the sky and blot out the sun. Soon the floor timber fell into the water. The structure was then beyond salvation; whereupon we left it, and set out in return to our lookout above the block-house.

For the howitzer there was no redemption, and Wiegel had gone to Tyler. I had the piece hauled out of the contracted earthwork behind which it had done good service. It might be carried off when the final retirement took place.

The arrival of the Third Brigade had been promised me by one o'clock. I continued to look for it with an anxiety that intensified with the passage of the minutes. Three regiments—such was the composition of the brigade—three like these then with Ricketts—had been worth full six in a time less serious. But they did not come. If I could only have got an order to the man in command!

The musketry had followed us with its peculiar noises, now a rattle, now a roll, up from the bridge; and, looking from our elevation, it was to see both the opposing lines engaged, that of the enemy and ours. A film of smoke whiter than morning mist hung over them; but it was only a film, transparent at that, and through it I could see the combatants, two or three hundred yards apart, and the flashing of twirling rammers, and the flags, and horsemen going to and fro. How busy they all were!

I remember the thrill I felt noticing the enemy brought to a stand-still along his whole front; then the thought, if the men of the "old Sixth" could do that much, it would not be strange if they yet did better.

Minutes passed. The firing became an unbroken roll. I could hear no sound else. Both sides were working under a repression too intense for cheering, a repression in which there could be but one intent—load, load, and fire, meaning kill, the more the better. Battle has no other philosophy.

Other minutes passed, and they seemed longer than any of the preceding, minutes during which the action grew so furious, so red-hot, as it were, I knew it was not in nature to continue. One line or the other must go to pieces.

The gunners out towards Frederick stopped; seeing the lines so close together, they doubtless feared doing their friends more harm than good. About that time, turning my glass to the southeast in the direction of the Thomas mansion, I saw a faltering on the part of the Confederates; it was very distinct—some of them were even running to the rear. This was well over towards their extreme right flank. It struck me a charge might start the break I was so anxiously expecting. I sent Ross to Ricketts with the suggestion; and he, meeting an aide of Colonel Treux,[4] who knew the general's whereabouts, gave him the suggestion for delivery in the form of an order, and returned to me.

A consideration of the time required for the transmission of this order will help one to a fair idea of the obstinacy of the struggle in progress. There are moments in which the mythical old man with scythe and hour-glass seems to disport himself with men and their solicitudes. I waited and waited, and while waiting thought of Father Weems's description of the ascension of souls at the Cowpens. At last two regiments—such they appeared to me—broke from the general line forward and advanced rapidly, firing and cheering as they moved. The effect was as if a sudden push had been given the enemy. They broke, resolved into a flying mass, and directly the whole opposing formation, catching the contagion of retreat, was going headlong in search of safety. I could see mounted officers raging in the rout, but in vain. The first triumph of the heroic "old Sixth" had taken place in a cornfield; this second one was scored in a wheat-field but recently reaped. Looking over it after the disappearance of men and flags in a woods on its southern boundary, the shacks were all down, and here and there, not infrequently either, there were black objects interspersed with the yellow sheaves; but whether they were of the dead or wounded, or of both, could only be surmised.

The shouting of the elated victors was long and loud. Landstreet's Eleventh Maryland, off a short distance to our right rear, arose to their feet and yelled with might and main. And we helped them all we could—I with my staff and orderlies. The expression may sound homely, but I could have hugged the two regiments that did the valorous deed. Then, in the very heat of our rejoicing, we were made to know that there were spectators whom we had not counted upon possessed of different emotions. The Confederates serving the scattered guns in battery beyond the river turned them upon our height and shelled it with a spite and venom not to be misunderstood. Again by the greatest good-fortune we all escaped harm, for which thanks were chiefly due to our elevation above the gunners. When the flurry was over I detached two of General Tyler's three pieces, sending them to Captain Alexander. They were doing no good where they were; perhaps he could make them useful.

I looked at my watch, and it was

---

[4]Captain W. H. Lanius. See *Eighty-seventh Pennsylvania Volunteers*, p. 182. The captain, it would appear, thought the time too short to advise with General Ricketts. In my name he ordered the Eighty-seventh Pennsylvania and the Fourteenth New Jersey to make the charge. Had it been less brilliantly done, with results more unquestionable, he might have heard from General Ricketts.

Two-forty-five o'Clock

—that is, it had taken Ricketts about forty minutes to dispose of this second attack; and forthwith I put them in the column of time against General Early, much as one hungry for a smoke puts pinches of tobacco in his pipe. Nearly eight hours now! Thus mentally I summed up.

There came then another spell of quiet, save only the gunners maintained their practice and the skirmishers kept belligerently spitting bullets at one another. I noticed this latter phase of the fight particularly. In their cover—a hollow in the ground or patches of weed and grass—the combatants, crouching low or flat on their backs, loaded their pieces: then, on their knees, they watched the irregular front offered by the enemy, and often, as a faint, white puff arose and was vanishing in the air, they fired aiming under it. Now and then the black smoke driving before the south wind from the burning bridge spread over that part of the valley, obscuring the exciting game; when it lifted, however, I could see our troops were retiring slowly back towards the river. And it was plain to me that the officer in charge, whoever he might be, understood the business engaging him, and had no thought of surrender. But the scheme of escape he nursed—what could it be? I failed to fathom it. If the big brass howitzer had been in condition, his rescue had been easy. This, it is worth saying, was absorbing to a degree to make me unmindful of other things in themselves very interesting. A cloud of dust on the road from Frederick at length drew me from it; then, in a short time, I made out a column of infantry in rapid movement going to my left by the same thoroughfare taken by their friends in the morning—reinforcements beyond question. While my glass circulated among the staff-officers, I reflected.

Should I get away? That were less difficult then. The enemy was undiscoverable in the fields or in the woods beyond them, and it would take an hour or more for the reinforcing column to cross the ford, particularly as it was followed by two batteries of four guns each. Another half-hour would be consumed in deploying the regiments into line with their brethren and getting the batteries into position. The time was ample, and it made the opportunity. I took no thought of self; but of the brave men here and there on the field, how many might pay the extreme penalty of delay? The urgency compressed debate into the narrowest limits and forced me to a decision.

I summoned Woodhull and Ross to my side and dictated—first, a telegram to General Grant, at City Point. Of this, both the duplicates having been lost, I can only give the substance:

"Monocacy Junction, Maryland,
"*July 9th*, 3 p.m.

"I have been fighting General Early here since seven o'clock. With General Ricketts' aid have repulsed two attacks. A third and heavier is making ready. It is evident now he is aiming at Washington. He has been fighting us with eighteen or twenty thousand men, and has others, apparently a corps, in reserve, with field artillery in proportion. If you have not already strengthened the defensive force at Washington, I respectfully suggest the necessity for doing it amply and immediately."

This I followed with a message to General Halleck, stating the fighting had, the result, and the probabilities—that the indications all were of an attempt on Washington; that Early had been actually engaging me with eighteen or twenty thousand infantry; that he had cavalry and artillery in full complement, with a body in reserve, apparently a corps.

The truth is, I worded the latter telegram thinking to scare General Halleck into action—he was, in my opinion, so constitutionally slow, if not timid.

The flight of the telegraph operator put me out sadly. As the next best thing, the only one in fact, I had Ross go look at the horses and bring me the best for the service; then to the owner I gave the messages, with directions to ride to Monrovia, or the nearest point on the railroad at which there was a telegraph-office and an operator. He was further instructed to see that the business had precedence of everything else, and to stand by the operator during the transmission; or, if that individual delayed or hesitated, he was to be threatened with President Garrett. The horse was not to be spared.

Then I sent to General Ricketts, requesting him to come to me for consultation.

About that time General Tyler passed up a courier, reporting that Colonel Brown was still on the west side of the river, holding his own. There was comfort in the report. Retreat was still possible.

General Ricketts responded promptly. The good soldier was dusty—hair, beard, and uniform—and red with heat and perspiration. He would have dismounted, but I told him to keep his saddle as long as the gunners over the river were disposed to let him alone.

"You did that very handsomely," I said, alluding to the repulses of the enemy.

"Thank you," he returned, wiping his face with his handkerchief.

The column of Confederates was yet in sight. I pointed to it.

"Guns?" he said.

"Yes, two four-gun batteries."

"Well, that means a division at least"; and he added, "God knows there were enough of them already."

"We can get away now," I then said. "Shall we go? What do you say?"

"What time is it?"

I looked at my watch, and replied:

"THREE-THIRTY O'CLOCK."

"A while longer"—he spoke deliberately— "and Early can't move before morning; and, if what I am told is true, that the ford is very rocky, it will be noon before he can get his artillery across the river."

"You are willing to stay, then?"

"Yes, at least until they show us what they have next. After whipping them twice, I don't like to run away."

"That is natural," I said; "and I am with you in opinion about holding on, but for another reason; and that is the other point about which I wanted to see you. Your Third Brigade is some hours overdue. What is the matter with it?"

Ricketts' brows contracted as he answered: "I don't know. If I live, I will know."

"He had his orders?"

"Yes, and cars in plenty."

"You don't know that he will not come?"

I saw the subject was exasperating him, and closed it, remarking: "The arrival of the brigade would be good when we have to retreat. As a rear-guard it would be infinitely serviceable. I will wait for it."

Ricketts swallowed his wrath and said: "Very well. When you think our time is up, let me know."

"I will send you the order."

And then I again explained that the retreat would be by the country roads north to the Baltimore pike; thence towards Baltimore.

"Do you need a guide?" I inquired.

"No. I can find the road."

"We understand each other, then?"

"Yes."

"As everything will depend upon the bridge on the Baltimore pike, it shall be held, if possible, until your command gets stretched out behind it."

"That will do," he said, gathering up his bridle-reins.

"Good-bye."

And he replied, "Good-bye"; then added, "If you see us coming back before your order reaches me, you should understand it is because we are out of ammunition."

"Is it getting low?"

"Yes, in some of the boxes. I have just had an inspection."

"God forbid!" I said.

"Yes, it would be ugly."

And with that he rode down the height to his command.

This conversation, condensed but substantially given, can hardly be misunderstood; so I leave it with the remark that General Ricketts and I were coincident in the opinion that we would be compelled to acknowledge the superiority of the enemy by yielding him the road to Washington. At the same time, we were both of a mind to tempt fortune by holding on yet longer—he partly out of soldierly pride, and I in the hope that his Third Brigade would arrive in time to cover the retreat. We were both agreed, moreover, that by persisting in the struggle it might be possible to make it noon next day before General Early could continue his march. At all events, I have always thought, and still think, the result justified me in the course taken. This is said with reference to my responsibility as ranking officer.

The withdrawal of an engaged line of battle is always a most difficult and dangerous resort, because it is so easy to turn it into an irretrievable rout; here, however, it was to be a thing of execution by veterans, and the reflection made me several degrees more hopeful. Nevertheless, I foresaw confusion, especially if the enemy was vigorous in making the most of his advantage, and I tried to determine how to reduce its probable consequences to a minimum of disaster. With that idea I sent for General Tyler and Colonel Landstreet.

General Tyler, it will be recollected, had command of all north of the railroad, including the stone bridge on the pike from Frederick to Baltimore. To him, in Landstreet's hearing, I exposed what was intended and in expectation. He received the explanation calmly, saying he was willing to do his utmost in making the retreat a success, only he wanted to know what I wanted him to do.

"You know the road to the Baltimore pike," I said, "the only one by which

Ricketts can bring his brigades off after withdrawing them, is narrow, rough, and for the most part through woods, all too narrow, in fact, to accommodate a column hard-pressed and in hasty movement. So the probabilities are that, instead of sticking to the road, individuals are certain to take courses for themselves until they gain the pike. There they will have become a mass more or less disordered; and, until they have time to reform, somebody must defend them from pressure and rear attack. That work, general, you must do. In other words, upon you more than any other man I can think of it now depends whether we are not all enclosed in the woods and killed or taken like a herd of sheep?"

"You want me to hold the bridge?"

"Yes, until Ricketts and his men gain the pike and are advanced well towards New Market; in fact, I want it held until the enemy following Ricketts through the woods show themselves in your rear."

"And then?" he asked.

"Let your men cut their way out, all who can—not a difficult thing to regiments like Gilpin's and Brown's, since the pursuers will be in disorder and few in numbers when they reach the pike. Should there be any who cannot cut their way out, order them to disperse, every man for himself, with New Market or Monrovia for rendezvous. It will be desperate work. What do you say?"

I watched General Tyler closely; and there was revelation of the man in his answer, simple, without bravado, unmelodramatic: "I will go to the bridge now, picking up my men on the way. They will not be needed except at the bridge."

"That reminds me," I said. "You have had two companies of Colonel Brown's regiment guarding the block-house here. Take them along with you."

"But what of the house?" Tyler asked.

I answered: "If only to deprive the enemy of the pleasure of burning it, I will burn it myself. Have your companies take out their movables immediately, and let them look after the howitzer."

Then I requested him to stay and hear what I had to say to Colonel Landstreet. That gentleman came to attention and saluted. He was not wanting in the technique of military manners. Still, it was very needful for me to be careful with him.

"You will take your regiments, marching rapidly, to the Baltimore pike," I said. "There turn to the right in the direction of Baltimore, and, when two miles out, halt, deploy, with your colors in the centre of the road, and face to the rear. Our men will come to you in numbers, disorganized, of course. Stop all of them who have guns and cartridges—stop all officers and make them help you rally the fugitives. Tyler, here, will have ultimately to abandon the bridge. When that takes place, cover his retreat as best you can, moving along the pike and halting when required to stay the pursuit." I wound the instructions up by what I thought an appeal to his pride. "In short, colonel, I mean your regiment to become our rear-guard, an important and, under the circumstances, a most honorable duty."

He saluted again, and, answering with confidence, left me, and shortly after was seen in the saddle leading his regiment from the height. Not long after General Tyler picked up his two companies and rode away.

I had now exhausted every resource, even to the last man; and again there was nothing for me but to wait on the enemy; *that*, however, was made appreciably easier by a feeling that he had given me time to do all possible for his reception, and that it had been done. A bitter pang struck me thinking of Ricketts' Third Brigade, so unaccountably absent. Where was it? Who held it back? Cowardice or treachery—which? In how many ways it could have been made useful in the extremity upon me!

FOUR O'CLOCK

Meantime the firing had almost ceased. Only at intervals a tentative shell spanned the field, leaving an arch of sound behind it. Once in a while, also, the skirmishers indulged in a spurt. Their fitful *rattling*, what moments it claimed my attention, left it evident that our people were crawling slowly back towards the river, and forced the reflection—what were they to do, what *could* they do, when the river was gained?

The men of my staff had nothing to say to me, and but little to one another. Like myself, they were impressed with the situation, and waiting. They knew as well as I that in all probability the preparation going on behind the screen of woods in the south would be decisive; and with them, as with me, the deliberation with which it was being conducted was ominous enough to edge their expectation with anxiety. Occasionally they remitted their watchfulness to follow the sound of a shell flying invisibly over the fields, golden-yellow with the ungarnered harvest of the respectable owner of the mansion fair to view in the southeast.

For my own part, I entertained myself with my watch, in hand the while, and with the small mental operation of counting the time from seven in the morning to the fraction of the hour of the observation.

"Eight o'clock"—and sometimes I counted the minutes.

Sometimes I varied the form of the calculation, saying to myself: "Eight hours and a quarter—or a half, or so many minutes. Early will not take to the road to-day, not even if he gets it. It is too late."

"Eight hours, and—!"

At moments, in my mind's eye, I could see my courier galloping through the white dust of the pike to the station, and there came a later moment when I said, still speaking to myself: "By this he has reached the station; now the message is off; now it is in Grant's hand, and, if troops are not already on the water, there is commotion at City Point, and much repetition around headquarters of the news. Early is marching on Washington. Washington is in peril!"

Four o'clock—at this point I turn to my official report for certainty—at four o'clock almost to the minute—four o'clock, in my account of time against General Early marking the ninth hour—and how I turned the finding over and over in my mind! The woods across the fields showed signs of renewed life. In the fringing of scattered trees, by looking closely, I could see what I thought moving figures. Now and then these appeared in patches of sunlight of greater transparency than the general mass of late afternoon shadows, helping my glass bring them distinctly to view—men with slouched hats, and in dust-colored clothes—very reliable telltales, all of them, but not to be compared in that respect to the flashes electrically emitted by gun-barrels suddenly sunstruck. I passed the glass to the officer nearest me, and said, simply:

"They are coming."

And then to an orderly, the horses having been again taken down the hill: "Bring up the horses. We may have to ride."

"Yes," said Colonel Catlin, after a long look, "they come, and no mistake."

"Only see how long the line is!" said another of my officers.

And sure enough, out of the ragged fringe of trees there came a thin line of skirmishers—I say *line* out of grace, for there was no "dressing on guides"—that extended from the river up to the Thomas mansion, and beyond it, though how far I could form no idea on account of obstructions to the view; far enough, however, to overlap the extreme left of Ricketts' left regiment. And then, was the extension of the skirmishers a proper measure of the front of the main line advancing behind it? My hope, already faint, began shrivelling up like a child's rubber balloon while the air goes whistling out through an unlucky rent.

I turned the glass to where Ricketts was in holding, his brigades lying down, and looking for the most part like a far-stretched blue thread. The regiments on his left—two it seemed—were on the run, taking intervals in the direction of the Thomas house, a desperate expedient, but the only one left the good soldier, conscious of the necessity of saving his flank by equalizing fronts as best he could. But how thin the formation looked! I shivered, thinking of what would happen to it in the face of the rush of a solid line of battle.

And presently the slouch-hatted skirmishers began firing. Then, as at a signal, the battle broke from its leash. All the guns on the thither side of the river awoke, reminding me of sleeping dogs responding to a kennel-cry. And again, drowning the crackle of the more distant skirmishers, and the yelping, they searched the low places and the high everywhere behind, over, and in front of Ricketts. In the common crash above the block-house we were not considered unworthy special attention. With a mighty *swishing*, comparable to nothing else I know of, though nearest the ragged tear of rushing locomotives, the missiles rent the air over our heads seemingly not more than an arm's-length too high. The tempest spent, we counted one another, thankful for another escape; and when I got a breathing time to give attention to the situation in the field proper, the skirmishers were giving place to a line of battle emerged from the woods, and reaching from near the river's bluff out of sight almost solidly. I saw the flags in furious waving, and the mounted officers galloping to and fro in the rear. Then I became interested in the number of regiments moving into action, and while trying to count the flags in sight, the whole long array under them began firing. This brought them to a slower movement; whereupon a misty, pale-blue envelopment which I knew to be musketry smoke dimmed them to the eye; while out of it arose the inevitable "*Yelp, yelp, yelp,*" a vent to battle passion strangely unlike that of any other of the great fighting Anglo-Saxon families.

I turned my glass anxiously upon the blue showing of Ricketts' line. The ground it occupied was friendly, being in many places broken by rain-washed ditches and shallow irregularities, precious nevertheless to old soldiers rich with the wisdom of many battles. And now these, on their bellies or knees, half-hidden, were countering the comparatively harmless fury of the tempest sweeping over them. Their flags, though hazy in the rising smoke, were in display clear to the Thomas mansion, and they were so steady in their uprightness, so motionless, I knew their sharp steel shoes had been driven into the earth *to stay*. Occasionally the folds blew out in the breeze, and what touches of roselike color the scene then borrowed from them!

Bringing my observation down closer to the stand-point I occupied, I noticed next a bare space of a hundred or more yards between the regiment on the extreme right of the line and the river. Slowly and inadvertently the forma-tion had drawn itself leftward. The discovery was the more disquieting, since I could not soothe myself with a hope that the enemy would fail to see the lapse and hurry a battery into it. While thinking what to do, a cheering and an out-burst of musketry arose beyond the railroad bridge; and looking thither, a sight broke upon me in the stress of which all interest else was for the moment smothered.

I looked, as did my officers, and we were all astonished—I never more so.

In the allusion to the skirmishers in the direction of Frederick, a page or so back, I described them as shifting from their original position by crawling back towards the river, with what hopeful purpose I could not make out. Hours had come and gone, hours of painful retirement, during which the good men, undiscouraged, undaunted by the abandonment so discernible after the burn-ing of the wooden bridge, literally wormed themselves off the field, stopping at intervals to fight the enemy off, and keeping the railroad bridge always in mind. Now they had reached the bridge. By what signal I do not know, not unlikely by spontaneous impulse, they sprang up, and, unmindful of exposure, made a dash for liberty. And when I saw them they were on the bridge coming.

To judge this feat, and what of courage there was involved in it, the reader should keep in thought that the great steel structure was of goodly length, sixty or sixty-five yards at least, and unfloored, leaving passage over it afoot along cross-ties and girders. Nor should one's fancy stop there. Quite forty feet below the adventurers ran the water swiftly enough to make the head swim, and only too ready to catch a sufferer falling, and hide him in its remorseless, dark-brown current. Danger upon danger—and yet another. Every step taken was under fire of antagonists pressing forward furious at sight of the possible escape. Such the spectacle presented to us spellbound on the hill!

We saw two or three hundred reach the bridge—we saw them on the ties stepping short and carefully, as they needs must—we saw them from habit form in column order, not crowding, or pushing, or struggling to pass one another, or yelling. Now and then we could see one stop short, let go his musket, throw up his hands convulsively, and with a splash disappear in the stream beneath. Some of these may be there now unrecovered, buried forever in the whelming sand and silt. How many were thus overtaken may never be known. *Missing* was the simple record written on the next muster-roll over against their names. Fortunately, though holding the moving files in plain view, the artillerymen mercifully refrained from firing.

We watched the coming breathlessly; and when the crossing became assured I was the first of my party to speak.

"Hurry down," I said to Colonel Catlin, "and meet those men. The man in command is brave. I should like to know his name."

Catlin went running.

Upon our shore the fugitives halted, and while some of them turned for a last shot at the enemy, the others swung their caps and cheered, then reformed and in perfect order marched away as I supposed to their commands. I have not words to express my admiration. Enough that I cannot now recall an incident of occurrence under my eyes more desperate in the undertaking, yet more successful in outcome. From every point of view it was heroism.

Colonel Catlin brought me the name of the leader—Lieutenant George E. Davis, of the Tenth Vermont Infantry.[5]

"Lieutenant?" I said. "Only a lieutenant! There were captains over there. Where are they?"

I had this answer:

"The first companies were hundred-day men of Colonel Brown's, green in service, officers and privates. When Lieutenant Davis arrived, Brown's captains voluntarily offered to put themselves under his orders."

"Old or young?"

"As handsome a boy as I ever saw."

"You should have brought him to me."

"I suggested that," the colonel replied, "but he begged to be excused. His regiment was fighting, and he had not the time."

I followed the little column until it was out of sight in the low grounds by the old mill.

---

[5]Lieutenant Davis is yet living, a universally respected citizen of Burlington, Vermont. He was discharged at the end of the war a captain, a rank altogether disproportionate to his merits.

The battle, when I again reverted to it, was still in fierce progress, with the Confederates brought to a stand-still; a circumstance that was giving me great satisfaction, when Colonel Ross, whose blue eyes were clear as a baby's, and singularly far-sighted, spoke up in his quiet way: "There, in the edge of the wood beyond the cornfield, what is it?"

We all followed his pointing, I with my glass. One quick glance was enough.

"A second line, as I live. Here—what say you all? Look!"

The glass made the round. The men agreed with me. Every face showed excitement.

"They are halted, and waiting," I said; "and that means reserve."

Then Ross spoke again.

"Still another line! Look! It is in motion in rear of the one in the edge of the timber. I see brass pieces, and horses on the left. They are just coming up."

My heart jumped into my mouth. There could be no question about the new appearances. What was to be done? The call was for prompt action. It was no longer mine to say when Ricketts and his stubborn regiments should be brought off. They must go now. Heaven grant it was not too late! I thrust the glass into my pocket.

Calmly as I could I looked at my watch. My recollection is that the hands stood at

FOUR O'CLOCK AND TWENTY MINUTES

The shadows of the sun were stretching out, telling of evening and night, of the day almost gone. A sense of relief came to me: if the day was lost to me, General Early might not profit by it. Measured by his designs, and the importance of time to his cause, my loss was scarce worth a pinch of good old Scotch snuff; and so thinking, I betook myself to action.

*Promoted by Robert E. Lee to take command of a corps in the sum-
mer of 1864, Jubal Early took his troops north through the
Shenandoah Valley, crossing the Potomac into Maryland to march
eastward to threaten Washington. Early disparages the compe-
tence of his opponents, but overlooked in his memoir is the realiza-
tion that this was not the same war that Stonewall Jackson fought
in the Valley two years before. Back then, Jackson deftly danced
between converging Union forces poorly led by deadbeat generals.
Early was no less brave and audacious than Jackson, but in the
end, he lost the Valley. Fight as he might, Early could not change
the outcome against an enemy whose greater numbers he thought
were so badly led.*

A Memoir of the Last Year of the War for Independence in the Confederate States of America

BY JUBAL EARLY

Note by the Original Publisher.

The author of this work, having generously placed it at the disposal of the
Memorial Associations of Virginia,—engaged in the pious task of collecting the remains of the Southern soldiers who fell on Virginia battle-fields,
with the view of enclosing and marking their graves,—it is published at the
lowest possible cost, for the purpose of raising funds for this praiseworthy object. All the profits arising from the sale of the work will be
sacredly appropriated to the end in view. In a letter to the publisher Gen.
Early says: "Perhaps I might have made something by a sale of the work;
but I wanted to keep clear of all suspicion of writing a book for money."
He adds: "You can judge whether it is worthy of republication. One thing

is certain—it contains the truth." And nobody who knows Jubal A. Early as we know him, will question his veracity.

Apart from the intrinsic merits of the work,—as a valuable contribution to the history of the late war—revealing facts connected with a campaign that has not been understood even by our own people,—it is hoped that the laudable object of those who have incurred the expense of republishing it, will secure for this production of a gallant and meritorious officer an extended sale.

Preface.

Under a solemn sense of duty to my unhappy country, and to the brave soldiers who fought under me, as well as to myself, the following pages have been written.

When the question of practical secession from the United States arose, as a citizen of the State of Virginia, and a member of the Convention called by the authority of the Legislature of that State, I opposed secession with all the ability I possessed, with the hope that the horrors of civil war might be averted, and that a returning sense of duty and justice on the part of the masses of the Northern States, would induce them to respect the rights of the people of the South. While some Northern politicians and editors, who subsequently took rank among the most unscrupulous and vindictive of our enemies, and now hold me to be a traitor and rebel, were openly and sedulously justifying and encouraging secession, I was laboring honestly and earnestly to preserve the Union.

As a member of the Virginia Convention, I voted against the ordinance of secession on its passage by that body, with the hope that, even then, the collision of arms might be avoided, and some satisfactory adjustment arrived at. The adoption of that ordinance wrung from me bitter tears of grief; but I at once recognized my duty to abide the decision of my native State, and to defend her soil against invasion. Any scruples which I may have entertained as to the right of secession, were soon dispelled by the mad, wicked, and unconstitutional measures of the authorities at Washington, and the frenzied clamour of the people of the North for war upon their former brethren of the South. I then, and ever since have, regarded Abraham Lincoln, his counsellors and supporters, as the real traitors who had overthrown the constitution and government of the United States, and established in lieu thereof an odious despotism; and this opinion I entered on the journal of the Convention when I signed the ordinance of secession. I recognized the right of resistance and revolution as exercised by our fathers in 1776, and, without cavil as to the name by which it was called, I entered the military service of my State, willingly, cheerfully, and zealously.

When the State of Virginia became one of the Confederate States, and her troops were turned over to the Confederate Government, I embraced the cause of the whole Confederacy with equal ardour, and continued in the service, with the determination to devote all the energy and talent I possessed to the common defence. I fought through the entire war, without once regretting the course I had pursued; with an abiding faith in the justice of our cause; and I never saw the moment when I would have been willing to consent to any compromise or settlement short of the absolute independence of my country.

It was my fortune to participate in most of the great military operations in which the army in Virginia was engaged, both before and after General Lee assumed the command. In the last year of this momentous struggle, I commanded, at different times, a division and two corps of General Lee's Army, in the campaign from the Rapidan to James River, and, subsequently, a separate force which marched into Maryland, threatened Washington City, and then went through an eventful campaign in the Valley of Virginia. No detailed reports of the operations of these different commands were made before the close of the war, and the campaign in Maryland and the Valley of Virginia has been the subject of much comment and misapprehension. I have now written a narrative of the operations of all my commands during the closing year of the war, and lay it before the world as a contribution to the history of our great struggle for independence. In giving that narrative, I have made such statements of the positions and strength of the opposing forces in Virginia, and such reference to their general operations, as were necessary to enable the reader to understand it; but I do not pretend to detail the operations of other commanders.

I have not found it necessary to be guilty of the injustice of attempting to pull down the reputation of any of my fellow officers, in order to build up my own. My operations and my campaign stand on their own merits, whatever they may be. Nor, in anything I may have found it necessary to say in regard to the conduct of my troops, do I wish to be understood as, in way, decrying the soldiers who constituted the rank and file of my commands. I believe that the world has never produced a body of men superior, in courage, patriotism, and endurance, to the private soldiers of the Confederate armies. I have repeatedly seen those soldiers submit, with cheerfulness, to privations and hardships which would appear to be almost incredible; and the wild cheers of our brave men, (which were so different from the studied hurrahs of the Yankees,) when their thin lines sent back opposing hosts of Federal troops, staggering, reeling, and flying, have often thrilled every fibre in my heart. I have seen, with my own eyes, ragged, barefooted, and hungry Confederate soldiers perform deeds, which, if performed in days of yore by mailed warriors in glittering armour, would have inspired the harp of the minstrel and the pen of the poet.

I do not aspire to the character of a historian, but, having been a witness of and participator in great events, I have given a statement of what I saw and did, for the use of the future historian. Without breaking the thread of my narrative, as it proceeds, I have given, in notes, comments on some of the errors and inconsistencies committed by the commander of the Federal army, General Grant, and the Federal Secretary of War, Mr. Stanton, in their reports made since the close of the war; also some instances of cruelty and barbarity committed by the Federal commanders, which were brought to my immediate attention, as well as some other matters of interest.

As was to have been expected, our enemies have flooded the press with sketches and histories, in which all the appliances of a meretricious literature have been made use of, to glorify their own cause and its supporters, and to blacken ours. But some Southern writers also, who preferred the pen to the sword or musket, have not been able to resist the temptation to rush into print; and, accordingly, carping criticisms have been written by the light of after events, and even histories of the war attempted by persons, who imagined that the distinctness of their vision was enhanced by distance from the scene of conflict, and an exemption from the disturbing elements of whistling bullets and bursting shells. Perhaps other writers of the same class may follow, and various speculations be indulged in, as to the causes of our disasters. As for myself, I have not undertaken to speculate as to the causes of our failure, as I have seen abundant reason for it in the tremendous odds brought against us. Having had some means of judging, I will, however, say that, in my opinion, both President Davis and General Lee, in their respective spheres, did all for the success of our cause which it was possible for mortal men to do; and it is a great privilege and comfort for me so to believe, and to have been able to bring with me into exile a profound love and veneration for those great men.

In regard to my own services, all I have to say is, that I have the conscious-ness of having done my duty to my country, to the very best of my ability, and, whatever may be my fate, I would not exchange that consciousness for untold millions. I have come into exile rather than submit to the yoke of the oppressors of my country; but I have never thought of attributing aught of blame or censure to those true men who, after having nobly done their duty in the dreadful strug-gle through which we passed, now, that it has gone against us, remain to share the misfortunes of their people, and to aid and comfort them in their trials; on the contrary, I appreciate and honour their motives. I have not sought refuge in another land from insensibility to the wrongs and sufferings of my own country; but I feel deeply and continually for them, and could my life secure the redemp-tion of that country, as it has been often risked, so now it would be as freely given for that object.

There were men born and nurtured in the Southern States, and some of them in my own State, who took sides with our enemies, and aided in desolat-ing and humiliating the land of their own birth, and of the graves of their ances-tors. Some of them rose to high positions in the United States Army, and others to high civil positions. I envy them not their dearly bought prosperity. I had rather be the humblest private soldier who fought in the ranks of the Confeder-ate Army, and now, maimed and disabled, hobbles on his crutches from house to house, to receive his daily bread from the hands of the grateful women for whose homes he fought, than the highest of those renegades and traitors. Let them enjoy the advantages of their present positions as best they may! for the deep and bitter execrations of an entire people now attend them, and an immor-tality of infamy awaits them. As for all the enemies who have overrun or aided in overrunning my country, there is a wide and impassable gulf between us, in which I see the blood of slaughtered friends, comrades, and countrymen, which all the waters in the firmament above and the seas beneath cannot wash away. Those enemies have undertaken to render our cause odious and infa-mous; and among other atrocities committed by them in the effort to do so, an humble subordinate, poor Wirz, has been selected as a victim to a fiendish spirit, and basely murdered under an executive edict, founded on the sentence of a vindictive and illegal tribunal. Let them continue this system! they are but erecting monuments to their own eternal dishonour, and furnishing finger posts to guide the historian in his researches. They may employ the infamous Holt, with his "Bureau of Military Justice," to sacrifice other victims on the altars of their hatred, and provost marshals, and agents of the "Freedman's

Bureau," may riot in all the license of petty tyranny, but our enemies can no more control the verdict of impartial history, than they can escape that doom which awaits them at the final judgment.

During the war, slavery was used as a catchword to arouse the passions of a fanatical mob, and to some extent the prejudices of the civilized world were excited against us; but the war was not made on our part for slavery. High dignitaries in both church and state in Old England, and puritans in New England, had participated in the profits of a trade, by which the ignorant and barbarous natives of Africa were brought from that country, and sold into slavery in the American Colonies. The generation in the Southern States which defended their country in the late war, found amongst them, in a civilized and christianized condition, 4,000,000 of the descendants of those degraded Africans. The Almighty Creator of the Universe had stamped them, indelibly, with a different colour and an inferior physical and mental organization. He had not done this from mere caprice or whim, but for wise purposes. An amalgamation of the races was in contravention of His designs, or He would not have made them so different. This immense number of people could not have been transported back to the wilds from which their ancestors were taken, or if they could have been, it would have resulted in their relapse into barbarism. Reason, common sense, true humanity to the black, as well as the safety of the white race, required that the inferior race should be kept in a state of subordination. The condition of domestic slavery, as it existed in the South, had not only resulted in a great improvement in the moral and physical condition of the negro race, but had furnished a class of labourers as happy and contented as any in the world, if not more so. Their labour had not only developed the immense resources of the immediate country in which they were located, but was the main source of the great prosperity of the United States, and furnished the means for the employment of millions of the working classes in other countries. Nevertheless, the struggle made by the people of the South was not for the institution of slavery, but for the inestimable right of self-government, against the domination of a fanatical faction at the North; and slavery was the mere occasion of the development of the antagonism between the two sections. That right of self-government has been lost, and slavery violently abolished. Four millions of blacks have thus been thrown on their own resources, to starve, to die, and to relapse into barbarism; and inconceivable miseries have been entailed on the white race.

The civilized world will find, too late, that its philanthropy has been all false, and its religion all wrong on this subject; and the people of the United States will find that, under the pretence of "saving the life of the nation, and upholding the old flag," they have surrendered their own liberties into the hands of that worst of all tyrants, a body of senseless fanatics.

When the passions and infatuations of the day shall have been dissipated by time, and all the results of the late war shall have passed into irrevocable history, the future chronicler of that history will have a most important duty to perform, and posterity, while poring over its pages, will be lost in wonder at the follies and crimes committed in this generation.

My narrative is now given to the public, and the sole merit I claim for it is that of truthfulness. In writing it, I have received material aid from an accurate diary kept by Lieutenant William W. Old, aide to Major General Edward Johnson, who was with me during the campaign in Maryland and the Shenandoah Valley until the 12th of August, 1864, and the copious notes of Captain J. Kotchkiss, who acted as Topographical Engineer for the 2nd Corps and the Army of the Valley District, and recorded the events of each day, from the opening of the campaign on the Rapidan in May, 1864, until the affair at Waynesboro' in March, 1865.

J. A. EARLY
November, 1866.

Preface to Second Edition.

This work was written under an imperative sense of duty, as a matter of historical evidence; and, for reasons which will be understood, I determined from the beginning not to make it a source of personal profit. The first edition was published in Canada at my own expense for gratuitous distribution, and was necessarily limited. Some errors and inaccuracies which unavoidably crept into that edition,—the greater part being mere typographical mistakes,—have been corrected, though these corrections make no material change in any of the statements of facts contained in my narrative; and this edition is published for the benefit of the Ladies' Memorial Associations of Virginia, which have undertaken the work of collecting the remains and marking the graves of the Confederate dead, who fell on the battle-fields of that State. Let it not be supposed that this appropriation has been made because these Associations are in my own dearly loved State. No! the feelings which have dictated it are not confined to her limits, but embrace the whole South, from the Potomac to the Rio Grande.

Our enemies are in the habit of referring scoffingly to Virginia as the "sacred soil;" and in the hearts of all her true sons and daughters, her soil is, and from time immemorial has been held sacred; as well because of the associations connected with her history, as because it is the land of their birth, and with that soil mingle the ashes of their ancestors. This sentiment all true men everywhere must appreciate and honour. But the soil of Virginia is now, and henceforth will be, held sacred in the hearts of all true Southern men and women, because she has been baptized in the blood and has received into her bosom the remains of thousands upon thousands of the truest and noblest sons of the entire Confederacy. It is from this consideration that I have made the appropriation designated.

When the duty assumed by the ladies of Virginia shall have been fulfilled, it will carry consolation to the hearts of many mourning mothers and widows in the savannahs of the South, as well as upon the far distant plains of Texas, whose hearts will yearn with gratitude towards their noble sisters of the grand old State—grand even in her misfortunes.

J. A. Early.

Toronto, *February 1st*, 1867.

Campaign in Virginia, from the Rapidan to James River.

INTRODUCTION.

On the 3rd of May, 1864, the positions of the Confederate Army under General Lee, and the Federal Army under Lieutenant-General Grant, in Virginia, were as follows: General Lee held the southern bank of the Rapidan River, in Orange county, with his right resting near the mouth of Mine Run, and his left extending to Liberty Mills on the road from Gordonsville (via Madison Court House) to the Shenandoah Valley; while the crossings of the river on the right, and the roads on the left were watched by cavalry. Ewell's corps was on the right, Hill's on the left, and two divisions of Longstreet's corps were encamped in the rear; near Gordonsville. Grant's army (composed of the Army of the Potomac under Meade, and the 9th corps under Burnside,) occupied the north banks of the Rapidan and Robertson rivers; the main body being encamped in Culpeper county, and on the Rappahannock River.

I am satisfied that General Lee's army did not exceed 50,000 effective men of all arms. The report of the Federal Secretary of War, Stanton, shows that the "available force present for duty, May 1st, 1864," in Grant's army, was 141,166, to-wit: In the Army of the Potomac 120,386, and in the 9th corps 20,780. The draft in the United States was being energetically enforced, and volunteering had been greatly stimulated by high bounties. The North-Western States had tendered large bodies of troops to serve one hundred days, in order to relieve other troops on garrison and local duty, and this enabled Grant to put in the field a large number of troops which had been employed on that kind of duty. It was known that he was receiving heavy reinforcements up to the very time of his movement on the 4th of May, and afterwards; so that the statement of his force on the 1st of May, by Stanton, does not cover the whole force with which he commenced the campaign. Moreover, Secretary Stanton's report shows that there were, in the Department of Washington and the Middle Department, 47,751 available men for duty, the chief part of which, he says, was called to the front after the campaign began, "in order to repair the losses of the Army of the Potomac;" and Grant says that, at Spotsylvania Court House, "the 13th, 14th, 15th, 16th, 17th, and 18th [of May,] were consumed in manoeuvring and awaiting the arrival of reinforcements from Washington." His army, therefore, must have numbered very nearly, if not quite, 200,000 men, before a junction was effected with Butler.

On the 4th of May, it was discovered that Grant's Army was moving towards Germanna Ford on the Rapidan, which was ten or twelve miles from our right. This movement had begun on the night of the 3rd, and the enemy succeeded in seizing the ford, and effecting a crossing, as the river was guarded at that point by only a small cavalry picket. The direct road from Germanna Ford to Richmond passes by Spotsylvania Court House, and when Grant had effected his crossing, he was nearer to Richmond than General Lee was. From Orange Court House, near which were General Lee's headquarters, there are two nearly parallel roads running eastwardly to Fredericksburg—the one which is nearest to the river being called "The old Stone Pike," and the other "The Plank Road." The road from Germanna Ford to Spotsylvania Court House, crosses the old Stone Pike at the "Old Wilderness Tavern," and two or three miles further on, it crosses the Plank Road.

As soon as it was ascertained that Grant's movement was a serious one, preparations were made to meet him, and the troops of General Lee's Army were put in motion—Ewell's corps moving on the old Stone Pike, and Hill's corps on the Plank Road; into which latter road Longstreet's force also came, from his camp near Gordonsville.

Ewell's corps, to which my division belonged, crossed Mine Run, and encamped at Locust Grove, four miles beyond, on the afternoon of the 4th. When the rest of the corps moved, my division and Ramseur's brigade of Rodes' division were left to watch the fords of the Rapidan, until relieved by cavalry. As soon as this was done, I moved to the position occupied by the rest of the corps, carrying Ramseur with me.

Ewell's corps contained three divisions of infantry, to-wit: Johnson's, Rodes', and my own (Early's). At this time, one of my brigades (Hoke's) was absent, having been with Hoke in North Carolina; and I had only three present, to wit: Hays', Pegram's, and Gordon's. One of Rodes' brigades (R. D. Johnston's) was at Hanover Junction. I had about 4,000 muskets for duty; Johnson about the same number; and Rodes (including Johnston's brigade) about 6,000.

BATTLES OF THE WILDERNESS.

OPERATIONS OF EARLY'S DIVISION.

On the morning of the 5th, Ewell's corps was put in motion, my division bringing up the rear. A short distance from the Old Wilderness Tavern, and just in advance of the place where a road diverges to the left from the old Stone Pike to the Germanna Ford road, the enemy, in heavy force, was encountered, and Jones' brigade, of Johnson's division, and Battle's brigade, of Rodes' division, were driven back in some confusion. My division was ordered up, and formed across the pike; Gordon's brigade being on the right of the road. This brigade, as soon as it was brought into line, was ordered forward, and advanced, through a dense pine thicket, in gallant style. In conjunction with Daniel's Doles', and Ramseur's brigades, of Rodes' division, it drove the enemy back with heavy loss, capturing several hundred prisoners, and gaining a commanding position on the right. Johnson, at the same time, was heavily engaged in his front; his division being on the left of the pike, and extending across the road to the Germanna Ford road, which has been mentioned. After the enemy had been repulsed, Hays' brigade was sent to Johnson's left, in order to participate in a forward movement; and it did move forward, some half-a-mile or so, encountering the enemy in force; but, from some mistake, not meeting with the expected co-operation, except from one regiment of Jones' brigade (the 25th

Va.), the most of which was captured, it was drawn back to Johnson's line, and took position on his left.

Pegram's brigade was subsequently sent to take position on Hays' left; and, just before night, a very heavy attack was made on its front, which was repulsed with severe loss to the enemy. In this affair, General Pegram received a severe wound in the leg, which disabled him for the field for some months.

During the afternoon there was heavy skirmishing along the whole line, several attempts having been made by the enemy, without success, to regain the position from which he had been driven; and the fighting extended to General Lee's right, on the Plank Road. Gordon occupied the position which he had gained, on the right, until after dark, when he was withdrawn to the extreme left, and his place occupied by part of Rodes' division.

The troops encountered, in the beginning of the fight, consisted of the 5th corps, under Warren; but other troops were brought to his assistance. At the close of the day, Ewell's corps had captured over a thousand prisoners, besides inflicting on the enemy very heavy losses in killed and wounded. Two pieces of artillery had been abandoned by the enemy, just in front of the point at which Johnson's right and Rodes' left joined, and were subsequently secured by our troops.

After the withdrawal of Gordon's brigade from the right, the whole of my division was on the left of the road diverging from the pike, in extension of Johnson's line. All my brigades had behaved handsomely; and Gordon's advance, at the time of the confusion, in the beginning of the fight, was made with great energy and dispatch, and was just in time to prevent a serious disaster.

Early on the morning of the 6th, the fighting was resumed, and a very heavy attack was made on the front occupied by Pegram's brigade (now under the command of Colonel Hoffman, of the 31st Virginia Regiment); but it was handsomely repulsed, as were several subsequent attacks at the same point.

These attacks were so persistent, that two regiments of Johnson's division were moved to the rear of Pegram's brigade, for the purpose of supporting it; and, when an offer was made to relieve it, under the apprehension that its ammunition might be exhausted, the men of that gallant brigade begged that they might be allowed to retain their position, stating that they were getting along very well indeed, and wanted no help.

During the morning, the fact was communicated to General Ewell, by our cavalry scouts, that a column of the enemy's infantry was moving between our left and the river, with the apparent purpose of turning our left flank; and information was also received that Burnside's corps had crossed the river, and was in rear of the enemy's right. I received directions to watch this column, and take steps to prevent its getting to our rear; and Johnston's brigade, of Rodes' division, which had just arrived from Hanover Junction, was sent to me for that purpose. This brigade, with some artillery, was put in position, some distance to my left, so as to command some bye-roads coming in from the river. In the meantime General Gordon had sent out a scouting party on foot, which discovered what was supposed to be the enemy's right flank resting in the woods, in front of my division; and, during my absence while posting Johnston's brigade, he reported the fact to General Ewell, and suggested the propriety of attacking this flank of the enemy with his brigade, which was not engaged. On my return, the subject was mentioned to me by General Ewell, and I stated to him the danger and risk of making the attack under the circumstances, as a column was threatening our left flank, and Burnside's corps was in rear of the enemy's flank on which the attack was suggested. General Ewell concurred with me in this opinion, and the impolicy of the attempt at that time was obvious, as we had no reserves, and, if it failed, and the enemy showed any enterprise, a serious disaster would befall, not only our corps, but General Lee's whole army. In the afternoon, when the column threatening our left had been withdrawn, and it had been ascertained that Burnside had gone to Grant's left, on account of the heavy fighting on that flank, at my suggestion, General Ewell ordered the movement which Gordon had proposed. I determined to make it with Gordon's brigade supported by Johnston's, and to follow it up, if successful, with the rest of my division. Gordon's brigade was accordingly formed in line near the edge of the woods in which the enemy's right rested, and Johnston's in the rear, with orders to follow Gordon and obey his orders. I posted my Adjutant General, Major John W. Daniel, with a courier, in a position to be communicated with by Gordon, so as to inform me of the success attending the movement, and enable me to put in the other brigades at the right time. As soon as Gordon started, which was a very short time before sunset, I rode to my line and threw forward Pegram's brigade in a position to move when required. In the meantime Gordon had become engaged, and, while Pegram's brigade was being formed in line, I saw some of Gordon's men coming back in confusion, and Colonel Evans, of the 31st Georgia Regiment, endeavoring to rally them. Colonel Evans informed me that his regiment, which was on Gordon's right, had struck the enemy's breastworks and had given way. I immediately ordered Pegram's brigade forward, and directed Colonel Evans to guide it. Its advance was through a dense thicket of underbrush, but it crossed the road running through Johnson's line, and struck the enemy's works, and one of the regiments, the 13th Virginia, under Colonel Terrill, got possession of part of the line, when Colonel Hoffman ordered the brigade to retire, as it was getting dark, and there was much confusion produced by the difficulties of the advance. Gordon had struck the enemy's right flank behind breastworks, and a part of his brigade was thrown into disorder. In going through the woods, Johnston had obliqued too much and passed to Gordon's left, getting in rear of the enemy. Major Daniel, not hearing from Gordon, had endeavored to get to him, when, finding the condition of things, he attempted to lead one of Pegram's regiments to his assistance, and was shot down while behaving with great gallantry, receiving a wound in the leg which has permanently disabled him. Notwithstanding the confusion in part of his brigade, Gordon succeeded in throwing the enemy's right flank into great confusion, capturing two brigadier generals (Seymour and Shaler), and several hundred prisoners, all of the 6th Corps, under Sedgwick. The advance of Pegram's brigade, and the demonstration of Johnston's brigade in the rear, where it encountered a part of the enemy's force and captured some prisoners, contributed materially to the result. It was fortunate, however, that darkness came to close this affair, as the enemy, if he had been able to discover the disorder on our side, might have brought up fresh troops and availed himself of our condition. As it was, doubtless, the lateness of the hour caused him to be surprised, and the approaching darkness increased the confusion in his ranks, as he could not see the strength of the attacking force, and probably imagined it to be much more formidable than it really was. All of the brigades engaged in the attack were drawn back, and formed on a new line in front of the old one, and obliquely to it.

At light on the morning of the 7th, an advance was made, which disclosed the fact that the enemy had given up his line of works in front of my whole line, and a good portion of Johnson's. Between the lines, a large number of his dead had been left, and, at his breastworks, a large number of muskets and knapsacks had been abandoned, and there was every indication of great confusion. It was not till then, that we ascertained the full extent of the success attending the movement of the evening before. The enemy had entirely abandoned the left side of the road, across which Johnson's line extended, and my division and a part of his were thrown forward, occupying a part of the abandoned works on the right of the road, and leaving all those on the left in our rear. This rendered our line straight, the left having been previously thrown back, making a curve.

During this day there was some skirmishing, but no serious fighting in my front. The loss in my division during the fighting in the Wilderness was comparatively light.

On the morning of the 8th, it was discovered that the enemy was leaving our front and moving towards Spotsylvania Court House. General Lee's army was also put in motion; Ewell's corps moving along the line occupied by our troops on the day before, until it reached the Plank Road, where it struck across to Shady Grove, which is on the road from Orange Court House to Spotsylvania Court House.

On reaching the Plank Road, I received through General A. P. Hill, who was sick and unable to remain on duty, an order from General Lee, transferring Hays' brigade from my division to Johnson's, in order that it might be consolidated with another Louisiana brigade in that division, whose Brigadier-General had been killed at the Wilderness, and Johnston's brigade from Rodes' division to mine; and assigning me to the temporary command of Hill's corps, which was still in position across the Plank Road, and was to bring up the rear. I accordingly turned over the command of my division to Gordon, the senior Brigadier left with it, and assumed command of Hill's corps.*

---

*In his official report, Grant says: "Early on the 5th, the advance corps, the 5th, Major-General G. K. Warren commanding, met and engaged the enemy outside his entrenchments near Mine Run;" and further on he says: "On the morning of the 7th, reconnoissances showed that the enemy had fallen behind his entrenched lines, with pickets to the front covering a part of the battle-field. From this it was evident to my mind that the two days fighting had satisfied him of his inability to further maintain the contest in the open field, notwithstanding his advantage of position, and that he could wait an attack behind his works." In mentioning his movement toward Spotsylvania Court House, he says: "But the enemy having become aware of our movement, and having the shorter line, was enabled to reach there first." If these statements were true, the only legitimate inference is that General Lee had an entrenched line on, or near Mine Run, previously established; that the battle commenced immediately in front of the works on this line; and that, after the two days fighting, he had fallen behind them to wait an attack. Whereas the fact is, that the only entrenched line on, or near, Mine Run, was that made, on its west bank, when Meade crossed the river at the end of November, 1863, and which was used for that occasion only. The fighting in the Wilderness began eight or ten miles east of that line, and at no time during that fighting was it used for any purpose. The "entrenched lines" occupied by our army on the morning of the 7th, were slight temporary works thrown up, on, or in front of the battle-field, though

BATTLES AROUND SPOTSYLVANIA COURT HOUSE.

OPERATIONS OF HILL'S CORPS.

Hill's Corps was composed of Heth's, Wilcox's, and Mahone's (formerly Anderson's) divisions of infantry, and three battalions of artillery under Colonel Walker. When I took command of it, the infantry numbered about 13,000 muskets for duty.

General Lee's orders to me, were to move by Todd's tavern along the Brock Road to Spotsylvania Court House, as soon as our front was clear of the enemy. In order to get into that road, it was necessary to reopen an old one leading from Hill's right, by which I was enabled to take a cross road leading into the road from Shady Grove to Todd's tavern. The waggon trains and all the artillery, except one battalion, was sent around by Shady Grove. About a mile from the road from Shady Grove to Todd's tavern, the enemy's cavalry videttes were encountered, and Mahone's division was thrown forward to develope the enemy's force and position. Mahone encountered a force of infantry, which had moved up from Todd's tavern towards Shady Grove, and had quite a brisk engagement with it, causing it to fall back rapidly towards the former place. At the same time, General Hampton, who had communicated with me, after I left the Plank Road, moved with his cavalry on my right and struck the enemy on the flank and rear; but on account of want of knowledge of the country on our part, and the approach of darkness, the enemy was enabled to make his escape. This affair developed the fact that the enemy was in possession of Todd's tavern and the Brock Road, and a continuation of my march would have led through his entire army. We bivouacked for the night, at the

---

it is probable that, at some points, the line may not have been so far to the front, as our troops had advanced; as, in taking it, regard was necessarily had to the conformation of the ground. On our left, as will be seen above, the line was advanced in front of Grant's own line of the previous day.

Grant says General Lee had the advantage of position. As the latter had to move from his lines on the Rapidan and attack Grant in the Wilderness, how happened it that he was enabled to get the advantage of position, after the two days fighting. He also says that General Lee was enabled to reach Spotsylvania Court House, first, because he had the shorter line. The fact is, that, as the two armies lay in their positions at the Wilderness, their lines were parallel to the road to Spotsylvania Court House. Grant had the possession of the direct road to that place, and he had the start. General Lee had to move on the circuitous route by Shady Grove, and he was enabled to arrive at the Court House first with part of his infantry, because his cavalry held Grant's advance in check for nearly an entire day.

place from which Mahone had driven the enemy, and a force was thrown out towards Todd's tavern, which was about a mile distant.

Very early next morning, (the 9th,) I received an order from General Lee, through Hampton, to move on the Shady Grove road towards Spotsylvania Court House, which I did, crossing a small river called the Po, twice. After reaching the rear of the position occupied by the other two corps, I was ordered to Spotsylvania Court House, to take position on the right, and cover the road from that place to Fredericksburg. No enemy appeared in my front on this day, except at a distance on the Fredericksburg Road.

Early on the morning of the 10th, I was ordered to move one of my divisions back, to cover the crossing of the Po on the Shady Grove road; and to move with another division, to the rear and left, by the way of Spotsylvania Old Court House, and drive back a column of the enemy which had crossed the Po and taken possession of the Shady Grove road, thus threatening our rear and endangering our trains, which were on the road leading by the Old Court House to Louisa Court House.

Our line was then north of the Po, with its left, Field's division of Longstreet's corps, resting on that stream, just above the crossing of the Shady Grove road. The whole of the enemy's force was also north of the Po, prior to this movement of his. Mahone's division was sent to occupy the banks of the Po on Field's left, while, with Heth's division and a battalion of artillery, I moved to the rear, crossing the Po on the Louisa Court House Road, and then following that road until we reached one coming in from Waite's Shop on the Shady Grove Road. After moving about a mile on this road, we met Hampton gradually falling back before the enemy, who had pushed out a column of infantry considerably to the rear of our line. This column, was, in turn, forced back to the position on the Shady Grove Road, which was occupied by what was reported to be Hancock's corps. Following up and crossing a small stream just below a mill pond, we succeeded in reaching Waite's Shop, from whence an attack was made on the enemy, and the entire force which had crossed the Po was driven back with a loss of one piece of artillery, which fell into our hands, and a considerable number in killed and wounded. This relieved us from a very threatening danger, as the position the enemy had attained would have enabled him to completely enfilade Field's position, and get possession of the line of our communications to the rear, within a very short distance of which he was, when met by the force which drove him back. In this affair, Heth's division behaved very handsomely, all of the brigades, (Cook's, Davis', Kirkland's, and

Walker's,) being engaged in the attack. General H. H. Walker had the misfortune to receive a severe wound in the foot, which rendered amputation necessary, but, otherwise, our loss was slight. As soon as the road was cleared, Mahone's division crossed the Po, but it was not practicable to pursue the affair further, as the north bank of the stream at this point was covered by a heavily entrenched line, with a number of batteries, and night was approaching.

On the morning of the 11th, Heth was moved back to Spotsylvania Court House, and Mahone was left to occupy the position on the Shady Grove Road, from which the enemy had been driven.*

My line on the right had been connected with Ewell's right, and covered the Fredericksburg road, as also the road leading from Spotsylvania Court House across the Ny into the road from Fredericksburg to Hanover Junction. Wilcox was on my left uniting with Ewell, and Heth joined him. The enemy had extended his lines across the Fredericksburg Road, but there was no fighting on this front on the 10th or 11th, except some artillery firing.

On the afternoon of the 11th, the enemy was demonstrating to our left, up the Po, as if to get possession of Shady Grove and the road from thence to Louisa Court House. General Hampton reported a colum of infantry moving up the Po, and I was ordered by General Lee to take possession of Shady Grove, by light next morning, and hold it against the enemy. To aid in that purpose, two brigades of Wilcox's division, (Thomas' and Scales') were moved from the right, and Mahone was ordered to move before light to Shady Grove; but during the night it was discovered that the movement to our left was a feint, and that there was a real movement of the enemy towards our right.

Before daybreak on the morning of the 12th, Wilcox's brigades were returned to him, and at dawn, Mahone's division was moved to the right, leaving Wright's brigade of that division to cover the crossing of the Po on Field's left. On this morning, the enemy made a very heavy attack on Ewell's front, and broke the line where it was occupied by Johnson's division. A portion of the attacking force swept along Johnson's line to Wilcox's left, and was checked by a prompt movement on the part of Brigadier-General Lane, who was on that flank. As soon as the firing was heard, General Wilcox sent Thomas' and

---

*It will be seen that, after this affair, I held, for a time, both of General Lee's flanks, which was rather an anomaly, but it could not be avoided, as we had no reserves, and the two other corps, being immediately in front of the enemy, in line of battle, and almost constantly engaged, could not be moved without great risk. It was absolutely necessary to occupy the position hold on the left by Mahone, to avoid a renewal of the danger from which we had escaped.

Scales' brigades to Lane's assistance, and they arrived just as Lane's brigade had repulsed this body of the enemy, and they pursued it for a short distance. As soon as Mahone's division arrived from the left, Perrin's and Harris' brigades of that division, and subsequently, McGowan's brigade of Wilcox's division, were sent to General Ewell's assistance, and were carried into action under his orders. Brigadier-General Perrin was killed, and Brigadier-General McGowan severely wounded, while gallantly leading their respective brigades into action; and all the brigades sent to Ewell's assistance suffered severely.

Subsequently, on the same day, under orders from General Lee, Lane's brigade of Wilcox's division, and Mahone's own brigade (under Colonel Weisiger), were thrown to the front, for the purpose of moving to the left, and attacking the flank of the column of the enemy which had broken Ewell's line, to relieve the pressure on him, and, if possible, recover the part of the line which had been lost. Lane's brigade commenced the movement and had not proceeded far, when it encountered and attacked, in a piece of woods in front of my line, the 9th corps, under Burnside, moving up to attack a salient on my front. Lane captured over three hundred prisoners, and three battle flags, and his attack on the enemy's flank, taking him by surprise, no doubt, contributed materially to his repulse. Mahone's brigade did not become seriously engaged. The attacking column which Lane encountered, got up to within a very short distance of a salient defended by Walker's brigade of Heth's division, under Colonel Mayo, before it was discovered, as there was a pine thicket in front, under cover of which the advance was made. A heavy fire of musketry from Walker's brigade and Thomas' which was on its left, and a tire of artillery from a considerable number of guns on Heth's line, were opened with tremendous effect upon the attacking column, and it was driven back with heavy loss, leaving its dead in front of our works. This affair took place under the eye of General Lee himself. In the afternoon, another attempt was made to carry out the contemplated flank movement, with Mahone's brigade, and Cook's brigade of Heth's division, to be followed up by the other troops under my command; but it was discovered that the enemy had one or more intrenched lines in our front, to the fire from which our flanking column would have been exposed. Moreover, the ground between the lines was very rough, being full of rugged ravines and covered with thick pines and other growth; and it was thought advisable to desist from the attempt. The two brigades which were to have commenced the movement, were then thrown to the front on both sides of the Fredericksburg road, and, passing over two lines of breastworks, defended by a strong force of skirmishers, developed the existence of a third and much stronger line in rear, which would have afforded an almost insuperable obstacle to the proposed flank movement. This closed the operations of the corps under my command on the memorable 12th of May.

Between that day and the 19th, there was no serious attack on my front, but much manœuvring by the enemy. General Mahone made two or three recon-noissances to the front, which disclosed the fact that the enemy was gradually moving to our right. In making one of them, he encountered a body of the enemy which had got possession of Gayle's house, on the left of the road leading from our right towards the Fredericksburg and Hanover Junction road, at which a portion of our cavalry, under Brigadier General Chambliss, had been previously posted, and drove it back across the Ny.* Another reconnoissance, handsomely made by Brigadier-General Wright, who had been brought from the left, ascer-tained that a heavy force of the enemy was between the Ny and the Po, in front of my right, which was held by Mahone, and was along the road towards Hanover Junction. To meet this movement of the enemy, Field's division was brought from the left and placed on my right.

On the 19th, General Ewell made a movement against the enemy's right, and to create a diversion in his favour, Thomas' brigade was thrown forward, and drove the enemy into his works in front of the salient, against which Burn-side's attack had been made on the 12th, while the whole corps was held in readiness to co-operate with Ewell, should his attack prove successful; but, as he was compelled to retire, Thomas was withdrawn.

Subsequently, the enemy retired from Heth's and Wilcox's fronts; and, on the afternoon of the 21st, Wilcox was sent out on the road leading from Mahone's front across the Ny, with two of his brigades to feel the enemy, and found him still in force behind entrenched lines, and had a brisk engagement with that force.

While Wilcox was absent, an order was received by me, from General Lee, to turn over to General Hill the command of his corps, as he had reported for duty. I did so at once, and thus terminated my connection with this corps, which I had commanded during all the trying scenes around Spotsylvania

---

*The Mattapony River, which, by its junction with the Pamunkey, forms York River, is formed by the confluence of four streams, called respectively, the "Mat," "Ta," "Po," and "Ny." The Ny is north and east of Spotsylvania Court House, and behind it the enemy did most of his manœu-vring in my front. It unites with the Po, a few miles to the east and south of Spotsylvania Court House, and both streams are difficult to cross, except where there are bridges.

Court House. The officers and men of the corps had all behaved well, and contributed, in no little degree, to the result by which Grant was compelled to wait six days for reinforcements from Washington, before he could resume the offensive, or make another of his flank movements to get between General Lee's army and Richmond.

HANOVER JUNCTION.

OPERATIONS OF EARLY'S DIVISION.

The movement of the enemy to get between our army and Richmond had been discovered, and on the afternoon of the 21st, Ewell's corps was put in motion towards Hanover Junction.* After turning over to General Hill, the command of his corps, I rode in the direction taken by Ewell's corps, and overtook it, a short time before day on the morning of the 22nd. Hoke's brigade, under Lieutenant Colonel Lewis, this day joined us from Petersburg, and an order was issued, transferring Gordon's brigade, now under the command of Brigadier-General Evans, to Johnson's division, which was placed under the command of General Gordon, who had been made a Major General. This left me in command of three brigades, to wit: Pegram's, Hoke's, and Johnston's, all of which were very much reduced in strength. My Adjutant General, Major Daniel, had been disabled for life by a wound received at the Wilderness, and my Inspector General, Major Samuel Hale, had been mortally wounded at Spotsylvania Court House, on the 12th, while serving with the division and acting with great gallantry during the disorder which ensued after Ewell's line was broken. Both were serious losses to me.

On this day, (the 22nd), we moved to Hanover Junction, and, next day my division was posted on the extreme right, covering a ferry two or three miles below the railroad bridge across the North Anna. While at Hanover Junction my division was not engaged. At one time it was moved towards our left, for the purpose of supporting a part of the line on which an attack was expected, and

---

*Hanover Junction is about 22 miles from Richmond, and is at the intersection of the Richmond, Fredericksburg and Potomac railroad with the Central railroad from Richmond west, via Gordonsville and Staunton. It is on the direct road from both Spotsylvania Court House and Fredericksburg to Richmond. The North Anna River is north of the Junction about two miles, and the South Anna about three miles south of it. These two streams unite south of east, and a few miles from the Junction, and form the Pamunkey River.

moved back again without being required. It was, subsequently, placed temporarily on the left of the corps, relieving Rodes' division and a part of Field's while the line was being remodelled, and then took position on the right again.

During the night of the 26th, the enemy again withdrew from our front.*

BATTLES OF COLD HARBOUR.

OPERATIONS OF EWELL'S CORPS.

On the 27th, the enemy having withdrawn to the north bank of the North Anna, and commenced another flank movement by moving down the north bank of the Pamunkey, Ewell's corps, now under my command, by reason of General Ewell's sickness, was moved across the South Anna over the bridge of the Central railroad, and by a place called "Merry Oaks," leaving Ashland on the Richmond, Fredericksburg and Potomac railroad to the right, and bivouacked for the night at Hughes' cross road, the intersection of the road from Ashland to Atlee's station on the Central railroad with the road from the Merry Oaks to Richmond. Next morning I moved by Atlee's station to Hundley's corner, at the intersection of the road from Hanover Town, (the point at which Grant crossed the Pamunkey,) by Pole Green Church, to Richmond, with the road from Atlee's station, by Old Church in Hanover County, to the White House, on the Pamunkey. This is the point from which General Jackson commenced his famous attack on McClellan's flank and rear, in 1862, and it was very important that it should be occupied, as it intercepted Grant's direct march towards Richmond. All these movements were made under orders from General Lee.

My troops were placed in position, covering the road by Pole Green

---

*At Hanover Junction General Lee was joined by Pickett's division of Longstreet's corps, and Breckenridge with two small brigades of infantry, and a battalion of artillery. These, with Hoke's brigade, were the first and only reinforcements received by General Lee since the opening of the campaign. Yet, Grant's immense army, notwithstanding the advantage gained by it on the 12th of May, had been so crippled, that it was compelled to wait six days at Spotsylvania Court House for reinforcements from Washington, before it could resume the offensive. Breckenridge's infantry numbered less than 3,000 muskets; yet, Grant puts it 15,000, and he makes an absurd attempt to cast the whole blame for the failure of the campaign, so far, on Butler; to immolate whom, he makes a digression in his account of the operations at Hanover Junction, and says: "The army sent to operate against Richmond having hermetically sealed itself up at Bermuda Hundreds, the enemy was enabled to bring the most, if not all the reinforcements brought from the South by Beauregard against the Army of the Potomac." He therefore determined to try another flank movement, and to get more reinforcements from the army at Bermuda Hundreds.

Church, and also the road to Old Church, with my right resting near Beaver Dam Creek, a small stream running towards Mechanicsville and into the Chickahominy. Brigadier General Ramseur of Rodes' division, was this day assigned to the command of my division. Ewell's corps, the 2nd of the Army of Northern Virginia, now numbered less than 9,000 muskets for duty, its loss, on the 12th of May, having been very heavy.

On the 29th, the enemy having crossed the Tottopotomoy, (a creek running just north of Pole Green Church, and eastward to the Pamunkey,) appeared in my front on both roads, and there was some skirmishing, but no heavy fighting.

On the afternoon of the 30th, in accordance with orders from General Lee, I moved to the right across Beaver Dam, to the road from Old Church to Mechanicsville, and thence along that road towards Old Church, until we reached Bethesda Church. At this point the enemy was encountered, and his troops which occupied the road, were driven by Rodes' division towards the road from Hundley's corner, which unites with the road from Mechanicsville, east of Bethesda Church. Pegram's brigade, under the command of Colonel Edward Willis of the 12th Georgia regiment, was sent forward, with one of Rodes' brigades on its right, to feel the enemy, and ascertain its strength; but, meeting with a heavy force behind breastworks, it was compelled to retire, with the loss of some valuable officers and men, and among them were Colonel Willis, mortally wounded, and Colonel Terrell of the 13th Virginia regiment, and Lieutenant Colonel Watkins of the 52nd Virginia regiment, killed. This movement showed that the enemy was moving to our right flank, and at night, I withdrew a short distance on the Mechanicsville road, covering it with my force. When I made the movement from Hundley's corner, my position at that place was occupied by a part of Longstreet's corps, under Anderson.

On the next morning my troops were placed in position on the east side of Beaver Dam across the road to Mechanicsville, but Rodes was subsequently moved to the west side of the creek.

Grant's movement to our right, towards Cold Harbour, was continued on the 31st, and the 1st of June, and corresponding movements were made by General Lee to meet him, my command retaining its position with a heavy force in its front.

On the 2nd, all the troops on my left, except Heth's division of Hill's corps, had moved to the right, and, in the afternoon of that day, Rodes' division moved forward, along the road from Hundley's corner towards Old Church, and drove the enemy from his intrenchments, now occupied with heavy skirmish lines, and forced back his left towards Bethesda Church, where there was a heavy force. Gordon swung round so as to keep pace with Rodes, and Heth co-operated, following Rodes and taking position on his left flank. In this movement there was some heavy fighting and several hundred prisoners were taken by us. Brigadier-General Doles, a gallant officer of Rodes' division, was killed, but otherwise our loss was not severe.

On the next day (the 3rd), when Grant made an attack at Cold Harbour in which he suffered very heavily, there were repeated attacks on Rodes' and Heth's fronts, those on Cook's brigade, of Heth's division, being especially heavy, but all of them were repulsed. There was also heavy skirmishing on Gordon's front. During the day, Heth's left was threatened by the enemy's cavalry, but it was kept off by Walker's brigade under Colonel Fry, which covered that flank; and also repulsed an effort of the enemy's infantry to get to our rear. As it was necessary that Heth's division should join its corps on the right, and my flank in this position was very much exposed, I withdrew at the close of the day to the line previously occupied, and next morning Heth moved to the right.

My right now connected with the left of Longstreet's corps under General Anderson. The enemy subsequently evacuated his position at Bethesda Church and his lines in my front, and, having no opposing force to keep my troops in their lines, I made two efforts to attack the enemy on his right flank and rear. The first was made on the 6th, when I crossed the Matadaquean, (a small stream, running through wide swamps in the enemy's rear), and got in rear of his right flank, driving in his skirmishers until we came to a swamp, which could be crossed only on a narrow causeway defended by an intrenched line with artillery. General Anderson was to have co-operated with me, by moving down the other side of the Matadaquean, but the division sent for that purpose did not reach the position from which I started until near night, and I was therefore compelled to retire as my position was too much exposed.

On the next day (the 7th), a reconnoissance made in front of Anderson's line, showed that the greater part of it was uncovered, and, in accordance with instructions from General Lee, I moved in front of, and between it and the Matadaquean, until my progress was arrested by a ravine and swamp which prevented any further advance, but a number of pieces of artillery were opened upon the enemy's position in flank and reverse, so as to favour a movement from Anderson's front, which had been ordered but was not made; and at night I retired from this position to the rear of our lines.

Since the fighting at the Wilderness, Grant had made it an invariable practice to cover his front, flank, and rear, with a perfect network of intrenchments,
and all his movements were made under cover of such works. It was therefore
very difficult to get at him.

On the 11th, my command was moved to the rear of Hill's line, near
Gaines' Mill; and, on the 12th, I received orders to move, with the 2nd Corps,
to the Shenandoah Valley, to meet Hunter. This, therefore, closed my connection with the campaign from the Rapidan to James River.

When I moved, on the morning of the 13th., Grant had already put his
army in motion to join Butler, on James River, a position which he could have
reached, from his camps on the north of the Rapidan, by railroad and transports, without the loss of a man. In attempting to force his way by land, he had
already lost, in killed and wounded, more men than were in General Lee's
entire army; and he was compelled to give up, in despair, the attempt to reach
Richmond in that way.*

---

*Grant, in describing his movement from Spotsylvania Court House to Hanover Junction, says:
"But the enemy again having the shorter line, and being in possession of the main roads, was
enabled to reach the North-Anna in advance of us, and took position behind it." And when he
speaks of his final determination to join Butler, he says: "After the Battle of the Wilderness it was
evident that the enemy deemed it of the first importance to run no risk with the army he then had.
He acted purely on the defensive, behind breastworks, or, feebly on the offensive, immediately in
front of them, and where, in case of repulse, he could retire behind them. Without a greater sacrifice of life than I was willing to make, all could not be accomplished that I designed north of
Richmond."

Mr. Secretary Stanton, with a keenness of strategic acumen which is altogether unparalleled,
says: "Forty-three days of desperate fighting or marching, by day and night, forced back the rebel
army from the Rapidan to their intrenchments around Richmond, and carried the Army of the
Potomac to the south side of James River. The strength of the enemy's force when the campaign
opened, or the extent of his loss, is not known to this Department. Any inequality between Lee's
army and the Army of the Potomac, was fully compensated by the advantage of position."

We are left in the dark whether it was the desperate fighting or the desperate marching which
did all this; but, however that may be, it was a wonderful achievement, especially when it is considered that the Army of the Potomac might have been carried to the south side of James River by
transports, and Lee's army thereby forced back to the intrenchments around Richmond, without
the "Forty-three days of desperate fighting or marching, by day and by night," and without the
loss of men sustained by Grant. There are some who think Stanton is slyly making fun of Grant;
but, if he is not, and is in dead earnest, the question naturally arises, in the mind of one not as gifted
as the Federal Secretary of War: How happened it that, if Lee was being constantly forced back,
for forty-three days over a distance of more than eighty miles, he always had the shorter time, and
possession of the main roads, and got the advantage of position, and had time to fortify it?

I happen to know that General Lee always had the greatest anxiety to strike at Grant in the

Campaign in Maryland and the Valley of Virginia.

INTRODUCTION.

The Valley of Virginia, in its largest sense, embraces all that country lying between the Blue Ridge and Alleghany Mountains, which unite at its south-western end.

The Shenandoah Valley, which is a part of the Valley of Virginia, embraces the Counties of Augusta, Rockingham, Shenandoah, Page, Warren, Clarke, Frederick, Jefferson, and Berkeley. This valley is bounded on the north by the Potomac, on the south by the County of Rockbridge, on the east by the Blue Ridge, and on the west by the Great North Mountain and its ranges.

The Shenandoah River is composed of two branches, called, respectively, the "North Fork" and the "South Fork," which unite near Front Royal in War-

---

open field; and I should like to know when it was that the latter operated on the defensive, or offensive either, except behind, or immediately in front of, far better intrenchments than General Lee's army, with its limited means, was able to make. An inspection of the battle-fields, from the Rapidan to the James, will show that Grant's army did a vast deal more digging than General Lee's.

The truth is, that the one commander was a great captain, and perfect master of his art, while the other had none of the requisites of a great captain, but merely possessed the most ordinary brute courage, and had the control of unlimited numbers and means. Yet, it is claimed that Grant fights and writes better than Alexander, and Hannibal, and Caesar, and Napoleon, and all the rest; and when, in the exercise of his great powers of composition, he turns the batteries of his rhetoric on Butler, I say, in his own classic language, "Go in!" You can't him a lick amiss. I cannot, however, but be amused at the effort to make Butler the scape-goat; and cannot help thinking that Grant ought to have known, beforehand, that he (Butler) was unfit to make war, except on defenseless women and children, and that the trophies valued by him were not those won at the cannon's mouth.

Grant, in his report, has enunciated the leading principles of his strategy, and he is certainly entitled to the credit of having practised them, if not to the merit of originally. They were: "First, to use the greatest number of troops practicable against the armed force of the enemy;" and, Second, to hammer continuously against the armed force of the enemy, and his resources, until, by mere attrition, if by nothing else, there should be nothing left to him but an equal submission, with the loyal section of our common country, to the constitution and laws of the land." (Alas! what has become of the constitution and laws?) This latter principle was more concisely and forcibly expressed by Mr. Lincoln, when he declared his purpose to "keep a pegging." The plain English of the whole idea was to continue raising troops, and to oppose them, in overwhelming numbers, to the Confederate Army, until the latter should wear itself out whipping them, when a newly-recruited army might "go in and win." And, this was actually what took place in regard to General Lee's army.

ren County. The North Fork rises in the Great North Mountain, and runs east-wardly to within a short distance of New Market in Shenandoah County, and thence north-east by Mount Jackson to Strasburg, where it turns east to Front Royal. The South Fork is formed by the union of North River, Middle River, and South River. North River and Middle River, running from the west, unite near Port Republic in Rockingham County. South River rises in the south-eastern part of Augusta, and runs by Waynesboro', along the western base of the Blue Ridge, to Port Republic, where it unites with the stream formed by the junction of the North and Middle rivers. From Port Republic, the South Fork of the Shenandoah runs north-east, through the eastern border of Rockingham and the county of Page, to Front Royal in Warren county.

The North Fork and South Fork are separated by the Massanutten Moun-tain, which is connected with no other mountain, but terminates abruptly at both ends. Its northern end is washed at its base, just below Strasburg, by the North Fork. Its southern end terminates near the road between Harrisonburg and Conrad's Store on the South Fork, at which latter place the road through Swift Run Gap in the Blue Ridge crosses that stream. Two valleys are thus formed, the one on the North Fork being called "The Main Valley," and the other on the South Fork, and embracing the County of Page and part of the

---

Grant having established his fame as a writer, as well as fighter, I presume he will give the world the benefit of his ideas, and publish a work on strategy, which I would suggest ought to be called "The Lincoln-Grant or Pegging-Hammer Art of War."

He has made some observations, in his report, about the advantages of interior lines of com-munication, supposed to be possessed by the Confederate commanders, which are more spe-cious than sound. The Mississippi River divided the Confederacy into two parts, and the immense naval power of the enemy enabled him to render communication across that river, after the loss of New Orleans and Memphis, always difficult and finally to get entire possession of it. On the eastern side of it, the railroad communications were barely sufficient for the transporta-tion of supplies, and the transportation of troops over them was always tedious and difficult. The Ohio River, in the West, and the Potomac, in the East, with the mountains of Western Virginia, rendered it impossible for an invading army to march into the enemy's country, except at one or two fords on the Potomac, just east of the Blue Ridge, and two or three fords above Harper's Ferry. The possession of the seas and the blockade of our ports, as well as the possession of the Mississippi, the Ohio and Potomac Rivers, with the Baltimore and Ohio Railroad, and the rail-roads through Pennsylvania, Ohio, Indiana, Illinois, Kentucky and Tennessee, enabled the enemy to transport troops, from the most remote points, with more case and rapidity than they could be transported over the railroads under the control of the Confederate Government, all of which were in bad condition. The enemy, therefore, in fact, had all the advantages of interior lines; that is rapidity of communication and concentration, with the advantage, also, of unre-stricted communication with all the world, which his naval power gave him.

County of Warren, being usually known by the name of "The Luray Valley." The Luray Valley unites with the Main Valley at both ends of the mountain. There is a good road across Massanutten Mountain, from one valley to the other, and through a gap near New Market. South of this gap there is no road across the mountain, and north of it the roads are very rugged and not practicable for the march of a large army with its trains. At the northern or lower end of Massanutten Mountain, and between two branches of it, is a valley called "Powell's Fort Valley" or more commonly "The Fort." This valley is accessible only by the very rugged roads over the mountain which have been mentioned, and through a ravine at its lower end. From its isolated position, it was not the theatre of military operations of any consequence, but merely furnished a refuge for deserters, stragglers, and fugitives from the battle-fields.

From Front Royal the Shenandoah River runs along the western base of the Blue Ridge to Harper's Ferry, where it unites with the Potomac, which here bursts through the mountains. The mountain in extension of the range of the Blue Ridge from this point through Maryland and Pennsylvania is called "South Mountain."

Strictly speaking, the County of Berkeley and the greater part of Frederick are not in the Valley of the Shenandoah. The Opequon, rising south-west of Winchester, and crossing the Valley Pike four or five miles south of that place, turns to the north and empties into the Potomac some distance above its junction with the Shenandoah; the greater part of Frederick and nearly the whole of Berkeley being on the western side of the Opequon.

Little North Mountain, called in the lower valley "North Mountain," runs north-east, through the western portions of Shenandoah, Frederick, and Berkeley Counties, to the Potomac. At its northern end, where it is called North Mountain, it separates the waters of the Opequon from those of Back Creek.

Cedar Creek rises in Shenandoah County, west of Little North Mountain, and running north-east along its western base, passes through that mountain, four or five miles from Strasburg, and, then making a circuit, empties into the North Fork of the Shenandoah, about two miles below Strasburg.

The Baltimore and Ohio Railroad crosses the Potomac at Harper's Ferry, and passing through Martinsburg in Berkeley County, crosses Back Creek near its mouth, runs up the Potomac, crossing the South Branch of that river near its mouth, and then the North Branch to Cumberland in Maryland. From this place it runs into Virginia again and, passing through North Western Virginia, strikes the Ohio river by two stems terminating at Wheeling and Parkersburg, respectively.

There is a railroad from Harper's Ferry to Winchester, called "The Winchester and Potomac Railroad," and also one from Manassas Junction on the Orange and Alexandria Railroad, through Manassas Gap in the Blue Ridge, by Front Royal and Strasburg, to Mount Jackson, called "The Manassas Gap Railroad;" but both of these roads were torn up and rendered unserviceable in the year 1862, under the orders of General Jackson.

From Staunton in Augusta County, there is a fine macadamized road called "The Valley Pike," running through Mount Sidney, Mount Crawford, Harrisonburg, New Market, Mount Jackson, Edinburg, Woodstock, Strasburg, Middletown, Newtown, Bartonsville, and Kernstown to Winchester in Frederick County, and crossing Middle River seven miles from Staunton, North River at Mount Crawford eighteen miles from Staunton, the North Fork of the Shenandoah at Mount Jackson, Cedar Creek between Strasburg and Middletown, and the Opequon at Bartonsville, four or five miles from Winchester. There is also another road west of the Valley Pike, connecting these several villages, called the "Back Road," and, in some places, another road between the Valley Pike and the Back Road, which is called the "Middle Road."

From Winchester there is a macadamized road, via Martinsburg, to Williamsport on the Potomac in Maryland, and another, via Berryville in Clarke County, and Charlestown in Jefferson County, to Harper's Ferry. There is also a good pike from Winchester to Front Royal, which crosses both forks of the Shenandoah just above their junction; and from Front Royal there are good roads up the Luray Valley, and by the way of Conrad's Store and Port Republic, to Harrisonburg and Staunton.

From Staunton, south, there are good roads passing through Lexington, in Rockbridge County, and Buchanan, in Botetourt County, to several points on the Virginia and Tennessee Railroad; and others direct from Staunton and Lexington to Lynchburg.

The Central Railroad, from Richmond, passes through the Blue Ridge, with a tunnel at Rockfish Gap, and runs through Waynesboro and Staunton, westwardly to Jackson's River, which is one of the head-streams of James River.

This description of the country is given in order to render the following narrative intelligible without too much repetition.

In the spring of 1864, before the opening of the campaign, the lower Shenandoah Valley was held by the Federal troops, under Major-General Sigel, with his head-quarters at Winchester, while the upper Valley was held by Brigadier-General Imboden, of the Confederate Army, with one brigade of cavalry, or mounted infantry, and a battery of artillery. When the campaign opened, Sigel moved up the Valley, and Major-General Breckenridge moved from South-Western Virginia, with two brigades of infantry and a battalion of artillery, to meet him. Breckenridge, having united his forces with Imboden's, met and defeated Sigel, at New Market, on the 15th day of May, driving him back towards Winchester. Breckenridge then crossed the Blue Ridge, and joined General Lee, at Hanover Junction, with his two brigades of infantry and the battalion of artillery. Subsequently, the Federal General Hunter organized another and larger force than Sigel's, and moved up the Valley; and, on the 5th day of June, defeated Brigadier-General William E. Jones, at Piedmont, between Port Republic and Staunton—Jones' force being composed of a very small body of infantry, and a cavalry force which had been brought from South-Western Virginia, after Breckenridge's departure from the Valley. Jones was killed, and the remnant of his force, under Brigadier-General Vaughan, fell back to Waynesboro. Hunter's force then united with another column which had moved from Lewisburg, in Western Virginia, under the Federal General Crook. As soon as information was received of Jones' defeat and death, Breckenridge was sent back to the Valley, with the force he had brought with him.

MARCH TO LYNCHBURG, AND PURSUIT OF HUNTER.

On the 12th of June, while the 2nd Corps (Ewell's) of the Army of Northern Virginia was lying near Gaines' Mill; in rear of Hill's line at Cold Harbour, I received verbal orders from General Lee to hold the corps, with two of the battalions of artillery attached to it, in readiness to move to the Shenandoah Valley. Nelson's and Braxton's battalions were selected, and Brigadier-General Long was ordered to accompany me as Chief of Artillery. After dark, on the same day, written instructions were given me by General Lee, by which I was directed to move, with the force designated, at 3 o'clock next morning, for the Valley, by way of Louisa C. H. and Charlottesville, and through Brown's or Swift Run Gap in the Blue Ridge, as I might find most advisable; to strike Hunter's force in the rear, and, if possible, destroy it; then to move down the Valley, cross the Potomac near Leesburg in London County, or at or above Harper's Ferry, as I might find most practicable, and threaten Washington City. I was further directed to communicate with General Breckenridge, who would co-operate with me in the attack on Hunter, and the expedition into Maryland.

At this time the railroad and telegraph lines between Charlottesville and

Lynchburg had been cut by a cavalry force from Hunter's army; and those between Richmond and Charlottesville had been cut by Sheridan's cavalry, from Grant's army; so that there was no communication with Breckenridge. Hunter was supposed to be at Staunton with his whole force, and Breckenridge was supposed to be at Waynesboro, or Rockfish Gap. If such had been the case, the route designated by General Lee would have carried me into the Valley in Hunter's rear.

The 2nd Corps now numbered a little over 8,000 muskets for duty. It had been on active and arduous service in the field for forty days, and had been engaged in all the great battles from the Wilderness to Cold Harbour, sustaining very heavy losses at Spotsylvania C. H. where it lost nearly an entire division, including its commander, Major-General Johnson, who was made prisoner. Of the Brigadier-Generals with it at the commencement of the campaign, only one remained in command of his brigade. Two (Gordon and Ramseur) had been made Major-Generals; one (G. H. Steuart) had been captured; four (Pegram, Hays, J. A. Walker, and R. D. Johnston) had been severely wounded; and four (Stafford, J. M. Jones, Daniel, and Doles) had been killed in action. Constant exposure to the weather, a limited supply of provisions, and two weeks' service in the swamps north of the Chickahominy had told on the health of the men. Divisions were not stronger than brigades ought to have been, nor brigades than regiments.

On the morning of the 13th, at 2 o'clock, we commenced the march; and, on the 16th, arrived at the Rivanna River, near Charlottesville, having marched over eighty miles in four days.*

From Louisa C. H. I had sent a dispatch to Gordonsville, to be forwarded, by telegraph, to Breckenridge; and, on my arrival at Charlottesville,

---

*On the 15th, we passed over the ground, near Trevillian's depot, on which Hampton and Sheridan had fought, on the 11th and 12th. Hampton had defeated Sheridan, and was then in pursuit of him. Grant claims, in his report that, on the 11th, Sheridan drove our cavalry from the field, in complete rout;" and says, when he advanced towards Gordonsville, on the 12th, "he found the enemy reinforced by infantry, behind well-constructed rifle-pits about five miles from the latter place, and too strong to successfully assault."

This is thoroughly a fancy sketch as can well be manufactured. There was not an infantry soldier in arms nearer the scene of action than with General Lee's army, near Cold Harbour; and the "well-constructed rifle-pits" were nothing more than rails put up in the manner in which cavalry were accustomed to arrange them to prevent a charge. Sheridan mistook some of Hampton's cavalry, dismounted and fighting on foot, for infantry; and the statement was made to cover his defeat.

on the 16th, to which place I rode in advance of the troops, I received a telegram from him, dated at Lynchburg, informing me that Hunter was then in Bedford county, about twenty miles from that place, and moving on it.

The railroad and telegraph between Charlottesville and Lynchburg had been, fortunately, but slightly injured by the enemy's cavalry, and had been repaired. The distance between the two places was sixty miles, and there were no trains at Charlottesville, except one which belonged to the Central road, and was about starting for Waynesboro. I ordered this to be detained, and immediately directed, by telegram, all the trains of the two roads to be sent to me with all dispatch, for the purpose of transporting my troops to Lynchburg. The trains were not in readiness to take the troops on board until sunrise on the morning of the 17th, and then only enough were furnished to transport about half my infantry. Ramseur's division, one brigade of Gordon's division, and part of another were put on the trains, as soon they were ready, and started for Lynchburg. Rodes' division, and the residue of Gordon's, were ordered to move along the railroad, to meet the trains on their return. The artillery and wagon trains had been started on the ordinary roads at daylight.

I accompanied Ramseur's division, going on the front train, but the road and rolling stock were in such bad condition that I did not reach Lynchburg until about one o'clock in the afternoon, and the other trains were much later. I found General Breckenridge in bed, suffering from an injury received by the fall of a horse killed under him in action near Cold Harbour. He had moved from Rockfish Gap to Lynchburg by a forced march, as soon as Hunter's movement towards that place was discovered. When I showed him my instructions, he very readily and cordially offered to co-operate with me, and serve under my command.

Hunter's advance from Staunton had been impeded by a brigade of cavalry, under Brigadier-General McCausland, which had been managed with great skill, and kept in his front all the way, and he was reported to be then advancing on the old stone turnpike from Liberty, in Bedford County, by New London, and watched by Imboden with a small force of cavalry.

As General Breckenridge was unable to go out, at his request, General D. H. Hill, who happened to be in town, had made arrangements for the defence of the city, with such troops as were at hand. Brigadier-General Hays, who was an invalid from a wound received at Spotsylvania Court House, had tendered his services and also aided in making arrangements for the defence. I rode out with General Hill to examine the line selected by him, and make a reconnaissance of the country in front. Slight works had been hastily thrown up on College Hill, covering the turnpike and Forest roads from Liberty, which were manned by Breckenridge's infantry and the dismounted cavalry of the command which had been with Jones at Piedmont. The reserves, invalids from the hospitals, and the cadets from the Military Institute at Lexington, occupied other parts of the line. An inspection satisfied me that, while this arrangement was the best which could be made under the circumstances which General Hill found himself, yet it would leave the town exposed to the fire of the enemy's artillery, should he advance to the attack, and I therefore determined to meet the enemy with my troops in front.

We found Imboden about four miles out on the turnpike, near an old Quaker church, to which position he had been gradually forced back by the enemy's infantry. My troops, as they arrived, had been ordered in front of the works to bivouac, and I immediately sent orders for them to move out on this road, and two brigades of Ramseur's division arrived just in time to be thrown across the road, at a redoubt about two miles from the city, as Imboden's command was driven back by vastly superior numbers. These brigades, with two pieces of artillery in the redoubt, arrested the progress of the enemy, and Ramseur's other brigade, and the part of Gordon's division which had arrived, took position on the same line. The enemy opened a heavy fire of artillery on us, but, as night soon came on, he went into camp on our front.*

On my arrival at Lynchburg, orders had been given for the immediate return of the trains for the rest of my infantry, and I expected it to arrive by the morning of the 18th, but it did not get to Lynchburg until late in the afternoon of that day. Hunter's force was considerably larger than mine would have been, had it all been up, and as it was of the utmost consequence to the army at Richmond that he should not get into Lynchburg, I did not feel justified in attacking

---

*Hunter's delay in advancing from Staunton had been most remarkable, and can be accounted for only by the fact, that indulgence in petty acts of malignity and outrage upon private citizens was more congenial to his nature than bold operation, in the field. He had defeated Jones' small force at Piedmont about ten miles from Staunton, on the 5th, and united with Crook on the 8th, yet he did not arrive in front of Lynchburg until near night on the 17th. The route from Staunton to Lynchburg by which he moved, which was by Lexington, Buchanan, the Peaks of Otter, and Liberty, is about one hundred miles in distance. It is true McCausland had delayed his progress by keeping constantly in his front, but an energetic advance would have brushed away McCausland's small force, and Lynchburg, with all its manufacturing establishments and stores, would have fallen before assistance arrived. A subsequent passage over the greater part of the same route showed how Hunter had been employed.

him until I could do so with a fair prospect of success. I contented myself there-fore with acting on the defensive on the 18th, throwing Breckenridge's infantry and a part of his artillery on the front line, while that adopted by General Hill was occupied by the dismounted cavalry and the irregular troops. During the day, there was artillery firing and skirmishing along the line, and, in the after-noon, an attack was made on our line, to the right of the turnpike, which was handsomely repulsed with considerable loss to the enemy. A demonstration of the enemy's cavalry on the Forest road, was checked by part of Breckenridge's infantry under Wharton, and McCausland's cavalry.

On the arrival of the cars from Richmond this day, Major-Generals Elzey and Ransom reported for duty, the former to command the infantry and dis-mounted cavalry of Breckenridge's command, and the latter to command the cavalry. The mounted cavalry consisted of the remnants of several brigades divided into two commands, one under Imboden, and the other under McCausland. It was badly mounted and armed, and its efficiency much impaired by the defeat at Piedmont, and the arduous service it had recently gone through.

As soon as the remainder of my infantry arrived by the railroad, though none of my artillery had gotten up, arrangements were made for attacking Hunter at daylight on the 19th, but, sometime after midnight, it was discovered that he was moving, though it was not known whether he was retreating, or mov-ing so as to attack Lynchburg on the south where it was vulnerable, or to attempt to join Grant on the south side of James River. Pursuit could not, therefore, be made at once, as a mistake, if either of the last two objects had been contem-plated, would have been fatal. At light, however, the pursuit commenced, the 2nd Corps moving along the turnpike, over which it was discovered Hunter was retreating, and Elzey's command on the right, along the Forest road, while Ran-som was ordered to move on the right of Elzey, with McCausland's cavalry, and endeavor to strike the enemy at Liberty or the Peaks of Otter. Imboden, who was on the road from Lynchburg to Campbell Court House, to watch a body of the enemy's cavalry, which had moved in that direction the day before, was to have moved on the left towards Liberty, but orders did not reach him in time. The enemy's rear was overtaken at Liberty, twenty-five miles from Lynchburg, just before night, and driven through that place, after a brisk skirmish, by Ramseur's division. The days march on the old turnpike, which was very rough, had been terrible. McCausland had taken the wrong road and did not reach Liberty until after the enemy had been driven through the town.

It was here ascertained that Hunter had not retreated on the route by the Peaks of Otter, over which he had advanced, but had taken the road to Buford's depot, at the foot of the Blue Ridge, which would enable him to go either by Salem, Fincastle, or Buchanan. Ransom was, therefore, ordered to take the route, next day, by the Peaks of Otter, and endeavor to intercept the enemy should he move by Buchanan or Fincastle. The pursuit was resumed early on the morning of the 20th, and on our arrival in sight of Buford's, the enemy's rear guard was seen going into the mountain on the road towards Salem. As this left the road to Buchanan open, my aide, Lieutenant Pitzer, was sent across the mountain to that place, with orders to Ransom to move for Salem. Lieutenant Pitzer was also instructed to ride all night and send directions, by courier from Fincastle, and telegraph from Salem, to have the road through the mountains to Lewisburg and South-Western Virginia blockaded. The enemy was pursued into the mountains at Buford's Gap, but he had taken possession of the crest of the Blue Ridge, and put batteries in position commanding a gorge, through which the road passes, where it was impossible for a regiment to move in line. I had endeavored to ascertain if there was not another way across the mountain by which I could get around the enemy, but all the men, except the old ones, had gotten out of the way, and the latter, as well as the women and children, were in such a state of distress and alarm, that no reliable information could be obtained from them. We tried to throw forces up the sides of the mountains to get at the enemy, but they were so rugged that night came on before anything could be accomplished, and we had to desist, though not until a very late hour in the night.

By a mistake of the messenger, who was sent with orders to General Rodes, who was to be in the lead next morning, there was some delay in his movement on the 21st, but the pursuit was resumed very shortly after sun-rise. At the Big Lick, it was ascertained that the enemy had turned off from Salem towards Lewisburg on a road which passes through the mountains at a narrow pass called the "Hanging Rock," and my column was immediately turned towards that point, but on arriving there it was ascertained that the enemy's rear guard had passed through the gorge. McCausland had struck his column at this point and captured ten pieces of artillery, some waggons, and a number of prisoners; but, the enemy having brought up a heavy force, McCausland was compelled to fall back, carrying off, however, the prisoners, and a part of the artillery, and disabling the rest so that it could not be removed. As the enemy had got into the mountains, where nothing useful could be accomplished by pursuit, I did not deem it proper to continue it farther. A great part of my command had had nothing to eat for the last two days, except a little bacon which was obtained at Liberty. The cooking utensils were in the trains, and the effort to have bread baked at Lynchburg had failed. Neither the waggon trains, nor the artillery of the 2nd Corps, were up, and I knew that the country, through which Hunter's route led for forty or fifty miles, was, for the most part, a desolate mountain region; and that his troops were taking everything in the way of provisions and forage which they could lay their hands on. My field officers, except those of Breckenridge's command, were on foot, as their horses could not be transported on the trains from Charlottesville. I had seen our soldiers endure a great deal, but there was a limit to the endurance even of Confederate soldiers. A stern chase of infantry is a very difficult one, and Hunter's men were marching for their lives, his disabled being carried in his provision train which was now empty. My cavalry was not strong enough to accomplish anything of importance, and a further pursuit could only have resulted in disaster to my command from want of provisions and forage.

I was glad to see Hunter take the route to Lewisburg, as I knew he could not stop short of the Kanawha River, and he was, therefore, disposed of for some time. Had he moved to South-Western Virginia he would have done us incalculable mischief, as there was no troops of any consequence in that quarter, but plenty of supplies at that time. I should, therefore, have been compelled to follow him.*

My command had marched sixty miles, in the three days pursuit, over very

---

*Grant, in his report says: "General Hunter, owing to a want of ammunition to give battle, retired from before the place" (Lynchburg). This is a little remarkable, as it appears that this expedition had been long contemplated and was one of the prominent features of the campaign of 1864. Sheridan, with his cavalry, was to have united with Hunter at Lynchburg, and the two together were to have destroyed General Lee's communications and depots of supplies, and then have joined Grant. Can it be believed that Hunter set out on important an expedition with an insufficient supply of ammunition? He had fought only the battle of Piedmont, with a part of his force, and it was not a very severe one, as Jones force was a small one and composed mostly of cavalry. Crook's column not being there was not engaged. Had Sheridan defeated Hampton at Trevillian's, he would have reached Lynchburg after destroying the railroad on the way, and I could not have reached there in time to do any good. But Hampton defeated Sheridan, and the latter saw "infantry" "too strong to successfully assault." Had Hunter moved on Lynchburg, with energy, that place would have fallen before it was possible for me to get there. But he tarried on the way for purposes which will hereafter appear, and when he reached there, his heart failed him and he was afraid to fight an inferior force, and then there was discovered, "A want of ammunition to give battle."

rough roads, and that part of it from the Army of Northern Virginia had had no rest since leaving Gaines' Mill. I determined, therefore, to rest on the 22nd, so as to enable the waggons and artillery to get up, and prepare the men for the long march before them. Imboden had come up, following on the road through Salem after the enemy, and the cavalry was sent through Fincastle, to watch the enemy and annoy him as he passed through the mountains towards Lewisburg, and also ascertain whether he would endeavor to get into the Valley towards Lexington or Staunton.

MARCH DOWN THE VALLEY, AND OPERATIONS IN THE LOWER VALLEY AND MARYLAND.

At Lynchburg, I had received a telegram from General Lee, directing me, after disposing of Hunter, either to return to his army or carry out the original plan, as I might deem most expedient under the circumstances in which I found myself. After the pursuit had ceased, I received another dispatch from him, submitting it to my judgment whether the condition of my troops would permit the expedition across the Potomac to be carried out, and I determined to take the responsibility of continuing it. On the 23rd, the march was resumed and we reached Buchanan that night, where we struck again the route over which Hunter had advanced.* Ransom's cavalry moved by Clifton Forge, through the

---

*The scenes on Hunter's route from Lynchburg had been truly heart-rending. Houses had been burned, and helpless women and children left without shelter. The country had been stripped of provisions and many families left without a morsel to eat. Furniture and bedding had been cut to pieces, and old men and women and children robbed of all the clothing they had except that on their backs. Ladies trunks had been rifled and their dresses torn to pieces in mere wantonness. Even the negro girls had lost their little finery. We now had renewed evidences of the outrages committed by Hunter's orders in burning and plundering private houses. We saw the ruins of a number of houses to which the torch had been applied by his orders. At Lexington he had burned the Military Institute with all of its contents, including its library and scientific apparatus; and Washington College had been plundered and the statue of Washington stolen. The residence of Ex-Governor Letcher at that place had been burned by orders, and but a few minutes given Mrs. Letcher and her family to leave the house. In the same county a most excellent christian gentleman, a Mr. Creigh, had been hung, because, on a former occasion, he had killed a straggling and marauding Federal soldier while in the act of insulting and outraging the ladies of his family. These are but some of the outrages committed by Hunter or his orders, and I will not insult the memory of the ancient barbarians of the North by calling them "acts of Vandalism." If those old barbarians were savage and cruel, they at least had the manliness and daring of rude soldiers, with occasional traits of magnanimity. Hunter's deeds were those of a malignant and cowardly fanatic, who was better qualified to make war upon helpless women and children than upon armed soldiers. The time consumed in the perpetration of those deeds, was the salvation of Lynchburg, with its stores, foundries, and factories, which were so necessary to our army at Richmond.

western part of Rockbridge, to keep a lookout for Hunter and ascertain if he should attempt to get into the Valley again.

On the 26th, I reached Staunton in advance of the troops, and the latter came up next day, which was spent in reducing transportation and getting provisions from Waynesboro, to which point they had been sent over the railroad. Some of the guns and a number of the horses belonging to the artillery were now unfit for service, and the best of each were selected, and about a battalion taken from Breckenridge's artillery, under Lt. Col. King, to accompany us, in addition to the two battalions brought with the 2nd Corps. The rest were left behind with a portion of the officers and men in charge of them. The dismounted cavalry had been permitted to send for their horses which had been recruiting, and Col. Bradley T. Johnson, who had joined me at this place with a battalion of Maryland Cavalry, was assigned to the command of Jones' brigade, with the temporary rank of Brigadier-General, that brigade having been reorganized and the two Maryland battalions attached to it. General Breckenridge had accompanied us from Lynchburg, and, to give him a command commensurate with his proper one, and at the same time enable me to control the cavalry more readily, Gordon's division of infantry was assigned to his command in addition to the one under Elzey, and Ransom, in charge of the cavalry, was ordered to report to me directly. Major-General Elzey was relieved from duty at his own request, and the division under him was left under the temporary command of Brigadier-General Vaughan.

The official reports at this place showed about two thousand mounted men for duty in the cavalry, which was composed of four small brigades, to wit: Imboden's, McCausland's, Jackson's, and Jones' (now Johnson's). Vaughan's had not been mounted but the horses had been sent for from South-western Virginia. The official reports of the infantry showed 10,000 muskets for duty, including Vaughan's dismounted cavalry. Nearly, if not quite half of the company officers and men were barefooted or nearly so, and a dispatch had been sent from Salem by courier, and Lynchburg by telegraph, to Richmond, requesting shoes to be sent to Staunton, but they had not arrived.

Another telegram was received here from General Lee, stating that the circumstances under which my original orders were given had changed, and again submitting it to my judgment, in the altered state of things, whether the movement down the Valley and across the Potomac should be made. The accession to my command from Breckenridge's forces had not been as great as General Lee supposed it would be, on account of the disorganization consequent on

Jones' defeat at Piedmont, and the subsequent rapid movement to Lynchburg from Rockfish Gap, but I determined to carry out the original design at all hazards, and telegraphed to General Lee my purpose to continue the movement.

The march was resumed on the 28th with five days' rations in the waggons and two days in haversacks, empty waggons being left to bring the shoes when they arrived. Imboden was sent through Brock's Gap in the Great North Mountain to the Valley of the South Branch of the Potomac, with his brigade of cavalry and a battery of horse artillery, to destroy the railroad bridge over that stream and all the bridges on the Baltimore and Ohio railroad from that point to Martinsburg. The telegraph line was repaired to New Market as we marched down the Valley, and communications kept up with that point by signal stations. On the 2nd of July we reached Winchester,* and I here received a dispatch from General Lee, directing me to remain in the lower Valley until everything was in readiness to cross the Potomac, and to destroy the Baltimore and Ohio railroad and the Chesapeake and Ohio Canal as far as possible. This was in accordance with my previous determination, and its policy was obvious. My provisions were nearly exhausted and if I had moved through London, it would have been necessary for me to halt and thresh wheat and have it ground, as neither bread nor flour could be otherwise obtained; which would have caused much greater delay than was required on the other route, where we could take provisions from the enemy. Moreover unless the Baltimore and Ohio railroad was torn up, the enemy would have been able to move troops from the West over that road to Washington.

On the night of the 2nd, McCausland was sent across North Mountain, to move down Back Creek, and burn the railroad bridge at its mouth, and then to move by North Mountain depot to Hainesville, on the road from Martinsburg to Williamsport; and, early on the morning of the 3rd, Bradley Johnson was sent by Smithfield and Leetown, to cross the railroad at Kearneysville, east

---

*On this day we passed through Newtown where several houses, including that of a Methodist minister, had been burned by Hunter's orders, because a part of Mosby's command had attacked a train of supplies for Sigel's force, at this place. The original order was to burn the whole town, but the officer sent to execute it had revolted at the cruel mandate of his superior, and another had been sent who but partially executed it, after having forced the people to take an oath of allegiance to the United States to save their houses. Mosby's battalion, though called "guerillas" by the enemy, was a regular organization in the Confederate Army, and was merely serving on detached duty under General Lee's orders. The attack on the train was an act of legitimate warfare, and the order to burn Newtown, and the burning of the houses mentioned were most wanton, cruel, unjustifiable, and cowardly.

of Martinsburg, and unite with McCausland at Hainesville, so as to cut off the retreat of Sigel, who was at Martinsburg with a considerable force. Breckenridge moved, on the same morning, direct for Martinsburg, with his command preceded by Gilmor's battalion of cavalry, while I moved, with Rodes' and Ramseur's divisions, over the route taken by Johnson, to Leetown. On the approach of Breckenridge, Sigel, after very slight skirmishing, evacuated Martinsburg, leaving behind considerable stores, which fell into our hands. McCausland burned the bridge over Back Creek, captured the guard at North Mountain depot, and succeeded in reaching Hainesville; but Johnson encountered a force at Leetown, under Mulligan, which, after hard fighting, he drove across the railroad, when, Sigel, having united with Mulligan, Johnson's command was forced back, just before night, on Rodes' and Ramseur's divisions, which had arrived at Leetown, after a march of twenty-four miles. It was too late, and these divisions were too much exhausted, to go after the enemy; and, during the night, Sigel retreated across the Potomac, at Shepherdstown, to Maryland Heights.

On the 4th, Shepherdstown was occupied by a part of Ransom's cavalry. Rodes' and Ramseur's divisions moved to Harper's Ferry, and the enemy was driven from Bolivar Heights, and the Village of Bolivar, to an inner line of works under the cover of the guns from Maryland Heights. Breckenridge, after burning the railroad bridges at Martinsburg, and across the Opequon, moved to Duffield's depot, five miles from Harper's Ferry, destroying the road as he moved. During the night of the 4th, the enemy evacuated Harper's Ferry, burning the railroad and pontoon bridges across the Potomac.

It was not possible to occupy the town of Harper's Ferry, except with skirmishers, as it was thoroughly commanded by the heavy guns on Maryland Heights; and the 5th was spent by Rodes' and Ramseur's divisions in demonstrating at that place. In the afternoon, Breckenridge's command crossed the river at Shepherdstown, and Gordon's division was advanced over the Antietam, towards Maryland Heights. At night, considerable stores, which had been abandoned at Harper's Ferry, were secured; and, before day, Rodes' and Ramseur's divisions moved to Shepherdstown, and crossed the Potomac early on the 6th, Lewis' brigade, of Ramseur's division, being left to occupy Harper's Ferry with skirmishers.

On this day (the 6th) Gordon's division advanced towards Maryland Heights, and drove the enemy into his works. Working parties were employed in destroying the aqueduct of the canal over the Antietam, and the locks and canal boats.

On the 7th, Rodes moved through Rohersville, on the road to Crampton's Gap in South Mountain, and skirmished with a small force of the enemy, while Breckenridge demonstrated against Maryland Heights, with Gordon's division, supported by his other division, now under Brigadier-General Echols, who had reported for duty.

While these operations were going on, McCausland had occupied Hagerstown, and levied a contribution of $20,000, and Boonsboro' had been occupied by Johnson's cavalry. On the 6th I received a letter from General Lee, by special courier, informing me that, on the 12th, an effort would be made to release the prisoners at Point Lookout, and directing me to take steps to unite them with my command, if the attempt was successful; but I was not informed of the manner in which the attempt would be made—General Lee stating that he was not, himself, advised of the particulars.

My desire had been to manœuvre the enemy out of Maryland Heights, so as to enable me to move directly from Harper's Ferry for Washington; but he had taken refuge in his strongly-fortified works, and, as they could not be approached without great difficulty, and an attempt to carry them by assault would have resulted in greater loss than the advantage to be gained would justify, I determined to move through the gaps of South Mountain to the north of the Heights. On the 7th, the greater portion of the cavalry was sent across the mountain in the direction of Frederick; and, that night, the expected shoes having arrived and been distributed, orders were given for a general move next morning; and an officer (Lieut.-Col. Goodwin, of a Louisiana Regiment,) was ordered back to Winchester, with a small guard, to collect the stragglers at that place, and prevent them from following.

Imboden had reached the railroad, at the South Branch of the Potomac, and partially destroyed the bridge, but had not succeeded in dislodging the guard from the block-house at that place. He had been taken sick, and very little had been accomplished by the expedition; and his brigade, now under the command of Colonel George H. Smith, had returned.

Early on the morning of the 8th, the whole force moved; Rodes, through Crampton's Gap, to Jefferson; Breckenridge, through Fox's Gap; and Ramseur, with the trains, through Boonsboro' Gap, followed by Lewis' brigade, which had started from Harper's Ferry the night before, after burning the trestle-work on the railroad, and the stores which had not been brought off. Breckenridge and Ramseur encamped near Middletown, and Rodes near Jefferson. Ransom had occupied Catoctan Mountain, between Middletown and

Frederick, with his cavalry, and had skirmished heavily with a body of the enemy at the latter place. McCausland was ordered to move to the right, in the afternoon, and the next day cut the telegraph and railroad between Maryland Heights and Washington and Baltimore—cross the Monocacy, and, if possible, occupy the railroad bridge over that stream, at the Junction near Frederick.

Early on the 9th, Johnson with his brigade of cavalry, and a battery of horse artillery, moved to the north of Frederick, with orders to strike the railroads from Baltimore to Harrisburg and Philadelphia, burn the bridges over the Gunpowder, also to cut the railroad between Washington and Baltimore, and threaten the latter place; and then to move towards Point Lookout for the purpose of releasing the prisoners, if we should succeed in getting into Washington. The other troops also moved forward towards Monocacy Junction, and Ramseur's division passed through Frederick, driving a force of skirmishers before it.

BATTLE OF MONOCACY.

The enemy in considerable force under General Lew Wallace, was found strongly posted on the eastern bank of the Monocacy near the Junction, with an earthwork and two block houses commanding both the railroad bridge and the bridge on the Georgetown pike. Ramseur's division was deployed in front of the enemy, after driving his skirmishers across the river, and several batteries were put in position, when a sharp artillery fire opened from both sides. Rodes' division had come up from Jefferson and was placed on Ramseur's left, covering the roads from Baltimore and the crossings of the Monocacy above the Junction. Breckenridge's command, with the trains, was in the rear between Frederick and the Junction, while the residue of the cavalry was watching a force of the enemy's cavalry which had followed from Maryland Heights. The enemy's position was too strong, and the difficulties of crossing the Monocacy under fire too great, to attack in front without greater loss than I was willing to incur. I therefore made an examination in person to find a point at which the river could be crossed, so as to take the enemy in flank. While I was engaged in making this examination to my right, I discovered McCausland in the act of crossing the river with his brigade. As soon as he crossed he dismounted his men, and advanced rapidly against the enemy's left flank, which he threw into confusion, and he came very near capturing a battery of artillery, but the enemy concentrated on him, and he was gradually forced back obstinately contesting the ground. McCausland's movement which was very brilliantly executed, solved the problem for me, and, as soon as I discovered it, orders were sent to Breckenridge to move up rapidly with Gordon's division to McCausland's assistance, and to follow up his attack. This division crossed at the same place, and Gordon was ordered to move forward and strike the enemy on his left flank, and drive him from the positions commanding the crossings in Ramseur's front, so as to enable the latter to cross. This movement was executed under the personal superintendence of General Breckenridge, and, while Ramseur skirmished with the enemy in front, the attack was made by Gordon in gallant style, and, with the aid of several pieces of King's artillery which had been crossed over, and Nelson's artillery from the opposite side, he threw the enemy into great confusion and forced him from his position. Ramseur immediately crossed on the railroad bridge and pursued the enemy's flying forces, and Rodes crossed on the left and joined in the pursuit. Echols' division which had been left to guard the trains, was ordered up during the engagement, but was not needed. The pursuit was soon discontinued, as Wallace's entire force had taken the road towards Baltimore, and I did not want prisoners. Wallace's force I estimated at 8,000 or 10,000 men, and it was ascertained that one division of the 6th Corps (Rickett's) from Grant's army, was in the fight. Between 600 and 700 unwounded prisoners fell into our hands, and the enemy's loss in killed and wounded was very heavy. Our loss in killed and wounded was about 700, and among them were Brigadier-General Evans wounded, and Colonel Lamar of the 61st Georgia regiment, Lieutenant-Colonel Tavener, of the 17th Virginia Cavalry, and Lieutenant Hobson, of Nelson's artillery, killed. The action closed about sunset, and we had marched about fourteen miles before it commenced. All the troops and trains were crossed over the Monocacy that night, so as to resume the march early next day. Such of our wounded as could not be moved in ambulances or otherwise, were sent to the hospitals at Frederick under charge of competent medical officers, and our dead were buried. During the operations at Monocacy, a contribution of $200,000 in money, was levied on the city of Frederick, and some needed supplies were obtained.

OPERATIONS IN FRONT OF WASHINGTON, AND RECROSSING THE POTOMAC.

On the 10th, the march was resumed at daylight, and we bivouacked four miles from Rockville, on the Georgetown pike, having marched twenty miles.

Ramseur's division which had remained behind for a short time to protect a working party engaged in destroying the railroad bridge, was detained for a time in driving off the party of cavalry which had been following from Maryland Heights, and did not get up until one o'clock at night. McCausland, moving in front on this day, drove a body of the enemy's cavalry before him, and had quite a brisk engagement at Rockville, where he encamped after defeating and driving off the enemy.

We moved at daylight on the 11th; McCausland moving on the Georgetown pike, while the infantry, preceded by Imboden's cavalry under Colonel Smith, turned to the left at Rockville, so as to reach the 7th street pike which runs by Silver Spring into Washington. Jackson's cavalry moved on the left flank. The previous day had been very warm, and the roads were exceedingly dusty, as there had been no rain for several weeks. The heat during the night had been very oppressive, and but little rest had been obtained. This day was an exceedingly hot one, and there was no air stirring. While marching, the men were enveloped in a suffocating cloud of dust, and many of them fell by the way from exhaustion. Our progress was therefore very much impeded, but I pushed on as rapidly as possible, hoping to get into the fortifications around Washington before they could be manned. Smith drove a small body of cavalry before him into the works on the 7th street pike, and dismounted his men and deployed them as skirmishers. I rode ahead of the infantry, and arrived in sight of Fort Stevens on this road a short time after noon, when I discovered that the works were but feebly manned.

Rodes, whose division was in front, was immediately ordered to bring it into line as rapidly as possible, throw out skirmishers, and move into the works if he could. My whole column was then moving by flank, which was the only practicable mode of marching on the road we were on, and before Rodes' division could be brought up, we saw a cloud of dust in the rear of the works towards Washington, and soon a column of the enemy filed into them on the right and left, and skirmishers were thrown out in front, while an artillery fire was opened on us from a number of batteries. This defeated our hopes of getting possession of the works by surprise, and it became necessary to reconnoitre.

Rodes' skirmishers were thrown to the front, driving those of the enemy to the cover of the works, and we proceeded to examine the fortifications in order to ascertain if it was practicable to carry them by assault. They were found to be exceedingly strong, and consisted of what appeared to be enclosed forts for heavy artillery, with a tier of lower works in front of each pierced for an immense number of guns, the whole being connected by curtains with ditches in front, and strengthened by palisades and abattis. The timber had been felled within cannon range all around and left on the ground, making a formidable obstacle, and every possible approach was raked by artillery. On the right was Rock Creek, running through a deep ravine which had been rendered impassable by the felling of the timber on each side, and beyond were the works on the Georgetown pike which had been reported to be the strongest of all. On the left, as far as the eye could reach, the works appeared to be of the same impregnable character. The position was naturally strong for defence, and the examination showed, what might have been expected, that every appliance of science and unlimited means had been used to render the fortifications around Washington as strong as possible. This reconnoissance consumed the balance of the day.

The rapid marching which had broken down a number of the men who were barefooted or weakened by previous exposure, and had been left in the Valley and directed to be collected at Winchester, and the losses in killed and wounded at Harper's Ferry, Maryland Heights, and Monocacy, had reduced my infantry to about 8,000 muskets. Of those remaining, a very large number were greatly exhausted by the last two days marching, some having fallen by sunstroke, and I was satisfied, when we arrived in front of the fortifications, that not more than one-third of my force could have been carried into action. I had about forty pieces of field artillery, of which the largest were 12 pounder Napoleons, besides a few pieces of horse artillery with the cavalry. McCausland reported the works on the Georgetown pike too strongly manned for him to assault. We could not move to the right or the left without its being discovered from a signal station on the top of the "Soldier's Home," which overlooked the country, and the enemy would have been enabled to move in his works to meet us. Under the circumstances, to have rushed my men blindly against the fortifications, without understanding the state of things, would have been worse than folly. If we had any friends in Washington, none of them came out to give us information, and this satisfied me that the place was not undefended. I knew that troops had arrived from Grant's army, for prisoners had been captured from Rickett's division of the 6th Corps at Monocacy. From Sharpsburg I had sent a message to Mosby, by one of his men, requesting him to cross the Potomac below Harper's Ferry, cut the railroad and telegraph, and endeavour to find out the condition of things in Washington, but he had not crossed the river and I had received no information from him. A northern paper, which was obtained, gave the information that Hunter, after moving up the Ohio River in steamboats, was passing over the Baltimore and Ohio railroad, and I knew that he would be at Harper's Ferry soon, as Imboden had done very little damage to the road west of Martinsburg. After dark on the 11th, I held a consultation with Major-Generals Breckenridge, Rodes, Gordon and Ramseur, in which I stated to them the danger of remaining where we were, and the necessity of doing something immediately, as the probability was that the passes of the South Mountain and the fords of the upper Potomac would soon be closed against us. After interchanging views with them, being very reluctant to abandon the project of capturing Washington, I determined to make an assault on the enemy's works at daylight next morning, unless some information should be received before that time showing its impractibility, and so informed those officers. During the night a dispatch was received from Gen. Bradley Johnson from near Baltimore, informing me that he had received information, from a reliable source, that two corps had arrived from Gen. Grant's army, and that his whole army was probably in motion. This caused me to delay the attack until I could examine the works again, and, as soon as it was light enough to see, I rode to the front and found the parapets lined with troops. I had, therefore, reluctantly, to give up all hopes of capturing Washington, after I had arrived in sight of the dome of the Capitol, and given the Federal authorities a terrible fright.

Grant in his report says, in regard to the condition of things when I moved towards Washington: "The garrisons of Baltimore and Washington were at this time made up of heavy artillery regiments, hundred days men, and detachments from the invalid corps." And, in regard to the force of Wallace at Monocacy, he says: "His force was not sufficient to ensure success, but he fought the enemy nevertheless, and although it resulted in a defeat to our arms, yet it detained the enemy and thereby served to enable Gen. Wright to reach Washington with two divisions of the 6th Corps, and the advance of the 19th Corps, before him." Stanton says in his report: "Here (at Washington) they (we) were met by troops from the Army of the Potomac, consisting of the 6th Corps under General Wright, a part of the 8th Corps under General Gilmore, and a part of the 19th Corps, just arrived from New Orleans under General Emory." Taking Grant's statement of the troops which had arrived from his army as the most reliable, they were sufficient to hold the works against my troops, at least until others could arrive. But, in addition to those which had already arrived, there were the detachments from the invalid corps, called, I believe, the "Veteran Reserves" (of which I was informed there were about 5,000), the heavy artillery regiments, the hundred days' men, and, I suppose, the part of the 8th Corps mentioned by Stanton. To all these may be added the local troops, or militia, and the government employees. Some of the northern papers stated that, between Saturday and Monday, I could have entered the city; but on Saturday I was fighting at Monocacy, thirty-five miles from Washington, a force which I could not leave in my rear; and, after disposing of that force and moving as rapidly as it was possible for me to move, I did not arrive in front of the fortifications until after noon on Monday, and then my troops were exhausted, and it required time to bring them up into line. I had then made a march, over the circuitous route by Charlottesville, Lynchburg, and Salem, down the Valley, and through the passes of the South Mountain, which, notwithstanding the delays in dealing with Hunter's, Sigel's, and Wallace's forces, is, for its length and rapidity, I believe, without a parallel in this or any other modern war—the unopposed marauding excursion of the freebooter Sherman through Georgia, not excepted. My small force had been thrown up to the very walls of the Federal Capital, north of a river which could not be forded at any point within 40 miles, and with a heavy force and the South Mountain in my rear— the passes through which mountain could be held by a small number of troops. A glance at the map, when it is recollected that the Potomac is a wide river, and navigable to Washington for the largest vessels, will cause the intelligent reader to wonder, not why I failed to take Washington, but why I had the audacity to approach it as I did, with the small force under my command. It was supposed by some, who were not informed of the facts, that I delayed in the lower Valley longer than was necessary; but, an examination of the foregoing narrative will show that not one moment was spent in idleness, but that every one was employed in making some arrangement, or removing some difficulty in my way, which it was necessary to make or remove, so as to enable me to advance with a prospect of success. I could not move across the Potomac and through the passes of the South Mountain, with any safety, until Sigel was driven from, or safely housed in, the fortifications at Maryland Heights.

After abandoning the idea of capturing Washington, I determined to remain in front of the fortifications during the 12th, and retire at night, as I was satisfied that to remain longer would cause the loss of my entire force.

Johnson had burned the bridges over the Gunpowder, on the Harrisburg and Philadelphia roads, threatened Baltimore, and started for Point Lookout, but I sent an order for him to return. The attempt to release the prisoners of which I was informed by General Lee, was not made, as the enemy had received notice of it in some way. Major Harry Gilmor, who burned the bridge over the Gunpowder on the Philadelphia road, captured Major-General Franklin on a train at that point, but he was permitted to escape, either by the carelessness or exhaustion of the guard placed over him, before I was informed of the capture.

On the afternoon of the 12th, a heavy reconnoitering force was sent out by the enemy, which, after severe skirmishing, was driven back by Rodes' division with but slight loss to us. About dark we commenced retiring and did so without molestation.* Passing through Rockville and Poolsville, we crossed the Potomac at White's Ford, above Leesburg in London County, on the morning of the 14th, bringing off the prisoners captured at Monocacy and everything else in safety. There was some skirmishing in the rear between our cavalry and that of the enemy which was following, and, on the afternoon of the 14th, there was some artillery firing by the enemy, across the river, at our cavalry which was watching the fords. Besides the money levied in Hagerstown and Frederick, which was subsequently very useful in obtaining supplies, we brought off quite a large number of beef cattle, and the cavalry obtained a number of horses, some being also procured for the artillery.†

---

*Grant says: "On the 12th, a reconnaissance was thrown out in front of Fort Stevens to ascertain the enemy's position and force. A severe skirmish ensued, in which we lost 280 in killed and wounded. The enemy's loss was probably greater. He commenced retiring during the night." In regard to the same affair, Stanton says: "By those troops (Wright's, Gilmore's, and Emory's) the enemy was driven back from Washington and retreated hastily to Virginia, pursued by our forces under General Wright." Grant's statement is correct, with the exception of the estimate he places on our loss. Comment on Stanton's is unnecessary when it is compared with that of Grant.

†On the night of the 12th, the house of Postmaster-General Blair near Silver Spring was burned, and it was assumed by the enemy that it was burned by my orders. The fact is, that I had nothing to do with it, and do not yet know how the burning occurred. Though I believed that retaliation was fully justified by the previous acts of the enemy, yet I did not wish to incur the risk of any license on the part of my troops, and it was obviously impolitic to set the house on fire when we were retiring, as it amounted to notice of our movement. Some of my officers thought the burning was done by some person in the neighborhood, who took advantage of our presence to commit the set with impunity. It may have been occasioned by a sholl from the enemy's guns, some of which went in that direction late in the day, or it may have been the act of some of my men; and a number of them had abundant provocation for the act, in the sight of their own devastated homes as they marched down the Valley on Hunter's track. In retaliation for the burning of this house, two Federal gunboats with a body of soldiers on board were sent up the Rappahannock River, on which there was not a Confederate soldier, to burn the house of the widow of the brother of the Hon. James A. Soddon, the Confederate Secretary of War, and she and her little children were turned out of doors, and the house with all its contents consigned to the flames. A card was left, signed by Butler or his order, stating that the house was burned in retaliation for the burning of the Hon. Montgomery Blair's house. This retaliation upon a widowed lady and her orphan children, by a combined military and naval expedition, was worthy of the agent selected, and the

RETURN TO THE VALLEY, AND OPERATIONS THERE.

We rested, on the 14th and 15th, near Leesburg, and, on the morning of the 16th, resumed the march to the Valley, through Snicker's Gap in the Blue Ridge. Hunter had arrived at Harper's Ferry, and united with Sigel, and the whole force had moved from that place, under Crook, to Hillsboro', in Loudon, and a body of cavalry from it made a dash on our train, as we were moving towards the Valley, and succeeded in setting fire to a few waggons, but was soon driven off by troops from Rodes' and Ramseur's divisions, and one piece of artillery was captured from the enemy.

On the morning of the 17th, we crossed the Shenandoah, at Snicker's or Castleman's Ferry, and took position near Berryville—Breckenridge covering the ford at the ferry, and the river above and below, and Rodes' and Ramseur's divisions the roads from Harper's Ferry.

On the 18th, the enemy, having moved through Snicker's Gap, appeared on the banks of the Shenandoah, and there was some skirmishing. In the afternoon, a heavy column of his infantry made a clash at Parker's Ford, one mile below the ferry, and crossed over, after driving back the picket of one hundred men at that point. Breckenridge moved Gordon's and Echols' divisions to the front, and held the enemy in check, while Rodes' division was brought up from the left, and attacked and drove him across the river, with heavy loss, and in great confusion.

On the 19th, the enemy's main body still occupied the eastern bank of the Shenandoah, and smaller columns moved up and down the river, to effect a crossing. Imboden, with his own and McCausland's cavalry, resisted and repulsed one of these columns, which attempted to cross at Berry's Ferry, with considerable loss to the enemy. The horses of Vaughan's cavalry having been brought from South-western Virginia, his small force had been now mounted. On this day I received information that a column under Averill was moving from Martinsburg towards Winchester, and, as the position I held near Berryville left my trains exposed to expeditions in the rear from Martinsburg and Harper's Ferry, I determined to concentrate my force near Strasburg, so as

---

cause in which he was engaged. But, though it was very congenial to his nature, I do not regard Butler as alone responsible for this act. The odium of it should attach to his superiors Lincoln and Grant, he being the favorite of the former, and the subordinate of the latter, and at that time, serving under his immediate orders.

to enable me to put the trains in safety, and then move out and attack the enemy. This movement was commenced on the night of the 19th; Ramseur's division, with a battery of artillery, being sent to Winchester, to cover that place against Averill, while the stores, and the sick and wounded were being removed, and the other divisions moving through Millwood and White Post to the Valley Pike at Newtown and Middletown.

Vaughan's and Jackson's cavalry had been watching Averill, and, on the afternoon of the 20th, it was reported to General Ramseur, by General Vaughan, that Averill was at Stephenson's depot, with an inferior force, which could be captured, and Ramseur moved out from Winchester to attack him; but, relying on the accuracy of the information he had received, General Ramseur did not take the proper precautions in advancing, and his division, while moving by the flank, was suddenly met by a larger force, under Averill, advancing in line of battle, and the result was that Ramseur's force was thrown into confusion, and compelled to retire, with the loss of four pieces of artillery, and a number in killed and wounded—Brigadier-Generals Lewis and Lilly being among the wounded, and Col. Board, of the 58th Virginia Regiment, among the killed. Colonel Jackson made a vigorous charge with his cavalry, which enabled Ramseur to rally his men, restore order, and arrest the progress of Averill before he reached Winchester. The error committed, on this occasion, by this most gallant officer, was nobly retrieved in the subsequent part of the campaign. I received, at Newtown, the news of Ramseur's misfortune, and immediately moved to his assistance with Rodes' division; but, on arriving at Winchester, I found that the enemy, after being checked, had fallen back a short distance; and, as another and much larger column was moving through Berryville, I did not go after Averill, but moved the whole command to Newtown—the stores, and such of the wounded and sick as could be transported, having been gotten off.

On the 21st, my whole infantry force was concentrated near Middletown; and, on the 22nd, it was moved across Cedar Creek, towards Strasburg, and so posted as to cover all the roads from the direction of Winchester.

A report having been sent to me from Mt. Jackson, that a force of the enemy was moving from the Valley of the South Branch of the Potomac to that place, Imboden was sent to ascertain its truth, and it proved to be false. We rested on the 23rd, while waiting to ascertain the movements of the enemy, and during the day a report was received from the cavalry in front, that a large portion of the force sent after us from Washington, was returning, and that Crook and Averill had united, and were at Kernstown, near Winchester.

BATTLE OF KERNSTOWN.

On the reception of the foregoing information, I determined to attack the enemy at once; and, early on the morning of the 24th, my whole force was put in motion for Winchester. The enemy, under Crook, consisting of the "Army of West Virginia," and including Hunter's and Sigel's forces, and Averill's cavalry, was found in position at Kernstown, on the same ground occupied by Shields, at the time of General Jackson's fight with him, on the 23rd of March, 1862. Ramseur's division was sent to the left, at Bartonsville, to get around the enemy's right flank, while the other divisions moved along the Valley Pike, and formed on each side of it. Ransom's cavalry was ordered to move in two columns; one on the right along the road from Front Royal to Winchester; and the other on the left, and west of Winchester, so as to unite in rear of the latter place, and cut off the enemy's retreat. After the enemy's skirmishers were driven in, it was discovered that his left flank, extending through Kernstown, was exposed, and General Breckenridge was ordered to move Echols' division, now under Brig.-Gen. Wharton, under cover of some ravines on our right, and attack that flank. This movement, which was made under Gen. Breckenridge's personal superintendence, was handsomely executed, and the attacking division struck the enemy's left flank in open ground, doubling it up and throwing his whole line into great confusion. The other divisions then advanced, and the rout of the enemy became complete. He was pursued, by the infantry and artillery, through and beyond Winchester; and the pursuit was continued by Rodes' division to Stephenson's depot, six miles from Winchester—this division then having marched twenty-seven miles from its position west of Strasburg. The cavalry had not been moved according to my orders; and the enemy, having the advantage of an open country and a wide macadamized road, was enabled to make his escape with his artillery and most of his waggons. General Ransom had been in very bad health since he reported to me at Lynchburg, and unable to take the active command in the field; and all my operations had been impeded for the want of an efficient and energetic cavalry commander. I think, if I had had one on this occasion, the greater part of the enemy's force would have been captured or destroyed, for the rout was thorough. Our loss, in this action, was very light. The enemy's loss in killed and wounded was severe, and two or three hundred prisoners fell into our hands; and, among them, Colonel Mulligan, in command of a division, mortally wounded. The infantry was too much exhausted to continue the pursuit on the 25th, and only moved to Bunker Hill, twelve miles from Winchester. The pursuit was continued by our cavalry, and the enemy's rear guard of cavalry was encountered at Martinsburg; but, after slight skirmishing, it evacuated the place. The whole defeated force crossed the Potomac, and took refuge at Maryland Heights and Harper's Ferry. The road from Winchester, via Martinsburg, to Williamsport, was strewed with debris of the rapid retreat—twelve caissons and seventy-two waggons having been abandoned, and most of them burned.*

EXPEDITION INTO MARYLAND AND PENNSYLVANIA— BURNING OF CHAMBERSBURG.

On the 26th we moved to Martinsburg, the cavalry going to the Potomac. The 27th and 28th were employed in destroying the railroad, it having been repaired since we passed over it at the beginning of the month. While at Martinsburg, it was ascertained, beyond all doubt, that Hunter had been again indulging in his favourite mode of warfare, and that, after his return to the Valley, while we were near Washington, among other outrages, the private residences of Mr. Andrew Hunter, a member of the Virginia Senate, Mr. Alexander R. Boteler, an ex-member of the Confederate Congress, as well as of the United States Congress, and Edmund I. Lee, a distant relative of General Lee, all in Jefferson County, with their contents, had been burned by his orders, only time enough being given for the ladies to get out of the houses. A number of towns in the South, as well as private country houses, had been burned by the Federal troops, and the accounts had been heralded forth in some of the Northern papers in terms of exultation, and gloated over by their readers, while they were received with apathy by others. I now came to the conclusion that we had stood this mode of warfare long enough, and that it was time to open the eyes of the people of the North to its enormity, by an example in the way of retaliation. I did not select the cases mentioned, as having more merit or greater claims for

---

*Grant, in his report, entirely ignores this battle, in which the enemy's forces were superior to mine, and merely says: "About the 25th it became evident that the enemy was again advancing upon Maryland and Pennsylvania, and the 6th corps, which was at Washington, was ordered back to the vicinity of Harper's Ferry."

retaliation than others, but because they had occurred within the limits of the country covered by my command, and were brought more immediately to my attention.*

The town of Chambersburg in Pennsylvania was selected as the one on which retaliation should be made, and McCausland was ordered to proceed with his brigade and that of Johnson and a battery of artillery to that place, and demand of the municipal authorities the sum of $100,000 in gold, or $500,000 in United States currency, as a compensation for the destruction of the houses named and their contents; and, in default of payment, to lay the town in ashes, in retaliation for the burning of those houses and others in Virginia, as well as for the towns which had been burned in other Southern States. A written demand to that effect was sent to the municipal authorities, and they were informed what would be the result of a failure or refusal to comply with it. I desired to give the people of Chambersburg an opportunity of saving their town, by making compensation for part of the injury done, and hoped that the payment of such a sum would have the desired effect, and open the eyes of the people of other towns at the North, to the necessity of urging upon their government the adoption of a different policy. McCausland was also directed to proceed from Chambersburg towards Cumberland in Maryland, and levy contributions in money upon that and other towns able to bear them, and if possible destroy the machinery at the coal pits near Cumberland, and the machine shops, depots, and bridges on the Baltimore and Ohio railroad as far as practicable.

On the 29th, McCausland crossed the Potomac near Clear Spring, above Williamsport, and I moved with Rodes' and Ramseur's divisions and Vaughan's cavalry to the latter place, while Imboden demonstrated with his

---

*I had often seen delicate ladies, who had been plundered, insulted and rendered desolate by the acts of our most atrocious enemies, and while they did not call for it, yet in the anguished expressions of their features while narrating their misfortunes, there was a mute appeal to every manly sentiment of my bosom for retribution which I could no longer withstand. On my passage through the lower Valley into Maryland, a lady had said to me, with tears in her eyes, "Our lot is a hard one and we see no peace; but there are a few green spots in our lives, and they are, when the Confederate soldiers come along and we can do something for them." May God defend and bless those noble women of the Valley, who so often ministered to the wounded, sick and dying Confederate soldiers, and gave their last morsel of bread to the hungry! They bore with heroic courage the privations, sufferings, persecutions and dangers, to which the war which was constantly waged in their midst exposed them, and upon no portion of the Southern people did the disasters which finally befell our army and country, fall with more crashing effect than upon them.

and Jackson's cavalry towards Harper's Ferry, in order to withdraw attention from McCausland. Breckenridge remained at Martinsburg and continued the destruction of the railroad. Vaughan drove a force of cavalry from Williamsport, and went into Hagerstown, where he captured and destroyed a train of cars loaded with supplies. One of Rodes' brigades was crossed over at Williamsport and subsequently withdrawn. On the 30th, McCausland being well under way, I moved back to Martinsburg, and on the 31st the whole infantry force was moved to Bunker Hill, where we remained on the 1st, 2nd, and 3rd of August.

On the 4th, in order to enable McCausland to retire from Pennsylvania and Maryland, and to keep Hunter, who had been reinforced by the 6th and 19th Corps, and had been oscillating between Harper's Ferry and Monocacy Junction, in a state of uncertainty, I again moved to the Potomac with the infantry and Vaughan's and Jackson's cavalry, while Imboden demonstrated towards Harper's Ferry. On the 5th Rodes' and Ramseur's divisions crossed at Williamsport and took position near St. James' College, and Vaughan's cavalry went into Hagerstown. Breckenridge, with his command, and Jackson's cavalry, crossed at Shepherdstown, and took position at Sharpsburg. This position is in full view from Maryland Heights, and a cavalry force was sent out by the enemy to reconnoitre, which, after skirmishing with Jackson's cavalry, was driven off by the sharpshooters of Gordon's division. On the 6th, the whole force recrossed the Potomac at Williamsport, and moved towards Martinsburg; and on the 7th we returned to Bunker Hill.*

---

*While at Sharpsburg on this occasion, I rode over the ground on which the battle of Sharpsburg, or Antietam as it is called by the enemy, was fought, and I was surprised to see how few traces remained of that great battle. In the woods at the famous Dunkard or Tunker Church, where, from personal observation at the battle, I expected to find the trees terribly broken and shattered, a stranger would find difficulty in identifying the marks of the bullets and shells.

I will take occasion here to say that the public, North or South, has never known how small was the force with which General Lee fought that battle. McClellan's estimate is very wide of the mark. From personal observation and conversation with other officers engaged, including Gen. Lee himself, I am satisfied that the latter was not able to carry 30,000 men into action. The exhaustion of our men in the battles around Richmond, the subsequent battles near Manassas, and on the march to Maryland, when they were for days without anything to eat except green corn, was so great that the straggling was frightful before we crossed the Potomac. As an instance of our weakness, and a reminiscence worthy of being recorded, which was brought very forcibly to my mind while riding over the ground, I will state the following facts: In the early part of the day, all of Gen. Jackson's troops on the field except my brigade (A. P. Hill had not then arrived from Harper's Ferry) were driven from the field in great disorder, and Hood had taken their place

On the 30th of July McCausland reached Chambersburg, and made the demand as directed, reading to such of the authorities as presented themselves the paper sent by me. The demand was not complied with, the people stating that they were not afraid of having their town burned, and that a Federal force was approaching. The policy pursued by our army on former occasions had been so lenient, that they did not suppose the threat was in earnest this time, and they hoped for speedy relief. McCausland, however, proceeded to carry out his orders, and the greater part of the town was laid in ashes.* He then moved in the direction of Cumberland, but, on approaching that town, he found it defended by a force under Kelly too strong for him to attack, and he withdrew towards Hampshire County in Virginia, and crossed the Potomac near the mouth of the South Branch, capturing the garrison at that place and partially destroying the railroad bridge. He then invested the post on the railroad at New Creek, but finding it too strongly fortified to take by assault, he moved to Moorefield in Hardy County, near which place he halted to rest and recruit his men and horses, as the command was now considered safe from pur-

---

with his division. My brigade, which was on the extreme left supporting some artillery with which Stuart was operating, and had not been engaged, was sent for by General Jackson and posted in the left of the woods at the Dunkard Church. Hood was also forced back, and then the enemy advanced to this woods—Summer's Corps, which was fresh, advancing on our left flank. My brigade, then numbering about 1000 men for duty, with two or three hundred men of Jackson's own division, who had been rallied by Colonels Grigsby and Stafford, and when there was an interval of at least one half a mile between us and any other part of our line, held Summer's corps in check for some time, until Green's division of Mansfield's Corps penetrated into the interval in the woods between us and the rest of our line, when I was compelled to move by the flank and attack it. That division was driven out of the woods by my brigade, while Grigsby and Stafford skirmished with Summer's advancing force, when we turned on it, and, with the aid of three brigades—to wit: Anderson's, Semmes', and Barksdale's—which had just arrived to our assistance, drove it from the woods in great confusion and with heavy loss. So great was the disparity in the forces at this point that the wounded officers who were captured were greatly mortified, and commenced making excuses by stating that the troops in their front were raw troops, who stampeded and produced confusion in their ranks. McClellan, in his report, says that Summer's corps and Green's division encountered, in this woods, "overwhelming numbers behind breastworks," and he assigns the heavy losses and consequent demoralization in Summer's Corps as one of the reasons for not renewing the fight on the 18th. We had no breastworks nor anything like them in that woods on the 17th, and, on our part, it was a stand-up fight there altogether. The slight breastworks subsequently seen by McClellan were made on the 18th, when we were expecting a renewal of the battle.

*For this not I, alone, am responsible, as the officers engaged in it were simply executing my orders, and had no discretion left them. Notwithstanding the lapse of time which has occurred, and the result of the war, I am perfectly satisfied with my conduct on this occasion, and see no reason to regret it.

suit. Averill, however, had been pursuing from Chambersburg with a body of cavalry, and Johnson's brigade was surprised in camp, before day, on the morning of the 7th of August, and routed by Averill's force. This resulted also in the rout of McCausland's brigade, and the loss of the artillery (4 pieces) and about 300 prisoners from the whole command. The balance of the command made its way to Mount Jackson in great disorder, and much weakened. This affair had a very damaging effect upon my cavalry for the rest of the campaign.*

RETREAT TO FISHER'S HILL, AND SUBSEQUENT OPERATIONS, UNTIL THE BATTLE OF WINCHESTER.

On the 9th, Imboden reported that a large force had been concentrated at Harper's Ferry, consisting of the 6th, 19th, and Crook's Corps, under a new commander, and that it was moving towards Berryville, to our right. The new commander proved to be Major-General Sheridan, from Grant's army. On the 10th, we moved from Bunker Hill to the east of Winchester, to cover the roads from Charlestown and Berryville to that place; and Ramseur's division was moved to Winchester, to cover that place against a force reported to be advancing from the west; but, this report proving untrue, it was subsequently moved to the junction of the Millwood and Front Royal roads. On the morning of the 11th, it was discovered that the enemy was moving to our right, on the east of the Opequon, and my troops, which had been formed in line of battle covering Winchester, were moved to the right, towards Newtown, keeping between the enemy and the Valley Pike. Ramseur had a brisk skirmish with a body of the enemy's cavalry on the Millwood Road, and drove it back. Imboden's and Vaughan's brigades had a severe fight with another body of cavalry at the double toll-gate, at the intersection of the Front Royal road with the road from White Post to Newtown; and it was discovered that there had been a considerable accession to that arm from Grant's army. Just before night, Gordon had heavy skirmishing near Newtown, with a large force of cavalry, which advanced on the road from the double toll-gate, and drove it off. We encamped near Newtown; and, on the morning of the 12th, moved to Hupp's Hill, between Stras-

---

*Grant says, in reference to this expedition under McCausland: "They were met and defeated by General Kelly; and, with diminished numbers, escaped into the mountains of West Virginia;" and he makes no allusion whatever to Averill's affair. There was no defeat by Kelly, but there was one by Averill, as I have stated. This shows how loose Grant is as to his facts. So far as we were concerned, the defeat by Averill was worse than it could have been by Kelly.

burg and Cedar Creek. Finding that the enemy was advancing in much heavier force than I had yet encountered, I determined to take position at Fisher's Hill, above Strasburg, and await his attack there. Imboden, with his brigade, was sent to Luray Valley, to watch that route; and, in the afternoon, we moved to Fisher's Hill. I had received information a few days before, from General Lee, that General Anderson had moved with Kershaw's division of infantry and Fitz Lee's division of cavalry to Culpeper C. H.; and I sent a dispatch to Anderson, informing him of the state of things, and requesting him to move to Front Royal, so as to guard the Luray Valley.

Sheridan's advance appeared on the banks of Cedar Creek, on the 12th, and there was some skirmishing with it. My troops were posted at Fisher's Hill, with the right resting on the North Fork of the Shenandoah, and the left extending towards Little North Mountain; and we awaited the advance of the enemy. General Anderson moved to Front Royal, in compliance with my request, and took position to prevent an advance of the enemy on that route. Shortly after I took position at Fisher's Hill, Major-General Lomax reported to me to relieve Ransom, in command of the cavalry, and McCausland and Johnson joined us with the remnants of their brigades. Sheridan demonstrated at Hupp's Hill, within our view, for several days, and some severe skirmishing ensued.

Upon taking position at Fisher's Hill, I had established a signal-station on the end of Three Top Mountain, a branch of Massanutten Mountain, near Strasburg, which overlooked both camps and enabled me to communicate readily with General Anderson, in the Luray Valley. A small force from Sheridan's army ascended the mountain and drove off our signal-men, and possession was taken of the station by the enemy, who was in turn driven away; when several small but severe fights ensued over the station, possession of it being finally gained and held by a force of one hundred men under Captain Keller of Gordon's division.

On the morning of the 17th, it was discovered that the enemy was falling back, and I immediately moved forward in pursuit, requesting General Anderson, by signal, to cross the river at Front Royal, and move towards Winchester. Just before night, the enemy's cavalry and a body of infantry, reported to be a division, was encountered between Kernstown and Winchester, and driven through the latter place, after a sharp engagement, in which Wharton's division moved to the left, and attacked the enemy's infantry, and drove it from a strong position on Bower's Hill, south of Winchester, while Ramseur engaged it in front, and Gordon advanced against the cavalry on the right.*

On the 18th we took position to cover Winchester, and Gen. Anderson came up with Kershaw's division of infantry, Cutshaw's battalion of Artillery, and two brigades of cavalry under Fitz Lee. General Anderson ranked me, but he declined to take command, and offered to co-operate in any movement I might suggest. We had now discovered that Torbert's and Wilson's divisions of cavalry from Grant's army, had joined Sheridan's force, and that the latter was very large.

On the 19th, my main force moved to Bunker Hill and Lomax's cavalry made reconnoissances to Martinsburg and Shepherdstown, while Anderson's whole force remained near Winchester.

On the 20th, our cavalry had some skirmishing with the enemy's on the Opequon, and on the 21st, by concert, there was a general movement towards Harper's Ferry—my command moving through Smithfield towards Charlestown, and Anderson's on the direct road by Summit Point. A body of the enemy's cavalry was driven from the Opequon, and was pursued by part of our cavalry towards Summit Point. I encountered Sheridan's main force near

---

*When Hunter was relieved I had hoped that an end was put to his mode of warfare, but I had now to learn how the new commander proposed to carry on the war in behalf of "the best government the world ever saw," (so called). Sheridan had commenced burning barns, mills and stacks of small grain and hay, and the whole country was smoking. Among many others, the barn of a respectable farmer near Newtown, whose name was Chrisman, had been burned within a few steps of his house, and the latter saved with great difficulty, notwithstanding the fact that Mr. Chrisman had received from General Torbert, in command of the Federal cavalry, a written protection stating that for some weeks he had taken care of, and showed great kindness to, a badly wounded Federal soldier. In passing through Middletown, I was informed that one of my soldiers had been tried and hung as a spy. The grave at the foot of the gallows was opened, and the body was recognized by his brother and the officers of his company as a private of the 54th North Carolina regiment. This man had been found by the enemy in Middletown, in attendance on a Confederate soldier whose leg was amputated, and he had claimed to be a citizen, but a paper was found on his person showing that he had been formerly detailed as a nurse in the hospital. On this state of facts he was hung as a spy. He was not employed in any such capacity, and he was so illiterate, not being able to read or write, that his appearance and evident want of intelligence precluded the idea of his being so employed. I would have retaliated at once by hanging a commissioned officer, but the enquiry which I made furnished some reason for believing that the man had remained behind, and endeavored to pass for a citizen to avoid service in our army; and I did not therefore wish to risk the lives of my officers and men who were in the enemy's hands, by making his a case for retaliation. His execution by the enemy, however, was none the less wanton and barbarous.

Cameron's depot, about three miles from Charlestown, in a position which he commenced fortifying at once. Rodes' and Ramseur's divisions were advanced to the front, and very heavy skirmishing ensued and was continued until night, but I waited for General Anderson to arrive before making a general attack. He encountered Wilson's division of cavalry at Summit Point, and, after driving it off, went into camp at that place. At light next morning, it was discovered that the enemy had retired during the night, and his rear guard of cavalry was driven through Charlestown towards Hall-town, where Sheridan had taken a strong position under the protection of the heavy guns on Maryland Heights. I demonstrated on the enemy's front on the 22nd, 23rd, and 24th, and there was some skirmishing. General Anderson then consented to take my position in front of Charlestown and amuse the enemy with Kershaw's division of infantry, supported by McCausland's brigade of cavalry on the left and a regiment of Fitz Lee's cavalry on the right, while I moved with my infantry and artillery to Shepherdstown, and Fitz Lee with the rest of the cavalry to Williamsport, as if to cross into Maryland, in order to keep up the fear of an invasion of Maryland and Pennsylvania.

On the 25th Fitz Lee started by the way of Leetown and Martinsburg to Williamsport, and I moved through Leetown and crossed the railroad at Kearneysville to Shepherdstown. After Fitz Lee had passed on, I encountered a very large force of the enemy's cavalry between Leetown and Kearneysville, which was moving out with several days forage and rations for a raid in our rear. After a sharp engagement with small arms and artillery, this force was driven back through Shepherdstown, where we came very near surrounding and capturing a considerable portion of it, but it succeeded in making its escape across the Potomac. Gordon's division, which was moved around to intercept the enemy, became heavily engaged, and cut off the retreat of part of his force by one road, but it made its way down the river to the ford by another and thus escaped. In this affair, a valuable officer, Colonel Monaghan of the 6th Louisiana Regiment, was killed. Fitz Lee reached Williamsport, and had some skirmishing across the river at that place, and then moved to Shepherdstown.

On the 26th I moved to Leetown, and on the 27th I moved back to Bunker Hill; while Anderson who had confronted Sheridan, during the two days of my absence, with but a division of infantry and a brigade and a regiment of cavalry, moved to Stephenson's Depot.

On the 28th, our cavalry, which had been left holding a line from Charlestown to Shepherdstown, was compelled to retire across the Opequon, after having had a brisk engagement with the enemy's cavalry at Smithfield. On the 29th; the enemy's cavalry crossed the Opequon near Smithfield, driving in our cavalry pickets, when I advanced to the front with a part of my infantry, and drove the enemy across the stream again, and after a very sharp artillery duel, a portion of my command was crossed over and pursued the enemy through Smithfield towards Charlestown. We then retired, leaving a command of cavalry at Smithfield, but it was compelled to recross the Opequon, on the advance of a heavy force from the direction of Charlestown.

Quiet prevailed on the 30th, but on the 31st there were some demonstrations of cavalry by the enemy on the Opequon, which were met by ours. On this day, (31st), Anderson moved to Winchester, and Rodes with his division went to Martinsburg on a reconnoissance, drove a force of the enemy's cavalry from that place, interrupted the preparations for repairing the railroad, and then returned.

There was quiet on the 1st of September, but, on the 2nd, I broke up my camp at Bunker Hill, and moved with three divisions of infantry and part of McCausland's cavalry under Col. Ferguson, across the country towards Summit Point, on a reconnoissance, while the trains under the protection of Rodes' division were moved to Stephenson's depot. After I had crossed the Opequon and was moving towards Summit Point, Averill's cavalry attacked and drove back in some confusion, first Vaughan's, and then Johnson's cavalry, which were on the Martinsburg road, and the Opequon, but Rodes returned towards Bunker Hill and drove the enemy back in turn. This affair arrested my march, and I recrossed the Opequon and moved to Stephenson's depot, where I established my camp.

On the 3d Rodes moved to Bunker Hill in support of Lomax's cavalry, and drove the enemy's cavalry from and beyond that place.

A letter had been received from General Lee requesting that Kershaw's division should be returned to him, as he was very much in need of troops, and, after consultation with me, General Anderson determined to recross the Blue Ridge with that division and Fitz Lee's cavalry. On the 3rd he moved towards Berryville for the purpose of crossing the mountain at Ashby's Gap, and I was to have moved towards Charlestown next day, to occupy the enemy's attention during Anderson's movement. Sheridan, however, had started two divisions of cavalry through Berryville and White Post, on a raid to our rear, and his main force had moved towards Berryville. Anderson encountered Crook's corps at the latter place, and, after a sharp engagement, drove it back on the main body. Receiving information of this affair, I moved at daylight next morning, with three divisions, to Anderson's assistance, Gordon's division being left to cover Winchester. I found Kershaw's division extended out in a strong skirmish line confronting Sheridan's main force, which had taken position in rear of Berryville, across the road from Charlestown to that place, and was busily fortifying, while the cavalry force which had started on the raid was returning and passing between Berryville and the river to Sheridan's rear. As may be supposed, Anderson's position was one of great peril, if the enemy had possessed any enterprise, and it presented the appearance of the most extreme audacity for him thus to confront a force so vastly superior to his own, while, too, his trains were at the mercy of the enemy's cavalry, had the latter known it. Placing one of my divisions in line on Kershaw's left, I moved with the other two along the enemy's front towards his right, for the purpose of reconnoitring and attacking that flank, if a suitable opportunity offered. After moving in this way for two miles, I reached an elevated position from which the enemy's line was visible, and within artillery range of it. I at first thought that I had reached his right flank, and was about making arrangements to attack it, when casting my eye to my left, I discovered, as far as the eye could reach with the aid of field glasses, a line extending towards Summit Point. The position the enemy occupied was a strong one, and he was busily engaged fortifying it, having already made considerable progress. It was not until I had had this view that I realized the size of the enemy's force, and as I discovered that his line was too long for me to get around his flank, and the position was too strong to attack in front, I returned and informed General Anderson of the condition of things. After consultation with him, we thought it not advisable to attack the enemy in his intrenched lines, and we determined to move our forces back to the west side of the Opequon, and see if he would not move out of his works. The waggon trains were sent back early next morning (the 5th) towards Winchester, and about an hour by sun Kershaw's division, whose place had been taken by one of my divisions, moved towards the same point. About two o'clock in the afternoon my troops were withdrawn, and moved back to Stephenson's depot. This withdrawal was made while the skirmishers were in close proximity and firing at each other; yet there was no effort on the part of the enemy to molest us. Just as my front division (Rodes') reached Stephenson's depot, it met, and drove back, and pursued for some distance, Averill's cavalry, which was forcing towards Winchester that part of our cavalry which had been watching the Martinsburg road.

It was quiet on the 6th, but on the 7th the enemy's cavalry made demonstrations on the Martinsburg road and the Opequon at several points, and was repulsed.

On the 8th it was quiet again, but on the 9th a detachment of the enemy's cavalry came to the Opequon below Brucetown, burned some mills, and retreated before a division of infantry sent out to meet it.

On the 10th, my infantry moved by Bunker Hill to Darkesville and encountered a considerable force of the enemy's cavalry, which was driven off, and then pursued by Lomax through Martinsburg across the Opequon. We then returned to Bunker Hill, and the next day to Stephenson's depot, and there was quiet on the 12th.

On the 13th a large force of the enemy's cavalry, reported to be supported by infantry, advanced on the road from Summit Point and drove in our pickets from the Opequon, when two divisions of infantry were advanced to the front, driving the enemy across the Opequon again. A very sharp artillery duel across the creek then took place, and some of my infantry crossed over, when the enemy retired.

On the 14th General Anderson again started, with Kershaw's division and Cutshaw's battalion of artillery, to cross the Blue Ridge by the way of Front Royal, and was not molested. Fitz Lee's cavalry was left with me, and Ramseur's division was moved to Winchester to occupy Kershaw's position.

There was an affair between one of Kershaw's brigades and a division of the enemy's cavalry, while I was at Fisher's Hill and Anderson at Front Royal, in which some prisoners were lost; and, subsequently, there were two affairs, in which the outposts from Kershaw's command were attacked and captured by the enemy's cavalry, one in front of Winchester and the other in front of Charlestown, which I have not undertaken to detail, as they occurred when General Anderson was controlling the operations of that division, but it is proper to refer to them here as part of the operations in the Valley.

On the 15th and 16th my troops remained in camp undisturbed.

The positions of the opposing forces were now as follows: Ramseur's division and Nelson's battalion of artillery were on the road from Berryville to Winchester, one mile from the latter place. Rodes', Gordon's and Wharton's divisions, (the last two being under Breckenridge,) and Braxton's and King's battalions of artillery were at Stephenson's depot on the Winchester and

Potomac railroad, which is six miles from Winchester. Lomax's cavalry picketed in my front on the Opequon, and on my left from that stream to North Mountain, while Fitz Lee's cavalry watched the right, having small pickets across to the Shenandoah. Four principal roads, from positions held by the enemy, centered at Stephenson's depot, to wit: the Martinsburg road, the road from Charlestown via Smithfield, the road from the same place via Summit Point, and the road from Berryville via Jordan's Springs. Sheridan's main force was near Berryville, at the intrenched position which has been mentioned, while Averill was at Martinsburg with a division of cavalry. Berryville is ten miles from Winchester, nearly east, and Martinsburg twenty-two miles nearly north. The crossing of the Opequon on the Berryville road is four or five miles from Winchester. From Berryville there are two good roads to Front Royal, via Millwood and White Post, and from Millwood there is a macadamized road to Winchester, and also good roads via White Post to the Valley pike at Newtown and Middletown, the last two roads running east of the Opequon. The whole country is very open, being a limestone country, which is thickly settled and well cleared, and affords great facilities for the movement of troops and the operations of cavalry. From the enemy's fortifications on Maryland Heights, the country north and east of Winchester, and the main roads through it, are exposed to view.

The relative positions which we occupied rendered my communications to the rear very much exposed, but I could not avoid it without giving up the lower Valley. The object of my presence there was to keep up a threatening attitude towards Maryland and Pennsylvania, and prevent the use of the Baltimore and Ohio railroad, and the Chesapeake and Ohio canal, as well as to keep as large a force as possible from Grant's army to defend the Federal Capital. Had Sheridan, by a prompt movement, thrown his whole force on the line of my communications, I would have been compelled to attempt to cut my way through, as there was no escape for me to the right or left, and my force was too weak to cross the Potomac while he was in my rear. I knew my danger, but I could occupy no other position that would have enabled me to accomplish the desired object. If I had moved up the Valley at all, I could not have stopped short of New Market, for between that place and the country in which I was there was no forage for my horses; and this would have enabled the enemy to resume the use of the railroad and canal, and return all the troops from Grant's army to him. Being compelled to occupy the position where I was, and being aware of its danger as well as apprized of the fact that very great odds were opposed to me, my only resource was to use my forces so as to display them at different points with great rapidity, and thereby keep up the impression that they were much larger than they really were. The events of the last month had satisfied me that the commander opposed to me was without enterprise, and possessed an excessive caution which amounted to timidity. If it was his policy to produce the impression that his force was too weak to fight me, he did not succeed, but if it was to convince me that he was not an able or energetic commander, his strategy was a complete success, and subsequent events have not changed my opinion.

My infantry force at this time consisted of the three divisions of the 2nd Corps of the Army of Northern Virginia, and Wharton's division of Breckenridge's command. The 2nd Corps numbered a little over 8,000 muskets when it was detached in pursuit of Hunter, and it had now been reduced to about 7,000 muskets, by long and rapid marches and the various engagements and skirmishes in which it had participated. Wharton's division had been reduced to about 1,700 muskets by the same causes. Making a small allowance for details and those unfit for duty, I had about 8,500 muskets for duty. When I returned from Maryland, my cavalry consisted of the remnants of five small brigades, to wit: Imboden's, McCausland's, Johnson's Jackson's, and Vaughan's. Vaughan's had now been ordered to South-Western Virginia, most of the men having left without permission. The surprise and rout of McCausland's and Johnson's brigades by Averill at Moorefield, had resulted in the loss of a considerable number of horses and men, and such had been the loss in all the brigades, in the various fights and skirmishes in which they had been engaged, that the whole of this cavalry, now under Lomax, numbered only about 1,700 mounted men. Fitz Lee had brought with him two brigades, to-wit: Wickham's, and Lomax's old brigade (now under Colonel Payne), numbering about 1,200 mounted men. I had the three battalions of artillery which had been with me near Washington, and Fitz Lee had brought a few pieces of horse artillery. When I speak of divisions and brigades of my troops, it must be understood that they were mere skeletons of those organizations.

Since my return from Maryland, my supplies had been obtained principally from the lower Valley and the counties west of it, and the money which was obtained by contributions in Maryland was used for that purpose. Nearly the whole of our bread was obtained by threshing the wheat and then having it ground, by details from my command, and it sometimes happened that while my troops were fighting, the very flour which was to furnish them with bread for their next meal was being ground under the protection of their guns. Latterly our flour had been obtained from the upper Valley, but also by details sent for that purpose. The horses and mules, including the cavalry horses, were sustained almost entirely by grazing.

I have no means of stating with accuracy Sheridan's force, and can only form an estimate from such data as I have been able to procure. Citizens who had seen his force, stated that it was the largest which they had ever seen in the Valley on either side, and some estimated it as high as 60,000 or 70,000, but of course I made allowance for the usual exaggeration of inexperienced men. My estimate is from the following data: In Grant's letter to Hunter, dated at Monocacy, August 5th, 1864, and contained in the report of the former, is the following statement: "In detailing such a force, the brigade of cavalry now *en route* from Washington via Rockville, may be taken into account. There are now on their way to join you three other brigades of the best cavalry, numbering at least 5,000 men and horses." Sheridan relieved Hunter on the 6th, and Grant says in his report, "On the 7th of August, the Middle Department and the Department of West Virginia, Washington, and the Susquehanna were constituted into the Middle Military division, and Major-General Sheridan was assigned to the temporary command of the same. Two divisions of cavalry, commanded by Generals Torbert and Wilson were sent to Sheridan from the Army of the Potomac. The first reached him at Harper's Ferry on the 11th of August." Before this cavalry was sent to the Valley, there was already a division there commanded by Averill, besides some detachments which belonged to the department of West Virginia. A book containing the official reports of the chief surgeon of the cavalry corps of Sheridan's army, which was subsequently captured at Cedar Creek on the 19th of October, showed that there were present for duty in that Corps, during the first week in September, over 11,000 men, and present for duty during the week ending the 17th day of September, 10,100 men. The extracts from Grant's report go to confirm this statement, as, if three brigades numbered at least 5,000 men and horses, the two divisions, when the whole of them arrived, with Averill's cavalry, must have numbered over 10,000. I think, therefore, that I can safely estimate Sheridan's cavalry at the battle of Winchester, on the 19th of September, at 10,000. His infantry consisted of the 6th, 19th, and Crook's Corps, the latter being composed of the "Army of West Virginia," and one division of the 8th Corps. The report of Secretary Stanton shows that there was in the department of which the "Middle Military division" was composed, the following "available force present for duty May 1st, 1864," to-wit:

"Department of Washington .... .42,124"
"Department of West Virginia .... .30,782"
"Department of Susquehanna .... .2,970."
"Middle Department .... .5,627."

making an aggregate of 81,503; but, as the Federal Secretary of War in the same report says, "In order to repair the losses of the Army of the Potomac, the chief part of the force designed to guard the Middle Department and the Department of Washington was called forward to the front," we may assume that 40,000 men were used for that purpose, which would leave 41,503, minus the losses in battle before Sheridan relieved Hunter, in the Middle Military division, exclusive of the 6th and 19th Corps, and the cavalry from Grant's army. The infantry of the Army of the Potomac was composed of the 2nd, 5th, and 6th Corps, on the 1st of May, 1864, and Stanton says the "available force present for duty" in that army on that day, was 120,386 men. Allowing 30,000 for the artillery and cavalry of that army, which would be a very liberal allowance, and there would still be left 90,385 infantry; and it is fair to assume that the 6th Corps numbered one-third of the infantry, that is, 30,000 men on the 1st of May, 1864. If the losses of the Army of the Potomac had been such as to reduce the 6th Corps to less than 10,000 men, notwithstanding the reinforcements and recruits received, the carnage in Grant's army must have been frightful indeed. The 19th Corps was just from the Department of the Gulf and had not gone through a bloody campaign. A communication which was among the papers captured at Cedar Creek, in noticing some statement of a newspaper correspondent in regard to the conduct of that corps at Winchester, designated it as "a vile slander on 12,000 of the best soldiers in the Union army." In view of the foregoing data, without counting the troops in the Middle Department and the Departments of Washington and the Susquehanna, and making liberal allowances for losses in battle, and for troops detained on post and garrison duty in the Department of West Virginia, I think that I may assume that Sheridan had at least 35,000 infantry against me. The troops of the 6th Corps and of the Department of West Virginia, alone, without counting the 19th Corps, numbered on the 1st of May, 1864, 60,782. If with the 19th Corps, Sheridan did not have 35,000 infantry remaining from this force, what had become of the balance? Sheridan's artillery very greatly outnumbered mine, both in men and guns.

Having been informed that a force was at work on the railroad at Martinsburg, I moved on the afternoon of the 17th of September, with Rodes' and Gordon's division, and Braxton's artillery to Bunker Hill, and, on the morning of the 18th, with Gordon's division and a part of the artillery to Martinsburg, preceded by a part of Lomax's cavalry. Averill's division of cavalry was driven from the town across the Opequon in the direction of Charlestown, and we then returned to Bunker Hill. Gordon was left at Bunker Hill, with orders to move to Stephenson's depot by sunrise next morning, and Rodes' division moved to the latter place that night, to which I also returned. At Martinsburg, where the enemy had a telegraph office, I learned that Grant was with Sheridan that day, and I expected an early move.

BATTLE OF WINCHESTER.

At light on the morning of the 19th, our cavalry pickets at the crossing of the Opequon on the Berryville road were driven in, and information having been sent me of that fact, I immediately ordered all the troops at Stephenson's depot to be in readiness to move, directions being given for Gordon, who had arrived from Bunker Hill, to move at once; but, by some mistake on the part of my staff officer, the latter order was not delivered to General Breckenridge or Gordon. I rode at once to Ramseur's position, and found his troops in line across the Berryville road skirmishing with the enemy. Before reaching this point, I had ascertained that Gordon was not moving, and sent back for him, and now discovering that the enemy's advance was a real one and in heavy force, I sent orders for Breckenridge and Rodes to move up as rapidly as possible. The position occupied by Ramseur was about one mile and a half out from Winchester, on an elevated plateau between Abraham's Creek and Red Bud Run. Abraham's Creek crosses the Valley Pike one mile south of Winchester, and then crosses the Front Royal road about the same distance south-east of the town, and, running eastwardly, on the southern side of the Berryville road, crosses that road a short distance before it empties into the Opequon. Red Bud Run crosses the Martinsburg road about a mile and a half north of Winchester, and runs eastwardly, on the northern side of the Berryville road, to the Opequon. Ramseur was therefore in the obtuse angle formed by the Martinsburg and Front Royal roads. In front of and to the right of him, for some distance, the country was open. Abraham's Creek runs through a deep valley, and beyond it, on the right, is high open ground, at the intersection of the Front Royal and Millwood roads. To Ramseur's left, the country sloped off to the Red Bud, and there were some patches of woods which afforded cover for troops. To the north of the Red Bud, the country is very open, affording facilities for the movement of any kind of troops. Towards the Opequon, on the front, the Berryville road runs through a ravine, with hills and woods on each side, which enabled the enemy to move his troops under cover, and mask them out of range of artillery. Nelson's artillery was posted on Ramseur's line, covering the approaches as far as practicable; and Lomax, with Jackson's cavalry and part of Johnson's, was on the right, watching the valley of Abraham's Creek and the Front Royal road beyond, while Fitz Lee was on the left, across the Red Bud, with his cavalry and a battery of horse-artillery, and a detachment of Johnson's cavalry watched the interval between Ramseur's left and the Red Bud. These troops held the enemy's main force in cheek until Gordon's and Rodes' divisions arrived from Stephenson's depot. Gordon's division arrived first, a little after ten o'clock, A.M., and was placed under cover in rear of a piece of woods behind the interval between Ramseur's line and the Red Bud, the detachment of Johnson's cavalry having been removed to the right. Knowing that it would not do for us to await the shock of the enemy's attack, Gordon was directed to examine the ground on the left, with a view to attacking a force of the enemy which had taken position in a piece of wood in front of him, and while he was so engaged Rodes arrived with three of his brigades, and was directed to form on Gordon's right, in rear of another piece of woods. While this movement was being executed, we discovered very heavy columns of the enemy, which had been massed under cover between the Red Bud and the Berryville road, moving to attack Ramseur on his left flank, while another force pressed him in front. It was a moment of imminent and thrilling danger, as it was impossible for Ramseur's division, which numbered only about 1,700 muskets, to withstand the immense force advancing against it. The only chance for us was to hurl Rodes and Gordon upon the flank of the advancing columns, and they were ordered forward at once to the attack. They advanced in most gallant style through the woods into the open ground, and attacked with great vigor, while Nelson's artillery on the right, and Braxton's on the left, opened a destructive fire. But Evans' brigade of Gordon's division, which was on the extreme left of our infantry, received a check from a column of the enemy, and was forced back through the woods from behind which it had advanced, the enemy following to the very rear of the woods, and to within musket range of seven pieces of Braxton's artillery which were without support. This caused a pause in our advance, and the position was most critical, for it was apparent that unless this force was driven back the day was lost. Braxton's guns, in which now was our only hope, resolutely stood their ground, and, under the personal superintendence of Lieutenant Colonel Braxton and Colonel T. H. Carter, my then Chief of Artillery, opened with canister on the enemy. This fire was so rapid and well-directed that the enemy staggered, halted, and commenced falling back, leaving a battle-flag on the ground, whose bearer was cut down by a canister shot. Just then, Battle's brigade of Rodes' division, which had arrived and been formed in line for the purpose of advancing to the support of the rest of the division, moved forward and swept through the woods, driving the enemy before it, while Evans' brigade was rallied and brought back to the charge. Our advance, which had been suspended for a moment, was resumed, and the enemy's attacking columns were thrown into great confusion and driven from the field. This attacking force of the enemy proved to be the Sixth and Nineteenth corps, and it was a grand sight to see this immense body hurled back in utter disorder before my two divisions, numbering a very little over 5000 muskets. Ramseur's division had received the shock of the enemy's attack, and been forced back a little, but soon recovered itself. Lomax, on the right, had held the enemy's cavalry in check, and, with a part of his force, had made a gallant charge against a body of infantry, when Ramseur's line was being forced back, thus aiding the latter in recovering from the momentary disorder. Fitz Lee on the left, from across the Red Bud, had poured a galling fire into the enemy's columns with his sharpshooters and horse-artillery, while Nelson's and Braxton's battalions had performed wonders. This affair occurred about 11 A.M., and a splendid victory had been gained. The ground in front was strewn with the enemy's dead and wounded, and some prisoners had been taken. But on our side, Major General Rodes had been killed, in the very moment of triumph, while conducting the attack of his division with great gallantry and skill, and this was a heavy blow to me. Brigadier-General Godwin, of Ramseur's division, had been killed, and Brigadier-General York, of Gordon's division, had lost an arm. Other brave men and officers had fallen, and we could illy bear the loss of any of them. Had I then had a body of fresh troops to push our victory, the day would have been ours, but in this action, in the early part of the day, I had present only about 7000 muskets, about 2000 cavalry, and two battalions of artillery with about 30 guns; and they had all been engaged. Wharton's division and King's artillery had not arrived, and Imboden's cavalry under Colonel Smith, and McCausland's under Colonel Ferguson, were watching the enemy's cavalry on the left, on the Martinsburg road and the Opequon. The enemy had a fresh corps which had not been engaged, and there remained his heavy force of cavalry. Our lines were now formed across from Abraham's Creek to Red Bud and were very attenuated. The enemy was still to be seen in front in formidable force, and away to our right, across Abraham's Creek, at the junction of the Front Royal and Millwood roads, he had massed a division of cavalry with some artillery, overlapping us at least a mile, while the country was open between this force and the Valley Pike, and the Cedar Creek Pike back of the latter; which roads furnished my only means of retreat in the event of disaster. My line did not reach the Front Royal road on the right, or the Martinsburg road on the left.

When the order was sent for the troops to move from Stephenson's depot, General Breckenridge had moved to the front, with Wharton's division and King's artillery, to meet a cavalry force which had driven our pickets from the Opequon on the Charlestown road, and that division had become heavily engaged with the enemy, and sustained and repulsed several determined charges of his cavalry, while its own flanks were in great danger from the enemy's main force on the right, and a column of his cavalry moving up the Martinsburg road on the left. After much difficulty and some hard fighting, Gen. Breckenridge succeeded in extricating his force and moving up the Martinsburg road to join me, but he did not reach the field until about two o'clock in the afternoon.

In the meantime there had been heavy skirmishing along the line, and the reports from the front were that the enemy was massing for another attack, but it was impossible to tell where it would fall. As the danger from the enemy's cavalry on the right was very great and Lomax's force very weak, Wickham's brigade of Fitz Lee's cavalry had been sent from the left to Lomax's assistance. When Wharton's division arrived, Patton's brigade of that division was left to aid Fitz Lee in guarding the Martinsburg road, against the force of cavalry which was advancing on that road watched by Lomax's two small brigades; and the rest of the division was formed in rear of Rodes' division in the centre, in order to be moved to any point that might be attacked. Late in the afternoon, two divisions of the enemy's cavalry drove in the small force which had been watching it on the Martinsburg road, and the Crook's corps, which had not been engaged, advanced at the same time on that flank, on the north side of Red Bud, and, before this overwhelming force, Patton's brigade of infantry and Payne's brigade of cavalry under Fitz Lee were forced back. A considerable force of the enemy's cavalry then swept along the Martinsburg road to the very skirts of Winchester, thus getting in the rear of our left flank. Wharton's two other brigades were moved in double quick time to the left and rear, and, making a gallant charge on the enemy's cavalry, with the aid of King's artillery, and some of Braxton's guns which were turned to the rear, succeeded in driving it back. The division was then thrown into line by General Breckenridge, in rear of our left and at right angles with the Martinsburg road, and another charge of the enemy's cavalry was handsomely repulsed. But many of the men on our front line, hearing the fire in the rear, and thinking they were flanked and about to be cut off, commenced falling back, thus producing great confusion. At the same time, Crook advanced against our left, and Gordon threw Evans' brigade into line to meet him, but the disorder in the front line became so great that, after an obstinate resistance, that brigade was compelled to retire also. The whole front line had now given way, but a large portion of the men were rallied and formed behind an indifferent line of breastworks, which had been made just outside of Winchester during the first year of the war, and, with the aid of the artillery which was brought back to this position, the progress of the enemy's infantry was arrested. Wharton's division maintained its organization on the left, and Ramseur fell back in good order on the right. Wickham's brigade of cavalry had been brought from the right, and was in position on Fort Hill, just outside of Winchester on the west. Just after the advance of the enemy's infantry was checked by our artillery, it was reported to me that the enemy had got around our right flank, and as I knew this was perfectly practicable, and was expecting such a movement from the cavalry on the Front Royal road, I gave the order to retire, but instantly discovering that the supposed force of the enemy was Ramseur's division, which had merely moved back to keep in line with the other troops, I gave the order for the latter to return to the works before they had moved twenty paces. This order was obeyed by Wharton's division, but not so well by the others. The enemy's cavalry force, however, was too large for us, and having the advantage of open ground, it again succeeded in getting around our left, producing great confusion, for which there was no remedy. Nothing was now left for us but to retire through Winchester, and Ramseur's division, which maintained its organization, was moved on the east of the town to the south side of it, and put in position, forming the basis for a new line, while the other troops moved back through the town. Wickham's brigade, with some pieces of horse artillery on Fort Hill, covered this movement and checked the pursuit of the enemy's cavalry. When the new line was formed, the enemy's advance was checked until nightfall, and we then retired to Newtown without serious molestation. Lomax had held the enemy's cavalry on the Front Royal road in check, and a feeble attempt at pursuit was repulsed by Ramseur near Kernstown.

As soon as our reverse began, orders had been sent for the removal of the trains, stores, and sick and wounded in the hospitals, to Fisher's Hill, over the Cedar Creek Pike and the Back Road. This was done with safety, and all the wounded, except such as were not in a condition to be moved, and those which had not been brought from the field, were carried to the rear.

This battle, beginning with the skirmishing in Ramseur's front, had lasted from daylight until dark, and, at the close of it, we had been forced back two miles, after having repulsed the enemy's first attack with great slaughter to him, and subsequently contested every inch of ground with unsurpassed obstinacy. We deserved the victory, and would have had it, but for the enemy's immense superiority in cavalry, which alone gave it to him.

Three pieces of King's artillery, from which the horses were shot, and which therefore could not be brought off, were lost, but the enemy claimed five, and, if he captured that number, two were lost by the cavalry and not reported to me. My loss in killed, wounded and prisoners was severe for the size of my force, but it was only a fraction of that claimed by the enemy. Owing to its obedience to orders in returning to the works, the heaviest loss of prisoners was in Wharton's division. Among the killed were Major General Rodes and Brigadier General Godwin. Colonel G. W. Patton, commanding a brigade, was mortally wounded, and fell into the hands of the enemy. Major General Fitz Lee was severely wounded, and Brigadier General York lost an arm. In Major General Rodes I had to regret the loss not only of a most accomplished, skillful and gallant officer, upon whom I placed great reliance, but also of a personal friend, whose counsels had been of great service to me in the trying circumstances with which I had found myself surrounded. He fell at his post, doing a soldier's and patriot's duty to his country, and his memory will long be cherished by his comrades. General Godwin and Colonel Patton were both most gallant and efficient officers, and their loss was deeply felt, as was that of all the brave officers and men who fell in this battle. The enemy's loss in killed and wounded was very heavy, and some prisoners fell into our hands.

A skillful and energetic commander of the enemy's forces would have crushed Ramseur before any assistance could have reached him, and thus ensured the destruction of my whole force; and, later in the day, when the battle had turned against us, with the immense superiority in cavalry which Sheridan had, and the advantage of the open country, would have destroyed my whole force and captured everything I had. As it was, considering the immense disparity in numbers and equipment, the enemy had very little to boast of. I had lost a few pieces of artillery and some very valuable officers and men, but the main part of my force and all my trains had been saved, and the enemy's loss in killed and wounded was far greater than mine. When I look back to this battle, I can but attribute my escape from utter annihilation to the incapacity of my opponent.*

---

*The enemy has called this battle, "The Battle of the Opequon," but I know no claim it has to that title, unless it be in the fact that, after his repulse in the fore part of the day, some of his troops ran back across that stream. I have always thought that instead of being promoted, Sheridan ought to have been cashiered for this battle. He seems to be a sort of pet of Grant's, and I give the following extracts from the report of the latter, to show the strange inconsistency of which he is guilty to magnify Sheridan's services. In his Monocacy letter to Hunter, Grant says: "From Harper's Ferry, if it is found that the enemy has moved north of the Potomac in large force, push north, following him and attacking him wherever found; follow him if driven south of the Potomac as long as it is safe to do so. If it is ascertained that the enemy has but a small force north of the Potomac, then push south with the main force, detaching, under a competent commander, a sufficient force to look after the raiders and drive them to their homes." And further on in the same letter he says: "Bear in mind, the object is to drive the enemy south, and to do this, you want to keep him always in sight. Be guided in your course by the course he takes." When Sheridan relieved Hunter, this letter of instructions was ordered to be turned over to him, and two divisions of cavalry subsequently joined him; yet Grant says in regard to Sheridan's operations: "His operations during the month of August and the fore part of September were both of an offensive and defensive character, resulting in many severe skirmishes, principally by the cavalry, in which we were generally successful, but no general engagement took place. The two armies lay in such a position, the enemy on the west bank of the Opequon creek covering Winchester, and our forces in front of Berryville, that either could bring on a battle at any time. Defeat to us would open to the enemy the States of Maryland and Pennsylvania for long distances before another army could be interposed to check him. Under these circumstances, I hesitated about allowing the initiative to be taken. Finally the use of the Baltimore and Ohio Railroad and the Chesapeake and Ohio Canal, which were both obstructed by the enemy, became so indispensably necessary to us, and the importance of relieving Pennsylvania and Maryland from continuously threatened invasion so great, that I determined the risk should be taken. But fearing to telegraph the order for an attack without knowing more than I did of General Sheridan's feelings as to what would be the probable result, I left City Point on the 15th of September to visit him at his head-quarters, to decide after conference with him what should be done. I met him at Charlestown, and he pointed out so directly how each army lay, *what he would do the moment he was authorized*, and expressed such confidence of success, that I saw

AFFAIR AT FISHER'S HILL.

At light on the morning of the 20th, my troops moved to Fisher's Hill without molestation from the enemy, and again took position at that point on the old line—Wharton's division being on the right, then Gordon's, Ramseur's, and Rodes', in the order in which they are mentioned. Fitz Lee's cavalry, now under Brigadier-General Wickham, was sent up the Luray Valley to a narrow pass at Millford, to try and hold that valley against the enemy's cavalry. General Ramseur was transferred to the command of Rodes' division, and Brigadier-General Pegram who had reported for duty about the 1st of August, and been in command of his brigade since that time, was left in command of the division previously commanded by Ramseur. My infantry was not able to occupy the whole line at Fisher's Hill, notwithstanding it was extended out in an attenuated line, with considerable intervals. The greater part of Lomax's cavalry was therefore dismounted, and placed on Ramseur's left, near Little North Mountain, but the line could not then be fully occupied.

This was the only position in the whole Valley where a defensive line could be taken against an enemy moving up the Valley, and it had several weak points. To have retired beyond this point, would have rendered it necessary for me to fall back to some of the gaps of the Blue Ridge, at the upper part of the Valley, and I determined therefore to make a show of a stand here, with the hope that the enemy would be deterred from attacking me in this position, as had been the case in August.

On the second day after our arrival at this place, General Breckenridge received orders from Richmond, by telegraph, to return to South-Western Vir-

---

there were but two words of instruction necessary—go in." In the letter to Hunter there is no hesitation about the initiative, and yet, notwithstanding this letter was turned over to Sheridan for his guidance, and two divisions of cavalry subsequently sent to him, and the further fact that he had been operating both on the *offensive* and defensive during August and the fore part of September, the impression is sought to be made that his ardor was restrained by some sort of orders, of which no mention is made in Grant's report. Really this is very curious, and Grant's admission of his hesitation in allowing the initiative to be taken, and the statement that the Baltimore and Ohio Railroad and the Chesapeake and Ohio Canal were so obstructed, and the invasion of Pennsylvania and Maryland so constantly threatened, as to compel him to throw off that hesitation, convey a great compliment to the efficiency of my small force. The railroad is twenty-two miles from Winchester at the nearest point, and the canal over thirty and north of the Potomac, while Sheridan was much nearer to both. That Grant did find it necessary to say to Sheridan, "go in!" I can well believe, but that the latter was panting for the utterance of that classic phrase, I must be allowed to regard as apocryphal.

ginia, and I lost the benefit of his services. He had ably co-operated with me, and our personal relations had been of the most pleasant character.

In the afternoon of the 20th, Sheridan's forces appeared on the banks of Cedar Creek, about four miles from Fisher's Hill, and the 21st, and the greater part of the 22nd, were consumed by him in reconnoitring and gradually moving his forces to my front under cover of breast works. After some skirmishing, he attained a strong position immediately in my front and fortified it, and I began to think he was satisfied with the advantage he had gained and would not probably press it further; but on the afternoon of the 22nd, I discovered that another attack was contemplated, and orders were given for my troops to retire, after dark, as I knew my force was not strong enough to resist a determined assault. Just before sunset, however, Crook's corps, which had moved to our left on the side of Little North Mountain, and under cover of the woods, forced back Lomax's dismounted cavalry, and advanced against Ramseur's left. Ramseur made an attempt to meet this movement by throwing his brigades successfully into line to the left, and Wharton's division was sent for from the right but it did not arrive. Pegram's brigades were also thrown into line in the same manner as Ramseur's, but the movement produced some disorder in both divisions, and as soon as it was observed by the enemy, he advanced along his whole line, and the mischief could not be remedied. After a very brief contest, my whole force retired in considerable confusion, but the men and officers of the artillery behaved with great coolness, fighting to the very last, and I had to ride to some of the officers and order them to withdraw their guns, before they would move. In some cases, they had held out so long, and the roads leading from their positions into the Pike were so rugged, that eleven guns fell into the hands of the enemy. Vigorous pursuit was not made, and my force fell back through Woodstock to a place called the Narrow Passage, all the trains being carried off in safety.

Our loss in killed and wounded in this affair was slight, but some prisoners were taken by the enemy, the most of whom were captured while attempting to make their way across the North Fork to Massanutten Mountain, under the impression that the enemy had possession of the Valley Pike in our rear. I had the misfortune to lose my Adjutant General, Lieutenant Colonel A. S. Pendleton, a gallant and efficient young officer, who had served on General Jackson's staff during his Valley campaign, and subsequently to the time of the latter's death. Colonel Pendleton fell mortally wounded about dark, while posting a force across the Pike, a little in rear of Fisher's Hill, to check the enemy. He was acting with his accustomed gallantry, and his loss was deeply felt and regretted.*

RETREAT UP THE VALLEY, AND OPERATIONS UNTIL THE BATTLE OF CEDAR CREEK.

On the morning of the 23rd, I moved back to Mount Jackson, where I halted to enable the sick and wounded, and the hospital stores at that place to be carried off. In the afternoon Averill's division of cavalry came up in pursuit, and after some heavy skirmishing was driven back. I then moved to Rude's Hill between Mount Jackson and New Market.

On the morning of the 24th, a body of the enemy's cavalry crossed the North Fork below Mount Jackson, and attempted to get around my right flank, but was held in check. The enemy's infantry soon appeared at Mount Jackson, and commenced moving around my left flank, on the opposite side of the river from that on which my left rested. As the country was entirely open, and Rude's Hill an elevated position, I could see the whole movement of the enemy, and as soon as it was fully developed, I commenced retiring in line of battle, and in that manner retired through New Market to a point at which the road to Port Republic leaves the Valley Pike, nine miles from Rude's Hill. This movement was made through an entirely open country, and at every mile or two a halt was made, and artillery opened on the enemy, who was pursuing, which compelled him to commence deploying into line, when the retreat would be resumed. In this retreat, under fire in line, which is so trying to a retiring force, and tests the best qualities of the soldier, the conduct of my troops was most admirable, and they preserved perfect order and their line intact, notwithstanding their diminished numbers, and the fact that the enemy was pursuing in full force, and, every now and then, dashing up with horse artillery under the support of cavalry, and opening on the retiring lines. At the last halt, which was at a place

---

*In his account of the battle of Winchester, Grant says: "The enemy rallied and made a stand in a strong position at Fisher's Hill, where he was attacked and again defeated with heavy loss on the 20th." This makes Sheridan pursue and attack with great promptness and energy, if it were true, but it will be seen that the attack was not made until late on the afternoon of the 3rd day after the battle at Winchester, and that the movement on my left flank was again made by Crook. If Sheridan had not had subordinates of more ability and energy than himself, I should probably have had to write a different history of my Valley campaign.

called "Tenth Legion," near where the Port Republic road leaves the Pike, and was a little before sunset, I determined to resist any further advance, so as to enable my trains to get on the Port Republic road; and skirmishers were sent out and artillery opened on the advancing enemy, but, after some skirmishing, he went into camp in our view, and beyond the reach of our guns. At this point, a gallant officer of artillery, Captain Massie, was killed by a shell. As soon as it was dark, we retired five miles on the Port Republic road and bivouacked. In the morning Lomax's cavalry had been posted to our left, on the Middle and Back roads from Mount Jackson to Harrisonburg, but it was forced back by a superior force of the enemy's cavalry, and retired to the latter place in considerable disorder. Wickham's brigade had been sent for from the Luray Valley to join me through the New-Market Gap, but it arrived at that gap just as we were retiring through New-Market, and orders were sent for it to return to the Luray Valley and join me at Port Republic. In the meantime, Payne's small brigade had been driven from Millford by two divisions of cavalry under Torbert, which had moved up the Luray Valley and subsequently joined Sheridan through the New-Market Gap. This cavalry had been detained by Wickham with his and Payne's brigades, at Millford, a sufficient time to enable us to pass New-Market in safety. If, however, it had moved up the Luray Valley by Conrad's store, we would have been in a critical condition.

On the morning of the 25th, we moved towards Port Republic, which is in the fork of the South Fork and South River, and where the road through Brown's Gap in the Blue Ridge crosses those rivers, in order to unite with Kershaw's division, which had been ordered to join me from Culpepper C. II. We crossed the river below the junction, and took position between Port Republic and Brown's Gap. Fitz Lee's and Lomax's cavalry joined us here, and on the 26th, Kershaw's division with Cutshaw's battalion of artillery came up, after having crossed through Swift Run Gap, and encountered and repulsed, below Port Republic, a body of the enemy's cavalry. There was likewise heavy skirmishing on my front on the 26th with the enemy's cavalry, which made two efforts to advance towards Brown's Gap, both of which were repulsed after brisk fighting in which artillery was used.

Having ascertained that the enemy's infantry had halted at Harrisonburg, on the morning of the 27th I moved out and drove a division of his cavalry from Port Republic, and then encamped in the fork of the rivers. I here learned that two divisions of cavalry under Torbert had been sent through Staunton to Waynesboro, and were engaged in destroying the railroad bridge at the latter place, and the tunnel through the Blue Ridge at Rockfish Gap, and, on the 28th, I moved for those points. In making this movement I had the whole of the enemy's infantry on my right, while one division of cavalry was in my rear and two in my front, and on the left was the Blue Ridge. I had therefore to move with great circumspection. Wickham's brigade of cavalry was sent up South River, near the mountain, to get between the enemy and Rockfish Gap, while the infantry moved in two columns, one up South River with the trains guarded in front by Pegram's and Wharton's divisions, and in rear by Ramseur's division, and the other, composed of Kershaw's and Gordon's divisions, with the artillery, on the right through Mount Meridian, Piedmont and New Hope. McCauslaud's cavalry, under Colonel Ferguson, was left to blockade and hold Brown's Gap, while Lomax, with the rest of his cavalry and Payne's brigade, watched the right flank and rear. Wickham's brigade having got between Rockfish Gap and Waynesboro, drove the enemy's working parties from the latter place, and took position on a ridge in front of it, when a sharp artillery fight ensued. Pegram's division, driving a small body of cavalry before it, arrived just at night and advanced upon the enemy, when he retired in great haste, taking the roads through Staunton and west of the Valley Pike, back to the main body. A company of reserves, composed of boys under 18 years of age, which had been employed on special duty at Staunton, had moved to Rockfish Gap, and another company of reserves from Charlottesville, with two pieces of artillery, had moved to the same point, and when the enemy advanced towards the tunnel and before he got in range of the guns, they were opened, and he retired to Waynesboro.

On the 29th and 30th, we rested at Waynesboro, and an engineer party was put to work repairing the bridge, which had been but partially destroyed.

On the 1st of October, I moved my whole force across the country to Mount Sidney on the Valley Pike, and took position between that place and North River, the enemy's forces having been concentrated around Harrisonburg, and on the north bank of the river. In this position we remained until the 6th, awaiting the arrival of Rosser's brigade of cavalry which was on its way from General Lee's army. In the meantime there was some skirmishing with the enemy's cavalry on the North River, at the bridge near Mount Crawford and at Bridgewater above.*

---

*Grant says that, after the fight at Fisher's Hill, "Sheridan pursued him with great energy through Harrisonburg, Staunton, and the gaps of the Blue Ridge." With how much energy the pursuit was made, and how much truth there is in the statement that I was driven through "Har-

On the 5th, Rosser's brigade arrived and was temporarily attached to Fitz Lee's division, of which Rosser was given the command, as Brigadier-General Wickham had resigned. The horses of Rosser's brigade had been so much reduced by previous hard service and the long march from Richmond, that the brigade did not exceed six hundred mounted men for duty when it joined me. Kershaw's division numbered 2700 muskets for duty, and he had brought with him Cutshaw's battalion of artillery. These reinforcements about made up my losses at Winchester and Fisher's Hill, and I determined to attack the enemy in his position at Harrisonburg, and for that purpose made a reconnoissance on the 5th, but on the morning of the 6th, it was discovered that he had retired during the night down the Valley.*

When it was discovered that the enemy was retiring, I moved forward at once and arrived at New-Market with my infantry on the 7th. Rosser pushed forward on the Back and Middle Roads in pursuit of the enemy's cavalry, which was engaged in burning houses, mills, barns and stacks of wheat and hay, and had several skirmishes with it, while Lomax also moved forward on the Valley Pike and the roads east of it. I halted at New-Market with the infantry, but Rosser and Lomax moved down the Valley in pursuit, and skirmished successfully with the enemy's cavalry on the 8th; but on the 9th they encountered his whole cavalry force at Tom's Brook, in rear of Fisher's Hill, and both of their commands were driven back in considerable confusion, with a loss of some pieces of artillery; nine were reported to me as the number lost, but Grant claims eleven. Rosser rallied his command on the Back Road, at Columbia Fur-

risonburg, Staunton, and the gaps of the Blue Ridge," will be seen from the foregoing account. A portion of my cavalry passed through Harrisonburg, but none of my other troops, and none of them through Staunton, and I did not leave the Valley at all. Had Sheridan moved his infantry to Port Republic, I would have been compelled to retire through Brown's Gap, to get provisions and forage, and it would have been impossible for me to return to the Valley until he evacuated the upper part of it.

*While Sheridan's forces were near Harrisonburg, and mine were watching them, three of our cavalry scouts, in their uniforms and with arms, got around his lines near a little town called Dayton, and encountered Lieutenant Meigs, a Federal engineer officer, with two soldiers. These parties came upon each other suddenly, and Lieutenant Meigs was ordered to surrender by one of our scouts, to which he replied by shooting and wounding the scout, who in his turn fired and killed the Lieutenant. One of the men with Lieutenant Meigs was captured and the other escaped. For this act Sheridan ordered the town of Dayton to be burned, but for some reason that order was countermanded, and another substituted for burning a large number of private houses in the neighborhood, which was executed, thus inflicting on non-combatants and women and children a most wanton and cruel punishment for a justifiable act of war.

nace, opposite Edinburg, but a part of the enemy's cavalry swept along the Pike to Mount Jackson, and then retired on the approach of a part of my infantry. On the 10th, Rosser established his line of pickets across the Valley from Columbia Furnace to Edinburg, and on the 11th Lomax was sent to the Luray Valley to take position at Millford.

BATTLE OF CEDAR CREEK OR BELLE GROVE.

Having heard that Sheridan was preparing to send part of his troops to Grant, I moved down the Valley again on the 12th. On the morning of the 13th we reached Fisher's Hill, and I moved with part of my command to Hupp's Hill, between Strasburg and Cedar Creek, for the purpose of reconnoitring. The enemy was found posted on the North bank of Cedar Creek in strong force, and, while we were observing him, without displaying any of my force except a small body of cavalry, a division of his infantry was moved out to his left and stacked arms in an open field, when a battery of artillery was run out suddenly and opened on this division, scattering it in great confusion. The enemy then displayed a large force, and sent a division across the creek to capture the guns which had opened on him, but, when it had advanced near enough, Conner's brigade of Kershaw's division was sent forward to meet this division, and, after a sharp contest, drove it back in considerable confusion and with severe loss. Conner's brigade behaved very handsomely indeed, but unfortunately, after the enemy had been entirely repulsed, Brigadier-General Conner, a most accomplished and gallant officer, lost his leg by a shell from the opposite side of the creek. Some prisoners were taken from the enemy in this affair, and Colonel Wells, the division commander, fell into our hands mortally wounded. The object of the reconnoissance having been accomplished, I moved back to Fisher's Hill, and I subsequently learned that the 6th Corps had started for Grant's army but was brought back after this affair.

I remained at Fisher's Hill until the 16th observing the enemy, with the hope that he would move back from his very strong position on the north of Cedar Creek, and that we would be able to get at him in a different position; but he did not give any indications of an intention to move, nor did he evince any purpose of attacking us, though the two positions were in sight of each other. In the meantime there was some skirmishing at Hupp's Hill, and some with the cavalry at Cedar Creek on the Back Road. On the 16th Rosser's scouts reported a brigade of the enemy's cavalry encamped on the Back Road, and detached from the rest of his force, and Rosser was permitted to go that night, with a brigade of infantry mounted behind the same number of cavalry, to attempt the surprise and capture of the camp. He succeeded in surrounding and surprising the camp, but it proved to be that of only a strong picket, the whole of which was captured—the brigade having moved its location.

At light on the morning of the 17th, the whole of my troops were moved out in front of our lines, for the purpose of covering Rosser's return in case of difficulty, and, after he had returned, General Gordon was sent with a brigade of his division to Hupp's Hill, for the purpose of ascertaining by close inspection whether the enemy's position was fortified, and he returned with the information that it was. I was now compelled to move back for want of provisions and forage, or attack the enemy in his position with the hope of driving him from it, and I determined to attack. As I was not strong enough to attack the fortified position in front, I determined to get around one of the enemy's flanks and attack him by surprise if I could. After General Gordon's return from Hupp's Hill, he and Captain Hotchkiss, my topographical engineer, were sent to the signal station on the end of Massanutten Mountain, which had been re-established, for the purpose of examining the enemy's position from that point, and General Pegram was ordered to go as near as he could to Cedar Creek on the enemy's right flank, and see whether it was practicable to surprise him on that flank. Captain Hotchkiss returned to my headquarters after dark, and reported the result of his and General Gordon's examination, and he gave me a sketch of the enemy's position and camps. He informed me that the enemy's left flank, which rested near Cedar Creek, a short distance above its mouth, was lightly picketed, and that there was but a small cavalry picket on the North Fork of the Shenandoah, below the mouth of the creek, and he stated that, from information he had received, he thought it was practicable to move a column of infantry between the base of the mountain and the river, to a ford below the mouth of the creek. He also informed me that the main body of the enemy's cavalry was on his right flank on the Back Road to Winchester. The sketch made by Captain Hotchkiss, which proved to be correct, designated the roads in the enemy's rear, and the house of a Mr. Cooley at a favourable point for forming an attacking column, after it crossed the river, in order to move against the enemy and strike him on the Valley Pike in rear of his works. Upon this information, I determined to attack the enemy by moving over the ground designated by Captain Hotchkiss, if it should prove practicable to move a column between the base of the mountain and the river. Next morning, General Gordon confirmed the report of Captain Hotchkiss, expressing confidence that the attack could be successfully made on the enemy's left and rear, and General Pegram reported that a movement on the enemy's right flank would be attended with great difficulty, as the banks of Cedar Creek on that flank were high and precipitous and were well guarded. General Gordon and Captain Hotchkiss were then sent to examine and ascertain the practicability of the route at the base of the mountain, and General Pegram, at his request, was permitted to go to the signal station on the mountain to examine the enemy's position himself from that point. Directions were given, in the meantime, for everything to be in readiness to move that night (the 18th), and the division commanders were requested to be at my quarters at two o'clock in the afternoon, to receive their final instructions.

The river makes a circuit to the left in front of the right of the position at Fisher's Hill and around by Strasburg, leaving a considerable body of land between it and the mountain, on which are several farms. Whenever Fisher's Hill had been occupied by us, this bend of the river had been occupied by a portion of our cavalry, to prevent the enemy from turning the right of the position, and it was now occupied by Colonel Payne with his cavalry numbering about 300. In order to make the contemplated movement, it was necessary to cross the river into this bend, and then pass between the foot of the mountain and the river below Strasburg, where the passage was very narrow, and cross the river again below the mouth of Cedar Creek. The enemy's camps and positions were visible from a signal station on Round Hill in rear of Fisher's Hill, and had been examined by me from that point, but the distance was too great to see with distinctness. From the station on the mountain, which immediately overlooked the enemy's left, the view was very distinct, but I could not go to that point myself, as the ascent was very rugged, and it required several hours to go and come, and I could not leave my command for that time. I had therefore, necessarily, to rely on the reports of my officers.

General Gordon and Captain Hotchkiss, on their return, reported the route between the mountain and river, which was a blind path, to be practicable for infantry but not for artillery, and a temporary bridge was constructed under Captain Hotchkiss's superintendence, at the first crossing of the river on our right. The plan of attack on which I determined was to send the three divisions of the 2nd Corps, to-wit: Gordon's, Ramseur's, and Pegram's, under General Gordon, over the route which has been specified to the enemy's rear, to make the attack at 5 o'clock in the morning, which would be a little before daybreak—to move myself with Kershaw's and Wharton's divisions, and all the artillery, along the Pike through Strasburg, and attack the enemy on the front and left flank as soon as Gordon should become engaged, and for Rosser to move with his own and Wickham's brigade, on the Back Road across Cedar Creek, and attack the enemy's cavalry simultaneously with Gordon's attack, while Lomax should move by Front Royal, cross the river, and come to the Valley Pike, so as to strike the enemy wherever he might be, of which he was to judge by the sound of the firing.

At two o'clock, P. M., all the division commanders, except Pegram, who had not returned from the mountain, came to my headquarters, and I gave them their instructions. Gordon was directed to cross over into the bend of the river immediately after dark, and move to the foot of the mountain, where he would rest his troops, and move from there in time to cross the river again and get in position at Cooley's house, in the enemy's rear, so as to make the attack at the designated hour, and he was instructed, in advancing to the attack, to move for a house on the west side of the Valley Pike called the "Belle Grove House," at which it was known that Sheridan's headquarters were located. A guide who knew the country and the roads was ordered to be sent to General Gordon, and Colonel Payne was ordered to accompany him with his force of cavalry, and endeavor to capture Sheridan himself. Rosser was ordered to move before day, in time to attack at 5 o'clock next morning, and to endeavor to surprise the enemy's cavalry in camp. Kershaw and Wharton were ordered to move, at 1 o'clock in the morning, towards Strasburg under my personal superintendence, and the artillery was ordered to concentrate where the Pike passed through the lines at Fisher's Hill, and, at the hour appointed for the attack, to move at a gallop to Hupp's Hill—the movement of the artillery being thus delayed for fear of attracting the attention of the enemy by the rumbling of the wheels over the macadamized road. Swords and canteens were directed to be left in camp, so as to make as little noise as possible. The division commanders were particularly admonished as to the necessity for promptness and energy in all their movements, and they were instructed to press the enemy with vigour after he was encountered, and to allow him no time to form, but to continue the pursuit until his forces should be completely routed. They were also admonished of the danger to be apprehended from a disposition to plunder the enemy's camps by their men, and they were enjoined to take every possible precaution against it.

Gordon moved at the appointed time, and, after he had started, General

Pegram reported to me that he had discovered, from the signal station on the mountain, what he supposed to be an intrenchment thrown up across the road over which Gordon would have to advance after crossing the river the second time, and that the signal operators had informed him that it had been thrown up since Gordon and Hotchkiss made their examination; and he suggested the propriety of attacking the enemy's left flank at the same time Gordon made his attack, as he would probably have more difficulty than had been anticipated. I adopted this suggestion, and determined to cross Kershaw's division over Cedar Creek, at Bowman's Mill, a little above its mouth, and strike the enemy's left flank simultaneously with the other attacks, of which purpose notice was sent to General Gordon by General Pegram. At one o'clock on the morning of the 19th, Kershaw and Wharton moved, and I accompanied them. At Strasburg, Kershaw moved to the right on the road to Bowman's Mill, and Wharton moved along the Pike to Hupp's Hill, with instructions not to display his forces, but avoid the enemy's notice until the attack began, when he was to move forward, support the artillery when it came up, and send a force to get possession of the bridge on the Pike over the creek. I accompanied Kershaw's division, and we got in sight of the enemy's fires at half-past three o'clock. The moon was now shining and we could see the camps. The division was halted under cover to await the arrival of the proper time, and I pointed out to Kershaw, and the commander of his leading brigade, the enemy's position and described the nature of the ground, and directed them how the attack was to be made and followed up. Kershaw was directed to cross his division over the creek as quietly as possible, and to form it into column of brigades as he did so, and advance in that manner against the enemy's left breastwork, extending to the right or left as might be necessary. At half-past four he was ordered forward, and, a very short time after he started, the firing from Rosser on our left, and the picket firing at the ford at which Gordon was crossing were heard. Kershaw crossed the creek without molestation and formed his division as directed, and precisely at five o'clock his leading brigade, with little opposition, swept over the enemy's left work, capturing seven guns, which were at once turned on the enemy. As soon as this attack was made, I rode as rapidly as possible to the position on Hupp's Hill to which Wharton and the artillery had been ordered. I found the artillery just arriving, and a very heavy fire of musketry was now heard in the enemy's rear from Gordon's column. Wharton had advanced his skirmishers to the creek capturing some prisoners, but the enemy still held the works on our left of the Pike, commanding that road and the bridge, and opened with his artillery on us. Our artillery was immediately brought into action and opened on the enemy, but he soon evacuated his works, and our men from the other columns rushed into them. Just then the sun rose, and Wharton's division and the artillery were immediately ordered forward. I rode in advance of them across the creek, and met General Gordon on the opposite hill. Kershaw's division had swept along the enemy's works on the right of the Pike, which were occupied by Crook's corps, and he and Gordon had united at the Pike, and their divisions had pushed across it in pursuit of the enemy. The rear division of Gordon's column (Pegram's) was crossing the river at the time Kershaw's attack was made, and General Gordon moved rapidly to Cooley's house, formed his troops and advanced against the enemy with his own division on the left, under Brigadier General Evans, and Ramseur's on the right, with Pegram's in the rear supporting them. There had been a delay of an hour at the river before crossing it, either from a miscalculation of time in the dark, or because the cavalry which was to precede his column had not gotten up, and the delay thus caused, for which no blame is to be attached to General Gordon, enabled the enemy partially to form his lines after the alarm produced by Kershaw's attack, and Gordon's attack, which was after light, was therefore met with greater obstinacy by the enemy than it would otherwise have encountered, and the fighting had been severe. Gordon, however, pushed his attack with great energy, and the 19th and Crook's corps were in complete route, and their camps, with a number of pieces of artillery and a considerable quantity of small arms, abandoned. The 6th corps, which was on the enemy's right, and some distance from the point attacked, had had time to get under arms and take position so as to arrest our progress. General Gordon briefly informed me of the condition of things, and stated that Pegram's division, which had not been previously engaged, had been ordered in. He then rode to take command of his division, and I rode forward on the Pike to ascertain the position of the enemy, in order to continue the attack. There was now a heavy fog, and that, with the smoke from the artillery and small arms, so obscured objects that the enemy's position could not be seen; but I soon came to Generals Ramseur and Pegram, who informed me that Pegram's division had encountered a division of the 6th corps on the left of the Valley Pike, and, after a sharp engagement, had driven it back on the main body of that corps, which was in their front in a strong position. They further informed me that their divisions were in line confronting the 6th corps, but that there was a vacancy in the line on their right which ought to be filled. I ordered Wharton's division forward at once, and directed Generals

Ramseur and Pegram to put it where it was required. In a very short time, and while I was endeavoring to discover the enemy's line through the obscurity, Wharton's division came back in some confusion, and General Wharton informed me that, in advancing to the position pointed out to him by Generals Ramseur and Pegram, his division had been driven back by the 6th corps, which, he said, was advancing. He pointed out the direction from which he said the enemy was advancing, and some pieces of artillery which had come up were brought into action. The fog soon rose sufficiently for us to see the enemy's position on a ridge to the west of Middletown, and it was discovered to be a strong one. After driving back Wharton's division, he had not advanced, but opened on us with artillery, and orders were given for concentrating all our guns on him. In the mean time, a force of cavalry was advancing along the Pike, and through the fields to the right of Middletown, thus placing our right and rear in great danger, and Wharton was ordered to form his division at once, and take position to hold the enemy's cavalry in check. Wofford's brigade of Kershaw's division, which had become separated from the other brigades, was ordered up for the same purpose. Discovering that the 6th corps could not be attacked with advantage on its left flank, because the approach in that direction was through an open flat and across a boggy stream with deep banks, I directed Captain Powell, serving on General Gordon's staff, who rode up to me while the artillery was being placed in position, to tell the General to advance against the enemy's right flank, and attack it in conjunction with Kershaw, while a heavy fire of artillery was opened from our right; but as Captain Powell said he did not know where General Gordon was, and expressed some doubt about finding him, immediately after he started, I sent Lieutenant Page, of my own staff, with orders for both Generals Gordon and Kershaw to make the attack. In a short time Colonel Carter concentrated 18 or 20 guns on the enemy, and he was soon in retreat. Ramseur and Pegram advanced at once to the position from which the enemy was driven, and just then his cavalry commenced pressing heavily on the right, and Pegram's division was ordered to move to the north of Middletown, and take position across the Pike against the cavalry. Lieutenant Page had returned and informed me that he delivered my order to General Kershaw, but the latter informed him that his division was not in a condition to make the attack, as it was very much scattered, and there was a cavalry force threatening him in front. Lieutenant Page also stated that he had seen Gordon's division in Kershaw's rear reforming, and that it was also much scattered, and that he had not delivered the order to General Gordon, because he saw that neither his division nor Kershaw's was in a condition to execute it. As soon as Pegram moved, Kershaw was ordered from the left to supply his place. I then rode to Middletown to make provision against the enemy's cavalry, and discovered a large body of it seriously threatening that flank, which was very much exposed. Wharton's division and Wofford's brigade were put in position on Pegram's right, and several charges of the enemy's cavalry were repulsed. I had no cavalry on that flank except Payne's very small brigade, which had accompanied Gordon, and made some captures of prisoners and waggons. Lomax had not arrived, but I received a message from him, informing me that he had crossed the river after some delay from a cavalry force guarding it, and I sent a message to him requiring him to move to Middletown as quick as possible, but, as I subsequently ascertained, he did not receive that message. Rosser had attacked the enemy promptly at the appointed time, but he had not been able to surprise him, as he was found on the alert on that flank, doubtless owing to the attempt at a surprise on the night of the 16th. There was now one division of cavalry threatening my right flank, and two were on the left, near the Back Road, held in check by Rosser. The force of the latter was too weak to make any impression on the enemy's cavalry, and all he could do was to watch it. As I passed across Cedar Creek after the enemy was driven from it, I had discovered a number of men in the enemy's camps plundering, and one of Wharton's battalions was ordered to clear the camps, and drive the men to their commands. It was reported to me subsequently that a great number were at the same work, and I sent all my staff officers who could be spared, to stop it if possible, and orders were sent to the division commanders to send for their men.

After he was driven from his second position, the enemy had taken a new position about two miles north of Middletown, and, as soon as I had regulated matters on the right so as to prevent his cavalry from getting in rear of that flank, I rode to the left, for the purpose of ordering an advance. I found Ramseur and Kershaw in line with Pegram, but Gordon had not come up. In a short time, however, I found him coming up from the rear, and I ordered him to take position on Kershaw's left, and advance for the purpose of driving the enemy from his new position—Kershaw and Ramseur being ordered to advance at the same time. As the enemy's cavalry on our left was very strong, and had the benefit of an open country to the rear of that flank, a repulse at this time would have been disastrous, and I therefore directed General Gordon, if he found the enemy's line too strong to attack with success, not to make the assault. The advance was made for some distance, when Gordon's skirmishers came back reporting a line of battle in front behind breast works, and General Gordon did not make the attack. It was now apparent that it would not do to press my troops further. They had been up all night and were much jaded. In passing over rough ground to attack the enemy in the early morning, their own ranks had been much disordered, and the men scattered, and it had required time to reform them. Their ranks, moreover, were much thinned by the absence of the men engaged in plundering the enemy's camps. The delay which had unavoidably occurred, had enabled the enemy to rally a portion of his routed troops, and his immense force of cavalry, which remained intact, was threatening both of our flanks in an open country, which of itself rendered an advance extremely hazardous. I determined, therefore, to try and hold what had been gained, and orders were given for carrying off the captured and abandoned artillery, smalls arms, and waggons. A number of bold attempts were made during the subsequent part of the day, by the enemy's cavalry, to break our line on the right, but they were invariably repulsed. Late in the afternoon, the enemy's infantry advanced against Ramseur's, Kershaw's and Gordon's lines, and the attack on Ramseur's and Kershaw's fronts was handsomely repulsed in my view, and I hoped that the day was finally ours, but a portion of the enemy had penetrated an interval which was between Evans' brigade, on the extreme left, and the rest of the line, when that brigade gave way, and Gordon's other brigades soon followed. General Gordon made every possible effort to rally his men, and lead them back against the enemy, but without avail. The information of this affair, with exaggerations, passed rapidly along Kershaw's and Ramseur's lines, and their men, under the apprehension of being flanked, commenced falling back in disorder, though no enemy was pressing them, and this gave me the first intimation of Gordon's condition. At the same time the enemy's cavalry, observing the disorder in our ranks, made another charge on our right, but was again repulsed. Every effort was made to stop and rally Kershaw's and Ramseur's men, but the mass of them resisted all appeals, and continued to go to the rear without waiting for any effort to retrieve the partial disorder. Ramseur, however, succeeded in retaining with him two or three hundred men of his division, and Major Goggin of Kershaw's staff, who was in command of Conner's brigade, about the same number from that brigade; and these men, aided by several pieces of artillery, held the enemy's whole force on our left in check for one hour and a half, until Ramseur was shot down mortally wounded, and the ammunition of those pieces of artillery was exhausted. While the latter were being replaced by other guns, the force that had remained with Ramseur and

Goggin gave way also. Pegram's and Wharton's divisions, and Wofford's brigade had remained steadfast on the right, and resisted all efforts of the enemy's cavalry, but no portion of this force could be moved to the left without leaving the Pike open to the cavalry, which would have destroyed all hope at once. Every effort to rally the men in the rear having failed, I had now nothing left for me but to order these troops to retire also. When they commenced to move, the disorder soon extended to them, but General Pegram succeeded in bringing back a portion of his command across Cedar Creek in an organized condition, holding the enemy in check, but this small force soon dissolved. A part of Evans' brigade had been rallied in the rear, and held a ford above the bridge for a short time, but it followed the example of the rest. I tried to rally the men immediately after crossing Cedar Creek, and at Hupp's Hill, but without success. Could 500 men have been rallied, at either of these places, who would have stood by me, I am satisfied that all my artillery and waggons and the greater part of the captured artillery could have been saved, as the enemy's pursuit was very feeble. As it was, a bridge broke down on a very narrow part of the road between Strasburg and Fisher's Hill, just above Strasburg, where there was no other passway, thereby blocking up all the artillery, ordnance and medical waggons, and ambulances which had not passed that point; and, as there was no force to defend them, they were lost, a very small body of the enemy's cavalry capturing them.

The greater part of the infantry was halted at Fisher's Hill, and Rosser, whose command had retired in good order on the Back Road, was ordered to that point with his cavalry. The infantry moved back towards New Market at three o'clock next morning, and Rosser was left at Fisher's Hill to cover the retreat of the troops, and hold that position until they were beyond pursuit. He remained at Fisher's Hill until after ten o'clock on the 20th, and the enemy did not advance to that place while he was there. He then fell back without molestation to his former position, and established his line on Stony Creek, across from Columbia Furnace to Edinburg, seven miles below Mount Jackson. My other troops were halted at New Market, about seven miles from Mount Jackson, and there was an entirely open country between the two places, they being very nearly in sight of each other.*

---

*Grant says in his account of the battle of Cedar Greek: "The enemy was defeated with great slaughter, and the loss of the most of his artillery and trains, and the trophies he had captured in the morning. The wreck of his army escaped during the night, and fled in the direction of Stan-

Lomax had moved, on the day of the battle, on the Front Royal road towards Winchester, under the impression that the enemy was being forced back towards that place, and he did not reach me. When he ascertained the reverse which had taken place in the latter part of the day, he retired up the Luray Valley to his former position at Millford, without molestation.

My loss in the battle of Cedar Creek was twenty-three pieces of artillery, some ordnance and medical waggons and ambulances, which had been carried to the front for the use of the troops on the field; about 1860 in killed and wounded, and something over 1,000 prisoners. Major-General Ramseur fell into the hands of the enemy mortally wounded, and in him, not only my command, but the country sustained a heavy loss. He was a most gallant and energetic officer whom no disaster appalled, but his courage and energy seemed to gain new strength in the midst of confusion and disorder. He fell at his post fighting like a lion at bay, and his native State has reason to be proud of his memory. Brigadier-General Battle was wounded at the beginning of the fight, and other valuable officers were lost. Fifteen hundred prisoners were captured from the enemy and brought off, and his loss in killed and wounded in this action was very heavy.

This was the case of a glorious victory given up by my own troops after they had won it, and it is to be accounted for, on the ground of the partial demoralization caused by the plunder of the enemy's camps, and from the fact that the men undertook to judge for themselves when it was proper to retire. Had they but waited, the mischief on the left would have been remedied. I have never been able to satisfy myself that the enemy's attack, in the afternoon, was not a demonstration to cover his retreat during the night. It certainly was not a vigorous one, as is shown by the fact that the very small force with Ram-

---

ton and Lynchburg. Pursuit was made to Mount Jackson." Stanton, who seems to think it his duty to improve on all Grant's statements, says: "The routed forces of the enemy were pursued to Mount Jackson, where he arrived without an organized regiment of his army. All of his artillery and thousands of prisoners fell into Sheridan's hands. These successes closed military operations in the Shenandoah Valley, and a *rebel force appeared there no more during the war*." The recklessness of these statements, of both Grant and Stanton, will appear from the above narrative, as well as from my subsequent operations in the Shenandoah Valley. Would it be believed that this wreck of my army, which fled in such wild dismay before its pursuers, carried from the battle-field 1500 prisoners, who were sent to Richmond—subsequently confronted Sheridan's whole force north of Cedar Creek, for two days, without his attacking it, and sent out expeditions which captured two important posts, with over 1000 prisoners and several pieces of artillery, in the limits of Sheridan's command; Yet such was the case.

seur and Goggin held him in check so long; and the loss in killed and wounded in the division which first gave way, was not heavy, and was the least in numbers of all but one, though it was the third in strength, and its relative loss was the least of all the divisions. I read a sharp lecture to my troops, in an address published to them a few days after the battle, but I have never attributed the result to a want of courage on their part, for I had seen them perform too many prodigies of valor to doubt that. There was an individuality about the Confederate soldier which caused him to act often in battle according to his own opinions, and thereby impair his own efficiency; and the tempting bait offered by the rich plunder of the camps of the enemy's well-fed and well-clothed troops, was frequently too great for our destitute soldiers, and caused them to pause in the career of victory.

Had my cavalry been sufficient to contend with that of the enemy, the route in the morning would have been complete; as it was, I had only about 1200 cavalry on the field under Rosser, and Lomax's force, which numbered less than 1700, did not get up. My infantry and artillery was about the same strength as at Winchester. The reports of the ordnance officers showed in the hands of my troops about 8,800 muskets, in round numbers as follows: in Kershaw's division 2,700, Ramseur's 2,100, Gordon's 1,700, Pegram's 1,200, and Wharton's 1,100. Making a moderate allowance for the men left to guard the camps and the signal station on the mountain, as well as for a few sick and wounded, I went into this battle with about 8,500 muskets and a little over forty pieces of artillery.

The book containing the reports of the Chief Surgeon of Sheridan's cavalry corps, which has been mentioned as captured at this battle, showed that Sheridan's cavalry numbered about 8,700 men for duty a few days previous, and from information which I had received of reinforcements sent him, in the way of recruits and returned convalescents, I am satisfied that his infantry force was fully as large as at Winchester. Sheridan was absent in the morning at the beginning of the fight, and had returned in the afternoon before the change in the fortunes of the day. Nevertheless, I saw no reason to change the estimate I had formed of him.*

It may be asked, why with my small force I made the attack? I can only say we

---

*The retreat of the main body of his army had been arrested, and a new line formed behind breastworks of rails, before Sheridan arrived on the field; and he still had immense odds against me when he made the attack in the afternoon.

had been fighting large odds during the whole war, and I knew there was no chance of lessening them. It was of the utmost consequence that Sheridan should be prevented from sending troops to Grant, and General Lee, in a letter received a day or two before, had expressed an earnest desire that a victory should be gained in the Valley if possible, and it could not be gained without fighting for it. I did hope to gain one by surprising the enemy in his camp, and then thought and still think I would have had it, if my directions had been strictly complied with, and my troops had awaited my orders to retire.*

CLOSE OF THE VALLEY CAMPAIGN.

After the return from Cedar Creek, the main body of my troops remained in their camp for the rest of the month without disturbance, but on the 26th of October the enemy's cavalry attacked Lomax at Millford and, after sharp fighting, was repulsed. Having heard that Sheridan was preparing to send troops to Grant, and that the Manassas Gap Railroad was being repaired, I moved down the Valley again on the 10th of November. I had received no reinforcements, except about 350 cavalry under General Cosby from Breckenridge's department in Southwestern Virginia, some returned convalescents, and several hundred conscripts who had been on details which had been revoked. On the 11th, on our approach to Cedar Creek, it was found that the enemy had fallen back towards Winchester, after having fortified and occupied a position on Hupp's Hill subsequently to the battle of Cedar Creek. Colonel Payne drove a small body of cavalry through Middletown to Newtown, and I followed him and took position south of the latter place and in view of it. Sheridan's main force was

---

*A silly story was circulated and even published in the papers, that this battle was planned and conducted by one of my subordinates up to a certain point, when my arrival on the field stopped the pursuit and arrested the victory. No officer or soldier on that day received an order from me to halt, unless he was going to the rear. My orders were to press the enemy from the beginning and give him no time to form, and when I found that my troops had halted, I endeavoured to advance again, but I discovered it would not do to press them further. Those who have known me from my youth, as well as those who came in contact with me during the war, know that I was not likely to permit any other to plan a battle for me, or assume my duties in any particular. Yet I was always willing to receive and adopt valuable suggestions from any of my officers.

There was another false report as to my personal habits during the Valley Campaign, which obtained some circulation and credence, but which I would not notice, except for the fact that it was referred to on the floor of the Confederate Senate by two members of that body. The utter falsehood of this report was well known to all my staff and General officers, as well as to all others who associated with me.

found posted north of Newtown, in a position which he was engaged in fortifying. I remained in front of him during the 11th and 12th, Rosser being on my left flank on the Back Road, and Lomax on my right between the Valley Pike and the Front Royal road, with one brigade (McCausland's) at Cedarville on the latter road. Rosser had some skirmishing with the enemy's cavalry on the 11th, and on the 12th two divisions advanced against him, and after a heavy fight the enemy was repulsed and some prisoners captured. Colonel Payne, who was operating immediately in my front, likewise had a sharp engagement with a portion of the enemy's cavalry and defeated it. When Rosser was heavily engaged, Lomax was ordered to his assistance with a part of his command, and, during his absence, late in the afternoon, Powell's division of the enemy's cavalry attacked McCausland at Cedarville, and, after a severe fight, drove him back across the river with the loss of two pieces of artillery. At the time of this affair, a blustering wind was blowing and the firing could not be heard; and nothing was known of McCausland's misfortune until after we commenced retiring that night. In these cavalry fights three valuable officers were killed, namely: Lieutenant Colonel Marshall of Rosser's brigade, Colonel Radford of McCausland's brigade, and Captain Harvie of McCausland's staff.

Discovering that the enemy continued to fortify his position, and showed no disposition to come out of his lines with his infantry, and not being willing to attack him in his intrenchments, after the reverses I had met with, I determined to retire, as we were beyond the reach of supplies. After dark on the 12th, we moved to Fisher's Hill, and next day returned in the direction of New-Market, where we arrived on the 14th, no effort at pursuit being made. I discovered by this movement that no troops had been sent to Grant, and that the project of repairing the Manassas Gap Railroad had been abandoned.*

Shortly after our return to New-Market, Kershaw's division was returned to General Lee, and Cosby's cavalry to Breckenridge. On the 22nd of November two divisions of the enemy's cavalry advanced to Mount Jackson, after having driven in our cavalry pickets. A part of it crossed over the river into Meem's bottom at the foot of Rude's Hill, but was driven back by a portion of my

---

*From Grants account of the battle of Cedar Creek, it would be supposed that the 6th Corps was returned to the army of the Potomac immediately after that battle, but the truth is that no troops were sent from Sheridan's army until in December, when the cold weather had put an end to all operations in the field by infantry.

infantry, and the whole retreated, being pursued by Wickham's brigade, under Colonel Munford, to Woodstock.

On the 27th, Rosser crossed Great North Mountain into Hardy County, with his own and Payne's brigade, and, about the 29th, surprised and captured the fortified post at New Creek, on the Baltimore and Ohio rail-road. At this place, two regiments of cavalry with their arms and colours were captured, and eight pieces of artillery and a very large amount of ordnance, quarter master, and commissary stores fell into our hands. The prisoners, numbering 800, four pieces of artillery, and some waggons and horses, were brought off, the other guns, which were heavy siege pieces, being spiked, and their carriages and a greater part of the stores destroyed. Rosser also brought off several hundred cattle and a large number of sheep from Hampshire and Hardy counties.

This expedition closed the material operations of the campaign of 1864 in the Shenandoah Valley, and, at that time, the enemy held precisely the same portion of that valley, which he held before the opening of the campaign in the spring, and no more, and the headquarters of his troops were at the same place, to-wit: Winchester. There was this difference however: at the beginning of the campaign, he held it with comparatively a small force, and at the close, he was compelled to employ three corps of infantry and one of cavalry, for that purpose, and to guard the approaches to Washington, Maryland, and Pennsylvania. When I was detached from General Lee's army, Hunter was advancing on Lynchburg, 170 miles south of Winchester, with a very considerable force, and threatening all of General Lee's communications with a very serious danger. By a rapid movement, my force had been thrown to Lynchburg, just in time to arrest Hunter's march into that place, and he had been driven back and forced to escape into the mountains of Western Virginia, with a loss of ten pieces of artillery, and subsequent terrible suffering to his troops. Maryland and Pennsylvania had been invaded, Washington threatened and thrown into a state of frantic alarm, and Grant had been compelled to detach two corps of infantry and two divisions of cavalry from his army. Five or six thousand prisoners had been captured from the enemy and sent to Richmond, and, according to a published statement by Sheridan, his army had lost 13,831, in killed and wounded, after he took command of it. Heavy losses had been inflicted on that army by my command, before Sheridan went to the Valley, and the whole loss could not have been far from double my entire force. The enemy moreover had been deprived of the use of the Baltimore and Ohio rail-road, and the Chesapeake and Ohio canal, for three months. It is true that I had lost many valuable officers and men, and about 60 pieces of artillery, counting those lost by Ramseur and McCausland, and not deducting the 19 pieces captured from the enemy; but I think I may safely state that the fall of Lynchburg with its foundries and factories, and the consequent destruction of General Lee's communications, would have rendered necessary the evacuation of Richmond, and that, therefore, the fall of the latter place had been prevented; and, by my subsequent operations, Grant's operations against Lee's army had been materially impeded, and for some time substantially suspended.

My loss in killed, wounded, and prisoners, at Winchester and Fisher's Hill, had been less than 4,000, and, at Cedar Creek, about 3,000, but the enemy has attempted to magnify it to a much larger figure, claiming as prisoners several thousand more than my entire loss. How he makes out his estimate is not for me to explain. He was never scrupulous as to the kinds of persons of whom he made prisoners, and the statements of the Federal officers were not always confined to the truth, as the world has probably learned. I know that a number of prisoners fell into the enemy's hands, who did not belong to my command: such as cavalry men on details to get fresh horses, soldiers on leave of absence, conscripts on special details, citizens not in the service, men employed in getting supplies for the departments, and stragglers and deserters from other commands.

My army during the entire campaign had been self sustaining, so far as provisions and forage were concerned, and a considerable number of beef cattle had been sent to General Lee's army; and when the difficulties under which I laboured are considered, I think I may confidently assert that I had done as well as it was possible for me to do.*

---

*Some attempts have been made to compare my campaign in the Valley with that of General Jackson in the same district, in order to cast censure on me; but such comparison is not necessary for the vindication of the fame of that great leader, and it is most unjust to me, as the circumstances under which we operated were so entirely dissimilar. It was my fortune to serve under General Jackson, after his Valley campaign until his death, and I have the satisfaction of knowing that I enjoyed his confidence, which was signally shown in his last official act towards me; and no one admires his character and reveres his memory more than I do. It is not therefore with any view to detract from his merits, that I mention the following facts, but to show how improper it is to compare our campaigns, with a view of contrasting their merits. 1st. General Jackson did not have the odds opposed to him which I had, and his troops were composed entirely of the very best material which entered into the composition of our armies, that is, the men who came out voluntarily in the beginning of the war; while my command, though comprising all the principal organizations which were with him did not contain 1,500 of the men who had participated in the first Valley campaign, and there was a like falling off in the other organizations with me, which had not been with Gen. Jackson in that campaign. This was owing to the losses in killed and dis-

Shortly after Rosser's return from the New Creek expedition, Colonel Munford was sent with Wickham's brigade to the counties of Hardy and Pendleton, to procure forage for his horses, and, cold weather having now set in so as to prevent material operations in the field, the three divisions of the 2nd Corps were sent, in succession, to General Lee,—Wharton's division, the cavalry, and most of the artillery being retained with me.

On the 16th of December, I broke up the camp at New-Market, and moved back towards Staunton, for the purpose of establishing my troops on or near the Central railroad—Lomax's cavalry, except one brigade left to watch the Luray Valley, having previously moved across the Blue Ridge, so as to be able to procure forage. Cavalry pickets were left in front of New-Market, and telegraphic communications kept up with that place, from which there was communication with the lower Valley, by means of signal stations on the northern end of Massanutten Mountain, and at Ashby's Gap in the Blue Ridge, which overlooked the enemy's camps and the surrounding country.

The troops had barely arrived at their new camps, when information was received that the enemy's cavalry was in motion. On the 19th, Custar's division moved from Winchester towards Staunton, and, at the same time, two other divisions of cavalry, under Torbert or Merrit, moved across by Front Royal and Chester Gap towards Gordonsville. This information having been sent me by signal and telegraph, Wharton's division was moved, on the 20th, through a hail storm, towards Harrisonburg, and Rosser ordered to the front with all the cavalry he could collect. Custar's division reached Lacy's Spring, nine miles north

---

abled, and prisoners who were not exchanged. Besides the old soldiers whose numbers were so reduced, my command was composed of recruits and conscripts. 2nd. General Jackson's cavalry was not outnumbered by the enemy, and it was far superior in efficiency—Ashby being a host in himself; while my cavalry was more than trebled in numbers, and far excelled in arms, equipments, and horses, by that of the enemy. 3rd. The Valley, at the time of his campaign, was teeming with provisions and forage from one end to the other; while my command had very great difficulty in obtaining provisions for the men, and had to rely almost entirely on the grass in the open fields for forage. 4th. When General Jackson was pressed and had to retire, as well when he fell back before Banks in the spring of 1862, as, later, when he retired before Fremont to prevent Shields from getting in his rear, the condition of the water courses was such as to enable him to stop the advance of one column, by burning the bridges, and then fell upon and defeat another column; and, when hard pressed, place his troops in a position of security, until a favorable opportunity offered for attacking the enemy; while all the water courses were low and fordable, and the whole country was open in my front, on my flanks, and in my rear, during my entire campaign. These facts do not detract from the merits of General Jackson's campaign in the slightest degree, and far be it from me to attempt to obscure his well earned and richly deserved fame. They only show that I ought not to be condemned for not doing what he did.

of Harrisonburg, on the evening of the 20th, and, next morning before day, Rosser, with about 600 men of his own and Payne's brigades, attacked it in camp, and drove it back down the Valley in some confusion. Lomax had been advised of the movement towards Gordonsville, and, as soon as Custer was disposed of, Wharton's division was moved back, and on the 23rd a portion of it was run on the railroad to Charlottesville—Munford, who had now returned from across the great North Mountain, being ordered to the same place. On my arrival at Charlottesville on the 23rd, I found that the enemy's two divisions of cavalry, which had crossed the Blue Ridge had been held in check near Gordonsville by Lomax, until the arrival of a brigade of infantry from Richmond, when they retired precipitately. I returned to the Valley and established my headquarters at Staunton—Wharton's division and the artillery being encamped east of that place, and Rosser's cavalry west of it; and thus closed the operations of 1864 with me.*

---

*At the close of the year 1864, Grant's plans for the campaign in Virginia had been baffled, and he had merely attained a position on James River, which he might have occupied at the beginning of the campaign without opposition. So far as the two armies, with which the campaign was opened, were concerned, he had sustained a defeat, and, if the contest had been between those two armies alone, his would have been destroyed. But, unfortunately, he had the means of reinforcing and recruiting his army to an almost unlimited extent, and there were no means of recruiting General Lee's. Four years of an unexampled struggle had destroyed the finances of the Confederate Government, and exhausted the material out of which an army could be raised. General Lee had performed his task as a military commander, but the Government was unable to furnish him the means of properly continuing the war; and he had therefore to begin the campaign of 1865 with the remnant of his army of the previous year, while a now draft and heavy reinforcements from other quarters had furnished his opponent with a new army and largely increased numbers. The few detailed men sent to General Lee, after the revocation of their details, added nothing to the strength of his army, but were a positive injury to it. The mass of them had desired to keep out of the service, because they had no stomach for the fight, and when forced into it, they but served to disseminate dissatisfaction in the ranks of the army. Some writers who never exposed their own precious persons to the bullets of the enemy, have written very glibly about the desertions from the army. Now, God forbid that I should say one word in justification of desertion under any circumstances. I had no toleration for it during the war, and never failed to sanction and order the execution of sentences for the extreme penalty for that offence, when submitted to me; but some palliation was to be found for the conduct of many of those who did desert, in the fact that they did so to go to the aid of their families, who they knew were suffering for the necessaries of life, while many able-bodied young men remained at home, in pence and plenty, under exemptions and details. The duty to defend one's country exists independently of any law, and the latter is made to enforce, not create, the obligation. By the law, or the unwise administration of it, a man may be exempted from enforced service, but he cannot be released from the sacred duty of defending his country against invasion. Those able-bodied men who flocked abroad to avoid service, and were so blatant in their patriotism when beyond the reach of danger, as I have had occasion to learn in my wanderings, as well as those who sought

OPERATIONS IN 1865.

On the 2nd of January, 1865, I had a consultation with Gen. Lee at Richmond, about the difficulties of my position in the Valley, and he told me that he had left me there with the small command which still remained, in order to produce the impression that the force was much larger than it really was, and he instructed me to do the best I could.

Before I returned from Richmond, Rosser started, with between 300 and 400 picked cavalry, for the post of Beverly in Western Virginia, and, on the 11th, surprised and captured the place, securing over five hundred prisoners and some stores. This expedition was made over a very mountainous country, amid the snows of an unusually severe winter. Rosser's loss was very light, but Lieutenant-Colonel Cook of the 8th Virginia cavalry, a most gallant and efficient officer, lost his leg in the attack, and had to be left behind.

The great drought during the summer of 1864, had made the corn crop in the Valley a very short one, and, as Sheridan had destroyed a considerable quantity of small grain and hay, I found it impossible to sustain the horses of my cavalry and artillery where they were, and forage could not be obtained from elsewhere. I was therefore compelled to send Fitz Lee's two brigades to General Lee, and Lomax's cavalry was brought from across the Blue Ridge, where the country was exhausted of forage, and sent west into the counties of Pendleton, Highland, Bath, Alleghany, and Greenbrier, where hay could be obtained. Rosser's brigade had to be temporarily disbanded, and the men allowed to go to their homes with their horses, to sustain them, with orders to report when called on.—One or two companies, whose homes were down the Valley, being

---

exemptions and details under the law, with a view to avoid the dangers and hardships of the war, were to all intents and purposes deserters, and morally more criminal than the poor soldier, who, in the agony of his distress for the sufferings of his wife and little ones at home, yielded to the temptation to abandon his colours. There were some cases of exemptions and details, where the persons obtaining them could be more useful at home than in the field, and those who sought them honestly on that account are not subject to the above strictures, but there were many cases where the motives were very different. The men whose names form the roll of honor for the armies of the Confederate States, are those who voluntarily entered the service in the beginning of the war, or as soon as they were able to bear arms, and served faithfully to the end, or until killed or disabled; and I would advise the unmarried among my fair countrywomen to choose their husbands from among the survivors of this class, and not from among the skulkers. By following this advice, they may not obtain as much pelf, but they may rest assured that they will not be the mothers of cowards, and their posterity will have no cause to blush for the conduct of their progenitors.

required to picket and scout in front of New Market. The men and horses of Lieutenant-Colonel King's artillery were sent to South-Western Virginia to be wintered, and most of the horses of the other battalions were sent off, under care of some of the men, who undertook to forage them until spring. Nelson's battalion, with some pieces of artillery with their horses, was retained with me, and the remaining officers and men of the other battalions were sent, under the charge of Colonel Carter, to General Lee, to man stationary batteries on his lines. Brigadier-General Long, who had been absent on sick leave for some time and had returned, remained with me, and most of the guns which were without horses were sent to Lynchburg by railroad. This was a deplorable state of things, but it could not be avoided, as the horses of the cavalry and artillery would have perished had they been kept in the Valley.

Echols' brigade of Wharton's division was subsequently sent to South-Western Virginia, to report to General Echols for special duty, and McNeil's company of partizan rangers and Woodson's company of unattached Missouri cavalry were sent to the County of Hardy—Major Harry Gilmor being likewise ordered to that County, with the remnant of his battalion, to take charge of the whole, and operate against the Baltimore and Ohio railroad; but he was surprised and captured there, at a private house, soon after his arrival. Two very small brigades of Wharton's division, and Nelson's battalion with the few pieces of artillery which had been retained, were left as my whole available force, and these were in winter quarters near Fisherville, on the Central railroad between Staunton and Waynesboro. The telegraph to New Market and the signal stations from there to the lower Valley were kept up, and a few scouts sent to the rear of the enemy, and in this way was my front principally picketed, and I kept advised of the enemy's movements. Henceforth my efficient and energetic signal officer, Captain Wilbourn, was the commander of my advance picket line.

The winter was a severe one, and all material operations were suspended until its close. Late in February, Lieutenant Jesse McNeil, who was in command of his father's old company, with forty or fifty men of that company and Woodson's, made a dash into Cumberland, Maryland, at night, and captured and brought off Major-Generals Crook and Kelly with a staff officer of the latter, though there were at the time several thousand troops in and around Cumberland. The father of this gallant young officer had performed many daring exploits during the war, and had accompanied me into Maryland, doing good service. When Sheridan was at Harrisonburg, in October, 1864, Captain McNeil had burned the bridge at Edinburg in his rear, and had attacked and captured the guard at the bridge at Mount Jackson, but in this affair he received a very severe wound from which he subsequently died. Lieutenant Baylor of Rosser's brigade, who was in Jefferson County with his company, made one or two dashes on the enemy's outposts during the winter, and, on one occasion, captured a train loaded with supplies, on the Baltimore and Ohio railroad.

On the 20th of February, an order was issued by General Lee, extending my command over the Department of South-Western Virginia and East Tennessee, previously commanded by General Breckenridge—the latter having been made Secretary of War.

On the 27th, Sheridan started from Winchester up the Valley with a heavy force, consisting, according to the statement of Grant, in his report, of "two divisions of cavalry, numbering about 5,000 each." I had been informed of the preparations for a movement of some kind, some days previous, and the information had been telegraphed to General Lee. As soon as Sheridan started, I was informed of the fact by signs, and telegraph, and orders were immediately sent by telegraph to Lomax, whose headquarters were at Millboro, on the Central railroad, forty miles west of Staunton, to get together all of his cavalry as soon as possible. Rosser was also directed to collect all of his men that he could, and an order was sent by telegraph to General Echols, in South-Western Virginia, to send his brigade by rail to Lynchburg. My own headquarters were at Staunton, but there were no troops at that place except a local provost guard, and a company of reserves, composed of boys under 18 years of age, which was acting under orders of the Conscript Bureau. Orders were therefore given for the immediate removal of all stores from that place. Rosser succeeded in collecting a little over 100 men, and with these he attempted to check the enemy at North River, near Mount Crawford, on the 1st of March, but was unable to do so. On the afternoon of that day, the enemy approached to within three or four miles of Staunton, and I then telegraphed to Lomax to concentrate his cavalry at Pond Gap, in Augusta County, southwest of Staunton, and to follow and annoy the enemy should he move towards Lynchburg, and rode out of town towards Waynesboro, after all the stores had been removed.

Wharton and Nelson were ordered to move to Waynesboro by light next morning, and on that morning the (2nd) their commands were put in position on a ridge covering Waynesboro on the west and just outside of the town. My object, in taking this position was to secure the removal of five pieces of artillery for which there were no horses, and some stores still in Waynesboro, as well as to present a bold front to the enemy, and ascertain the object of his movement, which I could not do very well if I took refuge at once in the mountain. The last report for Wharton's command showed 1,200 men for duty; but, as it was exceedingly inclement, and raining and freezing, there were not more than 1,000 muskets on the line, and Nelson had six pieces of artillery. I did not intend making my final stand on this ground, yet I was satisfied that if my men would fight, which I had no reason to doubt, I could hold the enemy in check until night, and then cross the river and take position in Rockfish Gap; for I had done more difficult things than that during the war. About 12 o'clock in the day, it was reported to me that the enemy was advancing, and I rode out at once on the lines, and soon discovered about a brigade of cavalry coming up, on the road from Staunton, on which the artillery opened, when it retired out of range. The enemy manoeuvred for some time in our front keeping out of reach of our guns until late in the afternoon, when I discovered a force moving to our left. I immediately sent a messenger with notice of this fact to General Wharton, who was on that flank, and with orders for him to look out and provide for the enemy's advance; and another messenger, with notice to the guns on the left, and directions for them to fire towards the advancing force, which could not be seen from where they were. The enemy soon made an attack on our left flank, and I discovered the men on that flank giving back. Just then, General Wharton, who had not received my message, rode up to me and I pointed out to him the disorder in his line, and ordered him to ride immediately to that point and rectify it. Before he got back, the troops gave way on the left, after making very slight resistance, and soon everything was in a state of confusion and the men commenced crossing the river. I rode across it myself to try and stop them at the bridge and check the enemy, but they could not be rallied, and the enemy forded the river above and got in our rear. I now saw that everything was lost, and, after the enemy had got between the mountain and the position where I was, and retreat was thus cut off, I rode aside into the woods, and in that way escaped capture. I went to the top of a hill to reconnoitre, and had the mortification of seeing the greater part of my command being carried off as prisoners, and a force of the enemy moving rapidly towards Rockfish Gap. I then rode with the greater part of my staff and 15 or 20 others, including General Long, across the mountain, north of the Gap, with the hope of arriving at Greenwood depot, to which the stores had been removed, before the enemy reached that place; but, on getting near it, about dark, we discovered the enemy in possession. We then rode to Jarman's Gap, about three miles from the depot, and remained there all night, as the night was exceedingly dark, and the ice rendered it impossible for us to travel over the rugged roads.

The only solution of this affair which I can give, is that my men did not fight as I had expected them to do. Had they done so, I am satisfied that the enemy could have been repulsed; and I was and still am of opinion that the attack at Waynesboro was a mere demonstration to cover a movement to the south towards Lynchburg. Yet some excuse is to be made for my men, as they knew that they were weak and the enemy very strong.

The greater part of my command was captured, as was also the artillery, which, with five guns on the cars at Greenwood, made eleven pieces. Very few were killed or wounded on either side. The only person killed on our side that I have ever heard of was Colonel William H. Harmon, who had formerly been in the army, but then held a civil appointment; and he was shot in the streets of Waynesboro, either after he had been made prisoner, as some said, or while he was attempting to make his escape after everything was over. My aide, Lieutenant William G. Calloway, who had been sent to the left with one of the messages, and my medical director, Surgeon II. McGuire, had the misfortune to fall into the bands of the enemy. All the waggons of Wharton's command were absent getting supplies; but those we had with us, including the ordnance and medical waggons, and my own baggage waggon, fell into the hands of the enemy.*

---

* Grant, in speaking of this affair, says: "He (Sheridan) entered Staunton on the 2nd, the enemy having retreated on Waynesboro. Thence he pushed on to Waynesboro, where he found the enemy in force in an intrenched position, under General Early. Without stopping to make a reconnoissance, an immediate attack was made, the position was carried, and 1,600 prisoners, 11 pieces of artillery, with horses and caissons complete, 200 waggons and teams loaded with subsistence, and 17 battle-flags were captured." This is all very brilliant; but, unfortunately for its truth, Sheridan was not at Waynesboro, but was at Staunton, where he had stopped with a part of his force; while the affair at Waynesboro was conducted by one of his subordinates. The strength of my force has already been stated, and it was not in an intrenched position. I am not able to say how many prisoners were taken, but I know that they were more than my command numbered, as a very considerable number of recently exchanged and paroled prisoners were at the time in the Valley, on leave of absence from General Lee's army. I not only did not have 200 waggons or anything like it, but had no use for them. Where the 17 battic-flags could have been gotten, I cannot imagine.

On the 3rd, I rode, with the party that was with me, towards Charlottesville; but, on getting near that place, we found the enemy entering it. We had then to turn back and go by a circuitous route under the mountains to Gordonsville, as the Rivanna River and other streams were very much swollen. On arriving at Gordonsville I found General Wharton, who had made his escape to Charlottesville on the night of the affair at Waynesboro, and he was ordered to Lynchburg, by the way of the Central and Southside Railroads, to take command of Echols' brigade, and aid in the defence of the city. General Long was ordered to report to General Lee at Petersburg.

The affair at Waynesboro diverted Sheridan from Lynchburg, which he could have captured without difficulty, had he followed Hunter's route, and not jumped at the bait unwillingly offered him, by the capture of my force at the former place. His deflection from the direct route to the one by Charlottesville, was without adequate object, and resulted in the abandonment of the effort to capture Lynchburg, or to cross the James River to the south side. He halted at Charlottesville for two or three days, and then moved towards James River below Lynchburg, when, being unable to cross that river, he crossed over the Rivanna at its mouth, and then moved by the way of Frederick's Hall on the Central Railroad, and Ashland on the R. F. & P. Railroad, across the South and North Annas, and down the Pamunkey to the White House.

At Gordonsville about 200 cavalry were collected under Colonel Morgan, of the 1st Virginia Cavalry, and, with this force, I watched the enemy for several days while he was at Charlottesville, and when he was endeavoring to cross the James River. When Sheridan had abandoned this effort, and on the day he reached the vicinity of Ashland, while I was riding on the Louisa Court House and Richmond road, towards the bridge over the South Anna, with about 20 cavalry, I came very near being captured by a body of 300 cavalry sent after me, but I succeeded in eluding the enemy with most of those who were with me, and reached Richmond at two o'clock next morning, after passing twice between the enemy's camps and his pickets. My Adjutant General, Captain Moore, however, was captured, but made his escape.

Lomax had succeeded in collecting a portion of his cavalry and reaching Lynchburg, where he took position on the north bank of the river, but the enemy avoided that place. Rosser had collected a part of his brigade and made an attack, near New-Market, on the guard which was carrying back the prisoners captured at Waynesboro, with the view of releasing them, but he did not succeed in that object, though he captured a piece of artillery; the guard was compelled to retire in great haste. He then moved towards Richmond on Sheridan's track.

After consultation with General Lee, at his headquarters near Petersburg, Rosser's and McCausland's brigades were ordered to report to him under the command of General Rosser, and I started for the Valley, by the way of Lynchburg, to reorganize what was left of my command. At Lynchburg a dispatch was received from General Echols, stating that Thomas was moving in East Tennessee, and threatening Southwestern Virginia with a heavy force, and I immediately went on the cars to Wytheville. From that place I went with General Echols to Bristol, on the state line between Virginia and Tennessee, and it was ascertained beyond doubt that some important movement by the enemy was on foot. We then returned to Abingdon, and while I was engaged in endeavoring to organize the small force in that section, so as to meet the enemy in the best way we could, I received, on the 30th of March, a telegraphic dispatch from General Lee, directing me to turn over the command in Southwestern Virginia to General Echols, and in the Valley to General Lomax, and informing me that he would address a letter to me at my home. I complied at once with this order, and thus terminated my military career.

Conclusion.

In the afternoon of the 30th of March, after having turned over the command to General Echols, I rode to Marion in Smythe county, and was taken that night with a cold and cough so violent as to produce hemorrhage from the lungs, and prostrate me for several days in a very dangerous condition. While I was in this situation, a heavy cavalry force under Stoneman, from Thomas' army in Tennessee, moved through North Carolina to the east, and a part of it came into Virginia from the main column, and struck the Virginia and Tennessee Railroad at New River, east of Wytheville; whence, after destroying the bridge, it moved east, cutting off all communication with Richmond, and then crossed over into North Carolina. As soon as I was in a condition to be moved, I was carried on the railroad to Wytheville, and was proceeding thence to my home, in an ambulance under the charge of a surgeon, when I received, most unexpectedly, the news of the surrender of General Lee's army. Without the slightest feeling of irreverence, I will say, that the sound of the last trump would not have been more unwelcome to my ears.

Under the disheartening influence of the sad news I had received, I proceeded to my home, and I subsequently received a letter from General Lee, dated on the 30th of March, explaining the reasons for relieving me from command. As a copy of that letter has been published in Virginia, without any knowledge or agency on my part, it is appended to this narrative. The letter itself, which was written on the very day of the commencement of the attack on General Lee's lines which resulted in the evacuation of Richmond, and just ten days before the surrender of the Army of Northern Virginia, has a historical interest; for it shows that our great commander, even at that late day, was anxiously and earnestly contemplating the continuation of the struggle with unabated vigor, and a full determination to make available every element of success.

Immediately after the battle of Cedar Creek, I had written a letter to General Lee, stating my willingness to be relieved from command, if he deemed it necessary for the public interests, and I should have been content with the course pursued towards me, had his letter not contained the expressions of personal confidence in me which it does; for I knew that, in everything he did as commander of our armies, General Lee was actuated solely by an earnest and ardent desire for the success of the cause of his country. As to those among my countrymen who judged me harshly, I have not a word of reproach. When there was so much at stake, it was not unnatural that persons entirely ignorant of the facts, and forming their opinions from the many false reports set afloat in a time of terrible war and public suffering, should pass erroneous and severe judgments on those commanders who met with reverses.

I was not embraced in the terms of General Lee's surrender or that of General Johnston, and, as the order relieving me from command had also relieved me from all embarrassment as to the troops which had been under me, as soon as I was in a condition to travel, I started on horseback to the Trans-Mississippi Department, to join the army of General Kirby Smith, should it hold out; with the hope of at least meeting an honorable death while fighting under the flag of my country. Before I reached that Department, Smith's army had also been surrendered, and, without giving a parole or incurring any obligation whatever to the United States authorities, after a long, weary and dangerous ride from Virginia, through the States of North Carolina, South Carolina, Georgia, Alabama, Mississippi, Arkansas and Texas, I finally succeeded in leaving the country; a voluntary exile rather than submit to the rule of our enemies.

J. A. EARLY.

Closing Valediction

LEW WALLACE

Y ou know, sir, how prone men are in prosperity to forget the pangs of
adversity. Ordinarily, what cares the young spendthrift happy in the
waste of his father's fortune, for that father's life of toil and self-denial? It is to
be hoped that these flags will prevent such indifference on the part of our posterity. Think of them grouped all in one chamber! What descendant of a loyal
man could enter it and look upon them and not think of the ancestral sacrifices
they both attest and perpetuate? And when the foreigner, dreaming it may be
of invasion or conquest or ambition, political or military more dangerous now
than all the kings, come into their presence, as come they will, though they be
not oppressed with reverence or dumb-stricken with awe, as you and I and
others like us may be, doubt not that they will go away wiser than they came;
they will be reminded of what the Frenchman had not heard when he landed
his legions on the palmy shore of Mexico; of what rulers of England overlooked when they made such haste to recognize the Rebellion; of what the
trained leaders of the Rebellion themselves took not into account when they
led their misguided followers into the fields of war; they will be reminded that
this people, so given to peace, so devoted to trade, mechanics, and agriculture,
so occupied with schools and churches, and a government which does their
will through the noiseless agency of the ballot-box, have yet, when aroused, a

power of resistance sufficient for any need however great; that this nationality, yet in its youth's first freshness, is like a hive of human bees—stand by it quietly, and you will be charmed by its proofs of industry, its faculty of appliance, its well-ordered labor; but touch it, shake it rudely, menace its population, or put them in fear, and they will pour from their cells an armed myriad whom there is no confronting.

"Fellow-Citizens, Comrades:

"When we come visiting the old flags, and take out those more especially endeared to us because under them each rendered our individual service, such as it was, we will not fail to be reminded of those other comrades—alas, too many to be named!—who dropped one by one out of the ranks or the column, to answer at roll-call never more, whose honorable discharges were given them by the fever in the hospital or by a bullet in battle; whose bones lie in shallow graves in the cypress swamp, in the river's deepening bed, in the valley's Sabbath stillness, or on the mountain's breast, bleakened now by tempests human as well as elemental. For their sakes, let us resolve to come here with every recurrence of this day, and bring the old colors to the sunlight and carry them in procession, and salute them martially with roll of drums and thunder of guns. So will those other comrades of whom I speak know that they are remembered at least by us, and so will be remembered by them.

"In the armies of Persia was a chosen band called the Immortals. They numbered ten thousand; their ranks were always full, and their place was near the person of the king. The old poet sings of this resplendent host, as clad in the richest armor, and bearing spears pointed with pomegranates of silver and gold. We, too, have our Immortals! Only ours wear uniforms of light. And they number more than ten times ten thousand. And instead of a king to serve they have for leader and lover that man of God and the people, Lincoln the Martyr. On their rolls shine the heroic names, without regard to paltry distinctions as to rank or state; among them are no officers, no privates; in the bivouacs of heaven they are all alike Immortals. Of such are Ellsworth, Baker, Wadsworth. Sedgwick, and McPherson. Of such also are our Hackleman, Gerber, Tanner, Blinn, and Carroll, and that multitude of our soldiers who, victims of the war, are now 'at the front,' while we 'are waiting in reserve.'"

Published Source Materials

Custer, George A. "War Memoirs." *Galaxy*, XXII, September, 1876.

Doubleday, Abner. *Chancellorsville and Gettysburg*. Charles Scribner's Sons, 1882.

Early, Jubal A. *A Memoir of the Last Year of the War for Independence in the Confederate States of America*. Charles W. Button, 1867.

Hood, John Bell. *Advance and Retreat*.

Longstreet, James. *From Manassas to Appomattox*. J. P. Lippincott Company, 1896.

McClellan, George B. *McClellan's Own Story—The War for the Union*. Charles L. Webster & Company, 1887.

Mosby, John S. *Mosby's War Reminiscences*. Dodd, Mead & Company, 1887.

Sherman, William T. *Memoirs of General W. T. Sherman*. D. Appleton and Company, 1875.

Sorrel, G. Moxley. *Recollections of a Confederate Staff Officer*, 1905.

Wallace, Lew. *An Autobiography* (2 Volumes). Harper & Brothers, Publishers, 1906.

Excerpt introductions provided by William Terdoslavich